1443 Janie Av
Nashville TN 3

CW01640808

Color Correction with

DAVINCI RESOLVE 16

by Daria Fissoun, CSI

Color Correction with DaVinci Resolve 16

Daria Fissoun, CSI

Copyright © 2020 by Blackmagic Design Pty Ltd

Blackmagic Design

www.blackmagicdesign.com

To report errors, please send a note to learning@blackmagicdesign.com.

Series Editor: Patricia Montesion

Series Director: Dion Scoppettuolo

Editor: Bob Lindstrom

Contributing authors: Jason Druss, Mary Plummer, Dion Scoppettuolo, David Hover

Cover Design: Blackmagic Design

Notice of Rights

All rights reserved. No part of this book may be reproduced or transmitted in any form by any means, electronic, mechanical, photocopying, recording, or otherwise, without the prior written permission of the publisher. For information on getting permission for reprints and excerpts, contact learning@blackmagicdesign.com.

Notice of Liability

Neither the author nor Blackmagic Design shall have any liability to any person or entity for any loss or damage caused or alleged to be caused directly or indirectly by the information contained in this book, or by omissions from this book, or by the computer software and hardware products described within it.

Trademarks

Many of the designations used by manufacturers and sellers to distinguish their products are claimed as trademarks. Where those designations appear in this book, and Blackmagic Design was aware of a trademark claim, the designations appear as requested by the owner of the trademark. All other product names and services identified throughout this book are used in editorial fashion only and for the benefit of such companies with no intention of infringement of the trademark. No such use, or the use of any trade name, is intended to convey endorsement or other affiliation with this book.

macOS is a registered trademark of Apple Inc., registered in the U.S. and other countries. Windows is a registered trademarks of Microsoft Inc., registered in the U.S. and other countries.

ISBN: 978-1-7342279-2-5

Contents

Foreword

Welcome to **Color Correction with DaVinci Resolve 16**

DaVinci Resolve 16 is the only post production solution that brings editing, color correction, audio post and visual effects together in the same software application! The most exciting thing about DaVinci Resolve 16 is the revolutionary new cut page, which is designed specifically for editors that need to work quickly and on tight deadlines. It's an alternate edit page with a streamlined interface and new tools designed to help you work faster than ever before.

DaVinci Resolve 16 also includes even more advanced color correction, powerful new editing options on the traditional edit page, vastly improved Fairlight digital audio tools and even faster 2D and 3D visual effects compositing on the Fusion page. DaVinci Resolve 16 enables you to switch between creative tasks without having to export or translate files between different applications!

Best of all, DaVinci Resolve 16 is absolutely free! Plus, we've made sure that the free version of DaVinci Resolve actually has more features than any paid editing system. That's because at Blackmagic Design we believe everybody should have the tools to create professional, Hollywood caliber content without having to spend thousands of dollars.

I hope you'll enjoy using DaVinci Resolve 16 and we can't wait to see the amazing work you produce!

Grant Petty
Blackmagic Design

Getting Started

Welcome to **Color Correction with DaVinci Resolve 16**, an official Blackmagic Design-certified training book that teaches professionals and students how to get the most out of color correction using DaVinci Resolve 16. All you need is a Mac or Windows computer, the free download version of Resolve 16, and a passion to learn about color correction.

This guide blends practical, hands-on exercises with the aesthetics of the colorist's art to help you discover new techniques for whatever tasks you take on. You will learn how to use the program's many grading tools and workflows, and gain an in-depth understanding of advanced techniques and creative industry practices. Some exercises will even take you into the realm of compositing, which is an increasingly requested skill of contemporary colorists.

After completing this book, you are encouraged to take the 50-question online proficiency exam to receive a Certificate of Completion from Blackmagic Design. The link to the exam is located at the end of this book.

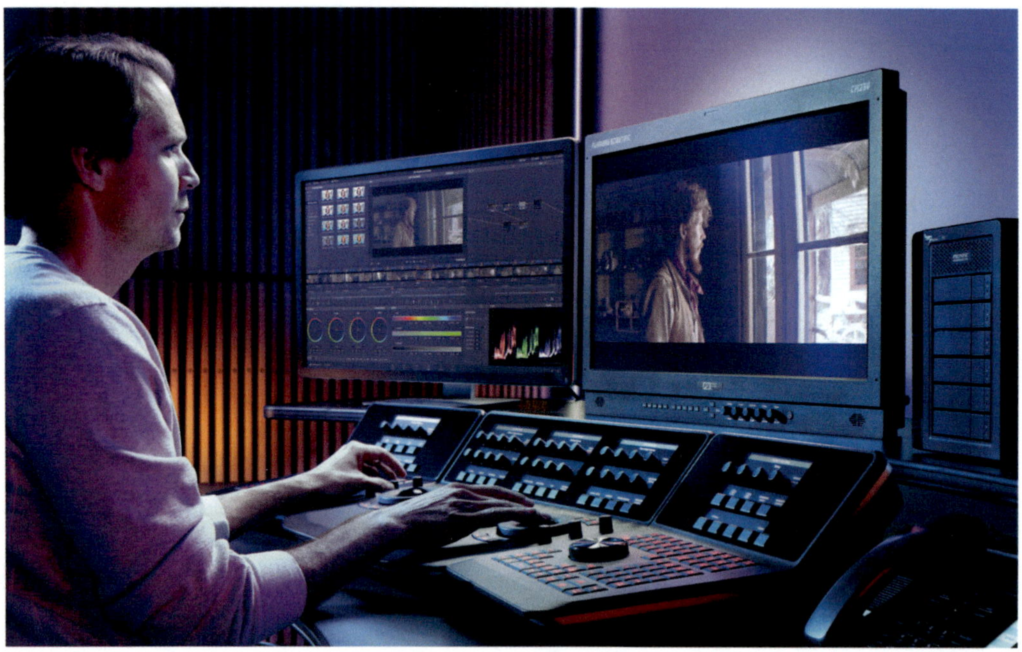

About DaVinci Resolve 16

DaVinci Resolve is the world's fastest growing and most advanced editing software. It also has a long history of being the world's most trusted application for color correction. In addition to its world-class color correction toolset, DaVinci Resolve 16 is a professional-level non-linear editing and effects application with a complete set of professional audio editing and mixing tools that enable you to complete projects using only one piece of software!

What you will Learn

In these lessons, you'll work with multiple projects to learn advanced, practical techniques used in several editing genres. You'll acquire real-world skills that you can apply to real-world productions.

Part I

Part I of the book will have you restoring a documentary edit from a Resolve archive file. The three lessons within this section focus on fundamental grading theory and practices. You will normalize and balance footage with the primary grading tools in Lesson 1, match the shots in the timeline for continuity in Lesson 2, and adopt secondary grading workflows in Lesson 3.

Part II

Part II looks at more advanced approaches to the grade node structure in the context of a feature film trailer. In Lesson 4, you will migrate the project to Resolve using an XML file format. In Lesson 5, you will more fully explore the importance of node order and consider incorporating mixer nodes when grading to ensure the optimal color outcome. In Lesson 6, you will practice different methods of managing and copying grades with an eye toward developing efficient, quick workflows.

Part III

Part III will focus more strongly on the optimization of grading workflows to ensure a quick, accurate grading process and output. In Lesson 7, you will look at a variety of methods of controlling the image frame and properties, as well as advanced keyframing, compositing, and noise-reduction techniques. Lesson 8 incorporates the classic grading workflow into a group-based pipeline that will allow you to grade entire segments of the timeline in one node tree. Lesson 9 demonstrates the many approaches you could take when starting a grading workflow with RAW media and emphasize its extended grading potential. Finally, Lesson 10 covers project delivery from basic preset setup to custom renders and DCP workflows.

The appendices at the end of the book provide additional information regarding the layout and functionality of the program, as well as the corresponding controls on the Blackmagic Design Mini Panel.

System Requirements

This book teaches Resolve 16 for macOS and Windows. If you have an older version of DaVinci Resolve, you must upgrade to the current version to follow along with the lessons. Fortunately, DaVinci Resolve 16 is a free upgrade from previous versions of DaVinci Resolve.

Downloading DaVinci Resolve 16

You can download the free version of DaVinci Resolve 16 from the Blackmagic Design website:

1. Open a web browser on your macOS, Windows, or Linux computer.
2. In the address field of your web browser, enter **www.blackmagicdesign.com/products/davinciresolve**.
3. On the DaVinci Resolve landing page, click the Download button.
4. Follow the installation instructions to complete the installation.

When you have completed the software installation, follow the instructions in the following section, "To Download and Install the Lesson Files," to download the content for this book.

Acquiring the Lesson Files

You must download three zipped lesson files to acquire the media files you'll use while performing the exercises in this book. After you download and save the compressed files to your hard disk, extract both zipped files and copy them to a single "BMD 16 - Advanced Color Correction" folder that you create in your Documents folder.

To Download and Install the Lesson Files:

When you are ready to download the three lesson files, follow these steps:

1. Connect to the Internet and navigate to: www.blackmagicdesign.com/dvres/grading-with-resolve16-pt1.

   The download will begin immediately.

   The BMD 16 CC - Project 01.zip file is 2.45 GB in size and should take roughly 15 minutes to download to your computer using a standard broadband connection.
2. Download the second part of the lesson files by navigating to www.blackmagicdesign.com/dvres/grading-with-resolve16-pt2.

   The BMD 16 CC - Project 02.zip file is 1.01 GB in size and should take roughly five minutes to download to your computer using a standard broadband connection.
3. Download the third part of the lesson files by navigating to www.blackmagicdesign.com/dvres/grading-with-resolve16-pt3.

   The BMD 16 CC - Project 03.zip file is 2.04 GB in size and should take roughly 10 minutes to download to your computer using a standard broadband connection.
4. After downloading the zip files to your computer, open your Downloads folder, and double-click both zip files to unzip them (if your computer doesn't unzip the file automatically).
5. In the Documents folder, create a new folder called **BMD 16 - Advanced Color Correction**.
6. From your Download folder, drag the BMD 16 CC - Project 01, BMD 16 CC - Project 02 and BMD 16 CC - Project 03 folders into the Documents > BMD 16 - Advanced Color Correction folder.

You are now ready to begin Lesson 1, "Balancing Footage."

The Blackmagic Design Learning Series

Blackmagic Design publishes several official certification books as part of the Blackmagic Design Learning Series. They include:

- The Definitive Guide to DaVinci Resolve 16
- Advanced Editing with DaVinci Resolve 16
- Color Correction with DaVinci Resolve 16
- Introduction to Fairlight Audio Post with DaVinci Resolve 16
- Fusion Visual Effects with DaVinci Resolve 16
- And more to come

Whether you want to learn more advanced editing techniques, color grading, or visual effects, certified training has a learning path for you.

After completing this book, you are encouraged to take a one-hour, 50-question online proficiency exam to receive a certificate of completion from Blackmagic Design. The link to this exam is located at the end of this book.

For more information on additional books in this series and Blackmagic Design certification training, visit www.blackmagicdesign.com/products/davinciresolve/training.

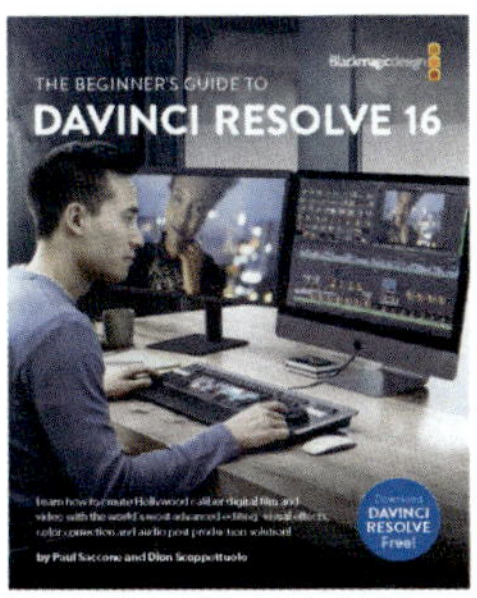

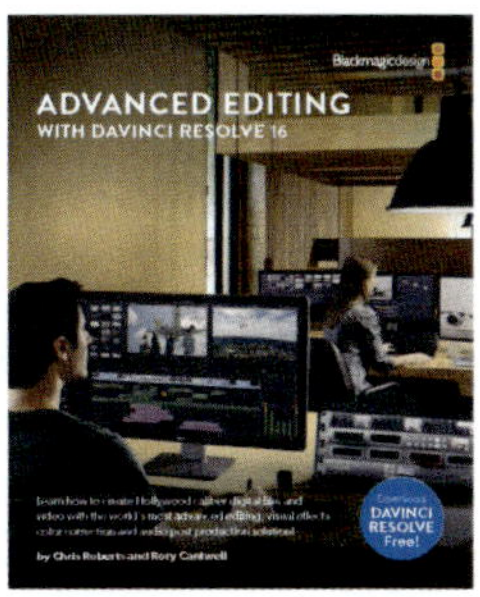

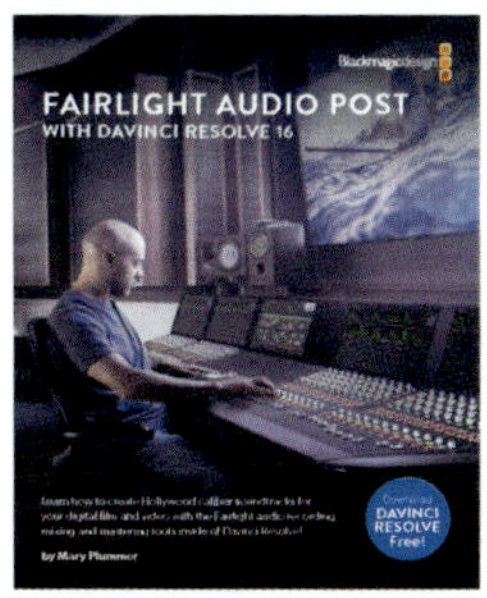

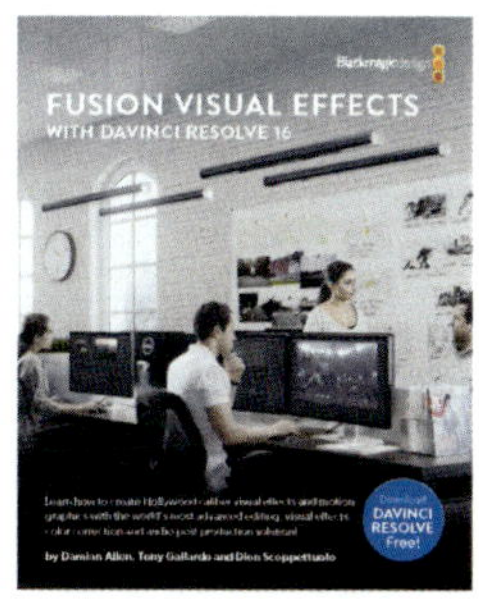

Getting Certified

After completing this book, you are encouraged to take the one-hour, 50-question online proficiency exam to receive a Certificate of Completion from Blackmagic Design. The link to this exam is located at the end of this book.

"No matter how much post experience you have, there's always something new to learn about DaVinci Resolve. I sometimes find that going back and reviewing the basics helps give you perspective on finding a new way to give clients the look they want quickly and efficiently. Highly recommended for newcomers and veteran colorists alike."

Marc Wielage, Senior Colorist - Chroma | Hollywood

Acknowledgments

With deepest gratitude to Patty Montesion and Dion Scoppettuolo for their mentorship and support during the writing process.

Special thanks and acknowledgements to Marc Wielage, David Hover, and Ollie Kenchington for their invaluable feedback during the test sessions of this training guide.

And extra super special thanks to editor Bob Lindstrom for his attention to detail, patience, and humor throughout the writing process.

Video Materials

Brian J Terwilliger (Terwilliger Productions) for "Living in the Age of Airplanes"

Sherwin Lau (Creative Media Institute, co-director) and Chris Lang (Organ Mountain Outfitters, co-director) for Organ Mountain Outfitters promo materials.

Aaron Walterscheid (Awal Visuals) and Nathan LeFever (LeFever Creative) from Organ Mountain Outfitters (organmountainoutfitters.com).

Interface Review

This section contains an overview of the Color page interface to remind you of its key functions and to establish the terminology that will be used throughout the book.

Color Page Layout

The default layout of the Color page contains the following panels:

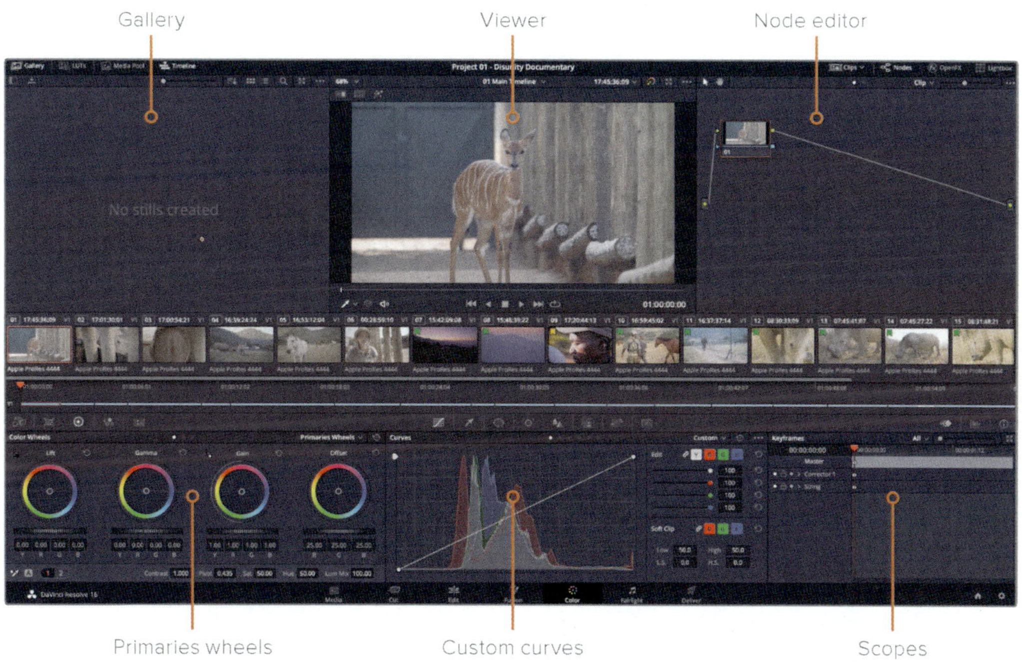

Gallery contains stills that can be used for visual comparison, or for copying grading data. Stills can be generated in Resolve or imported from an external source, and organized into albums.

Viewer displays and plays the selected clip, and offers additional interface controls.

Node graph allows grades and effects to be structured to maximize the visual quality of each clip.

Primaries wheels control the tonal and chromatic values of an image on the basis of three luminance ranges (highlights, midtones, and shadows).

Custom curves give precise control over the chromatic values of an image based on RGB and luminance curves.

Scopes provide graphic readouts of the luminance and chrominance values of an image for the purposes of balancing and matching.

A series of buttons the top of the interface allow you to show and hide panels as needed. Hiding panels (for example, the Timelines or the Gallery) will create more space for the Viewer and remaining panels.

Primaries Wheels

The Primaries wheels (and the corresponding bars and Log wheels) of the Color Wheel palette, allow you to affect the brightness and hue of the image by targeting specific luminance ranges.

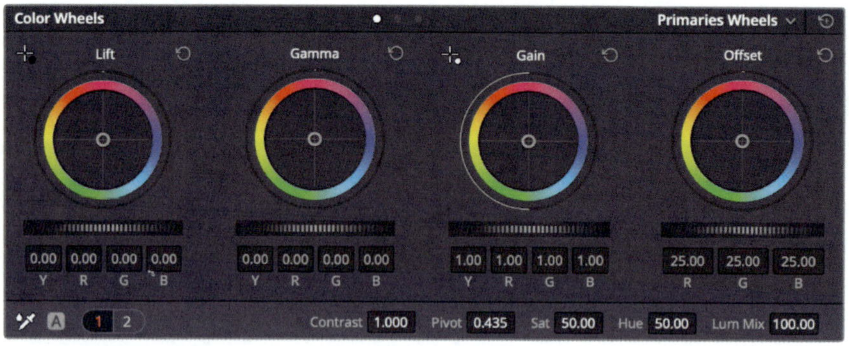

Lift targets the shadows of the image.

Gamma targets the midtones of the image.

Gain targets the highlights of the image.

Offset affects the entire image uniformly.

Master wheels are the dark horizontal sliders beneath the Color wheel that control the YRGB values of those respective ranges.

Clicking the Reset arrows in the upper-right corner of each wheel will neutralize the color and master wheel of that range. You can also reset the entire palette by clicking the general reset button next to the palette mode name.

The adjustment controls at the bottom of the Color wheel palette give additional control over the image with features such as contrast and saturation, temp and tint, and so on. Two buttons on the left allow you to switch between pages 1 and 2 of the adjustment controls.

Viewer

The Viewer shows the frame that the playhead is currently on. By default, clips are represented as they will appear upon final render. Some additional features allow you to temporarily bypass grades, see a representation of a clip's matte, and to compare clips to other media.

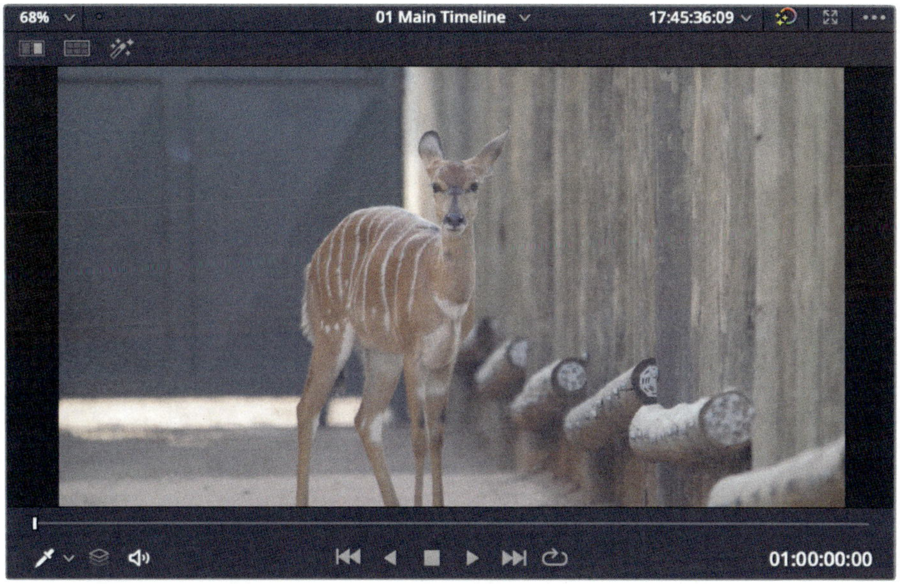

Some additional controls at the top and bottom of the Viewer maximize the functionality of the tools in the Color page.

> **TIP** You can position your mouse pointer over any tool in the Color page to see its name.

Image wipe enables you to wipe between a still, reference frame, or another clip in the Timeline for visual comparison and matching.

Split screen places clips alongside one another for review and comparison. It features several modes to allow comparison between clips on a timeline, in the same group, or even versions of grades within the same clip.

Highlight is enabled to reveal the matte that is associated with a selected node.

On-screen control menu is a pop-up menu in the lower-left of the Viewer that features a selection of UI controls associated with some of the palettes and functions of the Color page.

The bottom of the Viewer contains a scrubber and transport controls that allow you to navigate the clip as you would in the Edit page.

Palette Panel

A series of buttons under the Timeline enable you to navigate between the palettes available on the Color page. From left to right, these palettes are:

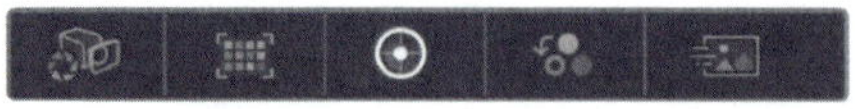

Left palettes—Camera RAW, Color Match, Color Wheels, RGB Mixer, Motion Effects

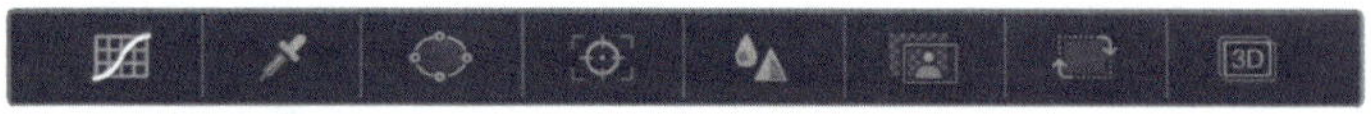

Central palettes—Curves, Qualifier, Window, Tracker, Blur, Key, Sizing, 3D

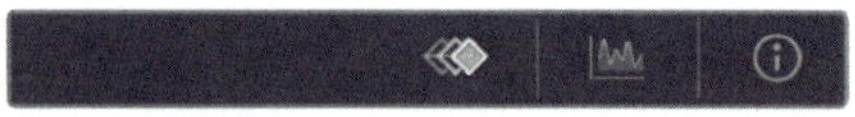

Keyframe editor—Keyframes, Scopes, Info

Use these buttons to navigate between palettes when prompted during the exercises. The name of each palette appears in the upper-left corner when clicked, as well as over the button itself when a mouse pointer is hovered over it.

Project File Locations and Solutions

You will find the training materials required to complete the exercises in this book divided into three project folders, which correspond to the 3 sections of the book (BMD 16 CC—Project 01, BMD 16 CC—Project 02 and BMD 16 CC—Project 03).

Follow the instructions at the start of every lesson to find the necessary folder, project, and timeline.

After you have completed an exercise, you have the option to review the completed timeline that is included in every project file provided with the media. Keep in mind that color grading is a subjective practice and your results will often differ from the completed timelines. Rather than attempting to match your work exactly, use them for general comparison and troubleshooting.

Introduction to the Color Panels

Blackmagic Design manufactures a wide range of control surfaces for use with DaVinci Resolve 16. Professional colorists working on commercials, television, and film prefer using control surfaces to using mouse and keyboard. Hardware control surfaces allow you to work faster and more efficiently because you can adjust multiple parameters simultaneously. Three control panels are available for Davinci Resolve: Micro, Mini, and Advanced.

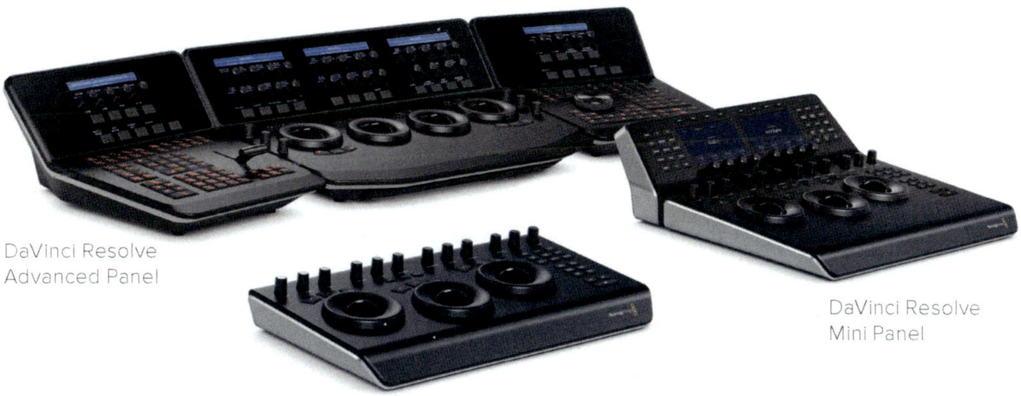

DaVinci Resolve Advanced Panel

DaVinci Resolve Mini Panel

DaVinci Resolve Micro Panel

DaVinci Resolve Micro Panel

The DaVinci Resolve Micro Panel is a high-quality, portable, low-profile panel that features three high-resolution trackballs and 12 precision-machined control knobs for accessing essential primary correction tools. If you're using a Micro Panel, it's important to know that all of the instructions regarding the primary color tools and setup are identical to the Mini Panel. Above the center trackball are keys for switching between Log and offset color correction, as well as a key to display DaVinci Resolve's full-screen viewer, which is great for use with laptops. Eighteen dedicated keys on the right side of the panel also give you access to many commonly used grading features and playback controls. The Davinci Resolve Micro Panel is perfect for anyone who needs a truly portable solution. It's great for use on set to quickly create looks and evaluate color; it's ideal for grading in broadcast trucks, excellent for education, and ideal for anyone who's work relies mostly on the primary color correction tools.

DaVinci Resolve Mini Panel

The DaVinci Resolve Mini Panel is a compact panel that's packed with a massive combination of features and controls. As with the Micro Panel, you get three professional trackballs along with a variety of buttons for switching tools, adding color correctors, and navigating your node tree. It also features two color LCD screens that display menus, controls, and parameter settings for the selected tool, along with buttons that give you direct access to the menus for specific features. The Mini Panel is ideal for users who regularly switch between editing and color grading, or for freelance colorists who need to carry a panel with them when moving between facilities. It's also great for colorists working on location shoots, for corporate and event videographers, for houses of worship, and more.

DaVinci Resolve Advanced Panel

For the ultimate in speed, power, and control, get the DaVinci Resolve Advanced Panel! The Advanced panel was designed in collaboration with professional colorists to work in total harmony with the software. This large panel consists of left, center, and right consoles that give you quick, one-touch access to virtually every parameter and control in DaVinci Resolve. The Advanced Panel lets colorists instinctively reach out and touch every part of the image, adjusting multiple parameters simultaneously with complete responsiveness for a smooth grading experience. When you're working with a client over your shoulder on a tight deadline, you need the DaVinci Resolve Advanced Panel.

Part 1: Color Correcting a DaVinci Resolve Timeline

Lessons

- Balance footage
- Create color continuity
- Correct and enhance isolated areas

Part 1 of Color Correction with DaVinci Resolve 16 focuses on establishing a strong practical foundation of primary and secondary grading techniques with additional focus on balancing and matching media in preparation for creative grading.

Each part of this guide focuses on its own project, and each project is set up to explore the variety of methods for starting a grade in Resolve. In Part 1, the project is accessed using Resolve's archiving feature.

Project File Location

You will find all the necessary content for this section in the "BMD 16 CC - Project 01" folder. Follow the instructions at the start of every lesson to find the necessary project, timeline, and media files. If you have not yet downloaded the first set of content files, go to the Getting Started section of this book for more information.

NOTE Although you can use DaVinci Resolve 16 for the majority of this guide, some exercises will require DaVinci Resolve Studio 16.

Lesson 1

Balancing Footage

The first project you will be grading is a documentary about protecting endangered rhinos. The workflow described is applicable to virtually all types of video project grading, but documentary cinematography is particularly sensitive to the following steps:

- **Balance footage**—Documentary videographers often change locations during a shoot, which means they have less shot-to-shot control over lighting conditions.
- **Match shots**—Scenes, interviews, and b-roll can be shot over many days with different cameras. You must visually match all content to create a cohesive narrative.
- **Improve imagery**—You can confine grading to specific portions of a shot to enhance skies, skin tones, and visual framing.

Time

This lesson takes approximately 60 minutes to complete.

Goals

Also, you wouldn't color grade a somber documentary about rhinoceros sanctuaries as you would grade a 30-second perfume ad featuring the latest Hollywood A-lister, even if both projects were shot on the same type of camera. So, in addition to addressing the technical requirements of the footage, you will also attend to the documentary's aesthetic considerations.

In this lesson, you'll familiarize yourself with the primary grading tools used to normalize and balance clips on a timeline, waveforms, and parade scopes for optimal matching, and employ secondary grading selection methods to enhance your final look. You will do so in the context of an overall grading workflow that addresses the needs of each timeline clip.

Opening a Resolve Archive

This book is divided into three distinct sections, each devoted to a different genre and using three different project setup methods. The first method uses a timeline edited and archived in DaVinci Resolve 16. This is one of the most efficient methods for sharing and launching timelines, as it uses the original project file and its associated media. By restoring the DRA folder, you can be certain you are seeing the timeline exactly as intended by the editor, with all of its transitions, layers, and retiming intact.

Blackmagic Design Mini Panel Operations

DaVinci Resolve control panels are designed to give you fluid, hands-on control over multiple parameters at the same time, so you can work faster and be more creative. See Appendix B, "Using the Blackmagic Design Mini Panel," for an overview of how a control panel can optimize your workflow in Resolve. Throughout this book, lesson notes will show how exercise workflows can be enhanced by using a Mini Panel.

NOTE For a quick refresher course on the DaVinci Resolve interface, see Appendix A, "Interface Review."

1. Open DaVinci Resolve 16.
2. Right-click in the project manager window, and choose Restore.
3. On your hard disk, locate the "BMD 16 CC - Project 1" folder.
4. Select the Project 01 - Disunity Documentary.dra file, and click Open.

5 In the project manager, double-click the Project 01 - Disunity Documentary thumbnail to open the project.

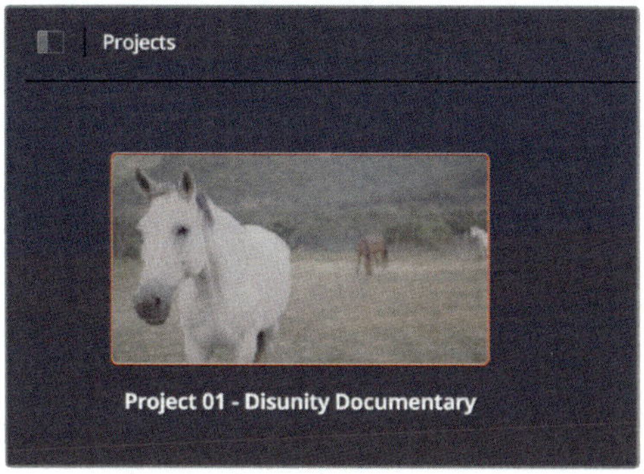

6 To enter the Color page, click the Color button at the bottom of the interface, or press Shift-6.

7 Verify that you are on the 01 Main Timeline. The name of the timeline appears above the viewer. You can select the current timeline by clicking the disclosure arrow next to the timeline name.

> **TIP** You can archive projects by right-clicking a project thumbnail in the project manager, and choosing Export Project Archive. Doing so will consolidate your project file, timelines, and media into a single folder for sharing or future retrieval.

You're almost ready to start grading! However, before you begin, you should make it a habit to verify that your project backup settings are enabled.

Setting up Project Backups

As soon you create or load an existing project, it is good practice to ensure that Resolve's Live Save feature is running in the background. Performing incremental background saves will keep track of every change you make to your project, as well as retain older variants of your project for future recall.

1 Open DaVinci Resolve > Preferences.

2 At the top of the Preferences pop-up window, switch from System to User.

3 Click "Project Save and Load" to the left to access Save Settings.

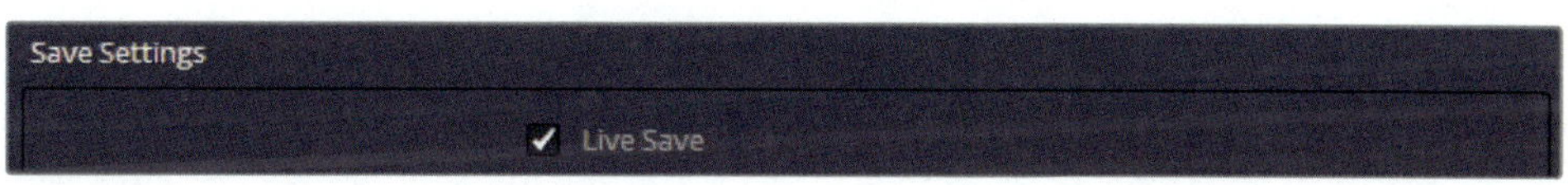

By default, Live Save is enabled, so DaVinci Resolve will overwrite your active project file every time you make a change, no matter how small. This setting is crucial to enable to minimize the risk of losing any project changes in the event of unexpected system or program shutdowns.

4 Choose Project Backups.

Selecting this option saves a new copy of your project file at regular intervals to a designated backup location.

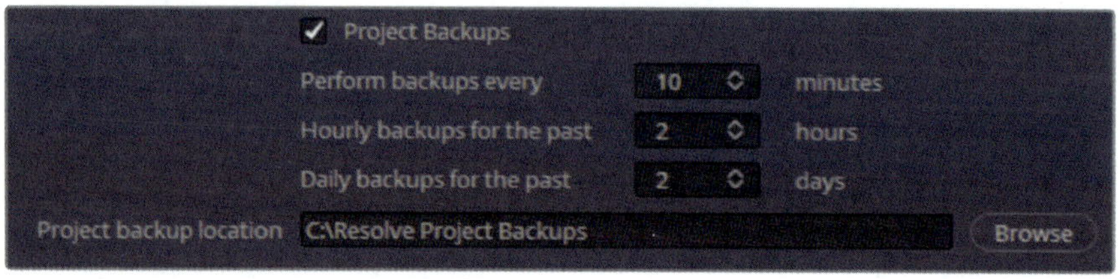

5 To select the backup location, click Browse, and specify a save destination on your workstation or external drive.

By default, a backup project is generated every 10 minutes, regardless of the number of changes that you made during that period. Eventually, older project backup files are cleared from the project storage, with the exception of files that extend over longer hourly and daily intervals. This behavior can be extremely helpful when working on long form projects because it allows you to return to the state of a project (from two weeks ago, for example) without sorting through thousands of project files.

6 Click Save to close Preferences and return to the project. You may now continue working on your project safe in the knowledge that your every change is backed up.

NOTE To open a backed-up project file, you can access the .drp file at the designated backup location on your drive; or you can open the project manager, right-click the thumbnail of the project you wish to restore, and choose Project Backups. In a pop-up window, you can select from a list of all of the backups associated with the project.

With the project loaded and Live Save enabled, you can proceed with actual color grading. But where to begin? When approaching an ungraded timeline, it's not always obvious where your starting point should be. The next section aims to establish a fundamental understanding of the grading process.

Understanding the Grading Workflow

It is good practice to have a clear idea of what your workflow is before beginning a grade. Your workflow is informed by a variety of factors including the color space and format of your footage, the way that the timeline edit was shared with you, and the project's content. Before continuing, let's review the common phases of a grading workflow.

Balancing and Shot Matching

Before you can grade footage creatively, you must adjust shot luminance and chrominance to create a level starting point for your grade. This process is akin to laying down a primer on a canvas before painting to ensure that the pigment is applied to a consistent surface.

A single grade applied to five balanced and matched shots will establish a visual continuity that flows naturally from one shot to the next; whereas the same grade applied to unbalanced and mismatched shots will continue to reflect each shot's differences.

This stage of grading is categorized as a *primary grade* because the entire frame of the image is adjusted. It is usually performed using techniques known as *normalization*, *balancing*, and *shot matching*.

Normalization and balancing involve creating a neutral starting point for clips in the timeline by consistently adjusting the luminance levels of each, and neutralizing any issues with their color balance.

Shot matching involves comparing clips and matching their contrasts and colors exactly. This technique is particularly advantageous when the majority of your clips already have a similar look, and you need to tweak only a few exceptional shots to create a smooth starting point for your scene.

Performing Secondary Grading

Secondary grading refers to any part of the grading process in which only a part of an image is altered. The potential for secondary grading is limitless, but it is mainly achieved by two means: *keying* and *masking*.

Keying targets a portion of an image based on a hue, saturation, or luminance range. In Resolve, the main tool for key extraction is the qualifier.

Masking employs geometric vector shapes to isolate a portion of an image. Resolve's masking interface—the Power Windows palette—features some standard shapes (linear, circle, polygon, and gradient), as well as a fully customizable power curve that enables you to generate garbage mattes and rotoscopes (animated masks).

Like the qualifier, Power Windows cannot alter the appearance of an image directly, but act as selectors for the grading tools.

Secondary grading is most powerful when the qualifier and Power Windows are used in tandem. While the qualifier focuses on extracting an element with a clean edge, a Power Window can confine the qualifier's influence to a specific portion of the screen. In this way, it is possible to target an object in areas of the shot that are of a similar key range.

Creating a Look

Once your clips are balanced and shot matched, and any individual secondary grading needs are met, your creative process can begin.

When performing creative grading, you should carefully consider the emotional and narrative implications of the scene. You can apply both primary and secondary grading techniques to influence an audience's emotional perception of an environment by tweaking the scene's color temperature to indicate positive (warm) or negative (cold) moods, and evoke a wide range of psychological color and tone associations. Additionally, a creative grade can communicate practical narrative elements such as a change in location or time (for non-linear stories).

> **NOTE** The grading workflow described here does not rigidly dictate the order in which these grades should be performed by the colorist. Although first completing the balancing and shot matching stage is strongly advised as a best practice, it is often necessary to readjust grades applied in earlier stages to ensure a consistent final output.

Visualizing the Grading Workflow in the Node Editor

The following chart represents a traditional grading workflow in the context of the Node Editor in Resolve's Color page.

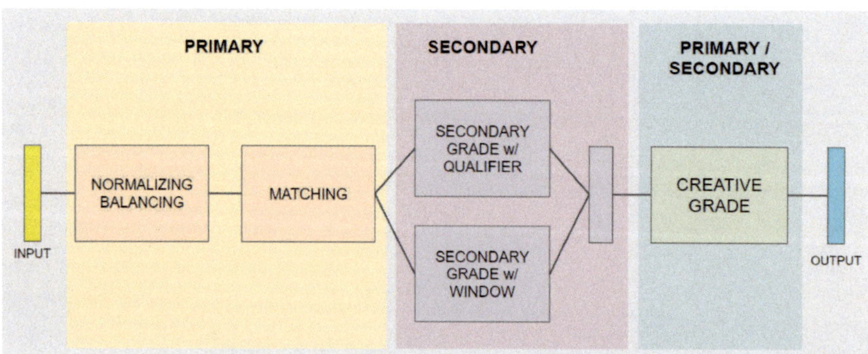

This graph is not intended as a literal guideline to how nodes should be structured, but a representative overview of how nodes relate to one another and their relative positions.

Setting Tonal Range and Contrast

The human eye is particularly sensitive to light sources and shadows, which is why it makes sense to begin the normalization and grading processes by establishing the luminance of an image.

In the following exercises, you will adjust luminance using Master Wheels and Custom curves while also learning about the waveform monitor.

Normalizing with Master Wheels

The Color Wheels are among the most integral primary color correction tools used to adjust image hue. Beneath them, the Master Wheels allow you to set the tonal range and contrast of an image by altering its luminance.

In this exercise, you will adjust the shadows and highlights using the Master Wheels. You'll also refer to the waveform scope to monitor your adjustments for unwanted clipping.

1 Select clip 02.

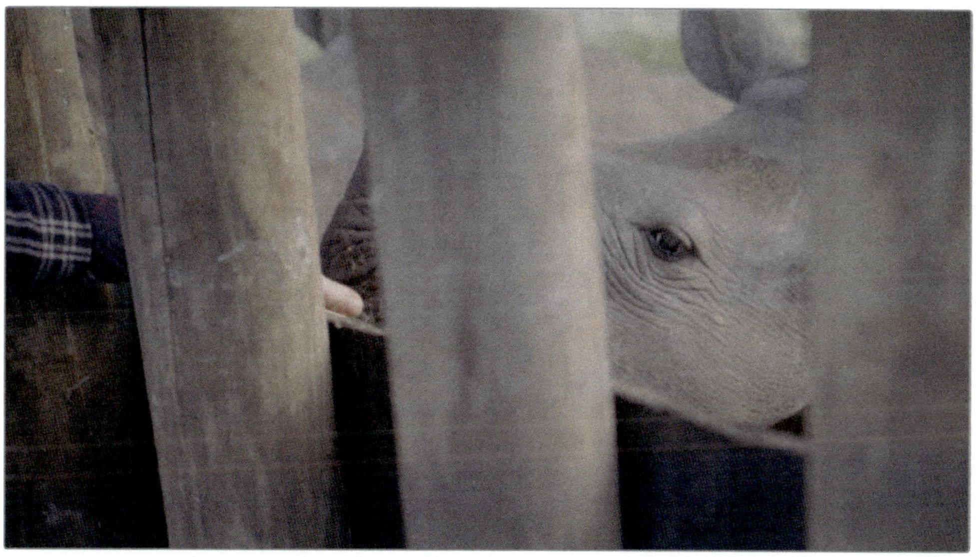

The palette in the lower-right corner of the DaVinci Resolve interface is currently set to the Scopes panel in Waveform mode.

The waveform scope displays the luminance and color channel values of the video at the precise timeline position of the playhead.

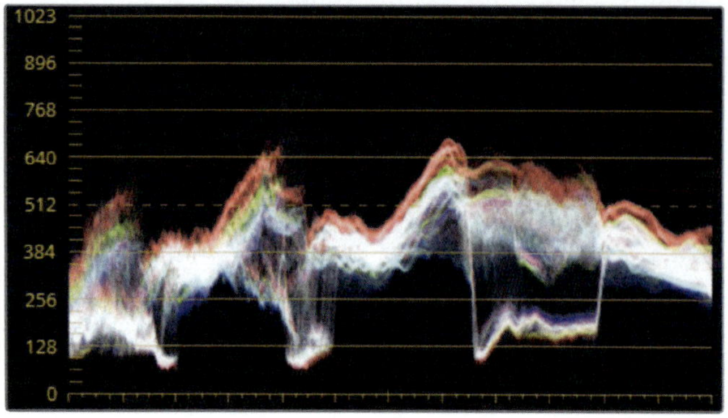

The vertical axis of the scope represents the entire luminance range of the image.

The bottom of the display represents the blackest black (0 in a 10-bit depth signal), and the top represents the whitest white (1023 in 10-bit). Everything between represents the full midtones range of the image in a grayscale format.

The horizontal axis represents the image itself and can be read across both the graph and the monitor. You can think of the display as showing the distribution of the pixels (the trace) across their respective vertical columns based on their luminance levels with darker areas of the footage toward the bottom of the graph, and lighter areas displayed toward the top.

Each color channel is overlapped in the trace. White in the trace indicates that each channel has an equal intensity. When adjusting tonality in an image, you can disable the RGB channels in the waveform and show only luminance.

2 In the upper-right corner of the waveform, click the settings button.

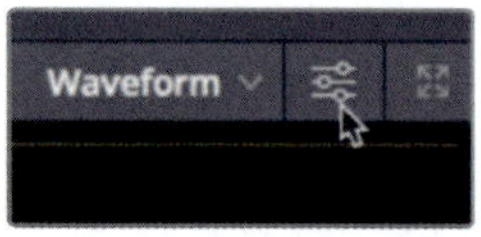

3 Click the Y channel button at the top to display only the luminance channel.

4 Deselect the Colorize option to display the trace with solid white pixels.

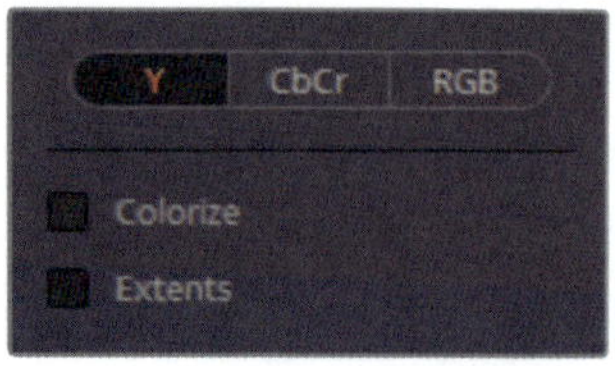

5 Click anywhere in Resolve to close the waveform settings window.

Any part of the trace that goes below 0 (black point) and above 1023 (white point) in the sRGB gamut will be clipped, which will result in a loss of image detail.

When initially normalizing footage, a good starting point is to ensure that the shadows are floating at around 5-10% above the black point (0) on the scope, while the pure white highlights (if any) should stop well under the white point (90%). This leaves the remaining 10% as headroom for superwhite elements such as blown out headlights, lens flares, or metallic specular highlights that can extend beyond the white point.

6 In the Color page, open the Color Wheels palette.

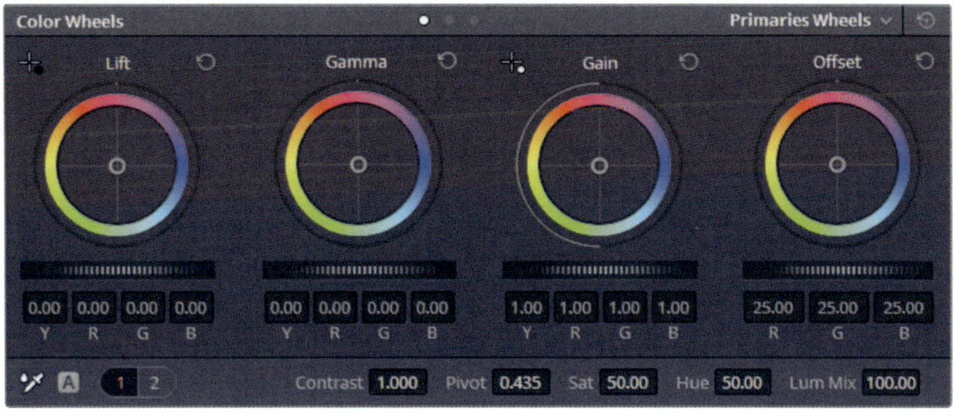

If you have already used DaVinci Resolve or read through Appendix A, "Interface Review," you know that the Lift wheel affects the image shadows, the Gamma wheel affects the midtones, and the Gain wheel affects the highlights. The Offset wheel impacts the entire image and can be thought of as a combination of all three wheels.

The horizontal wheels located under the Color wheels are called master wheels and impact the luminance values of their ranges.

7 Drag the Lift master wheel to the left to darken the shadows. Because this image has detail in the darkest areas of the wood, aim to place the lowest parts of the waveform trace far above 0 but below the 128 axis.

Notice that the three areas of the graph where the trace of the waveform dips toward the black level. Try to locate their respective positions in the frame.

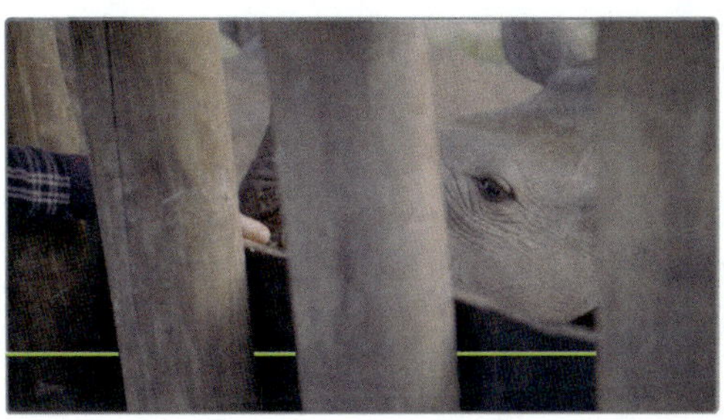

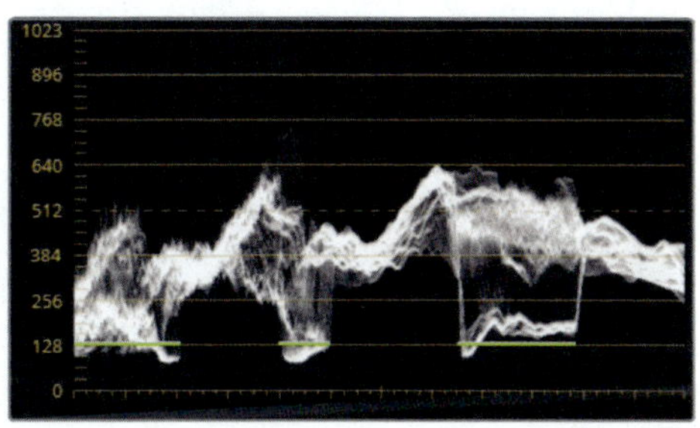

Those three dark areas correspond to places where the barrier is visible behind the wooden poles in the enclosure. The darkest areas of the barrier are represented by a pronounced dip in the graph.

8 You can use the Gain master wheel to brighten the lighter areas of the image. The image has no chart or reference for pure white, but you could use the thumb in the image as a luminance indicator. The highlights on skin should rest between 50-75% on the waveform graph. Drag the Gain master wheel so the tallest traces do not go higher than three-fourths of the waveform graph.

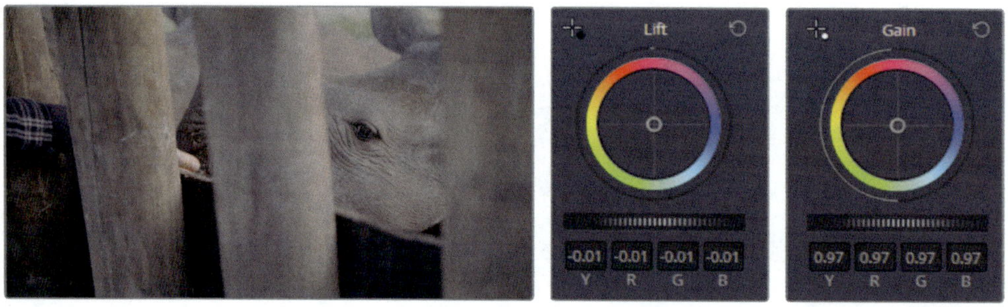

This is an example of using image context for balancing and grade adjustment. In future exercises, you will continue to identify elements that you could use as a guide for grading decisions.

With the shadow and highlight levels set, you will want to adjust the brightness of the midtones.

9 Drag the Gamma master wheel to the right to lighten the overall scene and enhance the details of the rhino's wrinkled skin.

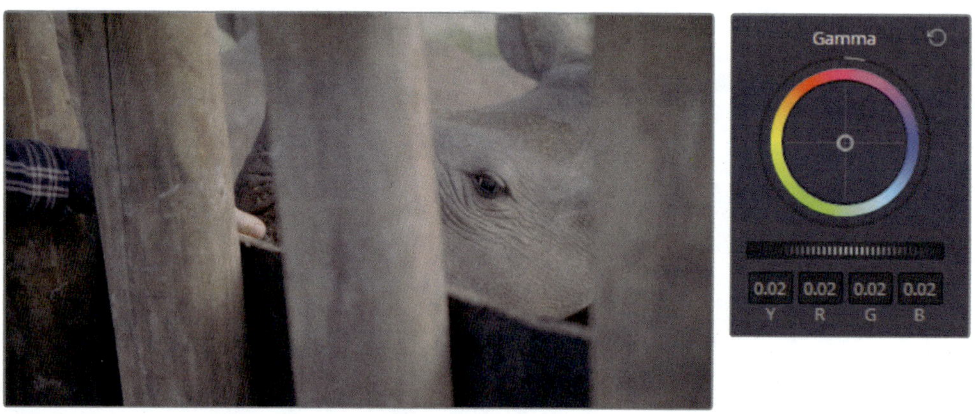

After setting the tonal range, you can further enhance the image details. The master wheels affect the luminance too broadly at this stage, so you should use the contrast control to refine the distinction between the darker and lighter areas.

10 At the bottom of the Color Wheels palette, in the adjustment controls, drag the contrast setting to the right to increase the level of detail in the skin and the wooden poles.

Your image may start look a little dark, but that's OK. So far you have been focusing on only the depth of the shadows, and the nature of the contrast.

11 To increase brightness while maintaining the shadows and level of contrast, drag the pivot control next to the contrast.

The pivot control establishes the contrast balance by placing more or less priority on either side of the luminance scale. By lifting the control, you will increase the overall brightness and clarity of the image, although at the inverse expense of the shadows, which will be reduced.

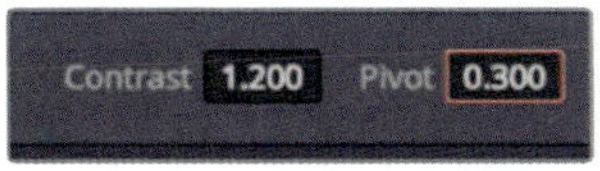

Finally, you will address the magenta tint in the resulting image. For that, you will need to access the second page of the adjustment controls.

12 Click the number 2 tab on the left of the adjustment controls bar.

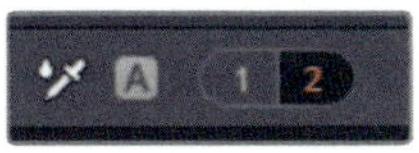

13 Drag the Tint field left until the pink tone of the rhino is reduced.

14 Drag the Temp field left to further "cool down" the image and turn the rhino gray.

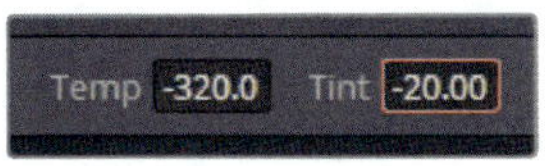

15 Press Cmd-D (macOS) or Ctrl-D (Windows) to toggle the bypass on and off. Compare your before and after results to evaluate how altering the contrast affected the image. Tweak the values if the grade appears overpowering.

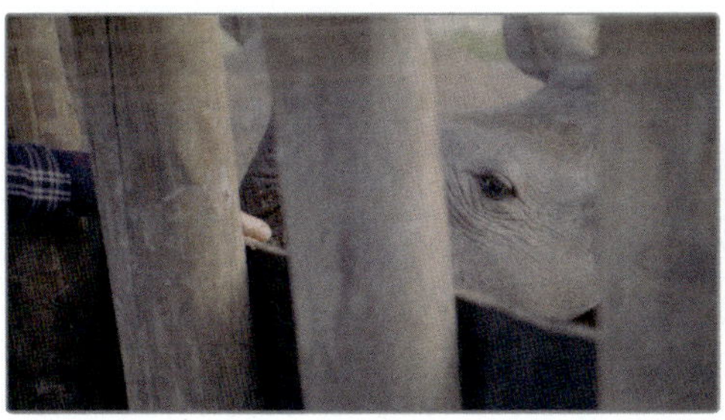
Bypassed

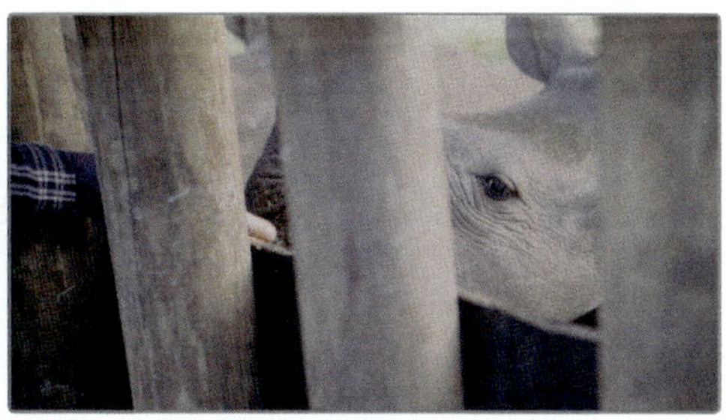
Graded

The grading process usually requires a lot of back-and-forth tweaking of palette values while monitoring the waveform. Some changes dramatically offset the effects of prior adjustments—as in this example, when increasing the contrast darkened the shadows and prompted additional tweaks. Iteration is a completely natural part of the grading process.

Using the Mini Panel—Offset Mode

Whereas the DaVinci Resolve 16 interface shows four wheels within the primary tool palette (Lift, Gamma, Gain, and Offset), you'll notice that the hardware-based Mini Panel has but three wheels and trackballs. To access the Offset wheel functionality, press the Offset button directly above the Gamma wheel. When the Offset button is illuminated, the Gain wheel and trackball will control the master offset. Just as when adjusting Lift, Gamma, or Gain, moving the wheel will control brightness and moving the trackball will control color.

Additionally, when in this "offset mode," the Lift and Gamma wheels control temperature and tint, respectively. To exit this offset mode, press the illuminated Offset button once again. When it no longer lights up, your trackballs and wheels will return to controlling Lift, Gamma, and Gain.

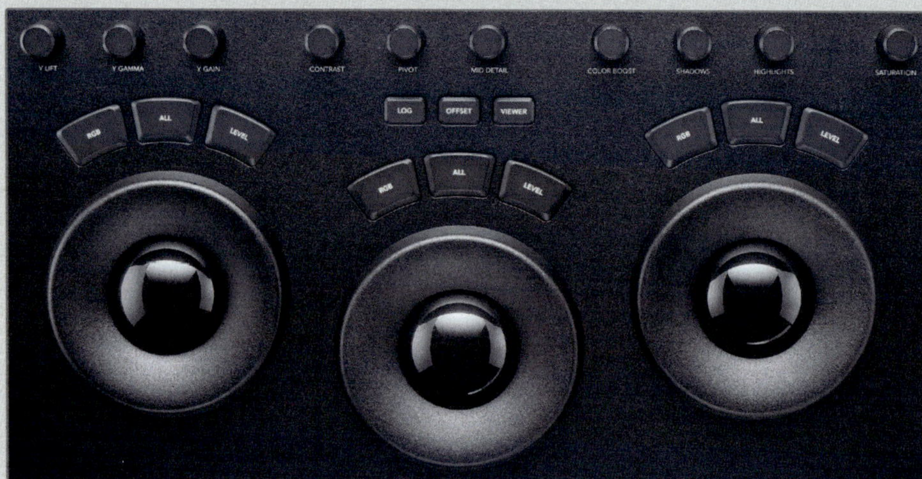

Setting Contrast with Increased Flexibility

Curves are another major grading tool used to perform primary and secondary adjustments. Whereas the master wheels target the luminance range of an image, the curves affect the image based on its luminance or RGB color channels.

The curves controls allow you to manipulate the image with great precision and flexibility.

1. In the timeline, click clip 03.

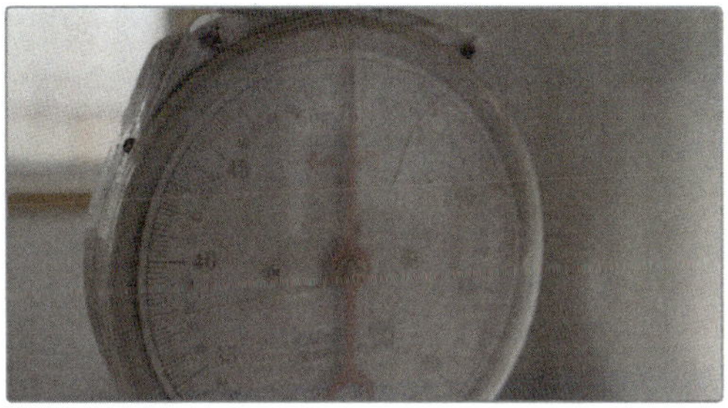

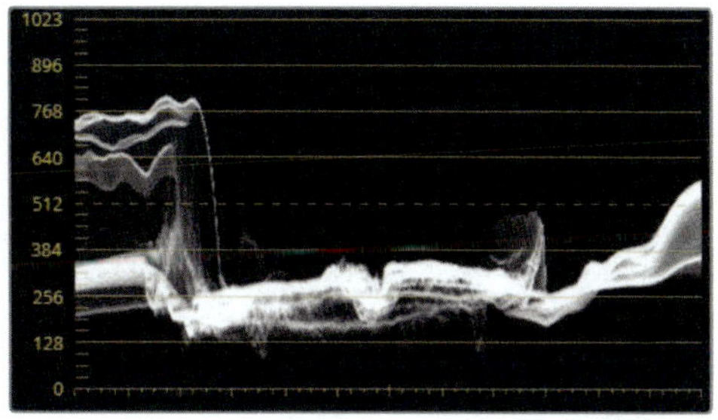

Because the colors in the image are flat, the majority of the waveform graph is condensed in the lower midtones. A significant elevation appears to the left, where a window is positioned behind the scale, and to the right you'll see a gentle peak where the light reflects off the plastic rim.

2. Choose Workspace > Viewer Mode > Enhanced Viewer, or press Option-F (macOS) or Alt-F (Windows) to enlarge the viewer.

   The Clips timeline and surrounding palettes collapse, dynamically enlarging the size of the viewer. The image becomes much easier to see for grading work.

3. Ensure that the custom Curves palette is active in the central palettes of the Color page.

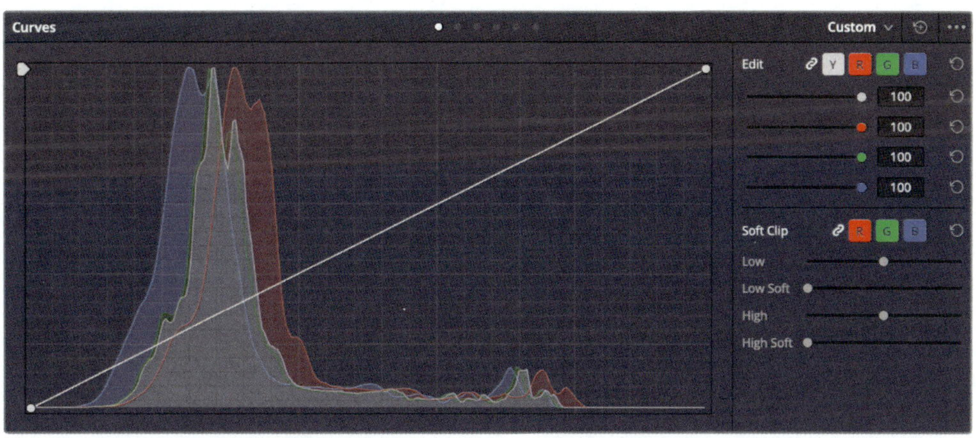

The lower-left of the curve graph represents the blackest potential point of the image, and the upper-right represents the whitest.

The horizontal axis represents the luminance range of the image itself, while the vertical axis represents the offset of that luminance range. By raising or lowering the two control points at either extreme of the curve, you can manipulate the distribution of the tonal range.

By default, the luminance curve (Y) will be visible for adjustment, ganged to all three color channels (R, G, B).

4 Click the Y channel button to ungang the channels.

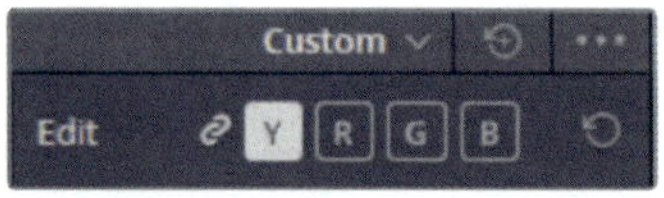

Now, instead of adjusting RGB values you will alter only the image luminance.

5 Drag the lowest control point on the luminance curve across the floor to the right.

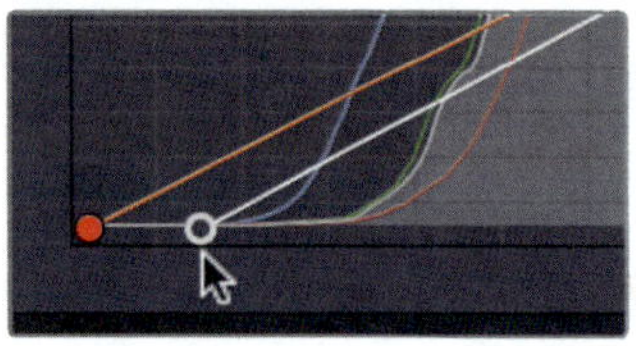

Doing so lowers the waveform of the image logarithmically, darkening the shadows more than the highlights.

6 Stop dragging the control point when the bottom of the trace is still above the 0 line of the waveform.

7 To raise the top of the waveform, drag the highest control point across the top of the graph.

Normally you'd stop when the top of the trace touches the second horizontal line in the Waveform graph (896); but because this part of the trace represents a very bright window in the video clip, it makes sense to continue raising it until the trace is almost halfway between the top horizontal lines on the graph.

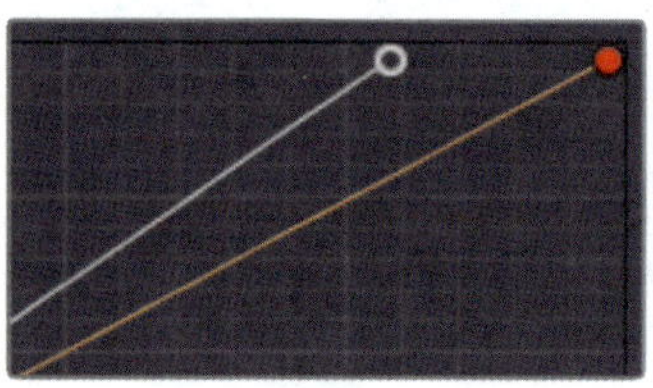

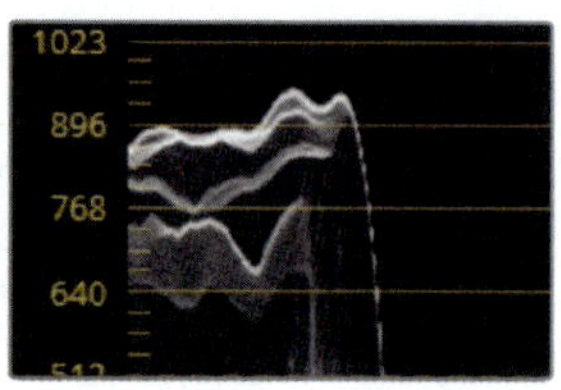

You can add more control points to the curve to manipulate the midtones of the image. Let's tackle the lower midtones that appear too dark after performing that black point adjustment.

8 Click the lower half of the curve to create a new control point to target the lower midtones.

> **TIP** When creating a control point, shift-click to prevent the curve from moving at the position of the mouse.

9 Drag the control point up to raise the lower midtones and brighten the face of the scale.

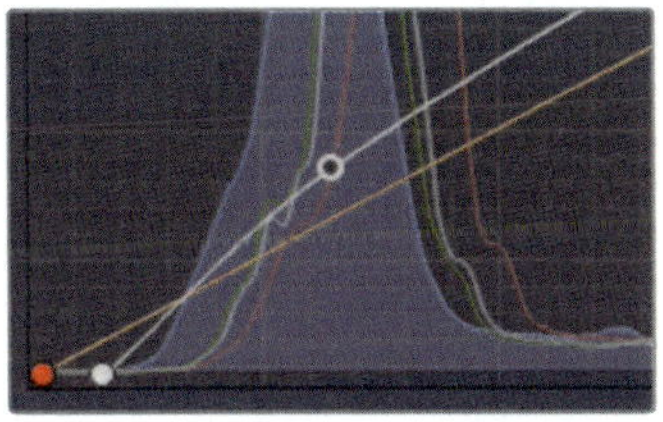

Many colorists prefer setting the tonal range and contrast in the custom curves because it offers much finer control over the contrast amount, the pivot point, and the intensity of each luminance level of the image.

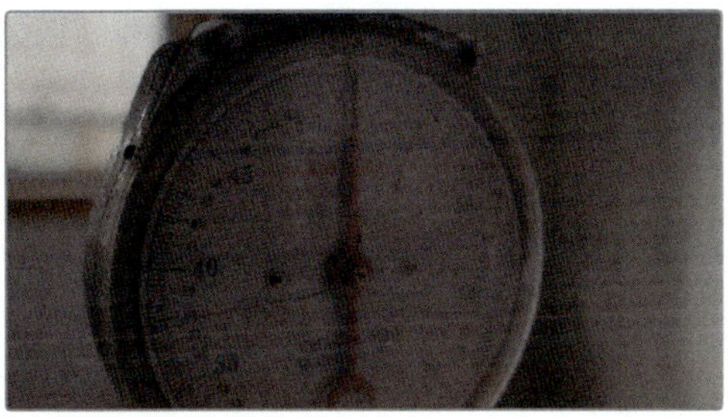

Bypassed

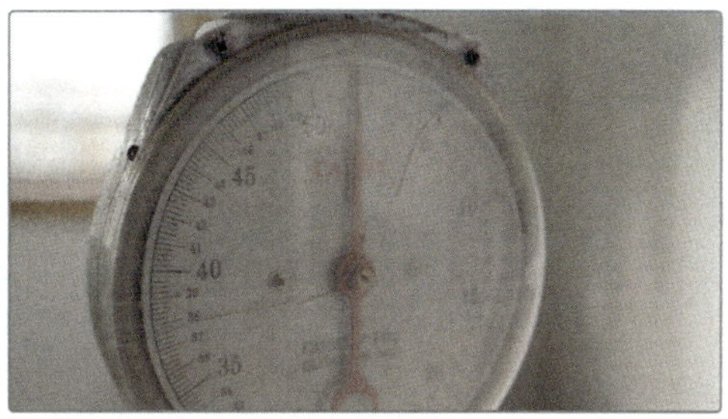

Graded

Balancing Colors

After adjusting the tonal range and contrast, you should carefully examine the colors and neutralize them in preparation for grading. An unbalanced image will affect the precision of your grade, along with the quality of any keyed elements; and will stand out in a sequence of balanced clips.

Balancing Color with Curves

You can use Custom curves to manipulate the three color channels in great detail by creating dedicated control points on each segment of the luminance on each channel.

1 Open the waveform settings, and click the RGB channel button to view the RGB channels.

2 Select the Colorize checkbox to view the individual color channel representations in the waveform trace.

When balancing an image using the waveform, all three channels making the trace appear white when the channels are aligned. In an image that should have white highlights, the trace will appear white at the top.

3 Review clip 03 alongside the waveform.

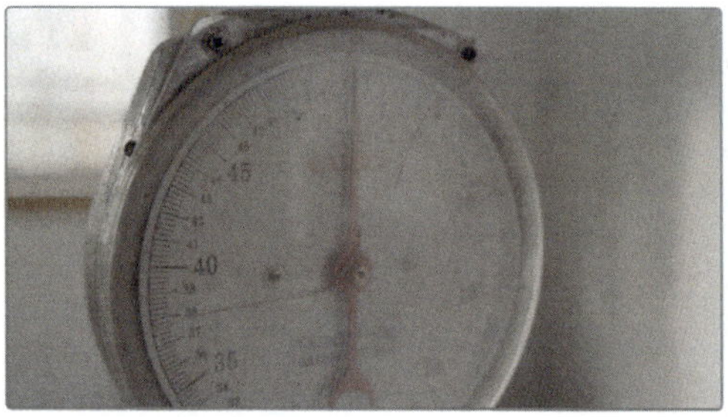

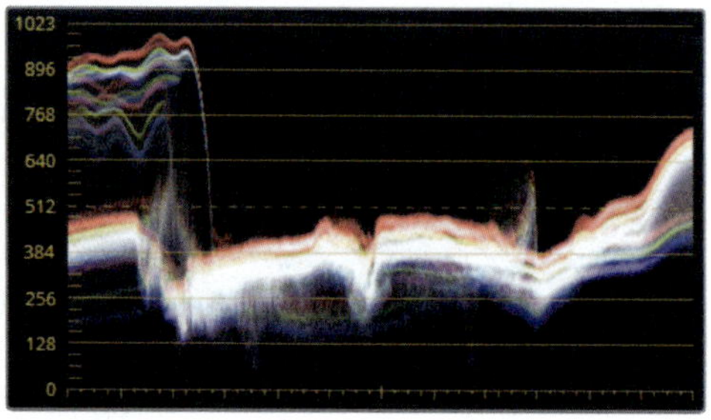

The red channel appears elevated above the other channels, which is giving the image a slightly warm tint.

4 In the Custom curves palette, Click the red (R) button to select the red channel.

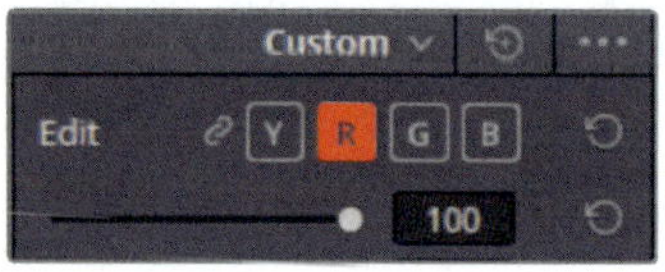

5 Click the top of the red curve and drag it downward. Pay attention to the waveform and drag until the red highlight overlaps the blue and green channels in the trace, resulting in white along the upper edge of the graph.

6 Create a second point on the red curve to perform the same action in the midtones. Drag until the lower half of the trace appears white.

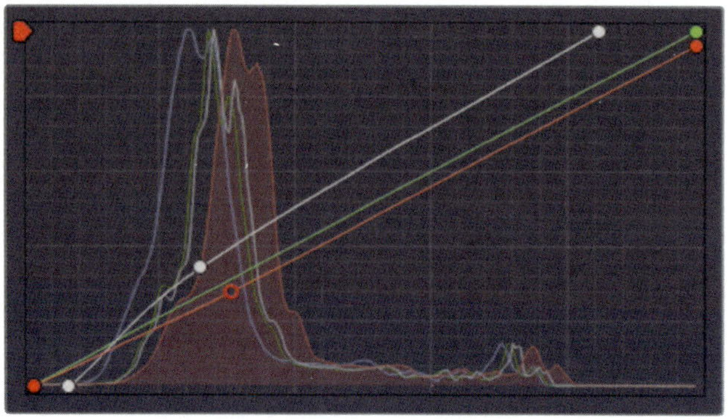

Though the red tint is corrected, the image now has a mild yellow tint because the blue channel has less presence in the highlights and midtones.

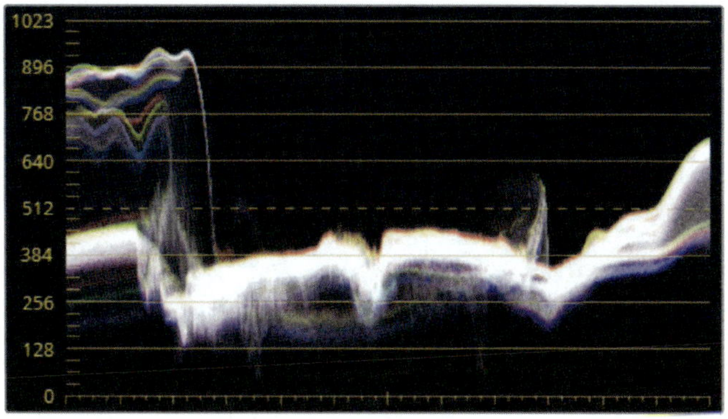

7 Click B to isolate the blue channel.

8 Click the center of the blue curve line to add a control point, and drag it up until the midtones in the waveform are aligned.

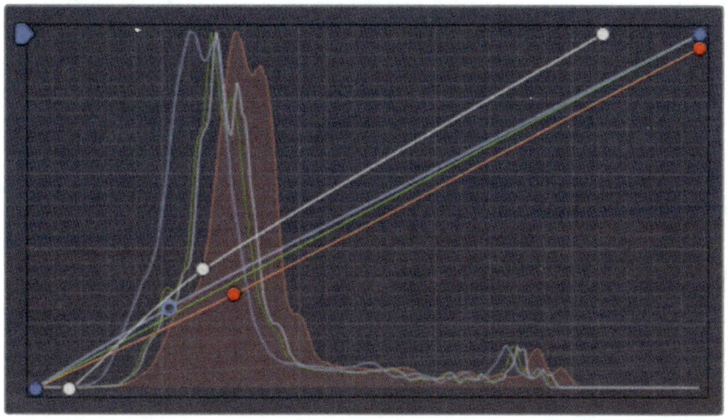

9 Press Cmd-D (macOS) or Ctrl-D (Windows) to disable color adjustments, then press it again to see the corrected image.

With the luminance of the overall image altered, you could opt to return to the Y curve and further adjust the tonal range and contrast of the image, if necessary.

Using the Mini Panel—Curves

You can use the Mini Panel to control all of your curves in DaVinci Resolve. If you used your keyboard and mouse in DaVinci Resolve, or any other image-processing application, chances are you've already worked with curves. While you might have previously used a mouse to control curves, the Mini Panel places dozens of preset curve points at your fingertips. You'll can enter Curves mode by pressing the Curves button in the upper-left of the Mini Panel.

If you've already selected a specific curve tool using your mouse, the Mini Panel will jump to that tool. Otherwise, the default curves that the Mini Panel will jump to are your Custom curves.

The curve tools provide an excellent way to explore the versatility and functionality of your Mini Panel. You may activate every major curve type featured in Resolve using the soft buttons above the five-inch screens. The knobs below those screens allow you to control specific points of the currently activated curve. For custom curves, intervals of 0%, 20%, 40%, 60%, 80%, and 100% may be adjusted. This functionality allows you to control more than one curve point at once, which will save time, increase your grading efficiency, and allow you to make more creative color grading decisions.

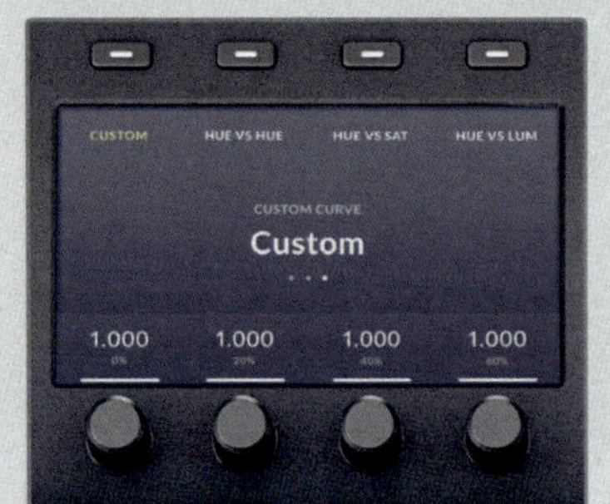

Understanding Log Controls and Primaries Wheels

Before you normalize the next clip, let's take a slight detour to understand another function that can be a fundamental part of primary grading and balancing: The Log color wheel.

It is easier to grasp the difference between the Primaries Wheels and the Log controls by observing a graphic example before moving on to image adjustment. Let's use the simple gradient image at the end of the timeline and manipulate its brightness to compare how the two adjustments affect it.

1 Choose Workspace > Viewer Mode > Enhanced Viewer, or press Option-F (macOS) or Alt-F (Windows), to see the timeline clips.

2 Select the last clip in the timeline (the grayscale image).

In the standard Primaries Wheels that you are familiar with, the Lift, Gamma, and Gain wheels target the luminance ranges as seen in the following figure.

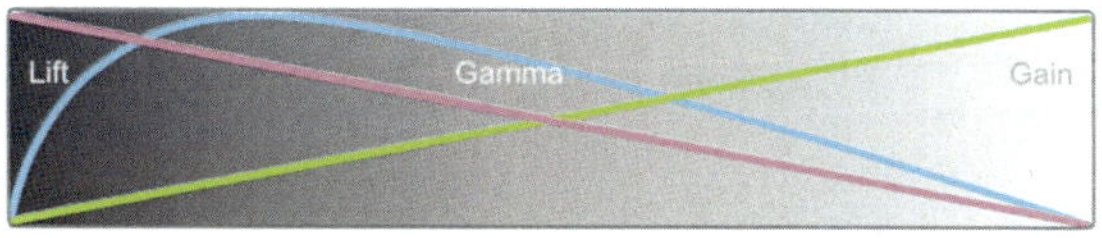

A wide overlap occurs between the segments. When you try to manipulate the shadows of the image using the Lift color or master wheels, the change also substantially affects the midtones, and even the brighter ranges of the image.

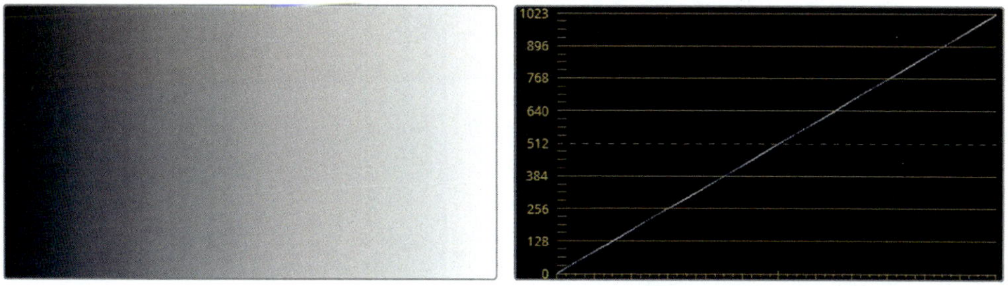

The waveform scope displays the gradient clip as a flat diagonal line extending left to right from 0 to 1023, thereby indicating its linear transition from black to white in the image.

3 Drag the Gain master wheel to the left to darken the upper ranges of the gradient.

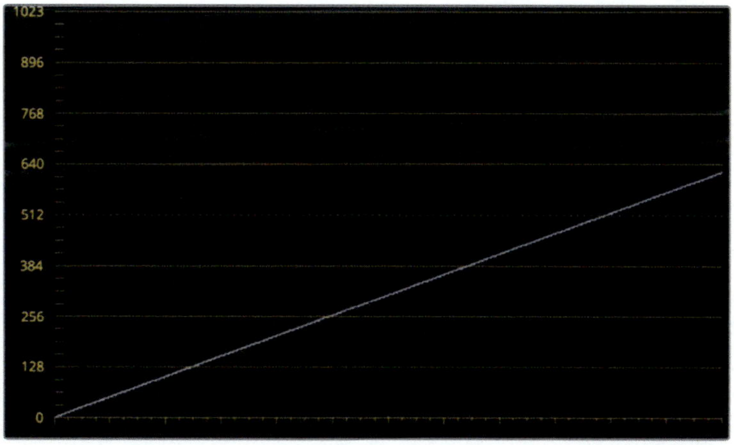

In the waveform, the bottom of the diagonal line remains connected to the black point. The brightest part of the gradient is affected most severely, but still exerts substantial impact on the rest of the luminance range.

4 Reset the Gain master wheel.

5 Drag the Lift master wheel to the right to brighten the lower ranges of the gradient.

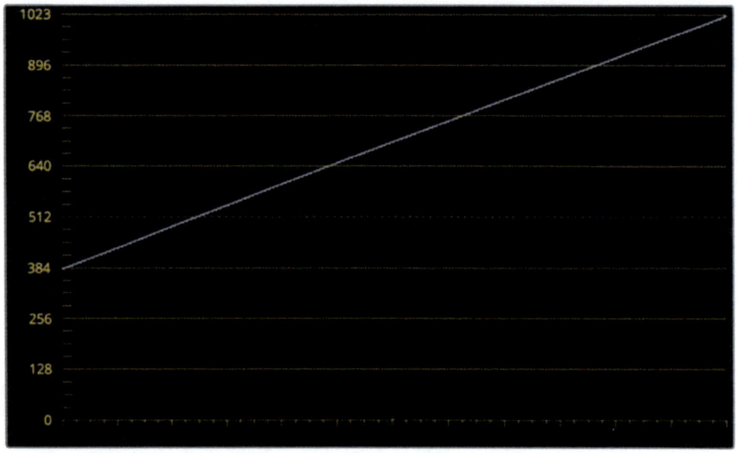

In contrast to the Gain wheel, the majority of the Lift wheel's impact is on the darkest portion of the gradient with the effect tapering off linearly as it reaches the top of the waveform.

The main point is that in both the gain and lift adjustments, the entire image is changed, except for the white and black points. This is intentional because a wide overlap creates nice, smooth transitions even in dramatic changes.

6 Reset the Lift master wheel.

When working in Log, the luminance ranges are much more defined:

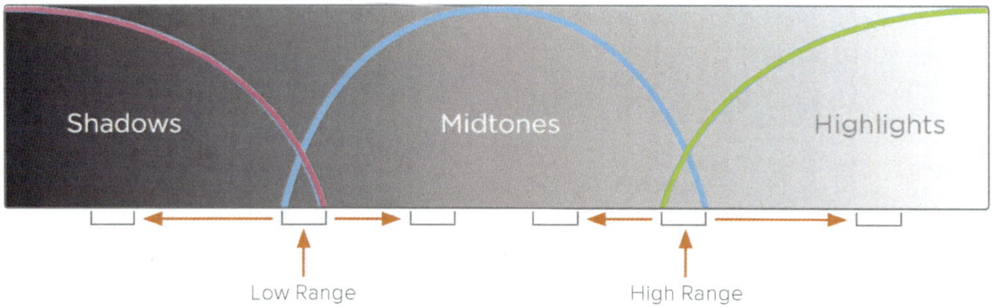

Manipulating the image shadows will have very little effect on the rest of the luminance range due to the small amount of overlap between the shadows and the midtones range.

7 In the options menu in the Color Wheel palette, choose Log.

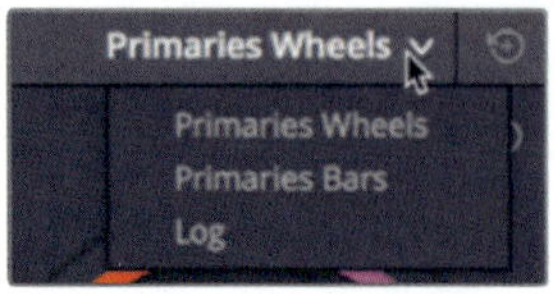

On the surface, this interface looks identical to the Primaries wheels. However, adjustments to the shadows, midtones, and highlights react very differently.

8 Drag the Highlight master wheel to the left to darken the highlights of the gradient.

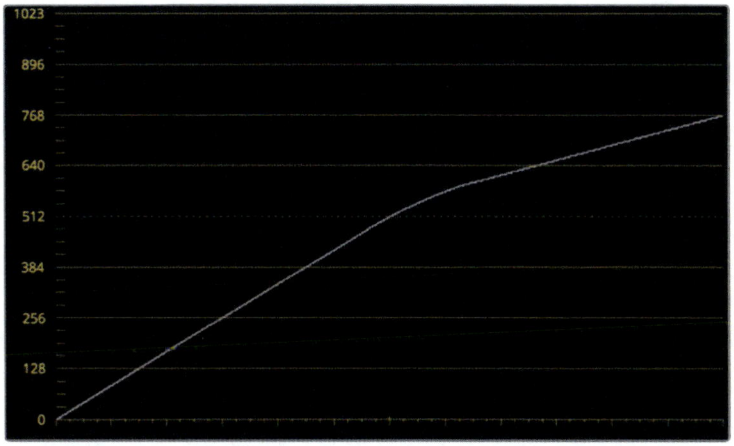

The upper-third of the waveform bends until it is horizontal, but this has no impact on the shadows. This behavior is reflected in the viewer, in which the brightest portion of the gradient are darkened, while the midtone and shadows remain the same.

9 Drag the Shadow master wheel to the right to brighten the dark ranges.

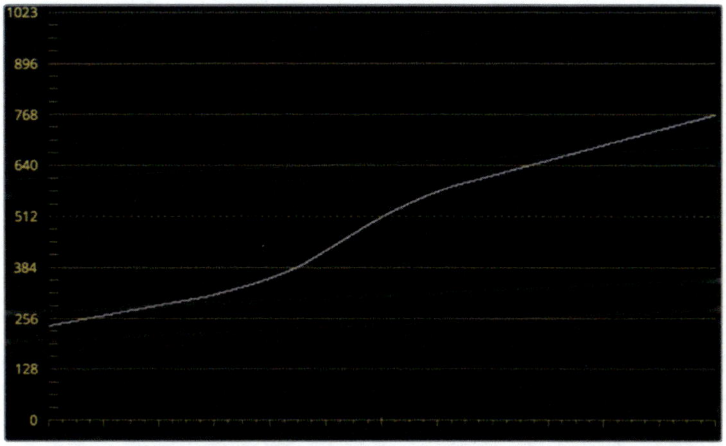

This time, the lower-third of the line rises until it is parallel to the horizon.

With the waveform in this position, it is easy to see how you can affect the position of overlap between the shadows and midtones (low range), and the midtones and highlights (high range).

10 In the adjustment settings under the Log wheels, drag the LR value to the left to move the low range down toward the shadows, thereby giving priority to the midtones controls.

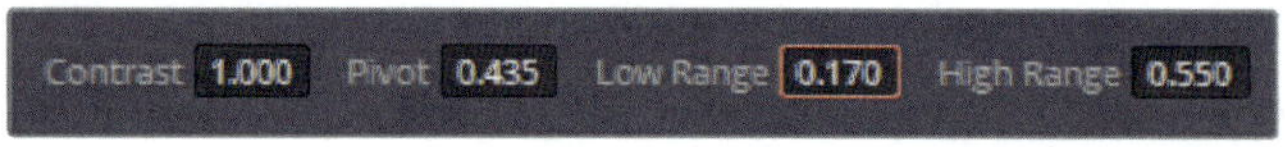

11 Drag the HR value to the right to move the high range toward the shadows for the same effect, but in reverse.

> **TIP** To further appreciate how primaries and Log differ, drag the color indicator inside the Lift and Shadow wheels to see how the gradient is affected. Adjusting the Lift wheel will cause the entire gradient to change hue, whereas dragging the Shadow wheel will constrain the color change to the darkest edge of the gradient.

The Log wheels can be extremely useful when you are attempting to change the luminance or chrominance of a narrower image luminance range. The next exercise will demonstrate a practical use of switching between Primaries and Log wheels.

Applying Log and Primaries Changes to an Image

With an understanding of how you can target the luminance ranges of an image, you can now more accurately adjust the tonal range and balance of an image.

1 Select clip 07.

The luma waveform indicates some room for adjusting the image's highlights.

2 Drag the Gain master wheel right to increase brightness until the trace reaches the second horizontal line from the top.

Even though the waveform appears to be intact, the sunset on the horizon might start to appear “blown out”. To understand why this is happening, let’s check the Parade scope to determine the presence of color in the luminance ranges.

3 Switch the scopes panel to Parade.

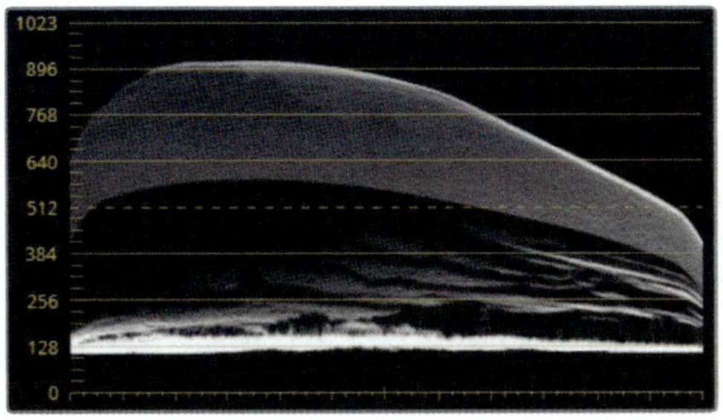

Waveform

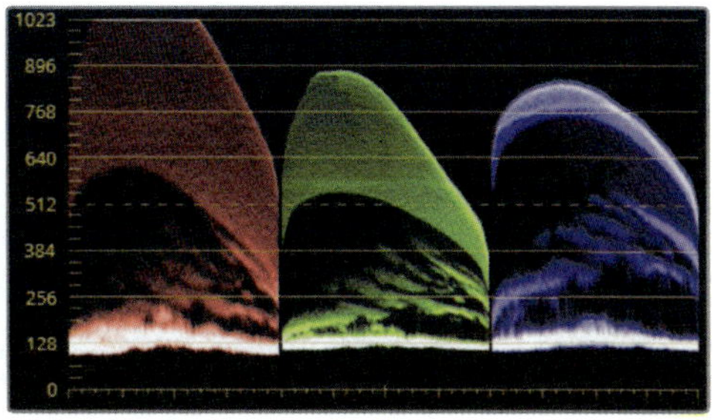

Parade

The waveform represents the combined luminance of the channels, but it does not take into account instances of clipping within individual channels in scenes with pronounced chromatic brightness (such as this sunset).

4 Drag the Gain master wheel to the left to decrease brightness until the top of the red channel is no longer clipped in the waveform scope.

With reliable white and black references in an image, standard procedure is to neutralize the three channels to achieve balance. Without references, context is important. In this case, the context is the sunset with its accompanying red skyline, which requires an exception to the balancing rule.

5 Switch the scopes back to Waveform. With the highlights analyzed, you can focus on the tonal range and the balance of the dark foreground elements.

6 To increase the overall brightness of the image without clipping its highlights, drag the Gamma master wheel to the right until you have raised the darkest parts of the image above the 128 line.

The image shadows appear to be compressed along a narrow luminance range which is causing loss of the detail in the image foreground. Adjusting the Lift master wheel will not sufficiently expand the compressed shadows.

7 To confirm this, drag the Lift master wheel to the left to see how dramatically it affects the foreground. The compressed shadows are pulled down until the entire image becomes too dark.

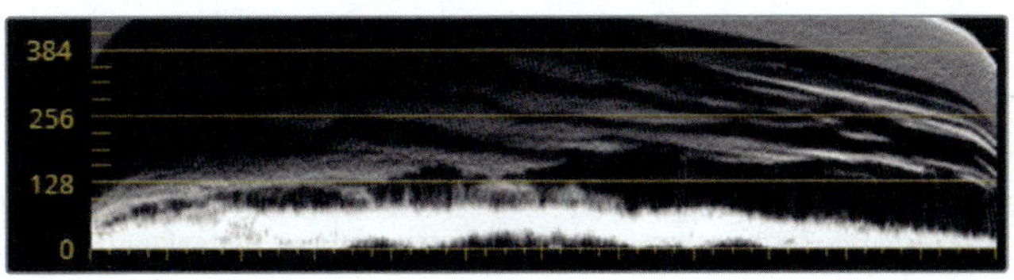

8 Reset the Lift wheel.

9 Switch the Color wheel palette to Log.

> **TIP** Press Option-Z (macOS) or Alt-Z (Windows) to toggle between the primaries and Log wheels.

10 Drag the Shadow master wheel to the left to lower the black point without clipping it. Note that the tree details begin to pop out against the mountains and ground.

11 In the adjustment controls, drag LR to the left to redefine the low range of the shadows. Because of this narrower shadow range, adjustments to the Shadow wheel will be more focused on altering the compressed shadows at the bottom of the image.

12 Drag the Shadow master wheel to the left to further expand the compressed shadow range. Keep adjusting the LR and Shadow master wheel controls until you see a good amount of detail in the foreground of the viewer.

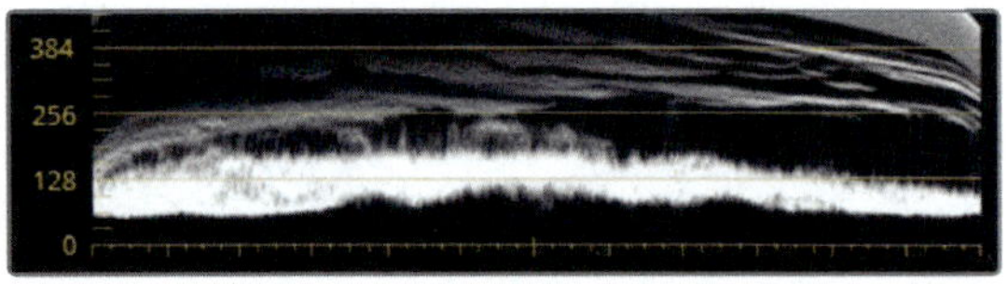

Because the Shadow wheel is more dedicated to the lower ranges of luminance, it is not affecting the midtones as dramatically as the Lift wheel did. With the contrast adjusted, you can now address the colors. This image is particularly tricky because of the conditions under which it was captured. The sun is still rising, resulting in beautiful peach, purple, and blue gradients throughout the sky. You will strive to retain these unusual hues, while normalizing the colors in the foreground—most notably, the magenta in the shadows.

13 Return to the Primaries wheels palette.

14 Gently drag the Gamma color wheel indicator away from the magenta side of the wheel and toward green. Stop dragging before the green in the shadows becomes too overpowering.

Bypassed

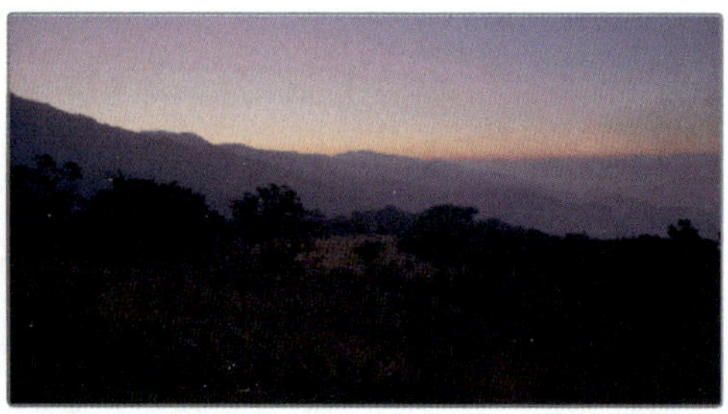
Graded

This adjustment removes the magenta tint from the shadows and lower midtones while preserving the hues in the mountains and the sky.

As you saw in this exercise, you can use Primaries and Log wheels together very effectively. You also can use the Primaries to establish tonal range and contrast. Log wheels behave like a secondary adjustment that can further refine the three luminance ranges.

Log wheels are particularly effective when working on under or overexposed footage. They allow for restorative work in the high and lower ranges, as well as minor tweaks to the brightness and hue of those ranges without seriously altering the remainder of the image.

Together with balancing and matching, Log wheels are also powerful tools for creating distinct creative looks.

Self-guided Exercises #1

Complete the following exercises in the 01 Main Timeline to test your understanding of the tools and workflows covered in this lesson.

Clip 01—Use Custom curves to normalize and balance this clip by eye. Place an additional control point in the high midtones of the Y channel to create a contrast and accentuate the details in the wood grain.

Clip 03—Use the contrast and pivot controls to enhance the details of the scale.

Clip 04, 05, 06, and 09—Use the Primaries wheels to establish a tonal range and contrast on these clips with the assistance of the waveform scope.

Clip 12, 16, and 17—Using custom curves, and using the Parade scope for reference, normalize these clips and balance the colors, as necessary.

When you've completed these exercises, open the 04 Completed Timeline to compare your balancing to the Balance node in this "solved" timeline. Note that normalization, balancing, and contrast in some of the clips was separated into individual actions in the Node editor. In the next lesson, you will also begin the practice of separating your grading stages into nodes.

Lesson Review

1. Does a DaVinci Resolve archive (.DRA) contain the original project media?
2. What does the Y in YRGB represent?
3. What does the pivot in the adjustment controls do?
4. How do you add additional control points to curves?
5. What is the difference between the Primaries Wheels and Log controls?

Answers

1. Yes. Archived projects (.DRA) consolidate all related project media within a single folder that can be restored through the project manager.
2. The Y refers to luminance.
3. Adjusts contrast balance
4. Click directly on a curve to add a new control point. Shift-click to add a new control point without adjusting the curve's position.
5. They target different tonal ranges of the image.

Lesson 2

Creating Color Continuity

When editing footage for a video project, the end goal often is to create a single running narrative that appears to be happening in real time. Much of the time—even in documentary filmmaking—this unity of time is an illusion. Materials for a single scene can take days or even weeks to photograph which can result in fluctuations in light, temperature, and tint as environmental factors influence the footage from one day to the next.

The goal of shot matching is to assess how multiple clips compare to one another when placed into a timeline, and to ensure that they create color continuity. When shots don't match, an audience becomes aware of their artificial sequencing (as opposed to events that were actually shot in real time) which breaks the illusion of cinema and compromises the viewer's suspension of disbelief.

Time

This lesson takes approximately 60 minutes to complete.

Goals

In the previous lesson, you looked at the most common tools and workflows for normalizing and balancing shots in preparation for a grade. In this lesson, you'll examine the shot-matching process.

Building a Shot-Matching Strategy

Your approach to shot matching will depend greatly upon the nature of the footage.

On a narrative production that was shot by an experienced cinematographer and camera crew, the quality of the raw content can have a reliable consistency throughout and require minimal normalization.

For documentaries, fluctuation in locations, light sources, and temperatures (not to mention the use of multiple, different cameras) may require a much more dedicated preparation.

It is normal to incorporate both balancing and shot matching during the first primary grade pass. You may opt to treat these as separate jobs and apply them to independent nodes, or you can forgo balancing on shots that you are matching to a single "key" shot in a scene.

Your shot-matching strategy may be narrowed down to the following approaches and considerations:

- **Balance all shots in a sequence.** This workflow assumes a shot-by-shot approach to normalizing the luminance range and balancing every shot in the sequence, which will result in a uniform sequence of shots. This is a time-consuming method that is best applied to projects with vastly mismatched media sources or lighting conditions (archival documentaries, promo videos, and so on).

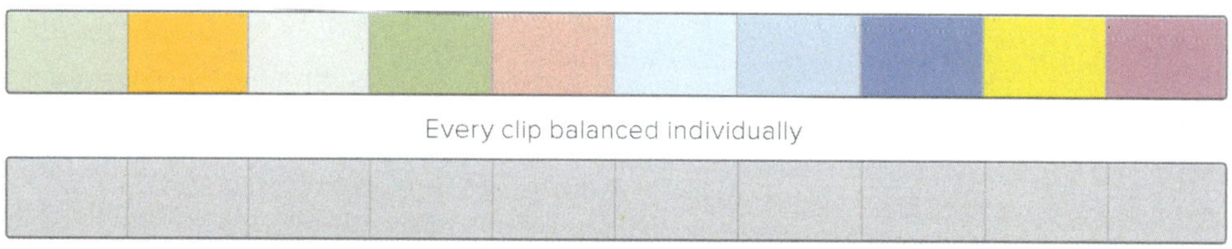

- **Adjust only mismatched shots in a sequence.** If only one or two shots in a sequence have a contrasting color balance, it makes sense to adjust only those shots to create an even starting point for the grade. This approach is more common to standard grading practices.

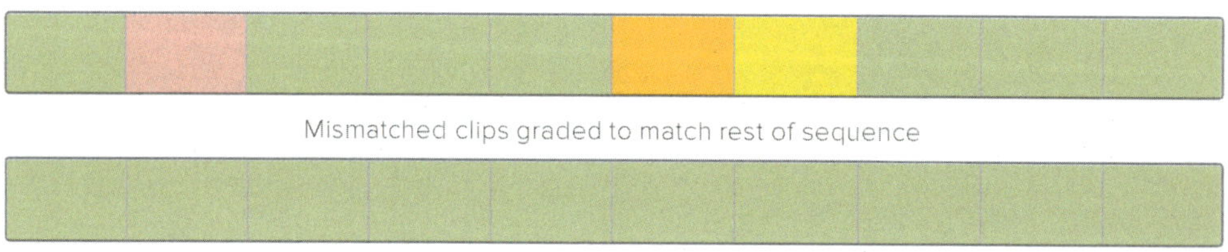

- **Select a master reference shot.** Sometimes you will have more than one clip that could you could use as a reference for matching. In those cases, you may opt to use the reference shot that will have a less extreme impact on the color tone of the other clips.

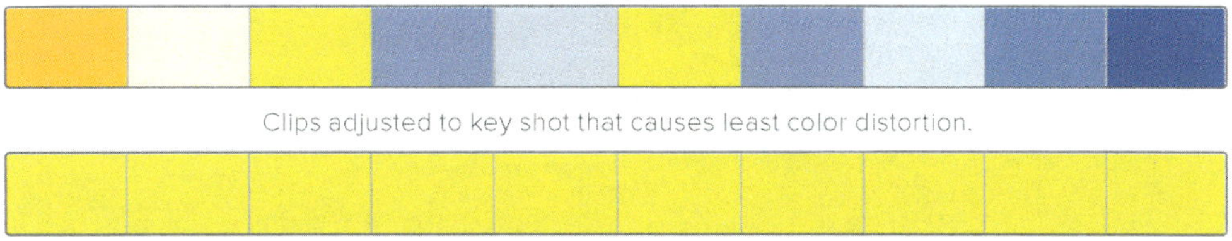

Clips adjusted to key shot that causes least color distortion.

Or, you might consider settling on the clip that is closest in appearance to your intended grade. In doing so, any further creative grading you perform will aim to enhance the colors and not undo them.

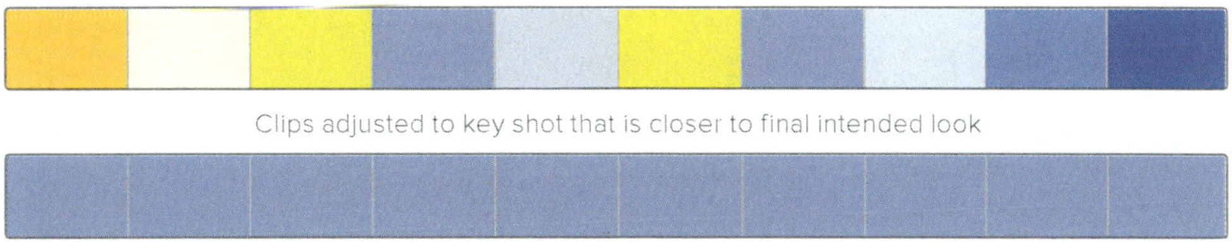

Clips adjusted to key shot that is closer to final intended look

> **TIP** When selecting a master reference shot, it is best to select a wide angle of the scene and match all other angles to it. A wide angle shot is likely to have the best overall representation of light sources and shadow tones, as well as include most of the physical elements in the scene such as actors, costumes, set design, walls, and so on. In contrast, a close-up might contain less reliable data for balancing and share few elements with other shots.

The exercises in the following lessons will focus on the practical implementation of shot matching based on these methods. Understanding the variety of matching methods that are available in DaVinci Resolve 16 will enable you to construct grading workflows that are best suited to your coloring abilities and project type.

Organizing Shots Using Flags and Filters

In the previous lesson, you clicked on individual clips throughout the Timeline. However, Resolve provides helpful organizational tools, called *flags*, that can assist you in identifying and categorizing clips based on any criteria that you define. For example, you might flag clips that have overexposed skies, clips that require green screen keying, or clips that need narrative-specific dynamic grades.

1 In the Timeline menu above the Viewer, open the 02 Balanced Timeline.

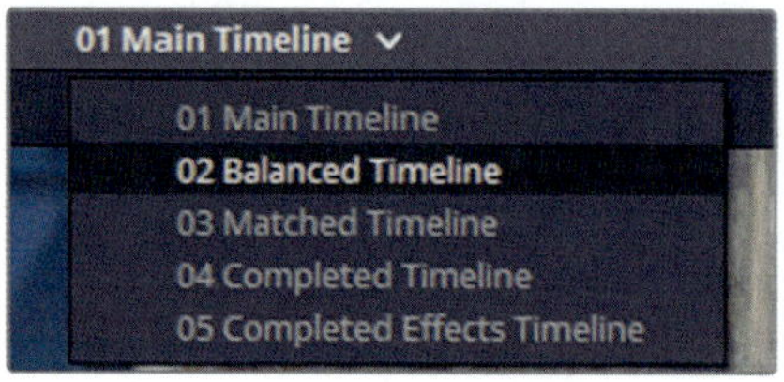

The timelines in this project already include some flags. You'll add a few more to identify those clips you will use for the matching exercises in this lesson.

2 In the Timeline, right-click clip 04, and choose Flags > Green.

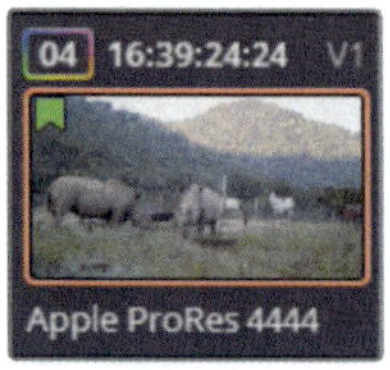

A green flag appears in the upper-left corner of the clip thumbnail to indicate that the clip is flagged.

Another method for applying flags is to use a keyboard shortcut.

3 Click clip 05. Press G on your keyboard to add another flag.

While this is a faster technique for applying flags, in this case, it applied the wrong color flag.

4 To change the flag to green, double-click the blue flag on the thumbnail to open the Flags dialog.

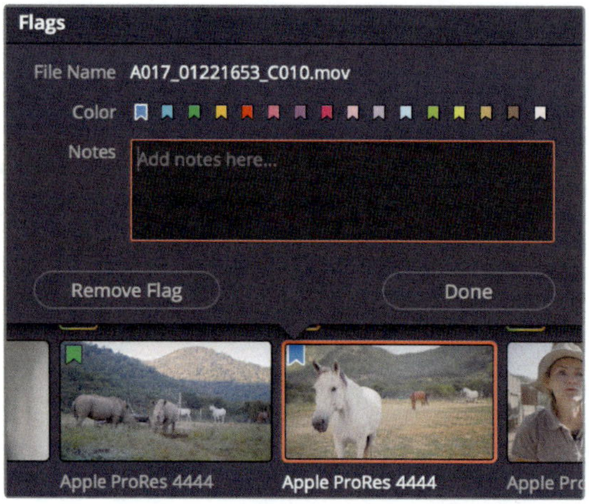

Note that the dialog window allows you to attach notes to flags, which is very handy for detailing future grading reference and visual adjustments.

5 Select the green-colored flag, and click Done to close the dialog.

The keyboard shortcut currently is configured to apply blue flags by default. To change the default flag color, you will need to change the flag color in the toolbar of the Edit page.

6 Go to the Edit page. In the toolbar, next to the flag icon, click the disclosure arrow, and choose Yellow.

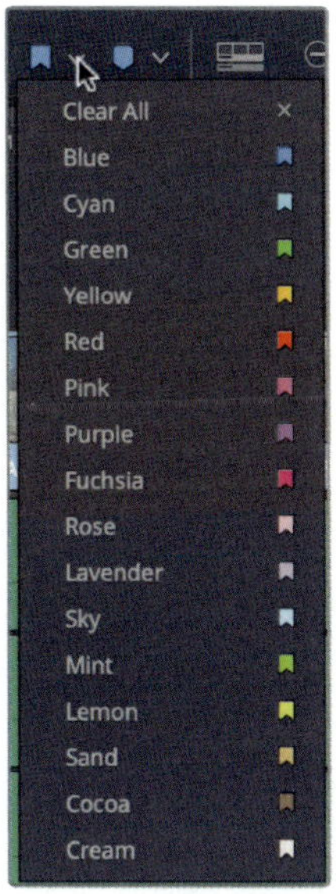

7 Return to the Color page, select clips 04 and 06, and press G to apply yellow flags to them.

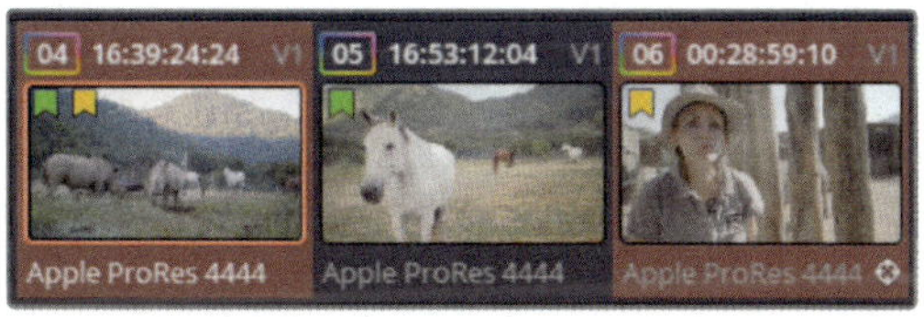

TIP You can apply a flag to multiple clips by selecting a range of thumbnails, and then using any of the methods described to apply the desired flag to the selected clips.

The green flags in the Timeline now identify the clips you will be working on throughout this lesson. You will find it easier to locate and navigate between them if you filter the Timeline to show only the green-flagged clips.

8 At the top of the color page, click the disclosure arrow next to the clips button, and choose Flagged Clips > Green Flag.

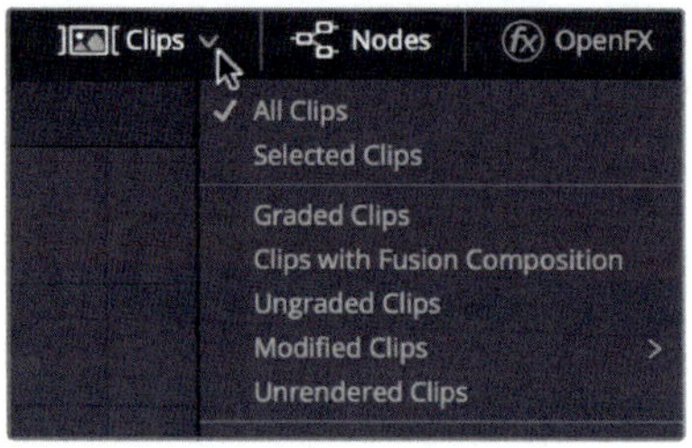

TIP When a filter is applied to a timeline, the Clips button is underlined in red to serve as a visual reminder that some clips in the Timeline might not be visible because of the filter.

You have temporarily hidden all clips that do not have a green flag. The result is a significantly simplified Timeline that will help you focus on those clips without the need to navigate around your Timeline and locate them.

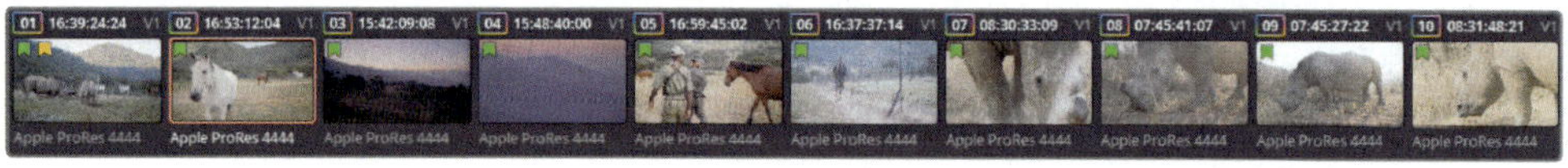

TIP Like flags, you can also use markers for filtering purposes. The difference compared to flags is that flags identify an entire clip (or source media), whereas markers identify out a specific frame or range on a single clip in the Timeline. In contrast, adding a flag to a clip applies it to every appearance of the source clip in the Timeline. Markers can be applied using a keyboard shortcut (M) and their default colors may be set in the toolbar of the Edit page.

9 Once again, click the disclosure arrow next to the Clips button, and choose Flagged Clips > Yellow Flag.

As you can see, clips may contain containing multiple flags. As a result, media classifications can overlap, which allows you to filter clips that have several workflow roles.

10 In the Clips pop-up menu, choose Yellow again to remove the yellow flags from the clip filter.

In Resolve, flags and filters can perform a wide variety of functions. You can use different flag colors to identify clips that must be reframed due to a visible boom, single out clips that were incorrectly white balanced, or isolate clips that require a flashback look. When the Timeline is filtered based on flag color, you can focus on addressing just one category of clips at a time.

Applying Shot Match

The shot match function in Resolve analyzes the colors in one image and reconfigures the balance of another image (or multiple images) to match it.

The results of any algorithmic grading function should be carefully evaluated after you apply it because an algorithm is unable to recognize the environmental factors behind scene colors. Even so, shot match can be a great starting operation for a match grade, and can enable you to quickly prepare shots for on-set review, or processing dailies.

1 In the green flag-filtered Timeline, select clip 01.

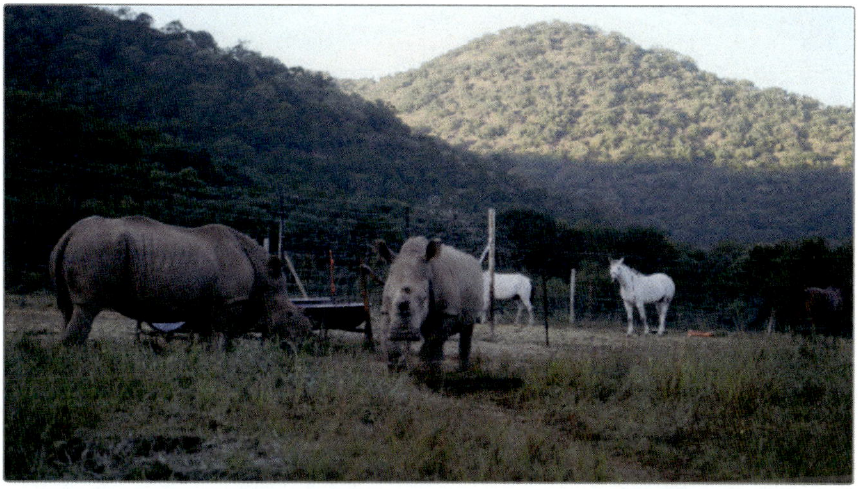

You will be matching the colors in this clip to the balanced clip 02 directly after it. In the interest of preserving the integrity of the video signal, you are advised to keep normalization, balancing, and matching on separate nodes.

2 In the Node editor, create a new serial node by right-clicking node 02, and choosing Add Node > Add Serial, or pressing Option-S (macOS) or Alt-S (Windows).

3 Right-click the new node, and choose Change Label. Name the node **Shot Match**.

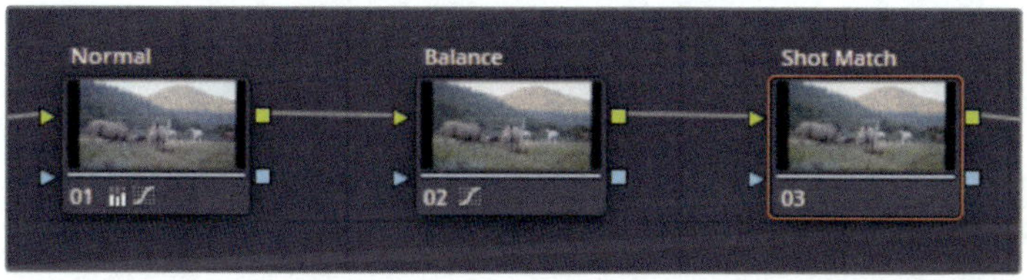

NOTE In the Balanced Timeline, the normalization and color balancing stages were organized into dedicated nodes. This method represents a common grading workflow that focuses on preserving the integrity of the RGB signal. You will explore it in greater depth in Part 2 of this book.

4 Right-click clip 02, and choose "Shot Match to This Clip". The shot match is performed on the active clip in the Timeline, which is currently clip 01.

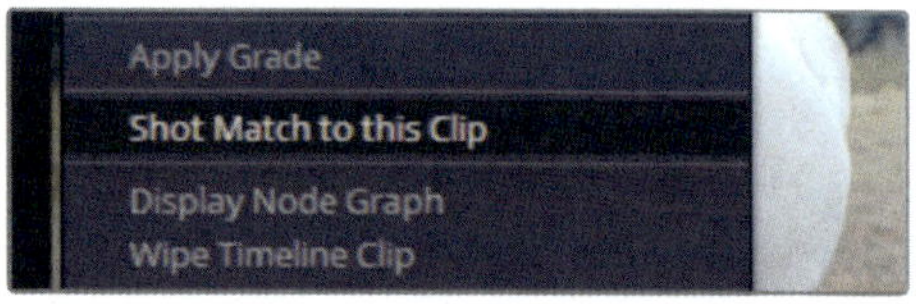

The result is a better match between the two images. Clip 01 becomes warmer and less contrasted to match the environment in clip 02. However, the shadows could be darkened to better match the mountains in the background, and the gamma brightened and made cooler to remove the strong red tones.

5 Drag the Lift master wheel left until the shadows of the waveforms in clips 01 and 02 more closely match.

6 Drag the Gamma master wheel right to brighten the image and increase contrast in the details.

7 Drag the Gamma color wheel indicator away from red until the rhinos appear more neutral in color.

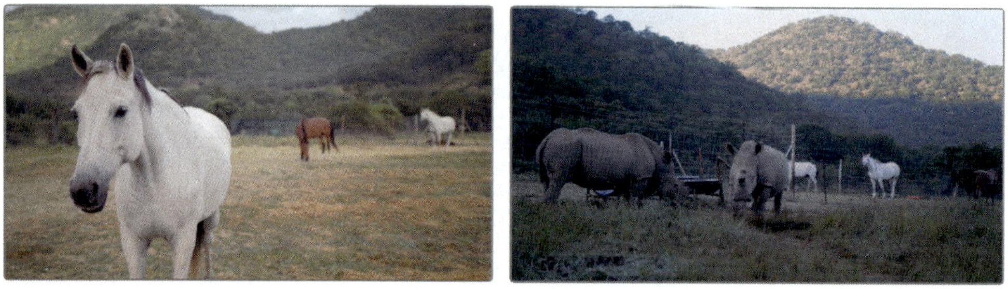

Before match

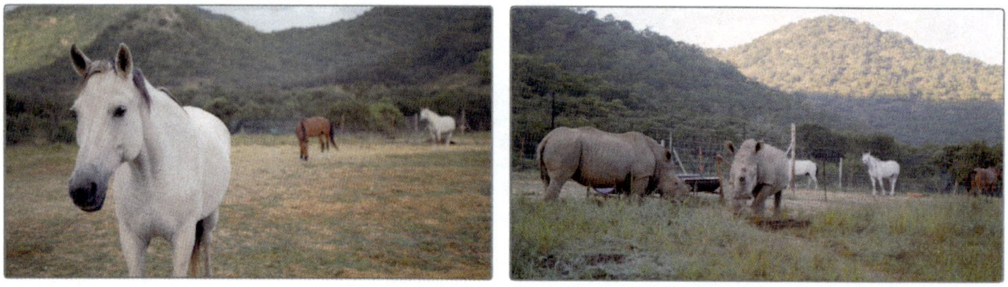

After match

Automatic shot matching is useful for quickly realizing an approximation of a match, to create a starting point for manual match grade, and to provide quick demonstrations to clients. But ultimately, you should still assess the image and check its video scopes to confirm an accurate match. If necessary, perform manual adjustments with the grading tools to refine the match.

Matching Shots Using Stills

Stills have a variety of functions in Resolve, as you will learn in lessons throughout this book. One of the most direct uses of stills is for visually comparing clips in the Viewer.

By superimposing a still, or snapshot, of a previous clip onto a current clip, you can visually assess their differences and similarities in contrast, saturation, and color dominance.

In this exercise, you will use stills to manually match clips.

1 In the green flag-filtered Timeline, select clip 05.

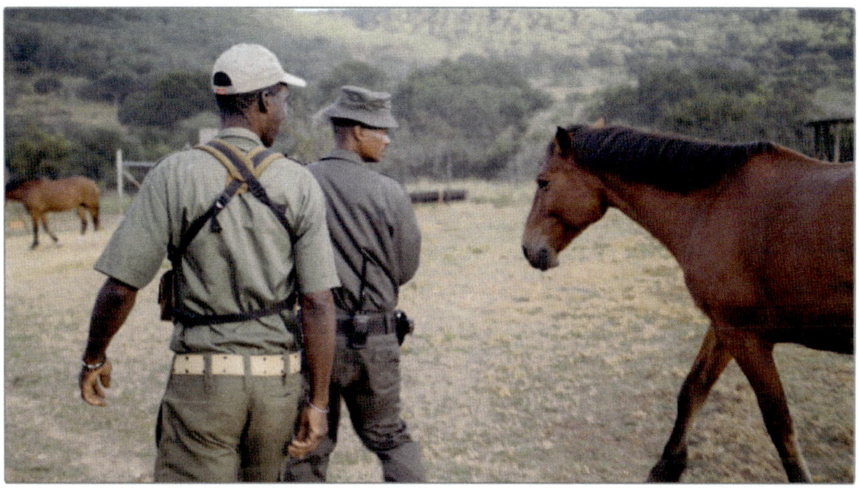

In the 02 Balanced Timeline, this clip already has its tonal range, balance, and contrast values set via the Primaries wheels.

2 Right-click in the Viewer, and choose Grab Still.

3 Double-click under the still that appears in the gallery, and label it **Match Reference**.

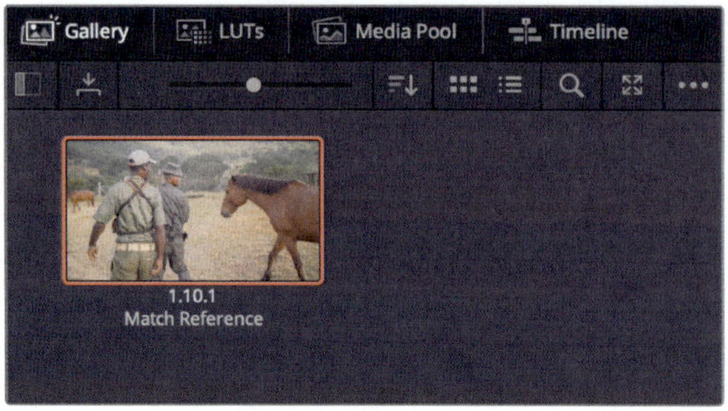

NOTE The numbers under the stills refer to the Timeline track, the clip number, and the number of stills generated for that clip.

4 In the Timeline, click clip 06. You will be using the Primaries bars and the Parade scope to match this shot to the still.

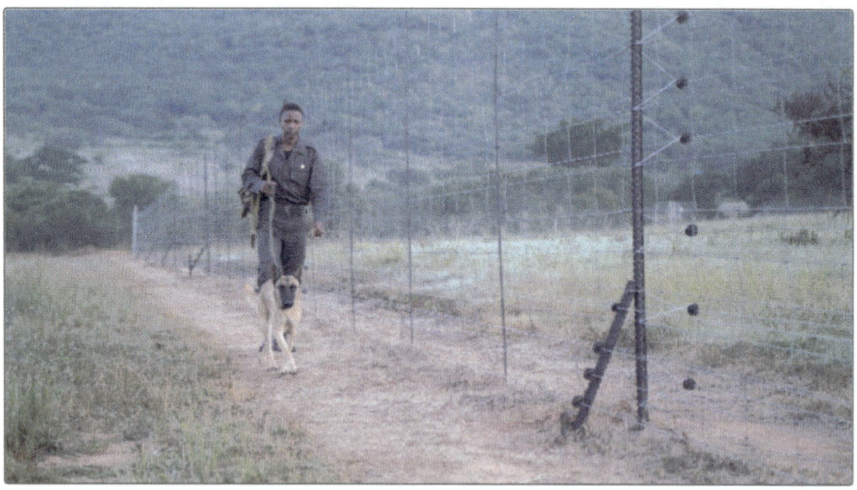

5 In the Scopes pop-up menu, choose Parade. This representation of the image is similar to that of the waveform scope, but with the luminance value of all three channels represented separately.

6 In the gallery window, double-click the Match Reference still.

You should now see the two clips in the Viewer, separated by a wipe line that you can drag.

TIP You can invert a wipe using the keyboard shortcuts Option-W (macOS) or Alt-W (Windows). Doing so will switch the frames for a reverse reference view.

The shot of the man by the fence is much cooler than the still with the men and the horse. The parade scope, which is also split in half, reveals this difference.

The channel traces on the reference still are much lower, which is an indication of higher contrast; and the reduced impact of the blue channel in the upper midtones and highlights produces a warmer look for the shot because the complementary color of blue in the additive color space is yellow. The absence of blue in a waveform normally translates to the presence of yellow.

7 In the node graph, change the label of node 01 in clip 06 to **Match**.

TIP Labelling nodes has many benefits. It clarifies the grading workflow by specifying each node's task, which enables you to make faster adjustments as you grade. Labels are also great for inserting reminders for future necessary returns to the clip grade.

To label nodes more quickly, consider creating a custom keyboard shortcut. Open DaVinci Resolve > Keyboard Customization, and in the lower-right corner of the pop-up interface, choose All Commands to reveal the full list of Resolve tools. Find the Label Selected Node command in the list below (use the search field at the top, if necessary), and press the keyboard shortcut you wish to associate with the command. The Tab key is a good option because it is not assigned to any default command.

8 In the Color Wheels palette, switch to the Primaries Bars.

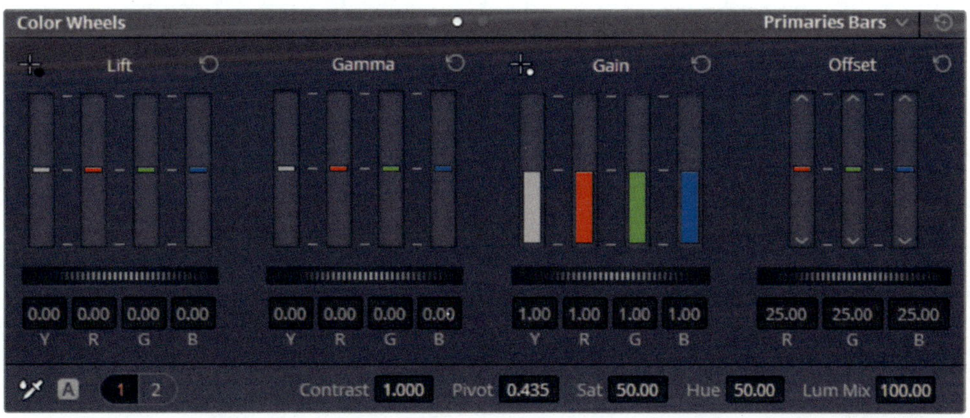

9 To match the shadows, drag the Lift Y (luminance) bar down until the shadows of clip 06 match the shadows in the still. Keep your eye on the green parade, in particular, and aim to set the lowest point of clip 05's trace (the man and dog) to a similar level as the shadow in clip 06.

> **TIP** Use the scroll wheel of your mouse to adjust the Primaries Bars with more precision.

The next step is to address the overall balance to match the reference.

10 Drag down the Blue Gain bar until the tops of the blue Parades align.

11 Drag up the Red and Green Gain bars to match the warmer reference look.

12 To address the coolness in the shadows of the mountains, drag up the Red Lift bar.

Finally, tweak the Gamma bars to offset any remaining color inconsistencies between the two images.

13 While keeping an eye on the middle pattern of the traces, drag up the Red Gamma bar and lower the Blue Gamma bar.

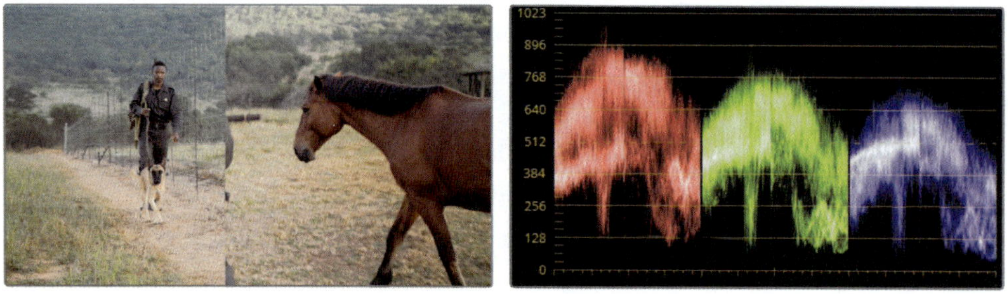

The result is a quick matching of the two clips using the Primaries Bars.

14 To turn off the reference wipe view, in the upper-left of the viewer, click the image wipe button; or right-click in the Viewer, and choose Show Reference Wipe.

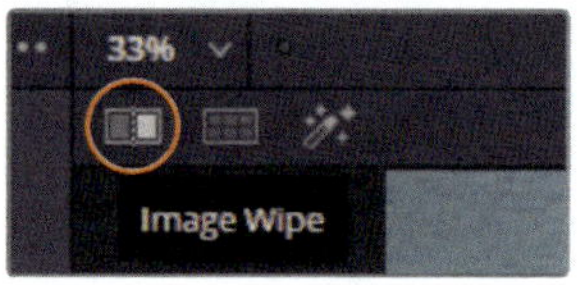

15 Toggle the grade bypass to compare clip 06 before and after the manual matching adjustment.

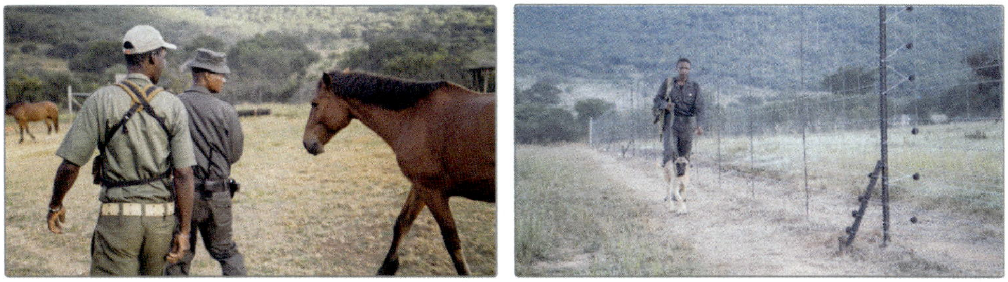

Before match

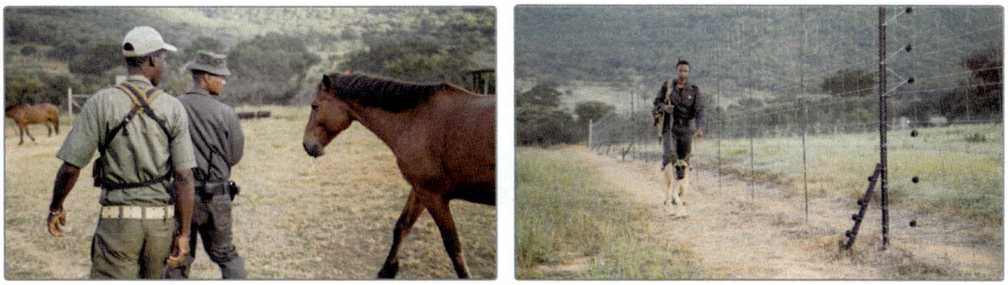

After match

NOTE The Y (luminance) bar of the Primaries Bars affects the image differently than the Primaries master wheel. The Master Wheel affects all RGB channels, which impacts saturation, whereas the bar targets only luminance.

When using stills for shot matching, your grading becomes even more precise when used in conjunction with video scopes. The scopes display a precise measure of the chroma and luma values of each frame, thereby allowing you to make very precise adjustments.

Stills have the additional benefit of carrying the grading data of the clips they were generated from. In later lessons, you will copy this data as a starting point for grading other clips in the Timeline.

Comparing and Matching Shots Manually

Unlike using the still wipe as in the previous exercise, you can grab a reference from any clip in the Timeline without generating a still in the gallery. In this exercise, you will extract a reference directly from the Timeline and match the images using custom curves.

1. In the green flag-filtered Timeline, click clip 04. You will be matching this clip to the previously balanced clip 03.
2. Review the parade scope for clip 04.

   You can see a distinct inconsistency in the shapes of the three channels. The red channel has the widest spread, extending beyond the green and blue channels in both the shadows and highlights. The blue channel's highest point is almost level with the green channel's, even though the blue channel is far more compressed within the midtone range.

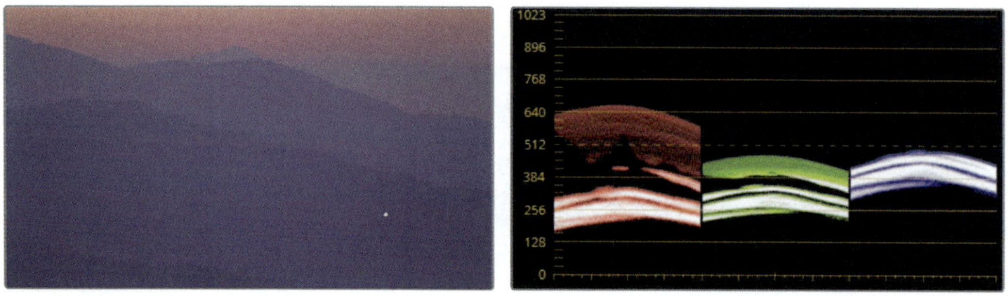

   When shot matching, the goal is not to spread out the parade channels to match each other. Instead, you must study the relationships of the three channels in the parade and try to recreate those relationships in the clip that you are matching.

3. Click clip 03, and review the channel relationships within its parade.

   The most obvious difference is in the overall spread and contrast of the channels. The shadows extend to the bottom of the graph, while the red shadows actually touch the black point line (0).

   In this situation, visual evaluation of the graph is vital. By understanding the context of the image, you can choose to ignore certain properties of the graph. Clip 09 contains a variety of elements that are not visible in the close-up in clip 10. The trees and field silhouetted against the mountains are portrayed as bunching at the bottom of the parades. You can ignore such elements when using the parade for shot matching.

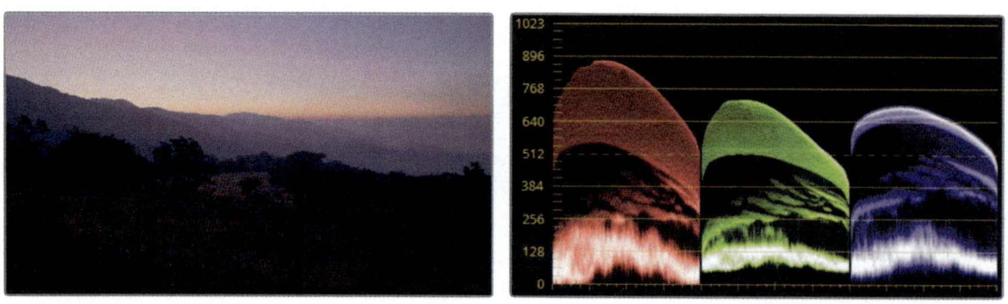

4 Click clip 04.

5 Right-click clip 03, and choose Wipe Timeline Clip.

Both clips become visible in the Viewer at the same time, divided by a wipe line.

> **TIP** Quickly toggle the wipe on and off by pressing Cmd-W (macOS) or Ctrl-W (Windows). Some colorists set their reference to fill up the whole screen and toggle the wipe continuously as they match the grade in the active clip.

One way to help you focus on relevant elements of the parade is to reframe the reference clip within the Viewer. Clip 03 is a much wider shot than clip 04, so you can zoom in and reposition it for better reference.

6 In the middle palettes, click the sizing button to open the Sizing palette.

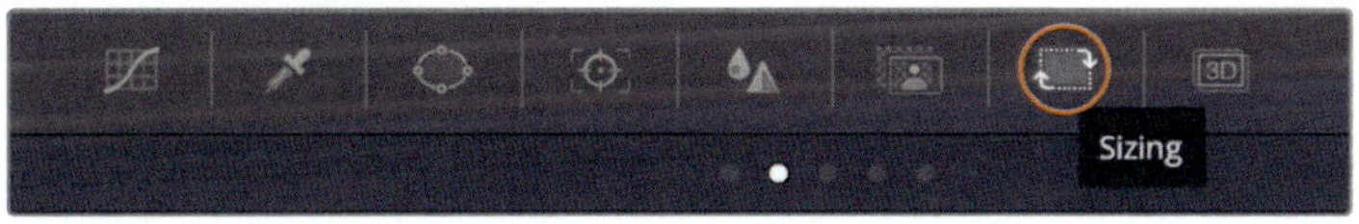

7 In the palette's upper-right corner pop-up menu, choose Reference Sizing.

The reference sizing applies the transform changes only to the reference image in the Viewer, not to the actual clip in the Timeline.

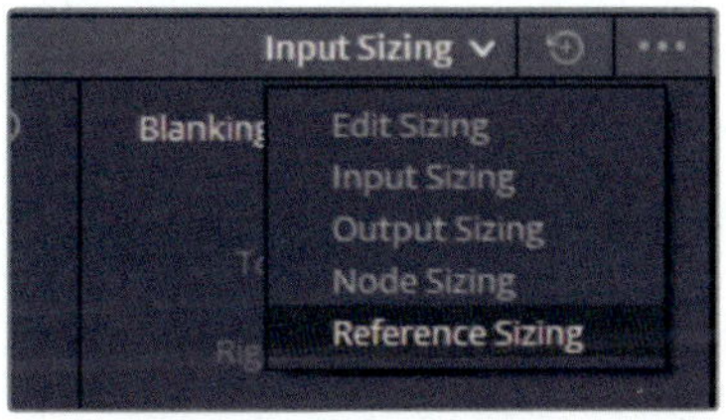

8 Use the sizing controls to zoom into the reference image (by a factor of about 8x).

9 Pan the image to the left, and tilt the image down until the framing starts to match clip 04.

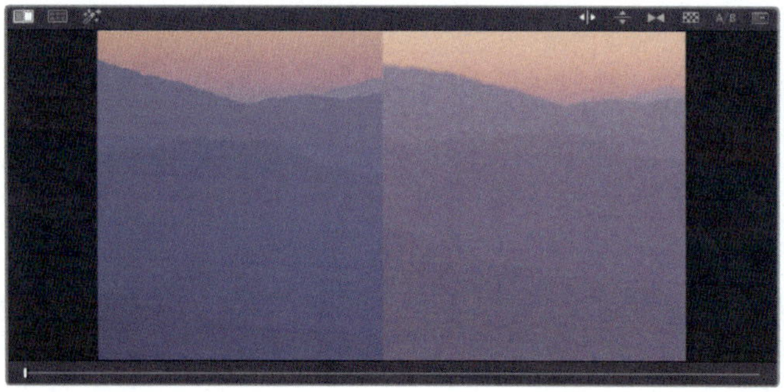

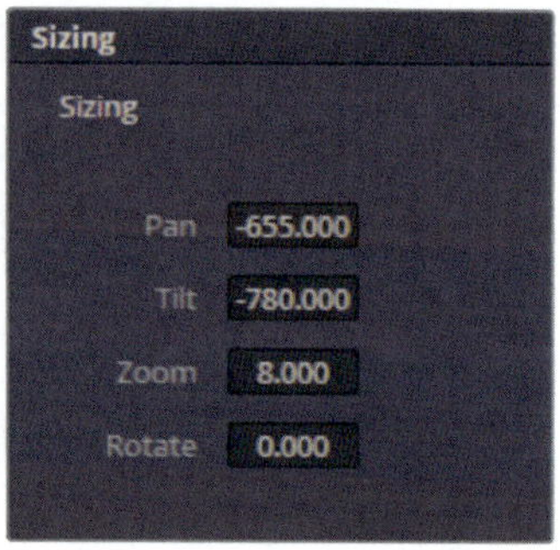

These transform changes place the reference image into a much better position for both visual reference and for the parade scope.

The side-by-side parade comparison reveals that the reference image is brighter overall with substantially more influence of the red color in the highlights. The overall spread of the green and blue channels is satisfactory, although they also need to be raised uniformly.

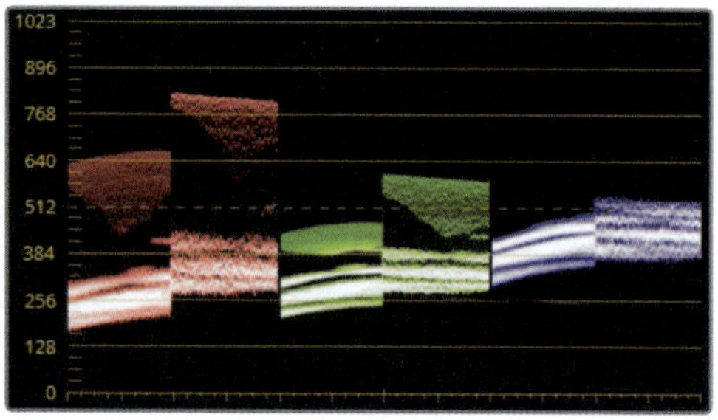

Remember, when matching, it is impossible to recreate the exact shape of the graphs, themselves. Instead, you should focus on matching the height, depths, and the midtone distributions of the graphs.

10 In the Node editor, rename node 01 as **Match**.

11 Open the custom curves palette. Let's perform a few adjustments to see how curves affect the parades.

12 Isolate the R curve, and drag the black point up and the white point left until the red channel in both parades has an equal spread.

13 Isolate the G curve, and drag the white point to the left.

As you drag the green control point, the two other channel parades shift to compensate, thereby affecting the output of the entire image. This happens because, by default,

Resolve tries to keep the luminance of the image constant when you change individual RGB channels in the Custom curves and Primaries Wheels palettes. This behavior is usually advantageous because it maintains the luminance of the image and allows you to adjust only the colors.

However, when shot matching, this behavior can be obstructive. To manipulate each channel independently, you need to indicate to Resolve that you do not wish to maintain a constant luminance.

14 Open the Color Wheel palette, and choose Primaries Wheels as the mode.

15 In the adjustment controls, select page 1, and drag Lum Mix down to 0.

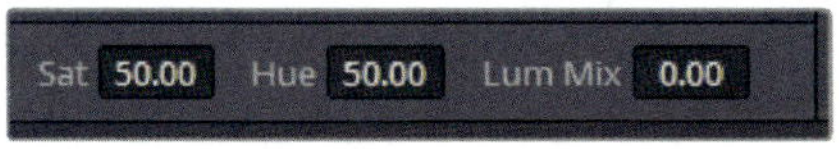

> **TIP** In the Project Settings, you can set Lum Mix to default to a value of 0 on every clip. Go to General Options > Color, and choose Luminance Mixer Defaults to Zero.

16 With the channels behaving independently, you can attempt to match up the curves once again. First, reset the Custom Curves palette.

> **TIP** When using the Master Wheels, you adjust the luminance together with the RGB channels which impacts the saturation of the image. To adjust only luminance without altering saturation, Option-drag (macOS) or Alt-drag (Windows) the Master Wheel or the indicator inside the Color wheel.

17 Isolate the R curve again, and drag the black and white points until the red channel in both parades has an equal spread.

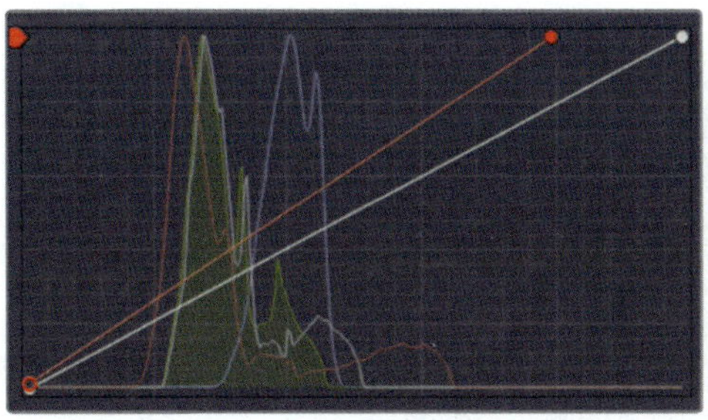

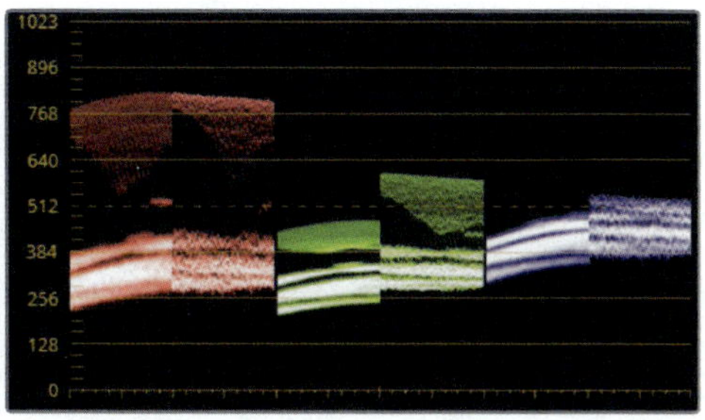

18 Isolate the G curve again, and reposition the black and white points to align the trace in the parade.

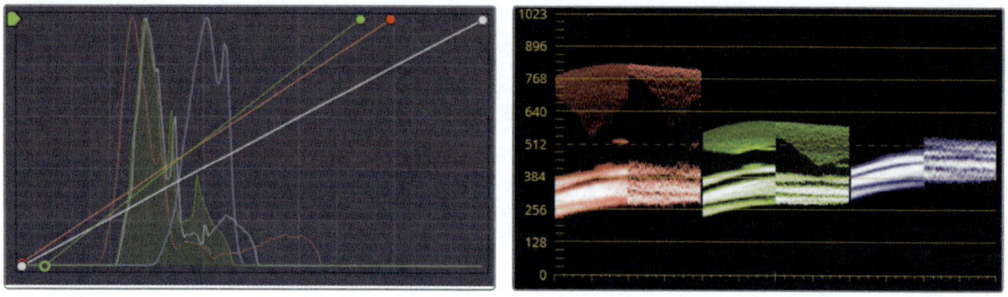

19 Isolate the B curve, and reposition the black and white points to align the trace in the parade.

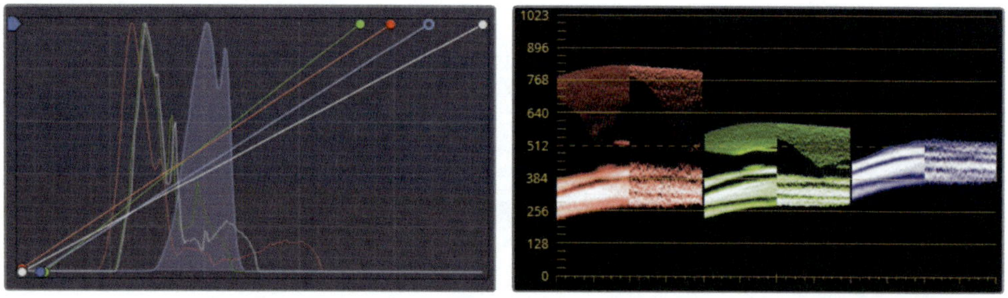

It appears that the parades now equally match each other, but the colors in clip 04 still do not match the reference in the Viewer. This is because you have been focusing only on the highlights and shadows of the images. The midtones are equally important and can have a profound impact on image appearance.

Notice the bunching occurring in the lower midtones of the channels. It represents the mountains in the image. Though the red and blue channels are aligned, the green channel is showing a substantial mismatch between clips 04 and 05.

20 Add control points to the green curve, and drag them until the midtones of the green channel line up more accurately.

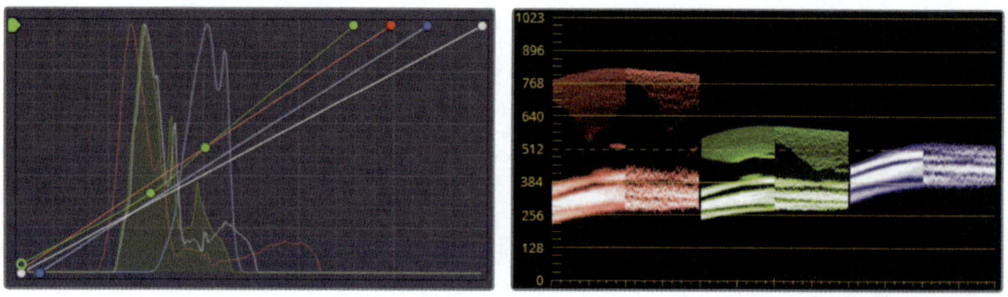

The match between the two parades results in a satisfactory visual similarity in the mountains and the sky. However, you can now continue to assess the match visually and further refine the result.

The close-up shot could use some contrast to create greater depth between the mountain ranges in clip 04.

21 In the adjustment controls, tweak the Contrast.

The depth is now accurate, but the contrast change results in the colors looking more saturated.

22 In the adjustment controls, reduce the Sat until you get a good visual match.

23 Open the Sizing palette. In Reference Sizing mode, click the reset arrow to return the reference image to its original placement.

If you do not reset this, all future reference images, including wiped stills from the gallery, will have the same transform placement in the Viewer.

24 Disable the image wipe.

25 Toggle between clips 03 and 04 to verify that the match is successful.

When matching contrast between clips, you aim to equalize the heights and depths of the pixel spread and match contrast bunching. By displaying an exact readout of the RGB values of each clip, scopes can help you remove the guesswork that might accompany the minute tweaking of midtone ranges and allow you to approach the image from a more empirical, yet creative mindset.

Using Split-Screen Views to Compare Multiple Clips

An alternative method of visually comparing clips within the Viewer is using a split-screen display. Instead of overlaying the still of a single image, you can display the frames of multiple clips side-by-side. The frames you use could be from other clips in the Timeline, stills in the gallery, different versions of grades, or other clips in the same group.

This comparison method is especially effective when you already have a collection of clips that are similar in appearance and wish to examine a wider visual reference of a scene or environment.

1 In the green flag-filtered Timeline, click clip 07. This clip is already normalized and balanced with Custom curves.

2 Shift-click clip 10 to highlight clips 07 to 10.

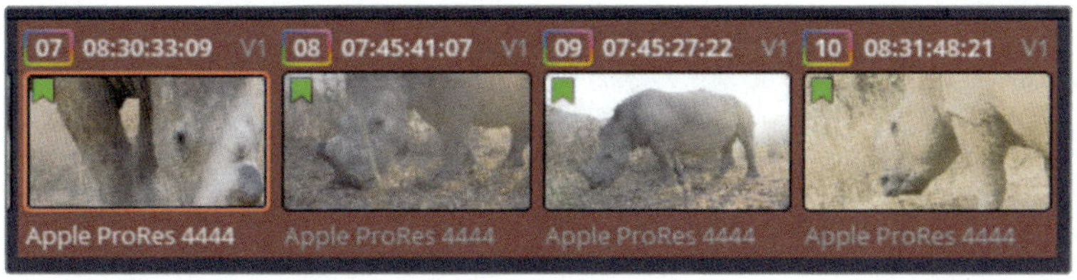

3 Right-click in the Viewer, and choose Split Screen > Selected Clips to display all four clips. For better visibility, press Option-F (macOS) or Alt-F (Windows) to enlarge the Viewer.

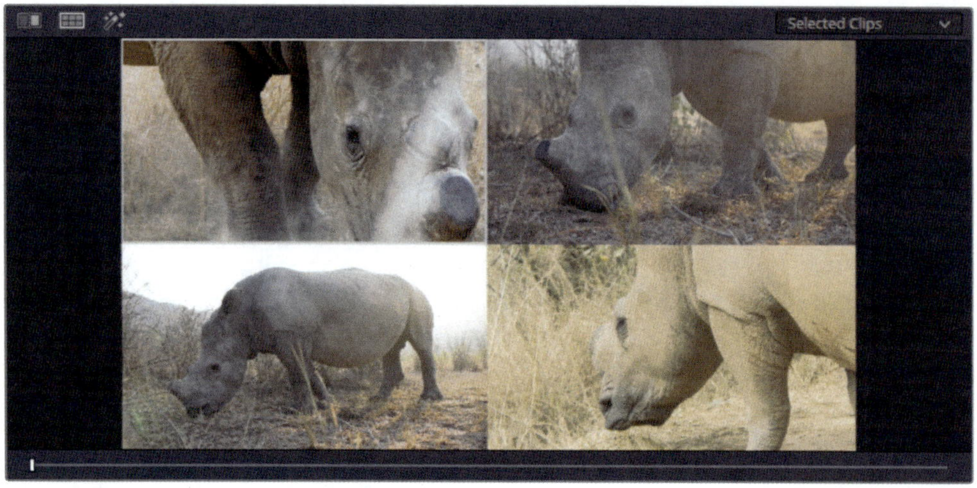

4 In the Viewer, click the upper-right image to select clip 08 on the Timeline. The selection is indicated by a white outline in the Viewer.

Changes made to the Color page palettes will impact whichever clip is actively selected in the split-screen view. You can perform quick grade matching by switching between clips in split-screen view, visually comparing them and making quick adjustments in the color wheel and curves.

Although reading the scopes and evaluating their data can be a straightforward process, you will need practice to acquire a level of finesse to accurately adjust the colors in the highlights, midtones, and shadows. Accurately adjusting and matching color is a highly valued skillset that requires plenty of experience and patience, so keep at it!

Self-guided Exercises #2

Complete the following exercises in the green flag-filtered 02 Balanced Timeline to test your understanding of the tools and workflows covered in this lesson.

Clips 08, 09, and 10—Match these clips to clip 07 using any of the methods covered in this lesson.

When you've completed these exercises, open the 04 Completed Timeline to compare your matching to the Match node in this "solved" Timeline.

Lesson Review

1. How do you prevent changes made to one color channel from affecting the waveform trace of the other two channels?
2. How can you filter the Timeline to show only clips with a flag?
3. When performing an automatic shot match, you might right-click the clip you have selected and *not* see "Shot Match to this Clip" in the contextual menu. Why?
4. Yes or no? It is possible to use a Timeline clip as a reference in the Viewer without first creating a still.
5. Which Viewer mode allows you to see multiple clips in the Viewer at the same time?

Answers

1. Set Lum Mix to 0.
2. Click the Clips button, and choose Flagged Clips.
3. The clip you have selected is the one that will be receiving the automatic shot match adjustment, so "Shot Match to this Clip" cannot be an option. Right-click any other clip on the Timeline and "Shot Match to this Clip" will appear in the contextual menu.
4. Yes. To do so, right-click a clip in the Timeline, and choose "Wipe Timeline Clip".
5. Split screen

Lesson 3

Correcting and Enhancing Isolated Areas

After you've completed balancing and shot matching, you will want to target details in the shots for more specific enhancement. This is the secondary color-grading stage.

Secondary color grading is not a standardized phase of the color grading process. Instead, it is a need-driven component of the workflow that is utilized only when a shot requires it. It enables you to achieve a wide variety of goals that improve the overall aesthetic and creative quality of the footage, as well as fix continuity errors.

In the first part of this lesson, you'll review some of the common applications of secondary grading using qualifiers and Power Windows. Your goal is to isolate areas of the image for color and effect enhancement with the purpose of drawing the viewer's eye.

Time

This lesson takes approximately 90 minutes to complete.

Goals

In the second part of the lesson, you will use more nuanced tools to clean up overcast (or overblown) skies, adjust regions of an image based on hue, and calibrate skin tones to enhance their warmth and smooth their details. Throughout the lesson, you will also employ some of the tools available in the OpenFX panel to see how subtle adjustments can exert enormous effect on the emotional impact of an image.

Controlling the Viewer's Eye

A film's musical score and sound effects can have a resounding impact on audience perception. Similarly, color and light play a critical role in manipulating the way an audience interprets a scene. In this lesson, you will focus on the fine art of shaping light to control the viewer's eye.

Drawing Attention Using Windows and Saturation

A simple alteration can dynamically reimagine the composition and mood of a shot by adjusting the saturation of colors in a specific part of the frame. In this exercise, you'll enhance the saturation in the vibrant, sunlit area of a field to give one scene a more dramatic feel.

1. In the Project 01 - Disunity Documentary project, open the 03 Matched Timeline.
2. In the Clips pop-up menu, choose All Clips to remove the green filter in the Timeline.
3. Filter the Timeline to show only those clips with yellow flags.

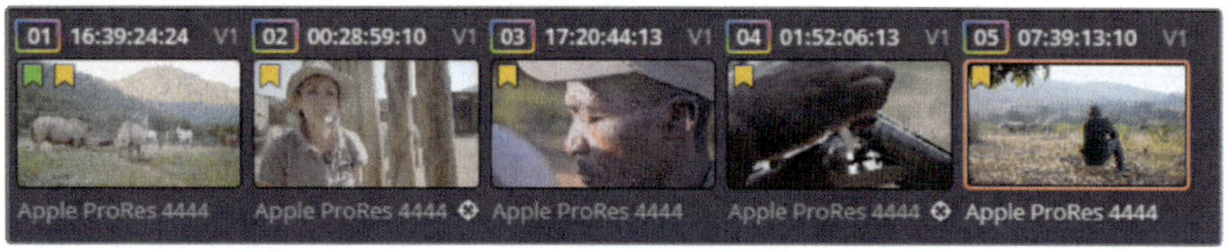

4. In the yellow flag-filtered Timeline, click clip 05. The clip already has a first node labelled Normal.

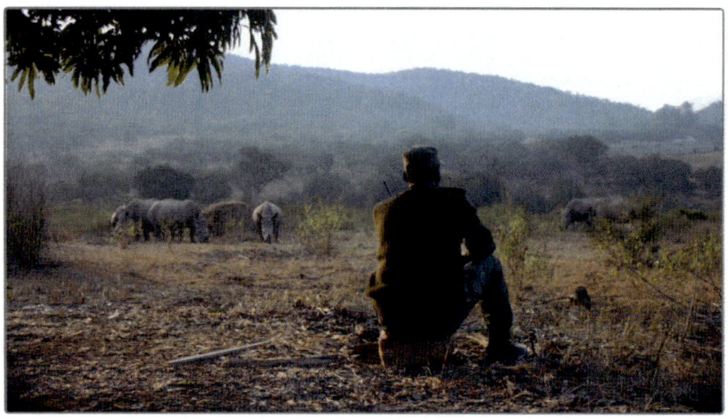

5. Create a second node and label it **Sunlight**.

6 In the central palettes toolbar, click the Window palette button. You will use a Power Window to specify the region of the image you will be grading.

7 Click the linear window button to activate it. It is the square-shaped window at the top of the default windows list.

When activated, the button will have an orange outline around it and you will see the outline of the window in the viewer.

8 Double-click next to the window thumbnail, and enter the name **Sunlight Area**.

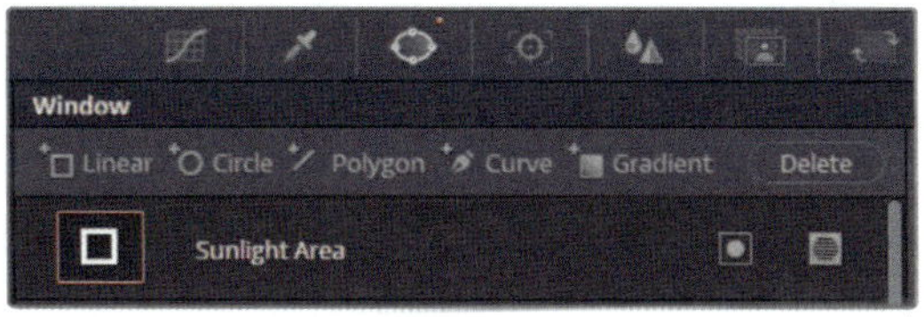

9 In the Viewer, move the four edges of the window to select the entire horizontal middle of the image where the sun hits the ground. Make sure to extend the shape to mimic the path of the sunlight.

10 In the Viewer, drag the red points on the window outline to increase the softness around its upper and lower edges.

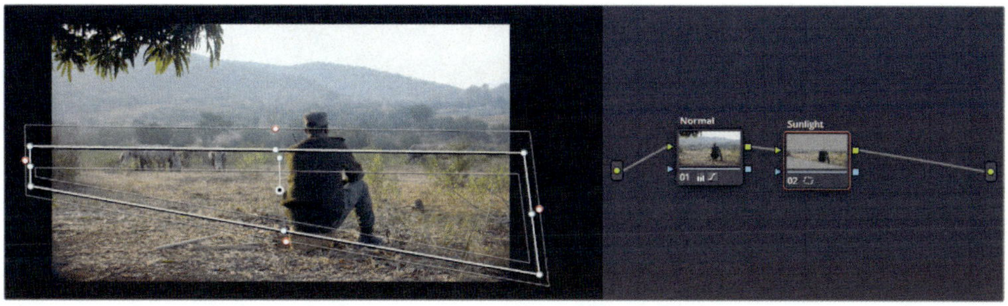

11 To review your Power Window selection in the viewer, click the Highlight button in the upper-left corner of the Viewer.

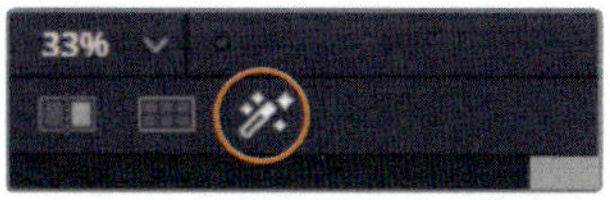

12 Click the Highlight button again to disable highlight mode and return to your full frame.

With the secondary selection created, you can begin to grade the image.

13 In the Color Wheel palette, increase the Sat to 65, and the Contrast to 1.1.

> **TIP** Toggle the window outline in the viewer by pressing Shift-~ (tilde) on your keyboard. You can use this keyboard shortcut to hide the outline and better see the impact of your grade on the image.

14 With the Sunlight node still selected in the Node editor, right-click it, and choose Add Node > Add Outside, or press Option-O (macOS) or Alt-O (Windows). This inverse selection will allow you to grade the environment around the sunlight.

15 Label node 03 as **Outside**.

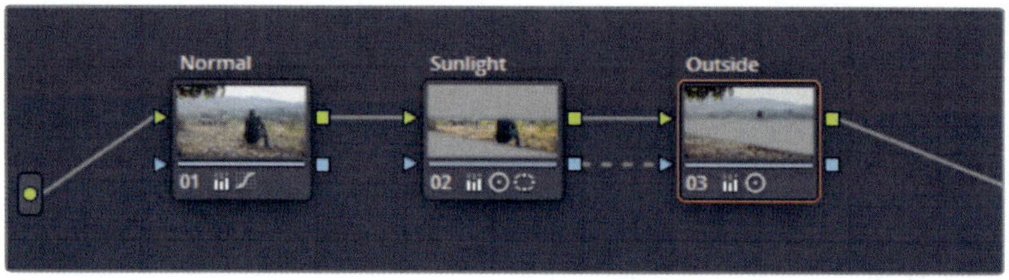

16 Drag the Gamma master wheel (-0.05) to decrease the brightness, and minimize Contrast (0.900).

Doing so creates a dark framing effect around the figure of the man and further draws the eye toward the sunlight on the field.

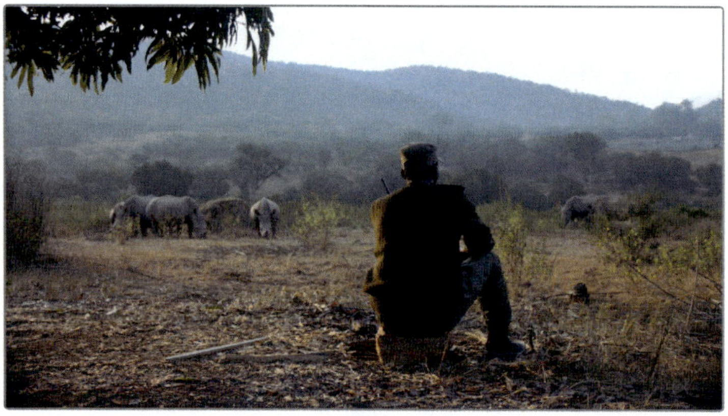

Before

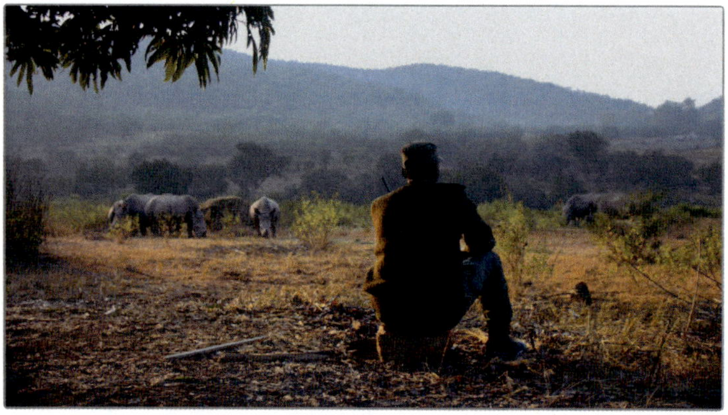

After

Mimicking a Shallow Depth of Field

ResolveFX are a series of filters included with DaVinci Resolve that enable you to adjust the physical or visual properties of your footage in creative ways that are often not possible using common grading tools.

NOTE The following exercise requires DaVinci Resolve Studio to complete.

The Tilt-Shift Blur effect imitates the look of a shallow focus lens to direct audience attention. However, you can also apply it to achieve effects that a lens could not—such as reducing the focus of elements contained within the same field and realizing a greater level of control over the blur type, amount, and angle. You will continue to work on clip 05 in the yellow flag-filtered timeline.

1. Create a new serial node (node 04) labelled **Tilt Shift**.
2. Click the OpenFX button to open its panel.

3. In the OpenFX panel, under ResolveFX Stylize, locate the Tilt-Shift Blur effect.
4. Drag the Tilt-Shift Blur effect onto the empty Tilt Shift node.

   The OpenFX library panel now displays a settings window in which you can tweak the Tilt-Shift Blur effect controls.
5. In the settings panel, in the Depth of Field category, select Depth Map Preview to see where the matte is currently located.

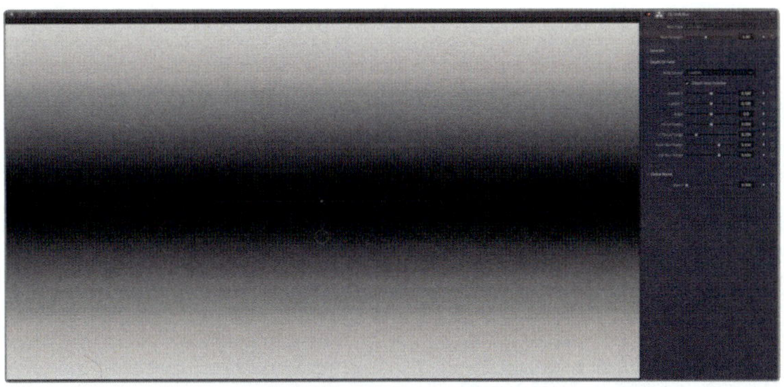

The matte represents the area where the effect is applied. Black indicates transparency, or the lack of selection in that area, whereas white represents full opacity, or a selected region. Gray implies semi-opacity and a diminished strength of selection.

Currently, the map is already placed level with the horizon and successfully targets the rhinos in the background. However, it is not an entirely realistic composite. The depth of field is too extreme at the top and bottom of the image, while maintaining focus on both the man in front of the camera and the rhinos hundreds of yards in front of him.

> **TIP** Repeatedly select and deselect Depth Map Preview to visually assess the position of the Tilt-Shift Blur matte in relation to the image.

6 Adjust the width of the matte by dragging the In Focus Range pointer to the right (0.330) to include more of the man in the focused range of the shot.

7 Adjust the height of the matte by dragging the Center Y value down (0.460) to ensure that the area directly behind the rhinos begins to go out of focus.

8 Deselect Depth Map Preview.

9 Slightly decrease the Near Blur Range (0.630) and Far Blur Range (0.630) values to control the severity of the blur and make it look more realistic.

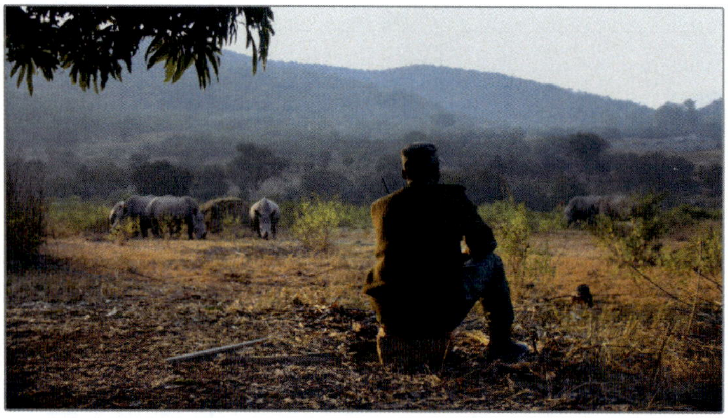

Before

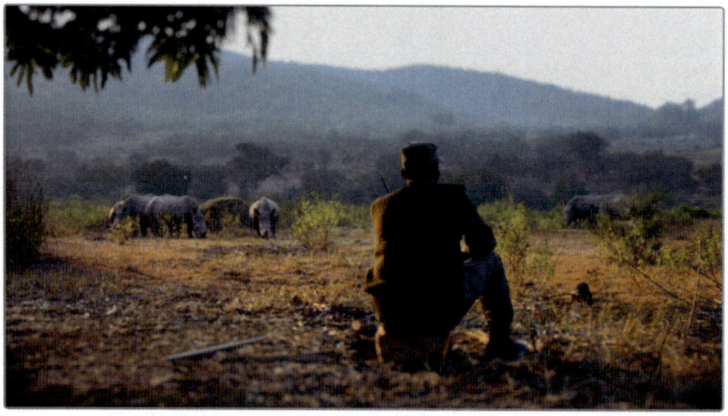

After

Focusing Attention with Vignettes

In classic filmmaking, a vignette refers to the darkened, soft edges of a film frame caused by the lens and matte box. With the advancement of camera equipment, and especially with the advent of digital film, natural vignettes are no longer an issue. However, their absence has caused an appreciation for the framing service they provided, and vignettes are now sought after for creative and compositing purposes as an effective method of directing the viewer's eye.

In this simple exercise, you will apply a circle window to a shot and reduce the brightness of the frame around it to create a vignette around the central subject. You will continue to work on clip 05 in the yellow flag-filtered timeline.

1. Create a new serial node labeled **Vignette**.
2. In the Window palette, click the circle window button.
3. Double-click the layer name field next to the circle window, and type **Vignette Frame**.
4. Vignettes are usually elliptical to reduce their visibility and enable easier blending into the footage, as compared to shapes with straight lines and corners.

   Use the onscreen transform controls to reposition and rescale the circle to completely fill the viewer frame.
5. In the onscreen controls, drag one of the red points to create a wide, soft edge around the selection.

   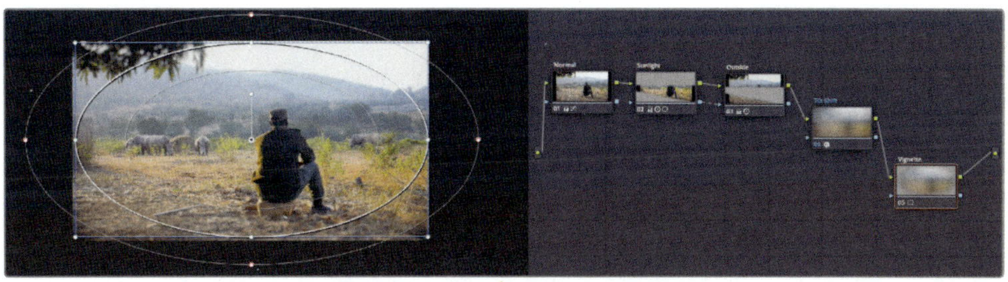

   In the Node editor, the Vignette node thumbnail preview shows that you have selected the subjects in the center of the frame. To use the node as a vignette, you will need to invert this selection.
6. In the Window palette, next to the circle window, click the invert symbol.

7. In the pop-up menu in the lower-left of the viewer, choose Off to hide the window outline.

8 Now that the vignette shape is made, you can proceed to use the grading tools to create a vignette effect on the image. Reduce the brightness of the selected area by dragging the Gamma master wheel to the left (-0.05). Using the gamma tonal range will ensure that you are not darkening overly bright areas of the footage (such as the overcast sky), which would make the vignette too obvious.

> **TIP** Vignettes are most effective when they are not noticeable. If you are concerned that your vignette may be too prominent, review the thumbnail of the clip in the timeline to determine if the vignette is too pronounced in the corners. If so, in the Key palette, lower the vignette node's Key output Gain to reduce its strength and further soften the Power Window's edges to more seamlessly blend it into the image.

You can also save the vignette you just generated for future use as a preset.

9 In the Window palette, ensure that the appropriate window (Vignette Frame) is selected in the window list.

10 In the upper-right corner of the palette, click the options button, and choose Save as New Preset.

11 Enter the preset name as **Vignette**.

From now on, when you want to apply this exact shape to a node in any other clip, you need only access the Window palette option menu, and choose the preset Vignette.

This basic adjustment allowed you to reduce the brightness of the majority of the image to focus attention on the subjects in its center. The softness around the vignette is crucial to ensure that the adjustment does not draw undue attention to itself.

> **TIP** A vignette preset is also available in the OpenFX library (in the ResolveFX stylize category) for quick application of a simple, customizable vignette.

It takes careful assembly and adjustment of secondary grading to draw the eye of the audience to the subject matter without calling attention to the image manipulation. When an audience becomes aware of the colorist's handiwork, it can break the illusion of realism and compromise viewer involvement with the content.

Using the Mini Panel—Power Windows

Using a DaVinci Resolve Mini Panel offers a great deal of time-saving potential when you're working with Power Windows. To make a Power Window on the Mini Panel, you have a few methods available. When you'd like to apply a Power Window to a node, press the Windows button in the upper-left of the panel. The five-inch screens will display a row of Power Window presets along the top.

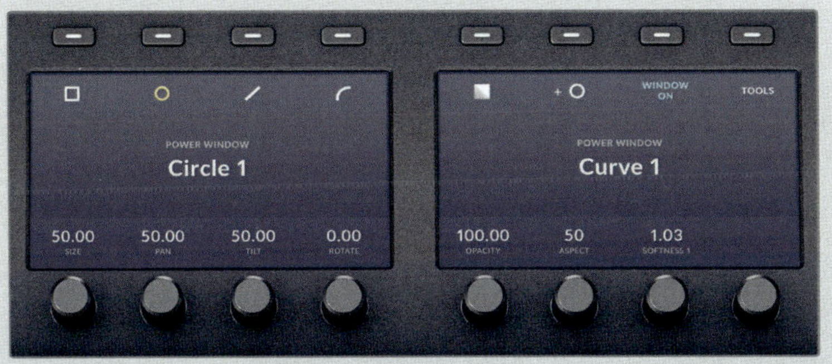

Select the desired window preset, and then press Window On to active it in the node.

Then use the knobs under the screens to simultaneously adjust the size, pan, tilt, aspect ratio, softness, and opacity of your window. With practice, you will find that this is a faster method for calibrating Power Windows than using a mouse.

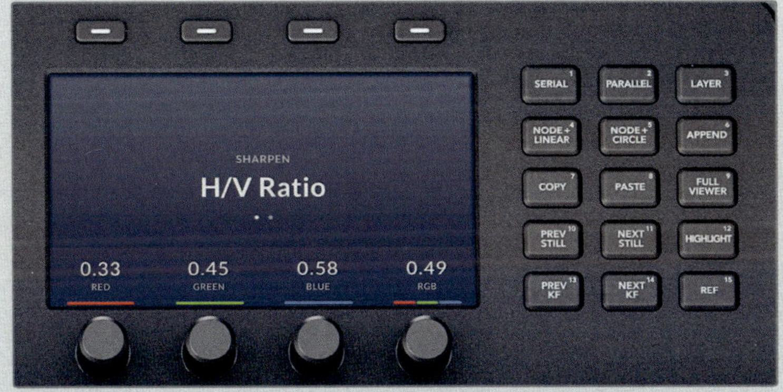

It's important to note that Power Windows also extend to the node controls on the Mini Panel. At the upper-right of the panel, node controls allow you to create several types of common nodes. You'll learn more about them throughout this book.

Right now, you'll want to pay attention to the node + buttons with which you can create a new serial node with a Power Window already activated, thereby turning two commonly used shortcuts into one. Pressing the Node + Circle button, for example, creates a new node with a circular Power Window.

Sharpening Key Elements

The Blur palette in the central palettes of the Color page also contains a sharpening mode. It works best when used conservatively and applied at the end of a grade. Too much artificial sharpening can stand out for the wrong reasons. When used precisely, sharpening can make details look extremely dynamic and draw the viewer's eye in a desired direction.

1 In the yellow flag-filtered timeline, click clip 04.

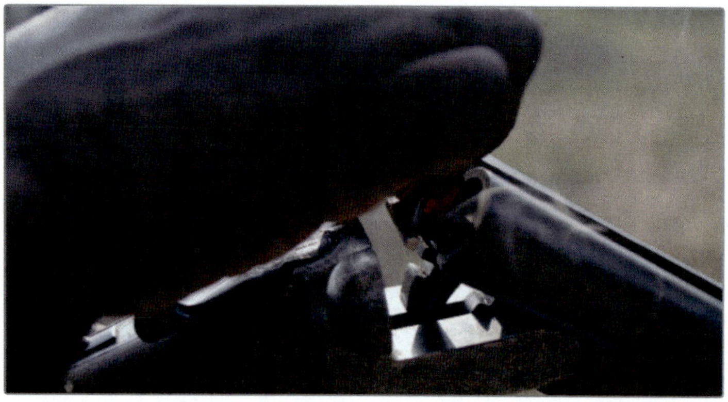

The clip begins with a man's hand obscuring the shot. In such cases, it is a good idea to play through the clip until you find a better point for grading and adding effects.

2 In the Viewer Timeline, drag the playhead to the center of the clip.

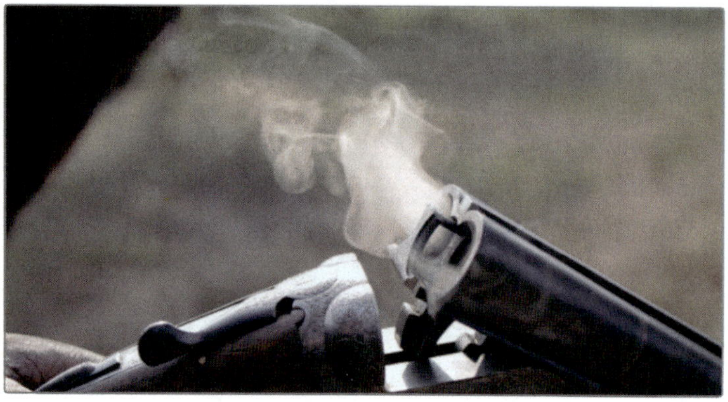

3 Create a second node called **Sharp**.

4 In the central palettes, open the Blur palette.

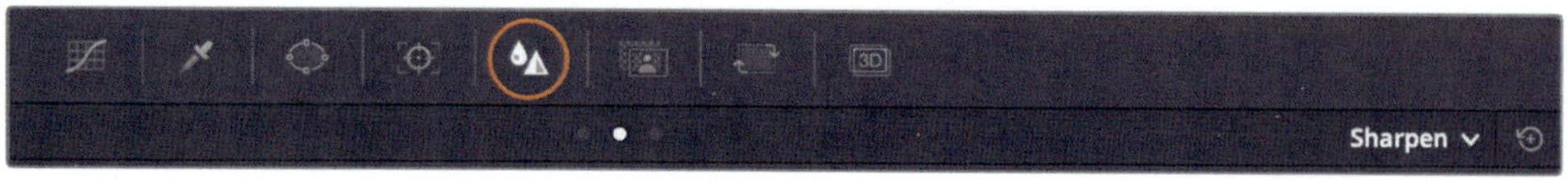

5 In the pop-up menu in the upper-right corner of the palette, choose Sharpen.

The main control in the Sharpen palette is the Radius. Dragging it upward will blur the image, and dragging it down will sharpen the edges of high-contrast detail.

6 Reduce the Radius to 0.40 by dragging down any of the three channel sliders under the Radius heading. The three channels are ganged together, so adjusting one will equally alter the other two.

Although it is easy to see that the engravings become more detailed, the impact that sharpening has on the rest of the image is more difficult to perceive.

7 Above the viewer, click the Highlight button, and then click the A/B Difference button in the right corner to display the edges found by the sharpening adjustment. You can also toggle this display on and off by pressing Cmd-Shift-H (macOS) or Ctrl-Shift-H (Windows).

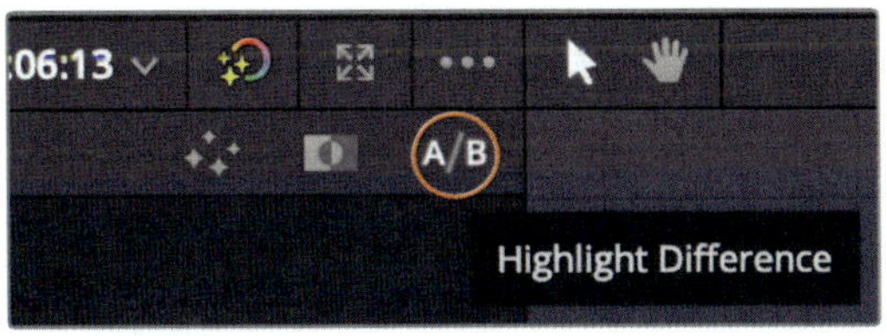

8 In the Sharpen palette, increase the scaling to 0.5. Doing so will multiply the result of the Radius adjustment.

The adjustments add a satisfactory level of detail to the engraving, but adds too much detail to the gun barrel and the smoke coming out of it. You can limit the sharpening effect using the Coring Softness and Level controls at the bottom of the palette. Start by increasing the Level control to set a threshold for the sharpening.

9 Increase the Level (around 10-15) until the detail in the smoke and on the barrel of the gun disappears.

10 Increase the Coring Softness to around 5 to recover some of the sharpening between the level threshold setting and the most detailed areas.

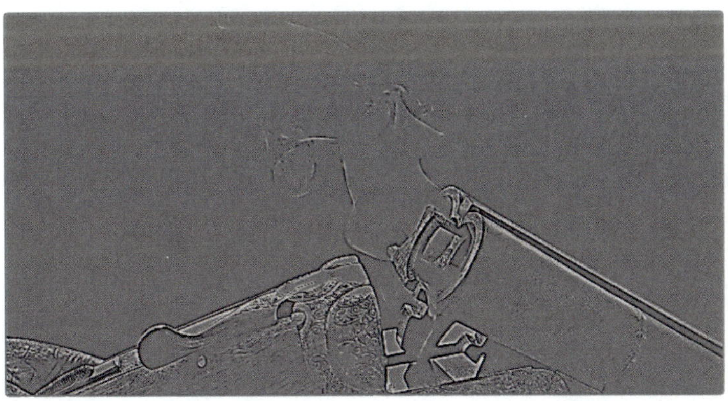

To see the results on the image, you can disable the difference highlight.

11 Click the Highlight button above the Viewer, or press Cmd-Shift-H (macOS) or Ctrl-Shift-H (Windows).

12 Press Cmd-D (macOS) or Ctrl-D (Windows) to bypass the Sharp node and compare your results to the original image.

> **TIP** You could also achieve this effect using Sharpen Edge ResolveFX in the OpenFX palette. This filter includes an edge display in the settings controls, as well as other fine-tuning parameters.

Although the sharpness looks very nice on the engravings, it's causing some ringing on the hand in the left corner of the screen, as well producing some pixel artifacting on the shotgun shell at the start of the clip. However, you can use a window to limit an effect to a specific area in the shot.

Tracking Obscured Objects

Adding a simple circular window to the sharpening node will allow you to confine the sharpening to the engravings and shotgun barrel.

1 In the Sharp node of clip 04, create a circle window, and name it **Barrel Detail**.

2 Resize the circle, and place it directly over the engravings on the shotgun.

3 Make the circle narrower and rotate it so it confines the sharpening effect to just the engravings on the handle.

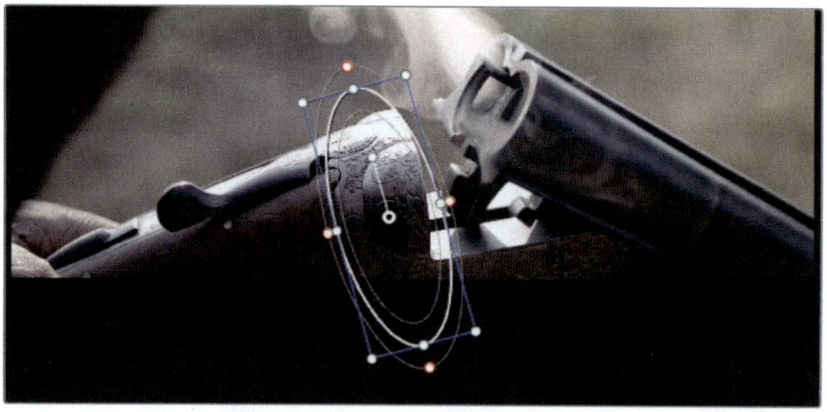

4 Drag the red control point on the window to soften the edges of the mask. The sharpening is now successfully isolated to the detail on the handle.

However, scrubbing through the clip will reveal that this is a handheld camera shot, and the shotgun is moved as it is loaded. You'll need to track the window for the effect to follow the engravings.

5 In the central palettes toolbar, click the Tracker button, which is located next to the Window button.

6 With the playhead still located in the center of the shot, and your circle window placed on the detail just under the barrel, click the Track Reverse button.

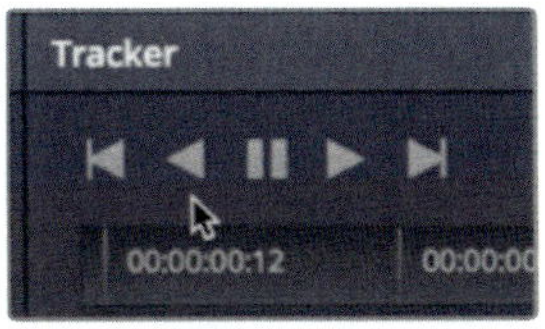

The analysis runs backward through the shot, recording the motion data for the gun barrel until the first frame of the clip is reached.

TIP It is common practice to track from the center or the end of a clip when doing so will provide more reliable tracking data.

7 When the tracking is completed, in the upper-right corner of the tracker graph, click the Keyframe button to return the playhead to the central keyframe.

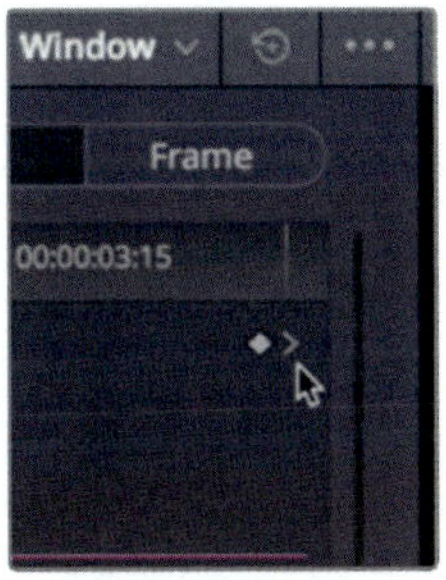

8 Click the Track Forward button to perform the rest of the track analysis in the second half of the clip.

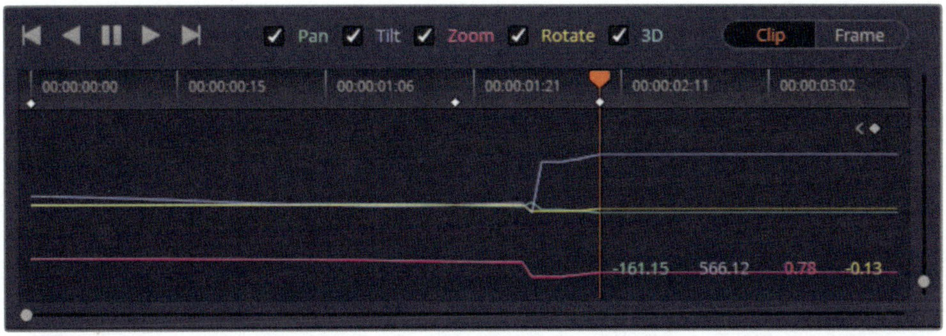

As the analysis runs, the window will be disconnected from the barrel detail due to the interference of the man's hand. This disconnection can occasionally occur during tracking, and it is useful to know how to quickly fix the issue.

In the Tracker palette, you can see a visual representation of the amount of motion applied to each transformation. Each colored line corresponds to the colored transformation label above the Tracker palette. Based on the sudden and dramatic movement on the pan and tilt graph lines in the second half of the graph, it is clear that the tracking data becomes distorted. To fix the track, you must first remove the bad tracking data.

9 Drag within the tracker graph to draw a dotted selection outline around the bad tracking data.

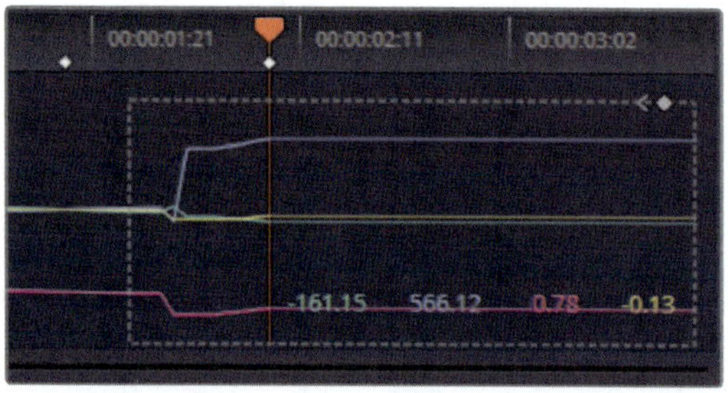

10 In the Tracker palette, in the options menu, choose Clear Selected Track Data.

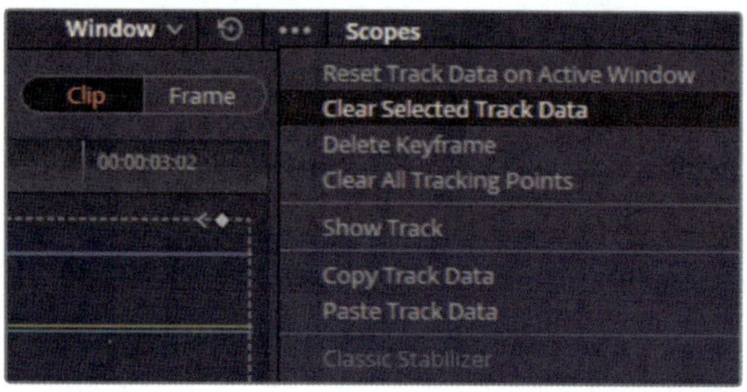

The tracking data in the selected area of the tracker graph is removed. Knowing that the track cannot be analyzed with the obstruction, you will need to manually adjust the movement of the window during the time that the hand is in the shot.

11 Switch the tracking to Frame mode.

In frame mode, any changes you make to the window in the viewer now will be recorded as a keyframe, as opposed to the Clip mode, which applies a uniform change to the window's position in relation to the key clip.

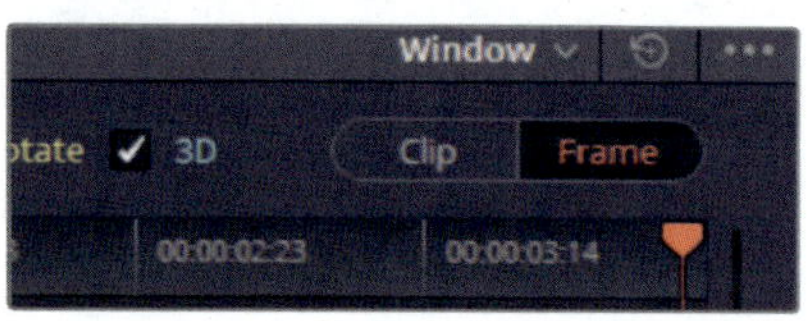

12 In the Viewer, drag the playhead to a point in time where the obstruction has passed, and the area appears to be trackable again.

13 Manually reposition the window to the area of the barrel that you were previously tracking. Use the anchor point in the center of the window as a visual guide, if necessary.

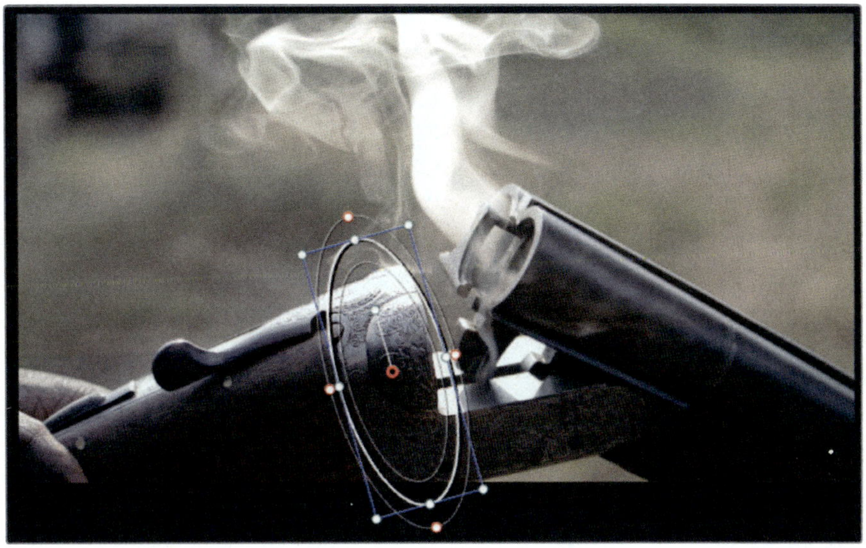

A new keyframe appears in the tracker graph, and tracking data is automatically generated between it and the last reliable tracked moment.

14 Click the Track Forward button to perform the rest of the track analysis.

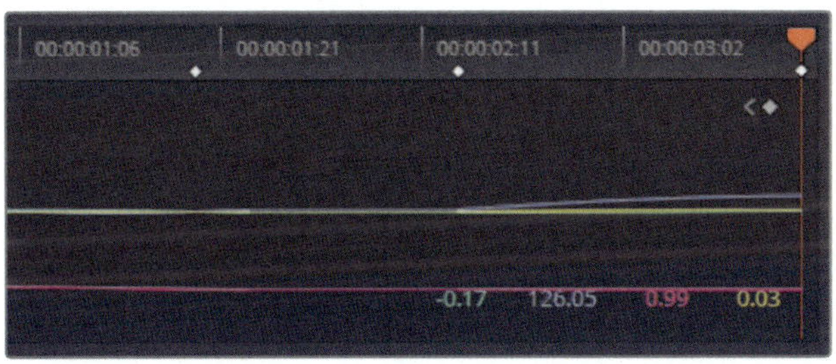

Using the Mini Panel—Tracking

You can use the Mini Panel to track Power Windows, and avoid using your mouse and keyboard by pressing the Tracker button at the upper-left of the panel.

By enabling Frame mode, you can keyframe Power Windows. Pressing the left and right arrow keys will display more advanced keyframe controls.

Fixing Overcast Skies

Capturing footage with skylines in-camera can sometimes be problematic. Subjects in the foreground usually require a substantial difference in their exposure levels compared to the sky. Opening the aperture or raising the ISO value usually results in better exposure in the foreground, but a blown-out sky.

In such cases, the best method of correction is to target the sky with a keying tool, such as the qualifier, and tweak the color using standard grading tools; or extract the sky altogether and composite an image/video of another sky in its place. In this exercise, you will practice the first method of sky correction.

1 In the yellow flag-filtered timeline, click clip 01. This clip was previously balanced and matched, and now needs secondary grading to address its overcast sky.

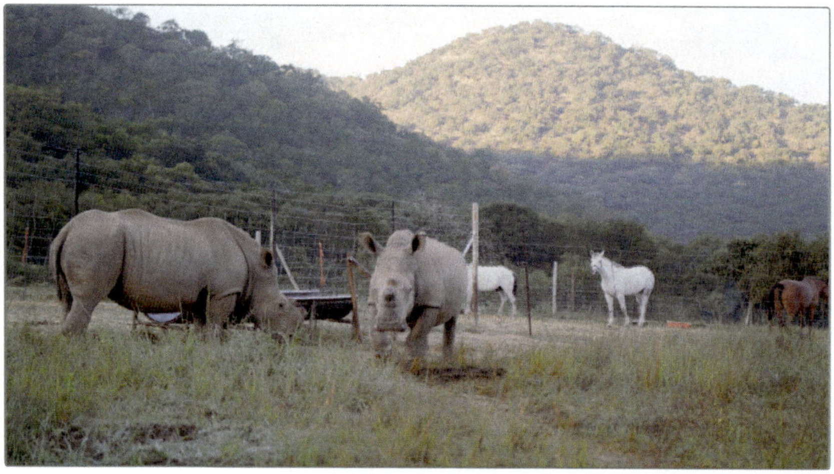

2 Create a fourth corrector node called **Sky**.

3 With the Sky node selected, in the central palettes, open the qualifier palette.

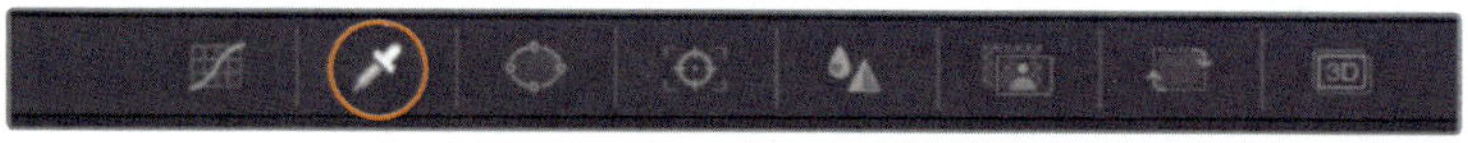

4 In the viewer, using the qualifier tool, click a portion of the sky. The thumbnail representation of the image in the Sky node will change to show the qualifier selection.

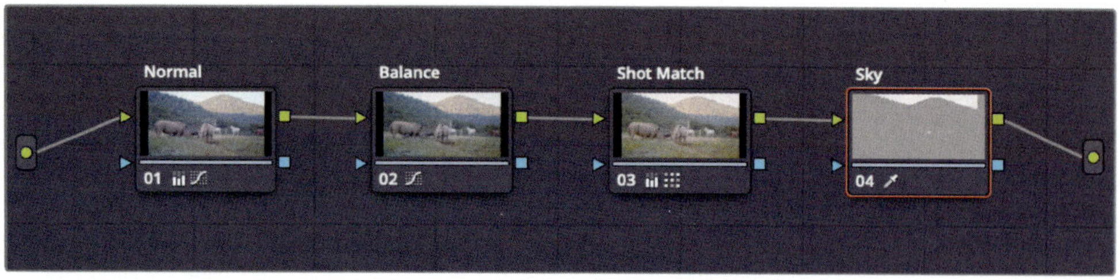

To perform further work with this selection, you must change the viewer mode to display only the qualifier extraction.

5 Switch the viewer to Highlight mode by clicking the Highlight button in the upper-left of the viewer. Ensure that the mode is set to Highlight in the upper-right corner.

The viewer now shows what the qualifier has selected by making the sky visible and turning everything else gray. This is a way to display the image matte.

Often, when a selection is first made using the qualifier, it will miss sections, or will include unwanted areas. You can use the HSL Qualifier palette to fine-tune the selection by dragging the Hue, Saturation, and Luminance sliders to define exactly what those respective values should be.

6 Toggle the Highlight button to compare the original image with the selection. You will see that areas of sky between the branches of the trees need refinement.

> **TIP** It can occasionally be unclear where you should click with the qualifier tool to identify the optimal starting selection. The best strategy is to click and drag close to an area from which you are trying to extract the selection. In this case, the best area is on the horizon directly above the mountains. Once the selection has a clean edge, you can easily isolate the remainder of the area using windows.

Using the Mini Panel—Qualifiers

After you make an initial qualifier selection, you can use the Mini Panel to refine it. When you press the qualifier button in the upper-left section of the panel, the two five-inch screens and their surrounding buttons and knobs become the controls you'll use to continue making adjustments.

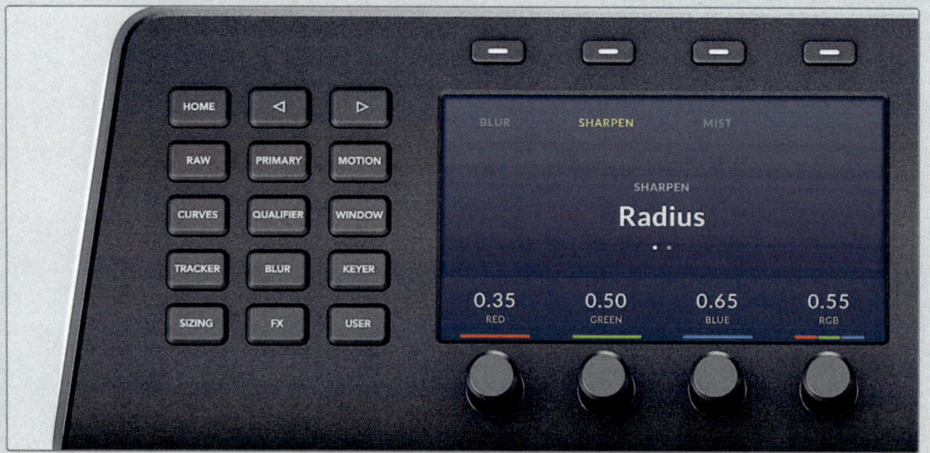

At first, you'll see the controls for Hue on the left screen and Saturation on the right. In the upper-left section of the panel, press the right arrow button to navigate to the luminance controls. In certain tools, you must use the left and right arrow buttons to access all of the functions that a specific tool has to offer.

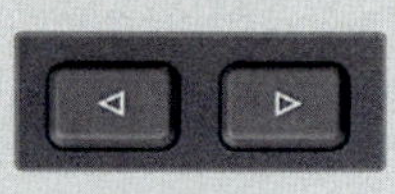

One more push of the right arrow button will bring you to the Matte Finesse tools, which you will use later in this exercise.

A good starting point to refining the HSL selection is to disable each value one-by-one to determine if its absence could improve the qualifier quality.

7 Click the orange toggle next to Hue to disable it.

Doing so has a positive effect on the selection. The horizon becomes refined and more areas of sky in the trees are included in the qualifier result. This result makes sense because the blown-out white sky is mostly made up of luminance data, not hue.

8 Drag the left side of the Luminance selection (Low) to refine the horizon selection. Aim to include the darker areas of sky between the trees.

The current focus is on ensuring the cleanest possible selection along the horizon; so, for now, you can ignore any other regions in the image that are also selected, such as the horses.

9 In the upper-right of the Viewer, click the Highlight B/W button to switch to a black-and-white representation of the matte. This is the traditional appearance of mattes with white indicating full opacity and black representing transparency.

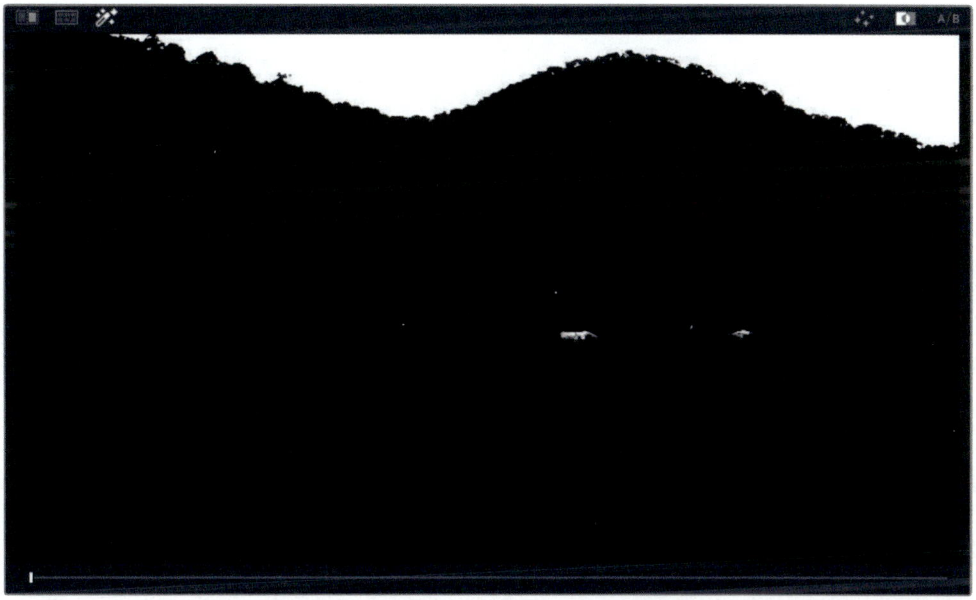

10 You can adjust the matte finesse controls in the HSL qualifier to further refine the selection. Adjusting Clean Black will reduce some of the minor spill-off occurring in the trees under the horizon. A setting of 20.0 should be enough for a satisfactory reduction.

11 Likewise, tweaking Clean White (20.0) can amplify the white between the tree branches for a cleaner overall result.

The clarity of the qualifier will often depend on the nature and quality of the footage. In this case, you might experience minor difficulty in getting a clean extraction from both mountain tops due to the difference in focal length between them. When one mountain has a clean key, the other appears too soft and vice versa. In such cases, the best approach is to break up the keying process into several nodes and combine them using a key mixer.

NOTE You can see the results of using a key mixer to clean up the sky selection on this clip in the 04 Completed Timeline. Open the timeline, right-click the clip, and under Local Versions, choose Mixed Key to see the version of the node pipeline with the key mixer.

Using Windows to Limit Qualifiers

If the HSL qualifier selection has extracted areas of the image that are not the sky, you will want to exclude them from the final matte.

1 Click the window palette next to the qualifier palette.

2 Click the linear window button to activate it. You will see the outline of the window in the viewer.

3 Double-click next to the window icon, and label it **Sky Window**.

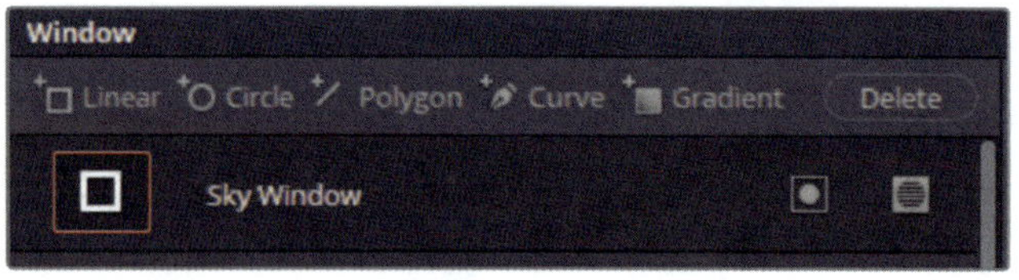

4 Drag its corners around the sky selection to exclude the lower regions of the matte.

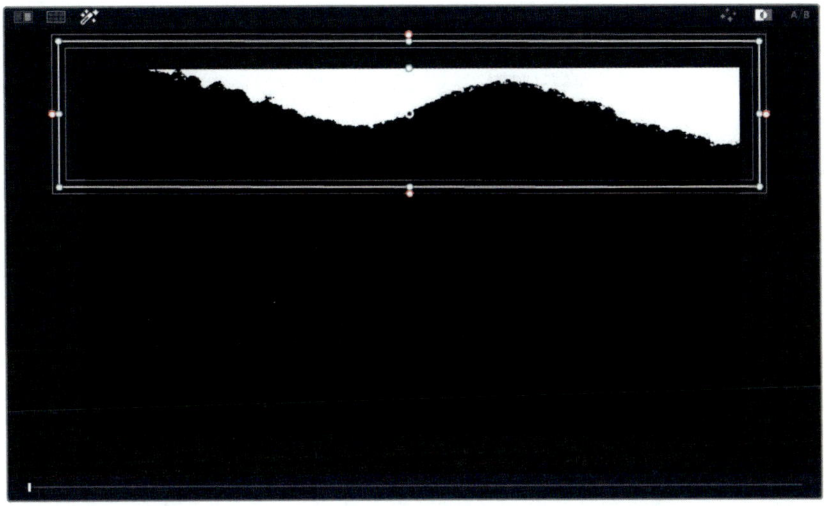

The sky should now be successfully selected and ready for color adjustment.

5 Click the Highlight button to disable the matte preview.

6 Drag the Gain master wheel to the left (0.95) to reduce the overexposure in the sky. By turning the white pixels gray, you will make them more receptive to hue and saturation changes.

7 Drag the Gain color wheel toward cyan/blue to introduce blue into the sky.

> **TIP** You could also use the Color Generator in the OpenFX panel to replace the sky color. It overwrites all the color data in a node with a single color hue without regard for any existing RGB data. It is ideal for working on elements that require a consistent color, but using it might not be optimal when you are trying to retain some of the natural variations of the hues and shadows in a selection.

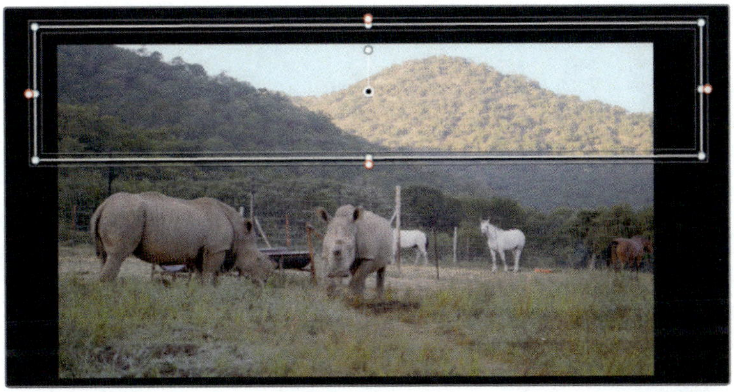

Finally, to soften the edges around the tops of the hills, you can gently blur the edge between the black and white portions of the matte.

8 In the qualifier palette, increase the Blur Radius (10.0) in the matte finesse controls.

A gentler edge will ensure a more organic-looking grade and hide any imperfections in the selection.

Adding Atmosphere

When you look into the distance through several miles of air, you can see the atmosphere reveal itself. In an air-polluted city, the atmosphere may have a hazy white, brown, or orange look; whereas, on a clear day, you would see a soft blue.

When you are enhancing a sky or replacing it altogether, you need to blend a blue hue into the shot's horizon to replicate that atmospheric refraction. Otherwise, the replacement sky might end up looking fake against the horizon.

1 In the Node editor, select and then right-click the Sky node, and choose Add Node > Add Outside, or press Option-O (macOS) or Alt-O (Windows). This inverse selection will allow you to blend the color of the sky into the horizon of the image.

2 Label node 05 as **Outside**.

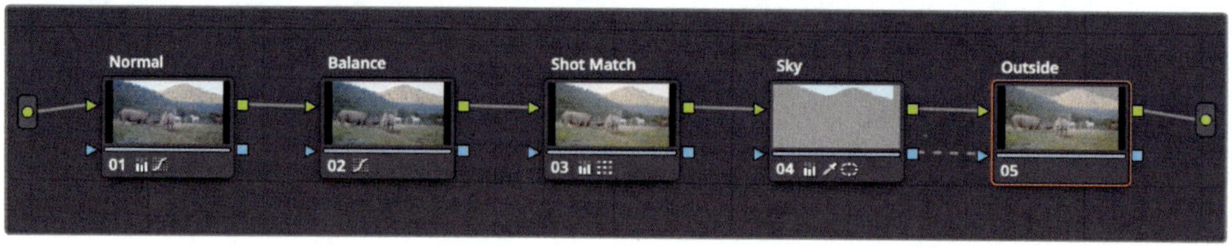

TIP You may need to pan and zoom out on the node graph by dragging with the middle mouse button to pan, and dragging the slider above the Node graph to zoom out.

3 With the Outside node selected, in the list of the Window palette, click the gradient window button.

An outline of the gradient controls appears in the viewer in the form of a line with a perpendicular arrow extending from it.

4 In the Window palette, double-click the layer name field next to the gradient icon, and type **Atmosphere**.

This gradient window works a bit differently compared to the other windows that you have created. Instead of defining a shape, you position a starting point and drag the arrow in the direction of the gradient fall-off. The further you drag the arrow, the softer the gradient will be.

5 Adjust the top of the gradient (the horizontal line) to start at the top of the distant mountain, and drag the arrow to taper off the gradient toward the bottom.

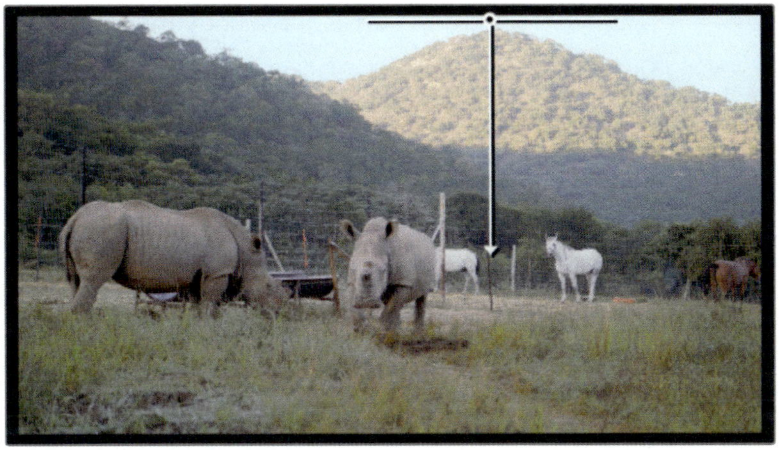

6 Drag the Offset master wheel in the direction of cyan, but not as far as you did for the sky change. The goal is to give the distant mountain a slight blue tint to convey the blue atmosphere in front of it.

7 Press Cmd-D (macOS) or Ctrl-D (Windows) to compare the results before and after your atmosphere addition.

The gradient looks good in the distance, but covers too much of the foreground mountain. You will want to create a new shape to select everything that you don't want altered by the atmosphere grade.

8 In the Node editor, disable the Outside node by clicking its number (5) or pressing Cmd-D (macOS) or Ctrl-D (Windows). Doing so will allow you to continue work without being distracted by the blue grade.

9 While still in the Window palette, click the Curve button.

10 In the viewer, click around the foreground hill and the lower-half of the frame to create a custom shape around it. To close the loop and define the shape, click the first point that you created.

> **TIP** When creating custom windows: click to create linear points, and drag to create rounded Bézier curves.

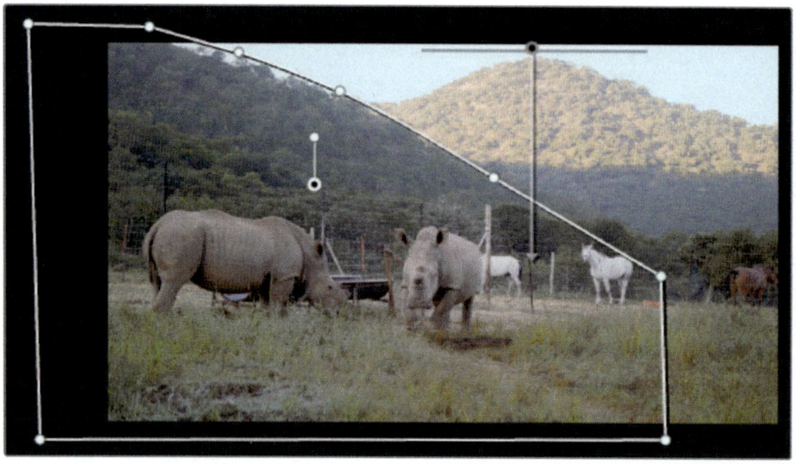

11 Double-click the layer name field next to the curve button, and enter the name **Foreground**. Enable the Outside node to see the result.

The cyan grade now affects both the background mountain and the entirety of the custom shape. By default, all windows are additive. You will need to indicate that you wish to subtract the selection from the final result.

12 In the curve field, next to the label, click the Subtract Mask button to extract this custom shape from the final output of the node.

13 To the right of the Window palette, adjust the Softness parameter to feather the edge of the Power curve. Drag the Inside and Outside fields to make the border of the window less aggressive between the two mountains.

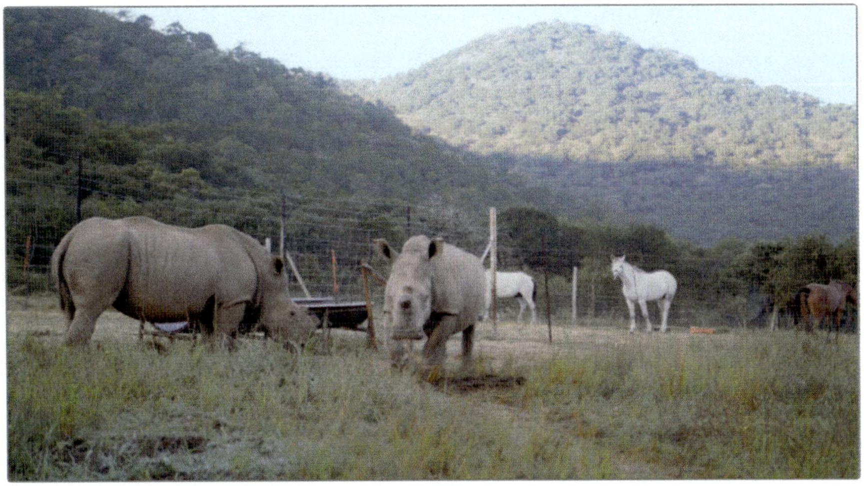

TIP When changing the sky color, another technique is to apply a gradient window on top of the sky selection node. By tapering off the artificial color toward the original hues at the bottom, you can also achieve a realistic-looking secondary grade.

Ordinarily, overblown skies can be addressed on the set using ND filters and focusing additional lighting on your talent. However, this solution may not always be an option for smaller productions or documentaries. In such cases, secondary grading becomes a viable option. It keeps the filming process light while ensuring a good shot at the end of the post-production process.

Warping Colors to a Target

On the surface, the Color Compressor filter allows you to select a single hue and flexibly blend it into the image by modifying various color characteristics. The filter begins to offer some impressive versatility when you start combining it with other selection methods, such as the qualifier. The method you'll learn in this exercise can be extremely useful when cleaning up skin tones, hair, and environment to give them a more consistent chromatic appearance.

NOTE This exercise requires DaVinci Resolve Studio to complete.

1 In the yellow flag-filtered timeline, ensure that clip 01 is selected.

2 Create a new serial node at the end of your pipeline called **Grass** (node 06).

3 Use the HSL qualifier to select the grass on the ground. Aim to grab a sample of the less vibrant, dry grass. The purpose of the exercise is to adjust its hue to a healthier shade.

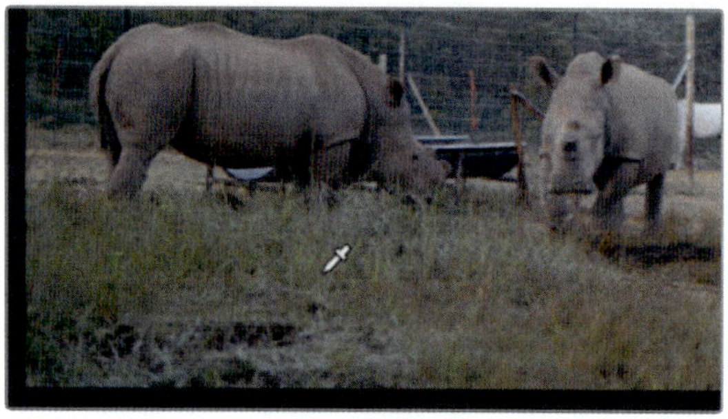

4 Switch the Viewer to Highlight mode and tweak the HSL sliders and matte finesse controls to clean up the selection.

You will notice that the trees are selected almost immediately due to their similarity to the color of the grass. You can temporarily ignore the trees, but pay particular attention to excluding the rhinos from the selection.

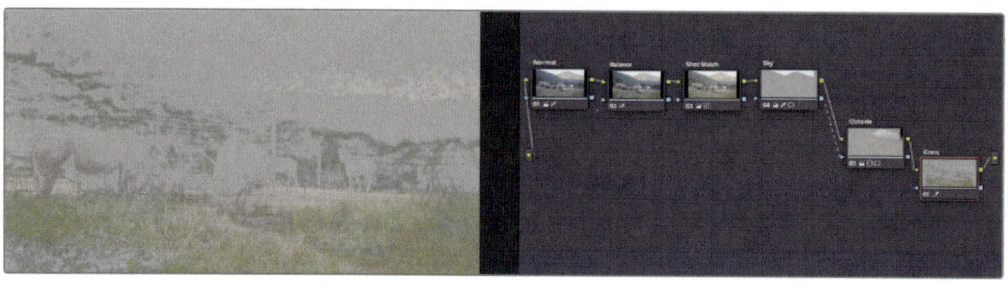

5 In the Window palette, create a linear window.

6 Name this window **Grass Matte**.

7 Drag the corners of the window around the grassy field in the foreground of the image.

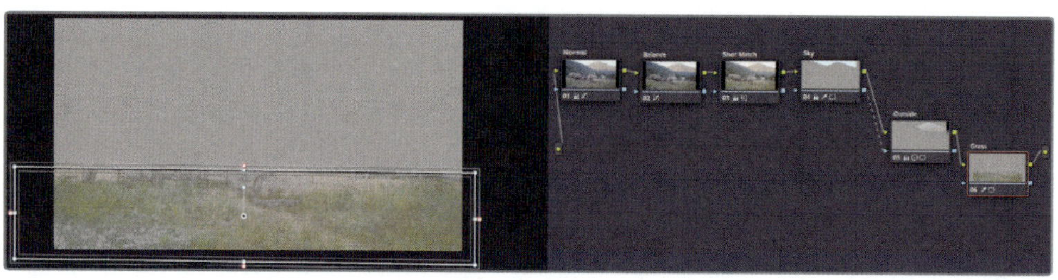

8 Turn off Highlight mode to see the original image.

9 Click the OpenFX button to open its palette.

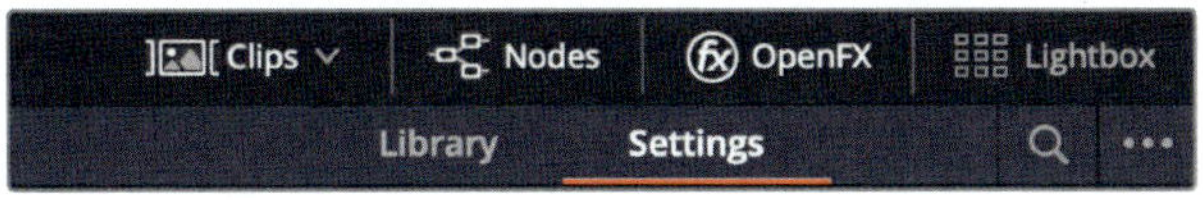

10 In the ResolveFX Color category, drag the Color Compressor effect onto the new node.

> **NOTE** If you are not using DaVinci Resolve Studio, a watermark will appear over the image. For the purpose of this exercise, you can dismiss the warning dialog and continue to work with the watermarked image.

You can work with ResolveFX more effectively by making the Viewer larger and displaying the Resolve FX setting panel to the right.

11 In the Workspace menu, choose Full Screen Viewer, or press Shift-F.

12 In the Color Compressor settings, double-click the box next to the Target Color field, and select a green hue for the grass.

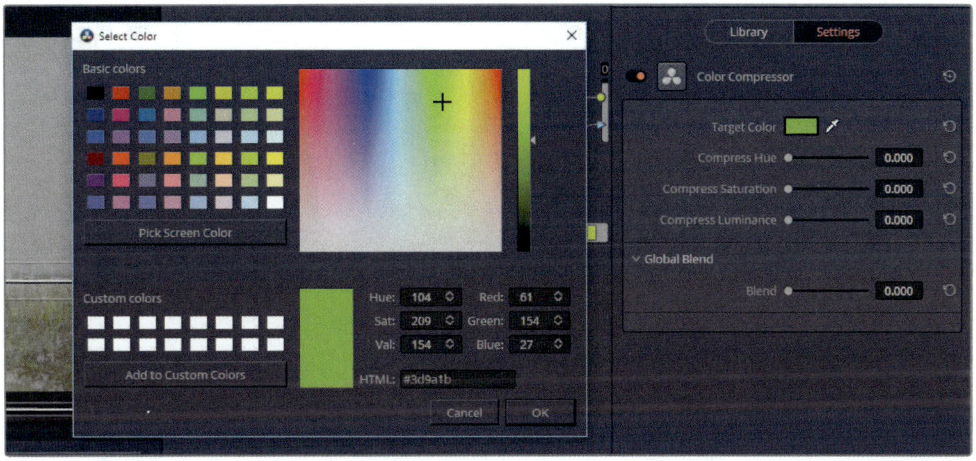

13 Raise the Compression Hue (0.350) and the Compression Saturation (0.050) values to increase the amount of the green in the selection and push its saturation.

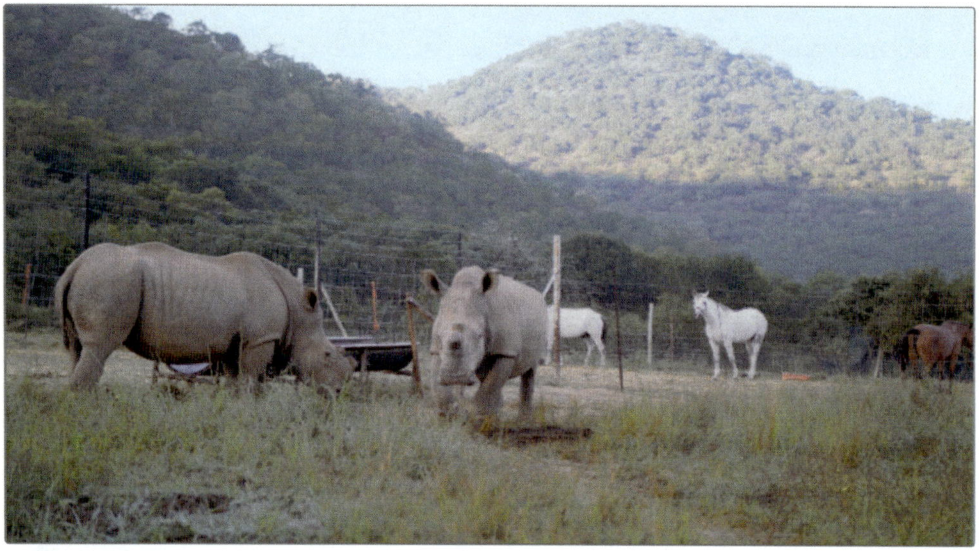

Before

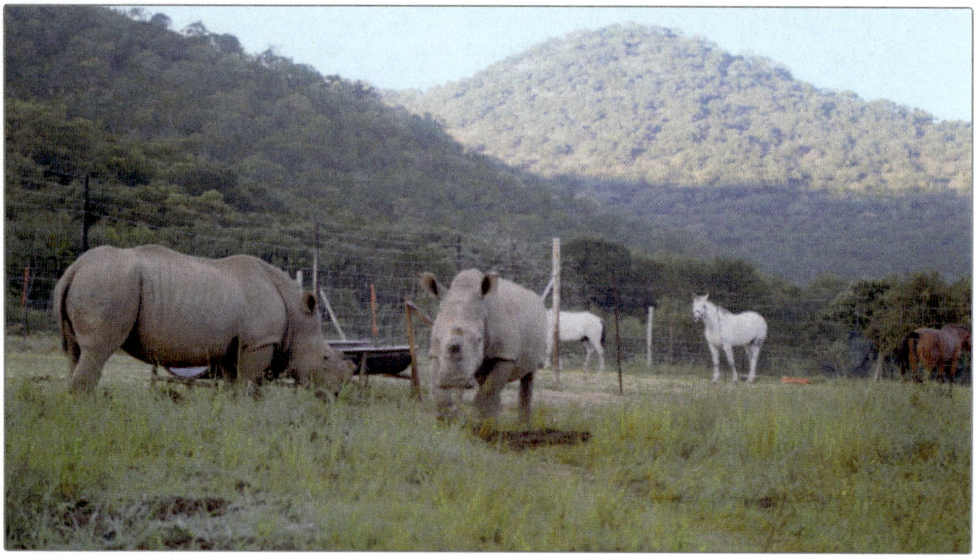

After

14 When you are done with the adjustments, choose Workspace > Full Screen Viewer, or press Shift-F, to exit Full Screen mode.

> **TIP** To remove a ResolveFX plug-in from a node, right-click the node, and choose Remove OFX Plugin.

As with all other effects, the Color Compressor can be keyframed, which gives you the ability to enhance a visual detail over time (dull hair grows vibrant, or a dry field turns green). You may also find purely aesthetic applications for the Color Compressor. For example, when compositing, you could blend a single hue into a backplate clip when a text layer or animation appears over it.

Enhancing Skin Tones with Face Refinement

A common task for secondary correction is to make skin tones look more natural. Whether you are working with a fictional narrative or a documentary, the audience will be paying the utmost attention to the actions (and, therefore, the faces) of the people on the screen. With this much focus from the audience, you want to be certain that skin tones do not cause a distraction.

NOTE This exercise requires DaVinci Resolve Studio to complete.

In this exercise, you'll start with a well-framed and properly exposed shot. The only issue is that the speaker is wearing a wide-brimmed hat on a sunny day, which is causing shadows that obscure her face. Your goal is to make her face stand out more, and then address general imperfections using the Face Refinement effect.

1. In the yellow flag-filtered timeline, select clip 02. In the Node editor, you can see that it has already been balanced on the first node.
2. Create a new serial node, and label it **Face**.
3. In the ResolveFX Refine category, drag the Face Refinement effect onto the Face node.

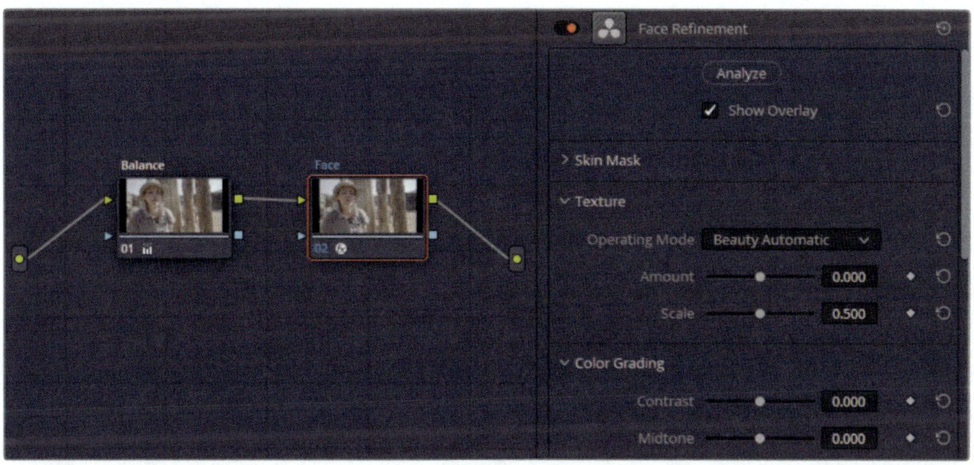

NOTE If you are not using DaVinci Resolve Studio, a watermark will appear over the image. You can dismiss the warning dialog and complete this exercise with the watermarked image.

Face Refinement includes a number of diagnostic and grading tools aimed specifically at enhancing the skin and details of a human face.

The effect analyzes the shot to automatically detect and track a moving face; and to recognize and adjust individual features such as eyes, lips, cheeks, chin, and forehead.

4 In the Face refinement settings, click Analyze. It will take some time for processing because the software detects the face and constructs a travelling matte.

When the analysis is complete, you will see a series of green trackers identifying the woman's facial features.

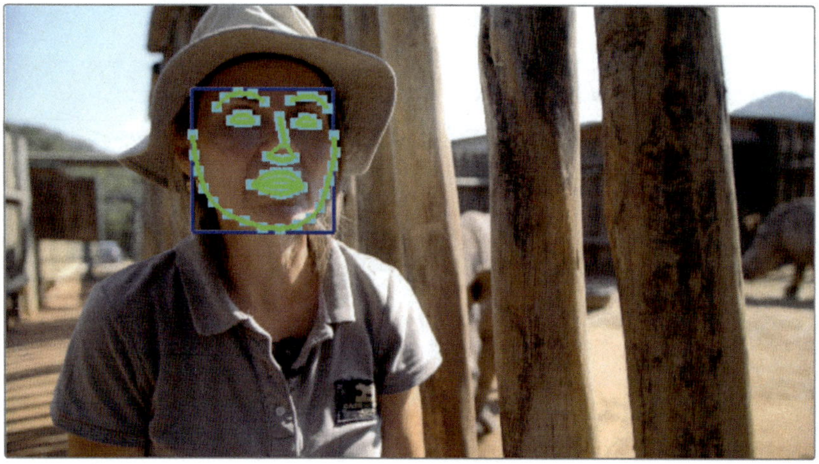

To ensure the highest quality of selection, you should check the matte of the face before proceeding with any adjustments. The matte quality can be compromised when analyzing a subject whose skin tones closely match their hair, clothes, or surroundings. In this example, the subject fits all three of these criteria.

5 Within the Face Refinement settings, double click the Skin Mask header to expand it and select Show Mask.

6 Deselect Show Overlay at the top of the settings to remove the green trackers from the Viewer.

7 Zoom inside the Viewer to get a clearer view of the subject's face.

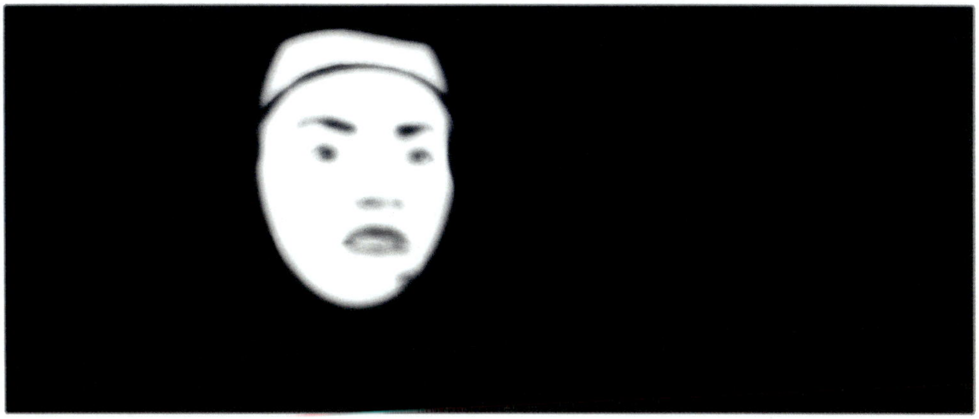

The selection is very clean overall. The only exception is the upper segment of the mask, which includes part of the tan hat that the woman is wearing.

Combining Windows with Face Refinement

To remove the unnecessary segment from Face Refinement, you will use a window to exclude the top of the matte from the selection.

1 Move the playhead to the last frame of the clip.

2 With the Face node still selected, open the Window palette.

3 Create a new circle window.

4 In the upper-right options menu of the Window palette, choose Convert to Bézier to transform the circle's points into Bézier curves. Label the resulting curve window, **Face**.

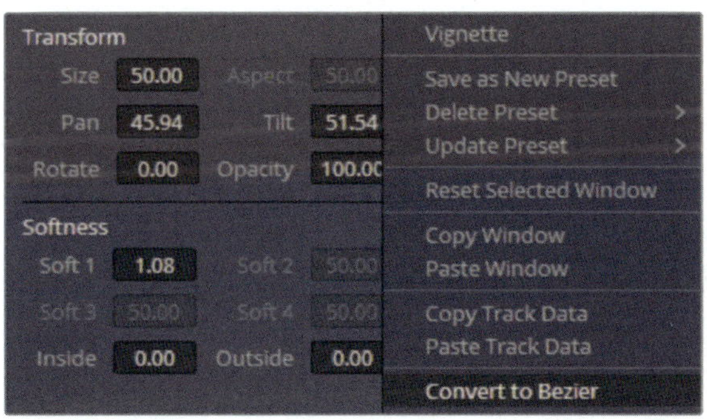

5 Adjust the points to fit around her face, paying extra attention to excluding the hat.

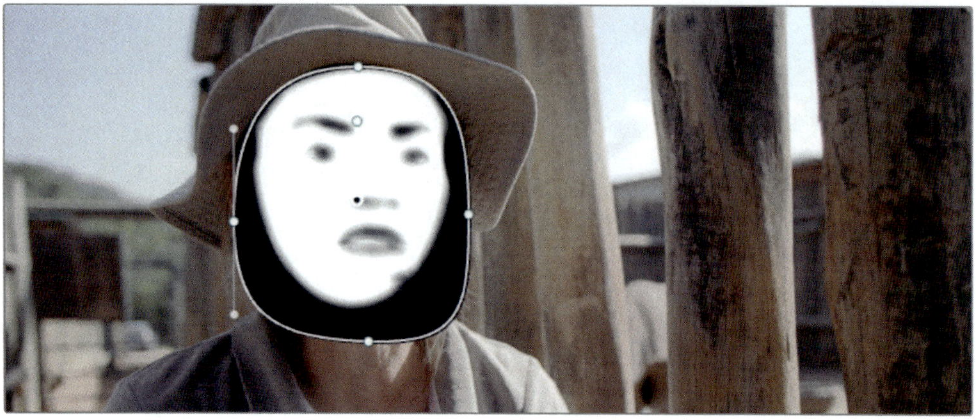

6 In the face refinement setting, deselect Show Mask.

7 Enter the Tracker palette.

8 Click the Track Reverse button to track the motion of her face backward through the clip.

9 When tracking is completed, refine the shape of the Face window, if necessary. Return to the Face Refinement settings when you are finished.

Improving Skin Quality

The bulk of the face refinement feature is about fixing skin tones. Skin tones might need adjustment for a variety of reasons:

General skin imperfections, such as variations of color, spots, dryness, oiliness, and so on—By applying the appropriate brightness, contrast, and blurring, you can reduce these issues and put the focus back on the performance.

Some skin types are prone to reflecting light with unpredictable tints—The most common variants are skin types that appear magenta or green under certain lights. The purpose of grading in this case is to remove the tint and match the performer to his surroundings and co-stars.

Overpowering primary grade—When a shot has been extremely graded at the primary stage to look a certain way (for example, to make the environment look cold), the skin can end up looking dead as a result. These kinds of flat grades can drain the shot of life and look dull. By bringing back the skin tone, the shot once again becomes vibrant.

In this exercise, you'll look at some of the commonly used settings of the face refinement feature.

1 In the Workspace menu, choose Full Screen Viewer, or press Shift-F, to expand the viewer to fill your screen while still allowing you to access the ResolveFX panel to the left.

2 In the Face Refinement settings, under Texture, adjust the Amount to 0.200. Doing so will gently blur the skin to soften minor wrinkles and imperfections.

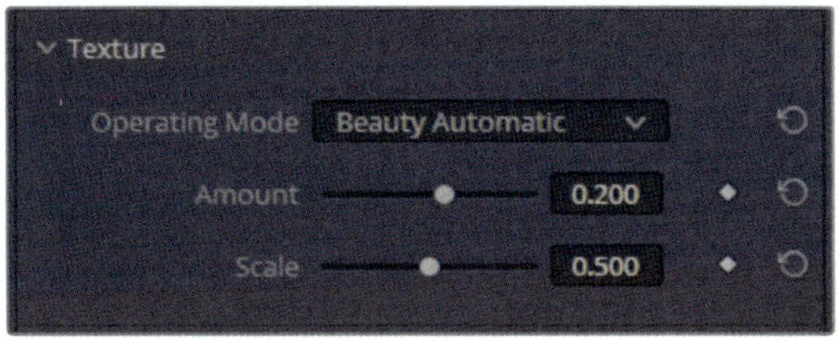

Be careful not to push this setting so far that skin starts to look plastic. You should not aim to remove wrinkles, but merely soften them.

> **TIP** For more precise skin smoothing options, change the Texture Operating mode to Smoothing or Beauty Advanced. These modes can break up the smoothing process into individual steps in which you can take into account skin texture and lighting.

3 Scroll down to the Color Grading section to begin work on the woman's skin tone grade.

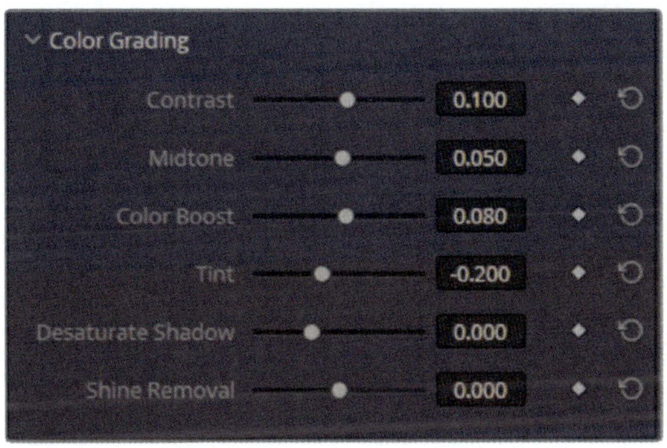

The Midtone control is responsible for the overall brightness of the skin, which you can adjust to negate the presence of shadows.

4 Drag the Midtone slider to the right (0.050) to brighten the skin, but do not pull it so far that the onscreen results become distracting.

Color Boost enhances the saturation in areas of the skin that are under-saturated.

5 Drag the color Boost slider to the right until you reach 0.080.

Tint is responsible for undoing the green or magenta color cast that some skin tones reflect.

6 Drag Tint to -0.200 to reduce the redness in the skin.

7 Raise the Contrast (0.100) to return some detail into the shadows of her face.

8 Next, scroll down to the Eye Retouching section and double-click to expand it.

The controls in this section allow you to enhance details in the iris of the speaker, as well as brighten up the reflections from light sources (known as *specular reflection*).

9 Set Sharpening to 0.050 to refine the pupil, eyelashes, and eye shape.

10 Set Brightening to 0.050 to brighten the color of the iris.

11 Set Eye Light to 0.050 to gently increase the brightness around the eye area.

12 Adjust Eyebag removal to 0.200 to brighten the area directly under her eyes.

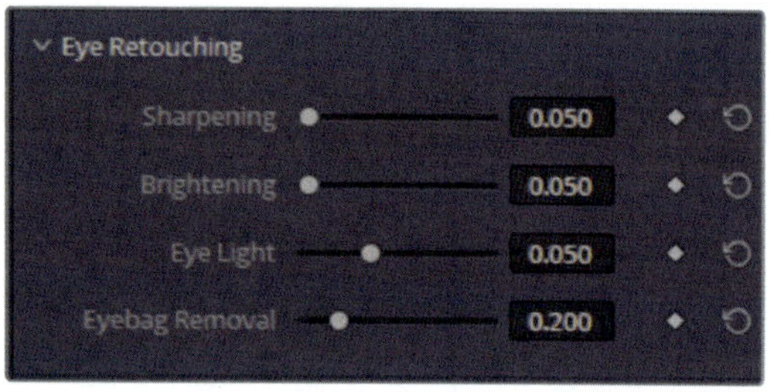

In addition to addressing general dark circles under eyes, Eyebag removal can reduce shadows caused by headwear as in this clip.

Lip Retouching allows you to saturate and change the hue of a subject's lip color and to smooth upper lip wrinkles in tighter close-ups. As usual, context is key. The park ranger in question is not wearing lipstick, nor do you have a justifiable reason to glamorize her as she talks about the issue of rhino poaching in South Africa. In this case, the Lip retouching tool is necessary only to add a minor contrast to her skin tone.

13 Raise Saturation to 0.200 to define her lips against her skin.

The same guidelines apply to the Blush retouching section.

14 Set Saturation just high enough (0.200) to define her face shape, without making it look like makeup.

15 Additionally, you could expand the Size to 0.500 to spread the gentle redness across either side of her face without concentrating it to the apples of her cheeks.

The final three sections (Forehead, Cheek, and Chin retouching) enable further hue adjustments to those specific areas. These controls can be beneficial when employing the traditional portraiture technique of "traffic lights," in which gentle yellow, red, and green hues are applied to the forehead, cheeks, and chin, respectively.

The Global Blend control at the bottom of the settings allow you to blend the original image back into the Face Refinement node. This is ideal when you are generally happy with your face refinement settings, but find that they are a touch too powerful.

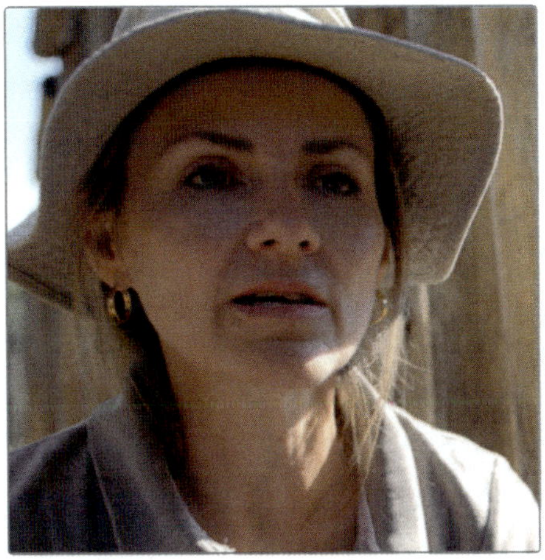
Before

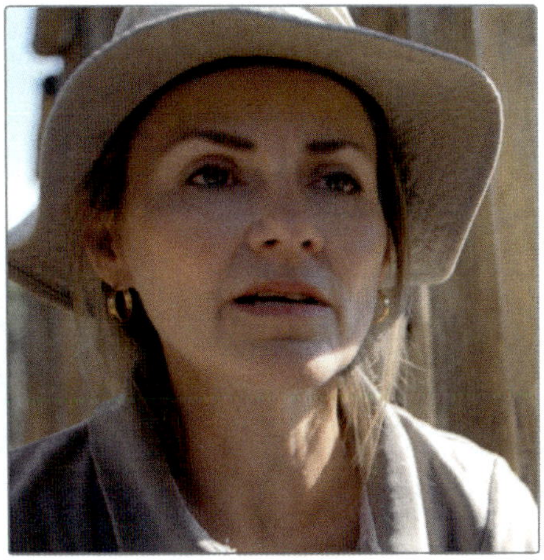
After

With just one node, you have successfully enhanced your subject's skin tone, made it more pronounced by brightening and warming it, and added chromatic detail into her features. In the original clip, it now becomes apparent how much the shadow of her hat was affecting the visibility of her face and facial expressions.

TIP You can apply ResolveFX to an existing corrector node or drag onto a connection line to create a ResolveFX node. ResolveFX nodes work slightly differently from normal Corrector nodes in that you cannot use grading tools, windows, or qualifiers on a ResolveFX node. They perform only the effect for which the filter was designed.

Adjusting Skin Tones Manually

As impressive as the Face Refinement ResolveFX feature is, it will not work for every skin refinement task. For example, when a face is turned away from the camera, the analysis tool will struggle to locate the facial features. When you are working on a profile shot, you'll need to use the standard selection and grading palettes.

In this example, the subject is in an uncontrolled lighting environment. He is simultaneously overexposed by direct sunlight, and underexposed in the shadows. Your aim will be to reduce this stark contrast and remove the magenta tint from his skin.

1 In the yellow flag-filtered timeline, select clip 03.

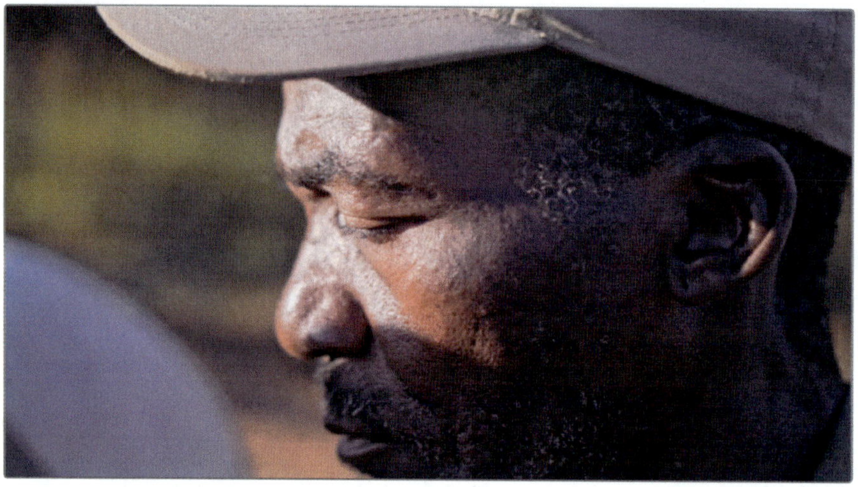

This clip already has a normalized tonal range via the primaries wheels in node 01.

2 Create a new serial node, and label it **Skin Hue** (node 02).

One possible approach to adjusting the man's skin tones would be to use the qualifier to extract his skin and treat it as a secondary grade. However, this is not necessarily the best approach. It takes times to create a clean key and the separation between the skin and the rest of the shot could end up looking too aggressive.

A gentler approach is to use the HSL curves which will allow you to target his skin range based on hue, luminance, and saturation.

3 Open the Custom curve palette, and in the mode pop-up menu, choose the Hue Vs Hue curve.

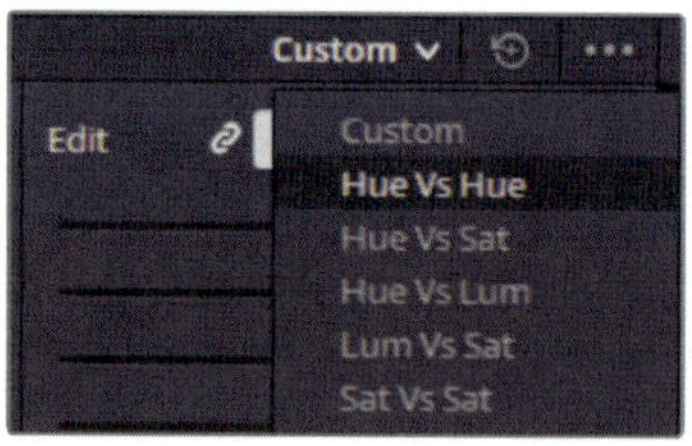

TIP The naming convention of the hue curves describes the selection method, followed by the change type. Hue Vs Sat implies that you are targeting a specific range of color (hue) to adjust its saturation (sat), whereas Sat Vs Sat suggests that you are targeting a certain range of saturation in an image with the aim of increasing or reducing it.

The Hue Vs Hue palette shows the full range of hues going left to right, looping through the red hue. It enables you to sample a specific color and shift it towards another hue.

One method of hue selection is to use the swatch buttons at the bottom of the curve graph. Another method is to click in the viewer to sample pixel values.

4 In the Viewer, click on an evenly exposed patch of the man's face.

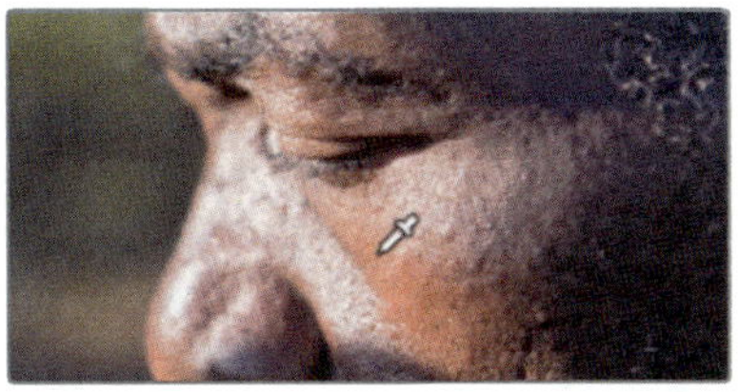

> **TIP** If a hue selection lands near the left or right edge of the palette, the range will smoothly cycle back around to the opposite edge.

Three control points are added to the Hue Vs Hue curve. The center point identifies the selected hue and the control points on either side limit the range of hue that is affected.

5 Drag the center control point down slightly to remove some of the red tint in the man's skin tone. Be careful not to introduce too much green. If necessary, drag the two control points on either side farther apart to define a wider hue for the skin tone.

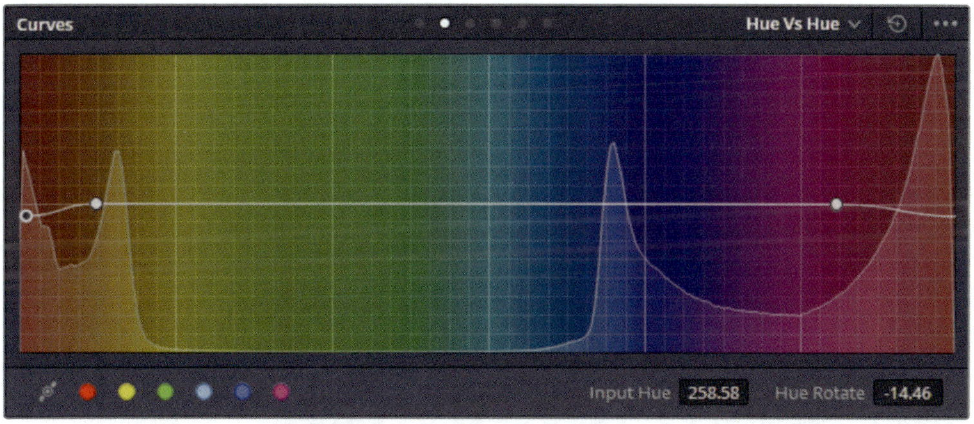

> **TIP** For more precision when moving a control point, use the Input Hue and Hue Rotation fields in the lower-right corner of the palette.

This may feel a bit like a guessing game. What is the right hue for his skin? To create more certainty in your adjustment, you will need to open the Vectorscope and check what the adjustment is doing to the skin.

The first thing you will need to do is to get a clean view of the face by using a window to remove interfering elements.

6 Open the Window palette.

7 Create a circle power curve window, and label it **Face Window**. Position it over the man's face to isolate a clean patch of skin.

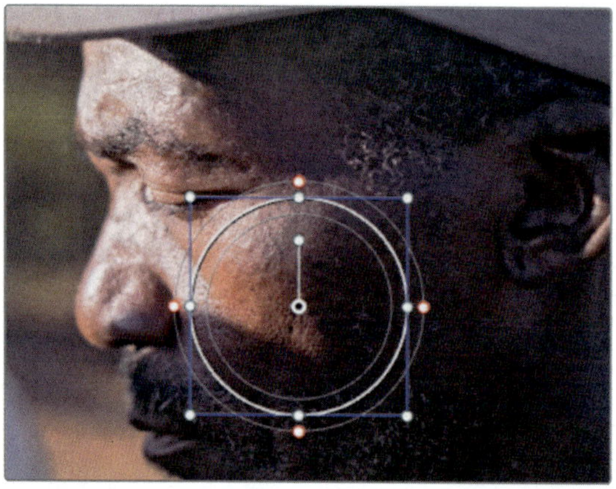

8 Remove the Softness Soft 1 on the window, and click the Highlight button.

This temporary window will aid in providing a clean readout of the skin tone to the Vectorscope.

9 In the Scopes palette, choose Vectorscope as the scope type.

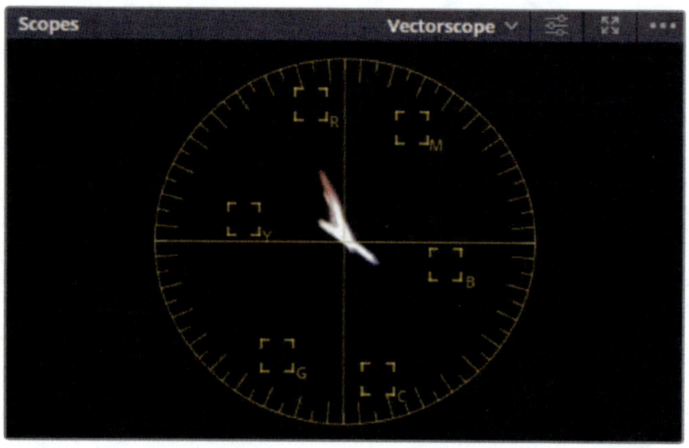

The Vectorscope distributes the visual data of an image on a circular graph representing the hues in the current frame and their saturation levels. A well-balanced image will generally appear as a cloud of pixels in the center of the Vectorscope with some deviations toward specific hues in images that contain prominent colors.

When working with skin tones, the Vectorscope can be invaluable for determining if a subject's skin is deviating toward the green, yellow, or magenta hues that can look unflattering.

The rule is to aim for the skin tone indicator line to ensure normal-toned skin.

10 In the upper-right corner, click the settings icon to adjust the appearance of the scope for easier readability.

11 Select Show 2x Zoom to increase the size of the scope.

12 Select Show Skin Tone Indicator to display a line that indicates a healthy skin tone range.

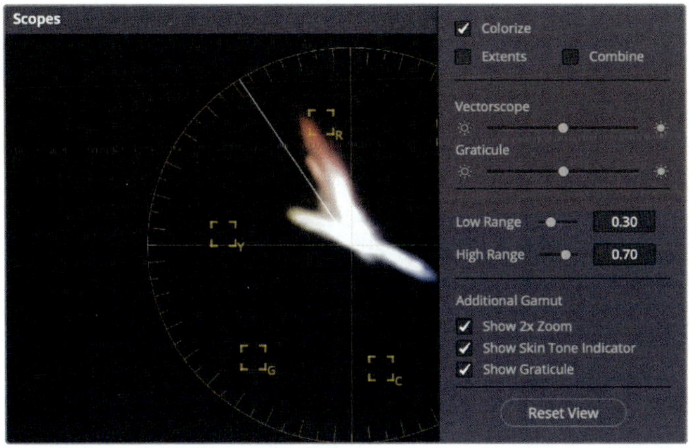

13 Click anywhere in the Color page to close the pop-up window.

14 Drag the center control point in the Hue Vs Hue palette up and down to view the movement in the Vectorscope. It's important to keep in mind that you are not trying to align the skin hue strictly to the Skin Tone Indicator line. Rather, you are using the Skin Tone Indicator to detect and gently reduce any obvious tone deviation in the skin tone.

15 A significant part of the man's skin is in shadow, where it appears to have a prominent magenta tint. Add additional control points in the Hue Vs Hue curve and move more of the skin data so that it falls closer to the skin tone line.

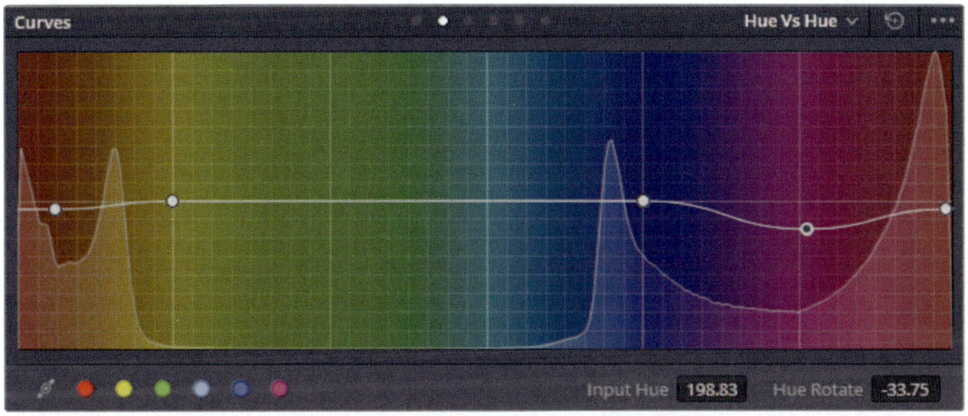

16 When you are happy with the skin tone hue, turn off Highlight mode to see the entire image, and remove the circle window by clicking the circle icon in the Windows palette.

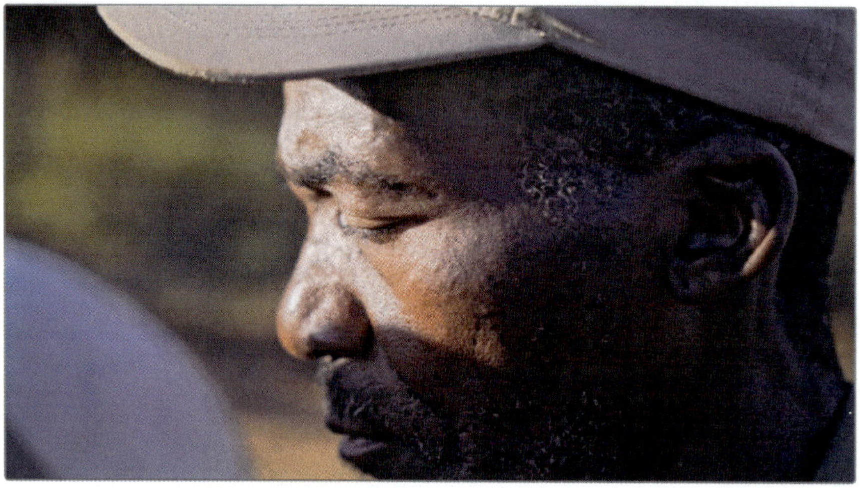

The hue curves should be your first choices when you are trying to quickly adjust the hue, saturation, or luminance of an object. If the result is not immediately satisfactory, you can then switch to working with the qualifier, which offers a greater degree of control over your matte selection. Also, keep in mind that you can use the hue curves in combination with the qualifiers and Power Windows for an even more refined selection.

Perfecting Skin Tone Saturation

The hue of the skin tone is critical because people view skin tones from memory. With an expectation of what a healthy skin tone should look like, a viewer will instinctively know if something is "off." You can use another hue curve on a separate node to address the saturation of the skin.

1. Create a new serial node, and label it **Skin Sat** (node 03).
2. In the Curve Mode pop-up menu, choose Hue Vs Sat.

   You can use Hue Vs Sat palette to make under-saturated items pop and highly saturated items more subdued. When dealing with skin tones, the right settings can be subjective. Generally, darker skin tones require the least amount of saturation, while lighter skin tones require the most before they begin to look distorted. In this case, the saturation in the man's skin needs a very slight adjustment.
3. In the Viewer, click a saturated patch of the man's face to drop the three points in the Hue Vs Sat curve. Drag the two surrounding control points to include a wider range of the skin.

4 Drag the central point up slightly to increase the height of the saturation in the Vectorscope.

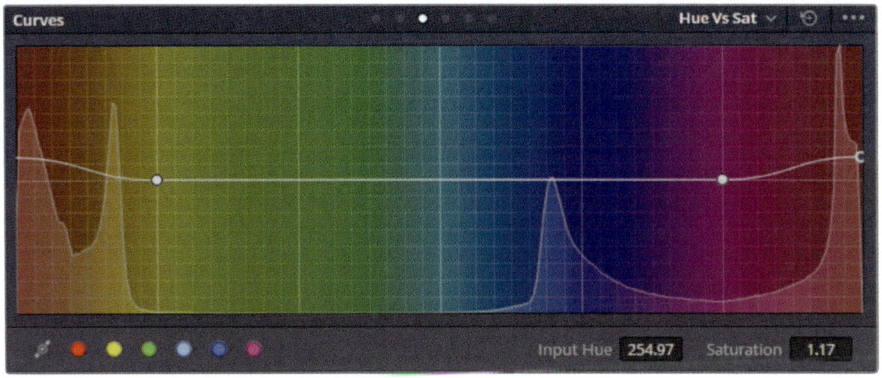

5 Press Cmd-D (macOS) or Ctrl-D (Windows) to disable the Hue Vs Sat node. Press the keyboard shortcut again to view the adjustment.

Memory Colors

Memory colors are colors for which human beings have an instinctive reference. The most common of those are sky, grass, and skin tones that tend to be closely imprinted in our perception of the world. It is particularly important to grade these colors accurately to ensure audience immersion, unless the narrative specifically calls for a distortion of these hues. Man-made objects tend to have less color memory associated with them, so you have more freedom to tweak the hue of a car or the saturation of a character's dress.

Be careful not to get too aggressive when adjusting skin tones. The aim is not to produce a magazine cover look, but to reduce minor imperfections and enhance the visibility and saturation of the face. Getting too aggressive with the ResolveFX or hue controls can result in plastic-looking skin that is even more distracting than imperfections.

Using the Mini Panel—Hue Curves

When switching between HSL curves, the color presets normally found in the interface are available using the knobs below the Mini Panel screens. You can find additional curves and tools by pressing the left and right arrow buttons on the panel.

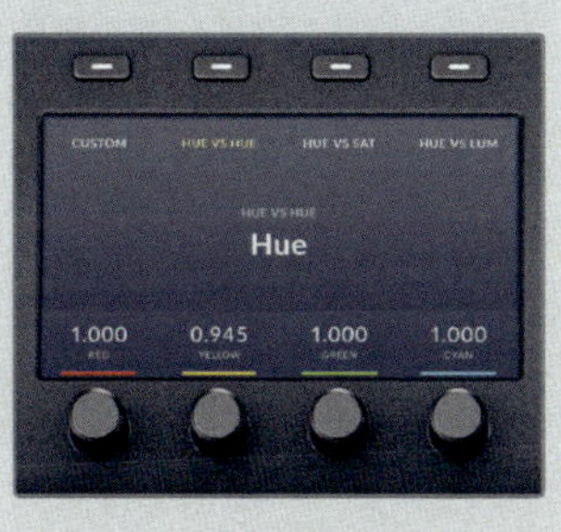

Continue using these techniques in new ways and combining qualifiers/Power Windows with your own footage. If you're uncertain how to proceed with a certain shot, write out a workflow to help determine how you want the final output to look, and then work backward to choose the tools and adjustments that will realize your goals. You'll always have several possible workflow options, so with experimentation and experience you will learn which are the most visually successful and time efficient for you.

Self-guided Exercises #3

Complete the following exercises in the unfiltered 03 Matched Timeline to test your understanding of the tools and workflows covered in this lesson.

Clip 01—Use Lum vs Sat in the HSL curves to increase the saturation of the deer in the center of the shot, but keep the saturation on the fence and ground low.

Clip 02—Apply a window to isolate the rhino's face between the bars, then apply the contrast Pop effect in ResolveFX to increase the contrast in that portion of the frame. The effect should immediately guide the eye without being overpowering.

Clip 03—Apply a window and use any of the sharpening methods covered in this lesson (Blur palette, Sharpen Edge FX, or Soften & Sharpen FX) to enhance the numbers on the scale and make them more readable. Track the window to the movement of the scale.

Clip 04—Apply a subtle circular vignette at the end of the pipeline in the shot with the rhinos and horses. Create another node *before* the vignette, and increase the brightness and contrast of the shot to enhance the color and detail.

Clip 05—Use the Color Compressor ResolveFX to tint the ground in the field green. Use the greenery in the mountains behind the horses as a reference for the shade of green you should use.

Clip 11—Use the Tilt-Shift Blur ResolveFX to create an artificial shallow depth of field in the shot with the man and his dog by the fence. Consider the depth of field in this clip – you might want to rotate the angle of the Depth of Field to be nearly vertical.

When you've completed these exercises, open the 05 Completed Effects Timeline to compare your work to the "solved" timeline.

Lesson Review

1. How are secondary color corrections different from primary color corrections?
2. How is an HSL qualifier selection refined?
3. What does the Hue vs Lum HSL curve do?
4. Which tool can you use to create a vignette?
5. True or False? Track data generated in the tracking palette can be copied and pasted onto another window or node.

Answers

1 Secondary color corrections affect only a part of the image, whereas primary corrections affect the whole frame.

2 Using the HSL selection ranges and matte finesse

3 Increases or decreases the brightness of a selected color. The naming convention of HSL curves is that the first word prompts the selection, and the second word affects the change.

4 Circle Power Window

5 True. The function to copy and paste track data is found in the options menu of the Tracker palette.

Part 2: Managing Nodes and Grades

Lessons

- Conforming from an XML Timeline
- Mastering the Node Processing Pipeline
- Managing Grades Across Clips and Timelines

In Part 2 of Color Correction with DaVinci Resolve 16, you'll look at workflows beyond primary and secondary color correction stages to improve your speed and productivity when grading. Along the way you'll learn how to conform Timelines from other applications, use stills and versions to copy and retain grade data, and perform some common compositing tasks.

Project File Location

You will find all the necessary content for this part of the book in the folder BMD 16 CC - Project 02. Follow the instructions at the start of every lesson to find the necessary folder, project, and Timeline. If you have not downloaded the second set of content files, see the Getting Started section of this book for instructions on how to do so.

Lesson 4

Conforming from an XML Timeline

XML and AAF are two file types frequently used to migrate Timelines between different software applications.

However, XML and AAF migration can occasionally fail to fully share Timeline structures dues to variances in application design. Migration inconsistencies can cause problems when you've received content edited in one application and want to grade and finish it in DaVinci Resolve 16. Upon import, you may find that some Timeline areas contain incorrect clips, or have failed to migrate transform changes or effects.

To ensure that an imported Timeline is an exact replica of the editor's work, you must use a verification process known as *conforming* to compare the reconstructed edit with a reference video and confirm that every cut and effect is reproduced within Resolve. When an element is mismatched or missing, you must manually alter it in the Timeline.

Time

This lesson takes approximately 55 minutes to complete.

Goals

In this lesson, you will look at the most common practices and issues associated with the conforming workflow. You will look at more advanced project setup practices by setting up scene-referred color for optimal grading conditions.

Importing an XML Timeline

The project you will be working on is a film trailer for a documentary called Age of Airplanes. Due to its non-linear nature, you will have more opportunity to experiment with grade construction and more dramatic looks on a clip-by-clip basis.

You will start by reconstructing the project Timeline from an XML file exported from the editing software.

1 Open DaVinci Resolve 16.

2 Right-click within the project manager window, and choose Import.

3 On your hard disk, locate the BMD 16 CC - Project 02 folder.

4 In the folder, select the Project 02 – Age of Airplanes Trailer.drp file, and click Import.

   The project is already set up with bins but contains no media or Timelines. You will be importing the Timelines required for the following exercises as XML files and associating the necessary media with them.

5 In the Edit page, select the empty Timelines bin as the destination for the XML Timeline, and choose File > Import Timeline > Import AAF, EDL, XML.

6 In the BMD 16 CC - Project 02 folder, navigate to the XMLs subfolder. Locate the Airplanes – 01 LQ Timeline.xml file, and click Open.

   The Load XML pop-up dialog appears in which you can set up how your XML Timeline and associated media are imported.

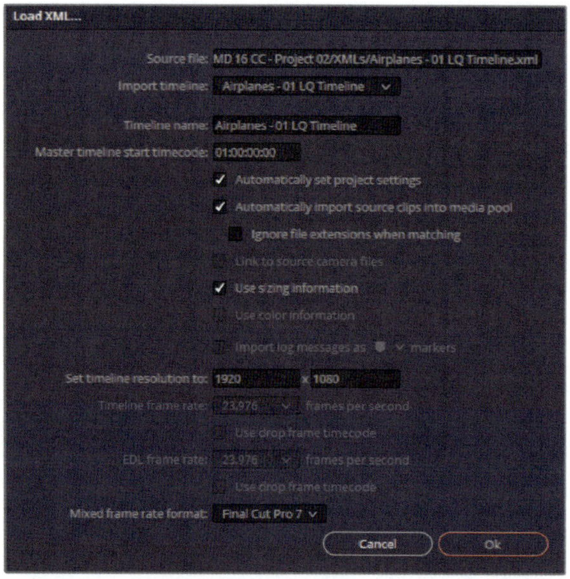

The default settings will work for this project because you want Resolve to find the media that belongs to this XML file.

> **TIP** Selecting "Ignore file extensions when matching" will allow you to choose media that is in a file format different from that of the original Timeline media. This option can be extremely useful when switching between offline and online workflows.

7 Click OK to close the dialog.

Resolve will search for the files based on their last known locations in relation to the XML file. Most of the time, drives and paths change during transfer, and a dialog will ask for help in locating the missing files.

8 If this dialog window appears, click Yes to locate the missing clips.

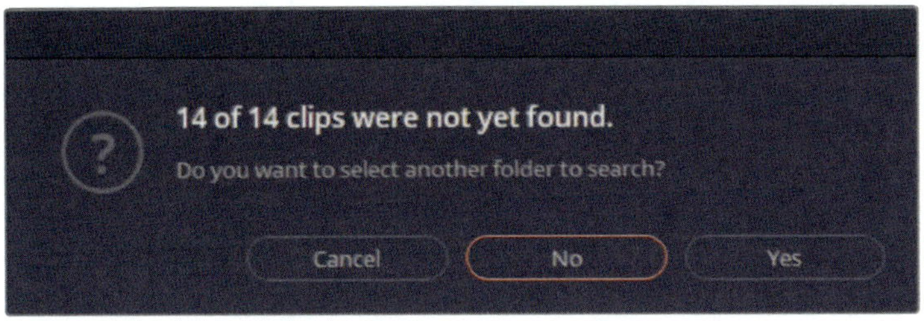

This Timeline should contain all of your low-quality video renders (LQ trancodes). You will need to be specific when indicating their location.

9 Navigate to the BMD 16 CC - Project 02 folder, and select the LQ Transcodes subfolder. Click OK at the bottom of the dialogue window.

This action should reconnect most of your media. However, the dialogue box will appear again, suggesting some remaining clips have not been located. You've specified the location of the video clips, but not the audio.

10 Click Yes again to find the audio.

11 In BMD 16 CC - Project 02, select the Audio subfolder, and click OK.

A few remaining clips will not be found. This sometimes occurs when video clips in the Timeline were renamed or changed after generating the XML file. Due to this change, Resolve cannot establish a connection with the media. You will resolve this during the conforming stage.

12 In the second dialog box, click No.

Another window will appear. The Log displays a summary of the migration process, including a confirmation of the imported Timeline and a list of migration issues (translation errors). This summary can help eliminate some of the guesswork from the conforming process.

13 Read the Log to see the name of the missing clips, and click Close when you are done.

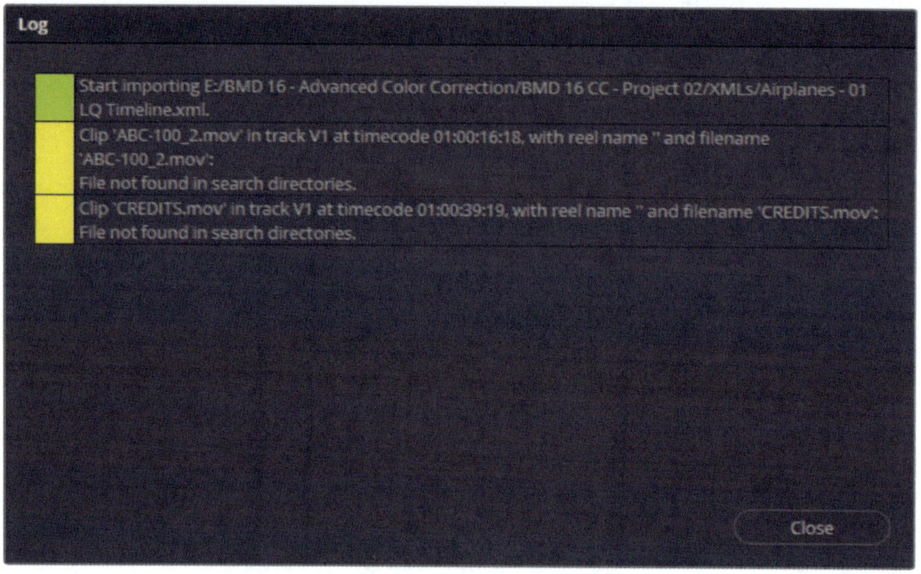

The Timeline should now appear in the Edit page, and its media in the media pool.

14 For easier project management, organize the imported files in the Media pool. The Timeline thumbnail (identified by an orange tick in the upper-right corner) can remain in the Timelines bin. The four audio files should be into the Audio bin, and the video files in the LQ Transcodes bin.

As long as the filenames of media files are not changed, relinking is a straightforward process. For this reason, it is highly advisable to never rename media, but work with the original camera filenames throughout the entire post-production process.

TIP When migrating with AAF files to and from Avid Media Composer, reel names are another piece of information that you must retain when creating low-resolution dailies and relinking to high-resolution original files. To do so, select the offline clips on the Timeline; choose File > Reconform from Media storage; and in the conform options, select "Assist using reel names from: embedded in source clip file".

Syncing an Offline Reference

With the XML Timeline imported and set up, you should now check the edit to ensure that every clip, cut, and effect was successfully migrated. To aid in this stage of the conforming process, the editor should provide a reference movie: a single exported video file of the final Timeline that you can use for visual verification of the migrated Timeline.

In this exercise, you'll associate a reference movie with a Timeline, and fix any issues that may have occurred during migration.

1 Go to the Media page.

2 In the Media pool, select the Reference bin as the target for the new clip you are about to import.

3 In the media storage browser, navigate to the BMD 16 CC - Project 02 folder.

4 In the Other folder, right-click the Age of Airplanes REFERENCE.mov file, and choose "Add as Offline Reference Clip."

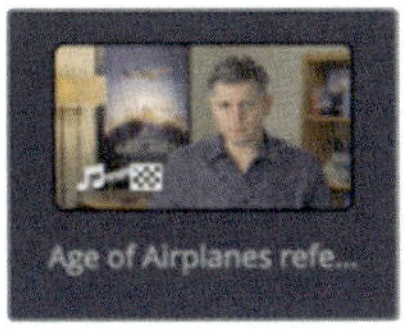

The reference video file is added to the Reference bin in the media pool with a checkerboard icon in the lower-left corner designating it as a reference movie.

5 In the Timelines bin of the media pool, right-click the Airplanes - 01 LQ Timeline thumbnail, and choose Timelines > Link Offline Reference Clip > Age of Airplanes REFERENCE.mov.

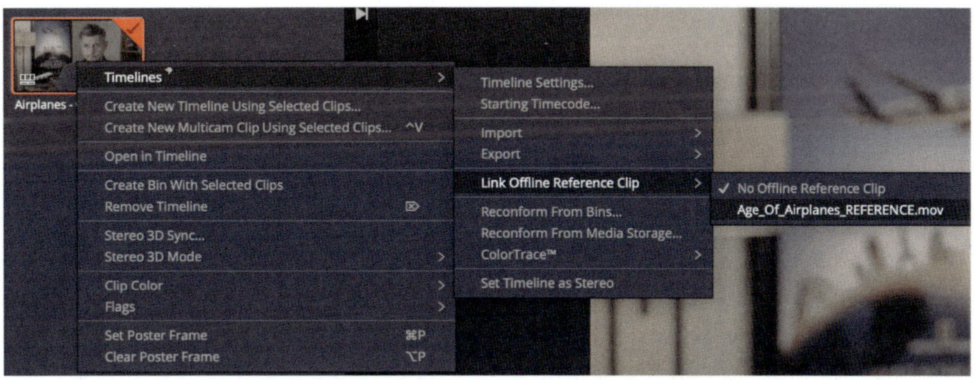

No obvious change will occur on the screen, but your reference movie is now associated with this Timeline. The next step is to display the reference movie in the source Viewer for visual comparison.

6 Open the Edit page.

7 In the lower-left corner of the source Viewer, in the Mode pop-up menu, choose Offline. Doing so will switch the source Viewer from showing source materials to displaying offline references associated with the active Timeline.

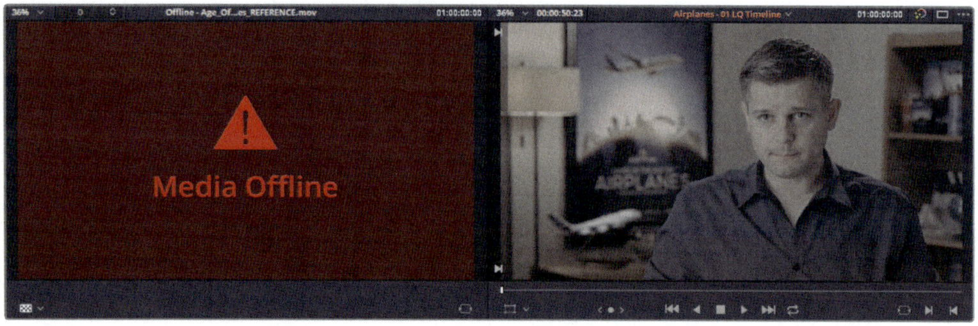

However, the Viewer currently shows the red Media Offline frame. One of the most common reasons a reference clip appears offline is because its timecode does not align with the Timeline timecode.

8 Select the Reference bin, and configure the media pool to list view.

9 In the Start TC column, view the start timecode of the reference clip and compare it to the start timecode of the Timeline.

Timelines in editing programs tend to begin at the one-hour timecode (01:00:00:00), whereas rendered video clips tend to begin at 00:00:00:00, as is the case with this reference. You can easily correct this by changing the start timecode of the reference clip to match the Timeline.

10 Move your playhead to the start of the Timeline.

11 Right-click the reference clip, and choose Clip Attributes.

12 In the Clip Attributes window, click the Timecode tab, and enter **01** as the Current Frame hour. Click OK to close the window.

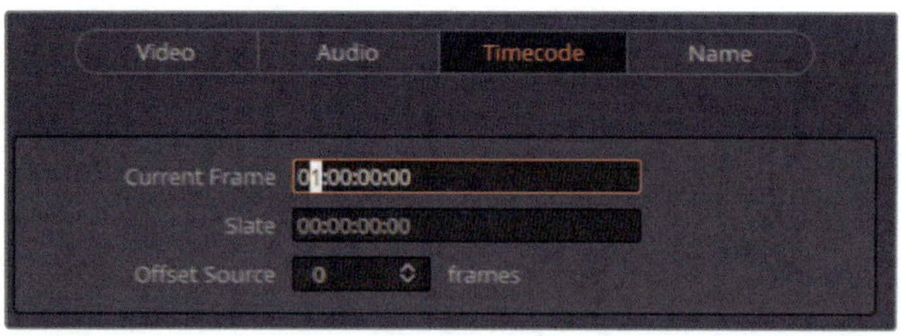

If the reference movie does not immediately appear in the source Viewer, check the Mode pop-up menu in the lower-left corner of the source Viewer to ensure that Offline is still chosen.

TIP You can designate any imported video clip as a reference movie in the Edit page. First, change the source Viewer to Offline mode using the source Viewer mode pop-up in the lower-left corner of the Viewer. Then, with your target Timeline open, drag the reference movie into the source Viewer to assign it as a reference.

Conforming a Timeline

With the reference movie in place, you may analyze of the Timeline to address any visual inconsistencies. During the first pass, you will make sure that the cuts occur at the right time and that the clips are in the right locations. To accomplish this, you must review the edit cut by cut.

1 Enter the Media page.

2 In the Media storage library, navigate to the BMD 16 CC - Project 02 folder, and enter the Other subfolder.

   The Log window listed the credits of the trailer among the missing media.

3 Drag CREDITS.mov into the Graphics bin of the media pool.

4 Return to the Edit page.

   The credits are automatically detected and can now be seen at the end of the film. If the source media maintains the same name as those in an XML file, it will immediately appear in the Timeline, even if imported after the XML construction.

5 Move the playhead to the start of the Airplanes - 01 LQ Timeline.

6 Press the Down Arrow on your keyboard until you navigate to the first video cut point at the start of the second clip on the Timeline.

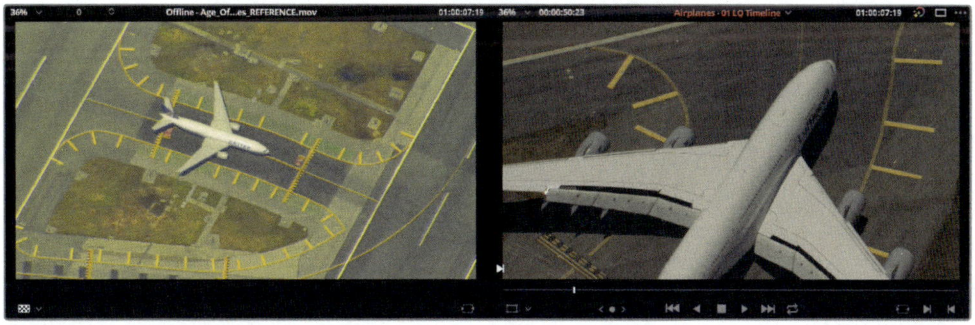

   It is apparent that the Timeline clip does not match the clip in the reference video. This could be due to a clash in tape/reel name, or due to the editor making a change after exporting the XML file. To resolve this, you can manually import and assign the correct clip to the Timeline.

7 Enter the Media page.

8 In the Media storage library, enter the Other LQ Transcodes subfolder .

9 Drag the AERIAL_SFO_02.mov video clip into the LQ Transcodes bin of the media pool.

10 Return to the Edit page.

11 In the LQ Transcodes bin of the media pool, click the AERIAL_SFO_02.mov thumbnail.

12 In the Timeline, right-click the second clip, and choose "Conform Lock with Media pool Clip". Doing so replaces the clip in the Timeline with the selected source media, which now matches the clip in the reference movie.

> **NOTE** If the clip in the media pool and the clip in the Timeline have the same timecode, the conform action will place the incoming clip using the same in and out points as the original cut. If the timecodes don't match, the first frame of the incoming clip will be aligned at the cut.

The contrast and saturation of the clips in the Viewers appears to be different. This is because the reference clip was rendered with a Rec.709 color gamut, while the source media is in a log color gamut. You will address color management at the end of this chapter.

Fixing Translation Errors

You can continue to navigate down the Timeline and look at the reference movie to check the clips, edit points, and effects to ensure that everything is successfully translated.

1 Press the Down Arrow to jump to the next video cut at the start of clip 3, TAKE_OFF_SFO.

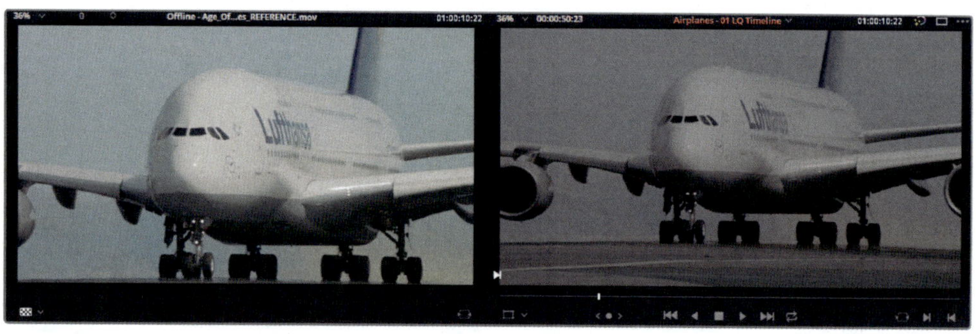

In addition to checking the Timeline clips and their edit points, your conforming process should ensure that all transitions and effects are present. A simple side-by-side comparison cannot always do this, so you have the option to superimpose the reference movie on the Timeline Viewer. This procedure helps to verify if the clips are framed identically.

2 Right-click the Timeline Viewer, and choose Horizontal Wipe.

The Timeline clip is displayed to the left while the reference clip is displayed to the right.

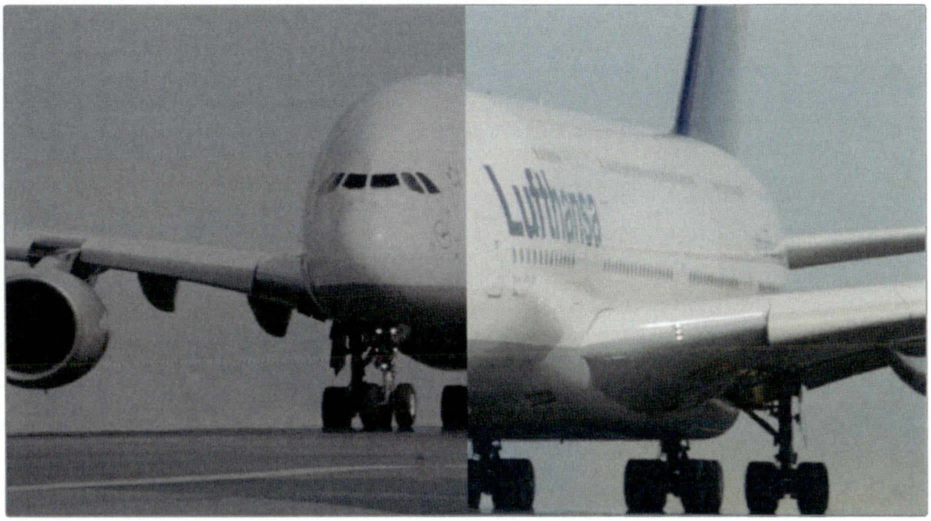

3 Drag the wipe left and right to compare the placement of the clip to the reference.

Using the wipe for comparison reveals a mismatch in the shot framing. To fix it, you can view a difference composite.

4 Right-click the Timeline Viewer, and choose Difference to highlight where the clip is misaligned.

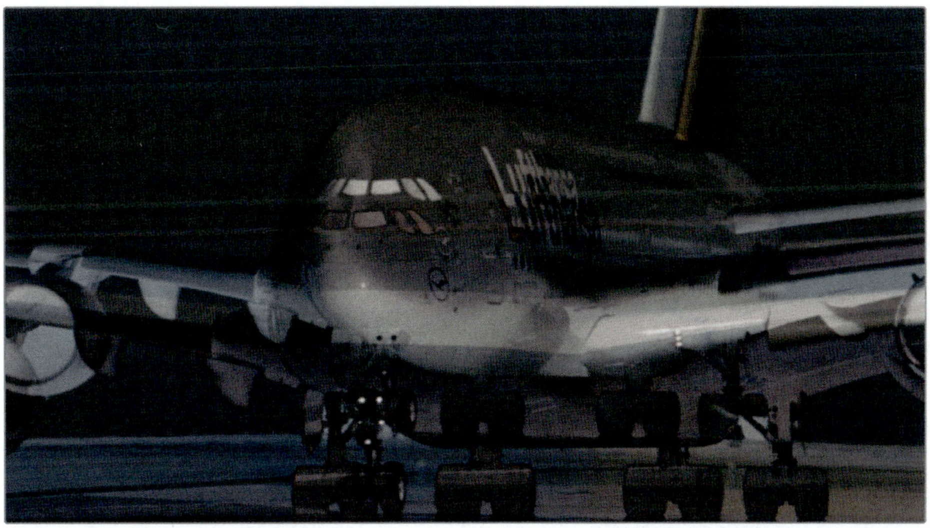

5 In the Timeline, click the TAKE_OFF_SFO clip, and open the inspector.

6 In Transform controls, increase the Zoom value until the size of the cockpit windows appear the same (1.200).

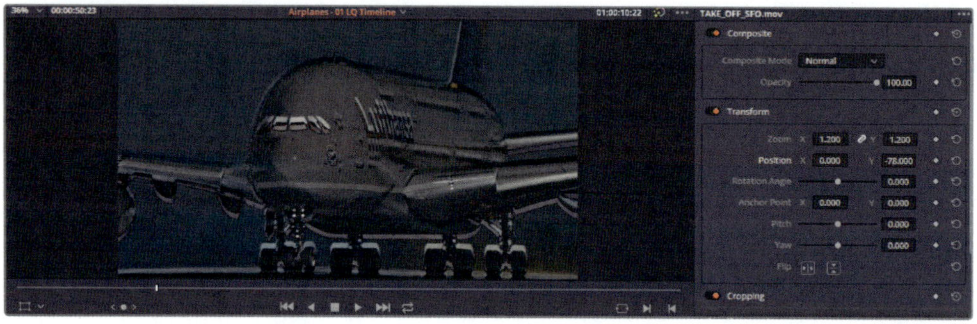

7 Because the windows and wings appear higher in the Timeline, drag the Y position down until the windows and wings overlap (-100.00). When visually performing these matches, you will need to go back and forth between the position parameters to get a perfect fit.

When you can no longer see a "double effect" in the Viewer, the framing is successfully replicated. If you were working on images with identical color gamuts, the Viewer would become black to signify that no visual differences remained between the clips.

8 Right-click the Timeline Viewer, and choose No Wipe to return to the normal Timeline Viewer.

9 Close the inspector to return to the offline reference Viewer.

10 Press the Down Arrow to navigate to the next video cut. This is the missing clip that was not found when the XML Timeline was imported.

11 Return to the Media page. In the Media storage browser, locate the Other folder, and open the Other LQ Transcodes subfolder.

12 Drag the BA4662_54 and BA4662_55 clips into the LQ Transcodes bin of the media pool, and return to the Edit page.

In the Timeline, one of the imported video clips has replaced the missing media. However, the clip does not match the reference movie in the source Viewer, perhaps because of a metadata clash between the source media.

13 Press Cmd-+ (plus sign) in macOS or Ctrl-+ (plus sign) in Windows to zoom in to the clip in the Timeline.

14 Right-click the clip, and choose Conform Lock Enabled. The clip is now receptive to all media that is associated with its metadata.

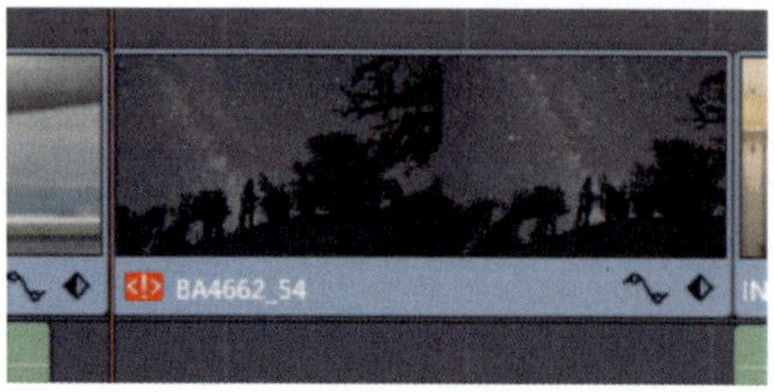

In the lower-left corner of the Timeline clip, a red attention badge icon indicates a potential metadata clash with another clip in the media pool.

15 Double-click the attention badge on the clip.

The conflict resolution window appears displaying all the clips in the bin that match the metadata of the clip in the Timeline. You can now select the correct clip according to the reference movie.

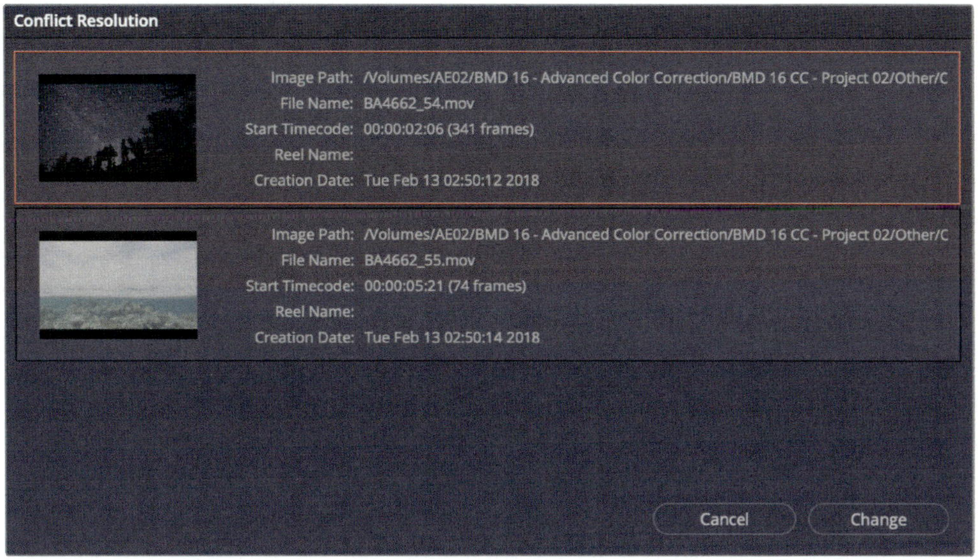

16 In the conflict resolution window, select the water shot BA4662_55 to change the media, and click Change to apply.

The correct clip is placed in the Timeline to match the reference movie. To remove the now black-colored resolved badge and confirm the new clip as the correct one, you can lock the conformed selection.

17 In the Timeline, right-click the clip, and choose Conform Lock Enabled.

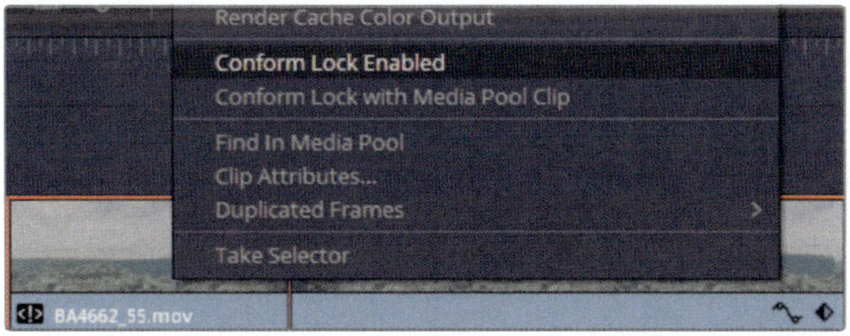

18 Continue to press the Down Arrow to check the remainder of the clips.

When you reach clip 08 (YELLOW_PLANE), you will notice that the clip has very different colors compared to the reference movie.

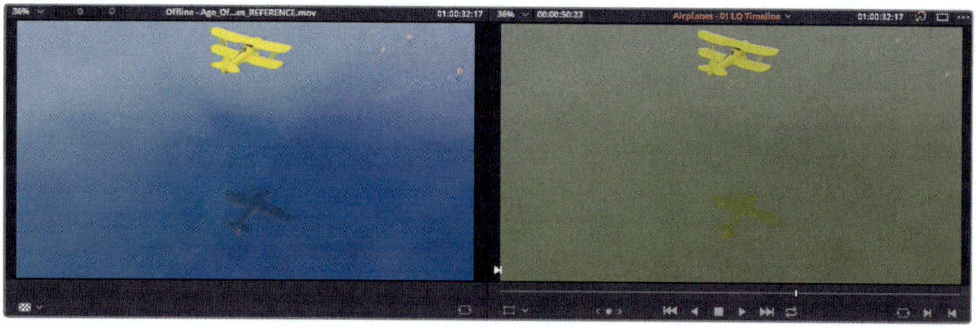

It is common practice for editors, directors of photography, or other creative directors to leave preliminary grades baked into the reference movie as a guide for the colorist. As a general rule, grading data does not come across in migration files unless the project is sent as a DRP file or it includes accompanying LUTs (look-up tables) or CDL (color decision list) data.

It will not be necessary to do anything with this clip at this time, but it will be useful when you begin the grading process.

Though it is natural to feel that something has gone wrong with your workflow when the Timeline presents issues during XML migration, it is important to remember that this is a completely normal and anticipated stage of post-production. It is encountered in projects of all calibers and it stems from the fact that no single migration standard exists among the dozens of applications that you may use when collaborating on a film project.

One of the major advantages of performing your entire post-production workflow in DaVinci Resolve is its substantial reduction of migration and project management issues. An edit can be ingested, edited, graded and delivered without the need to be conformed.

Associating HQ Footage with a Timeline for Online Workflows

The Timeline you reconstructed for this section is currently associated with media from the LQ Transcodes folder. These low-quality video files are generated from the source media with the intention of providing the editor with light video files that are easy to transfer and do not lag when played in real-time.

The accuracy of an image's pixel data is not vital to editors because they are focused on constructing a narrative and bringing a good flow to the edit. However, when the Timeline reaches the colorist, the quality of the image becomes paramount. Therefore, you will want to create a copy of the Timeline that links to the HQ video files that are optimal for grading.

1. In the Edit page, in the media pool, open the Timelines bin.
2. Click Airplanes – 01 LQ Timeline, and choose Edit > Copy, or press Cmd-C (macOS) or Ctrl-C (Windows).
3. Click in an empty area of the media pool, and choose Edit > Paste, or press Cmd-V (macOS) or Ctrl-V (Windows).
4. Slowly click twice on the name of the new Timeline, and rename it **Airplanes – 01 HQ Timeline**.
5. Double-click the HQ Timeline to open it in the Edit page Timeline window.
6. In the media pool, click the empty HQ Transcodes bin to select the destination for the HQ media.
7. In track V1, drag to select all of its video clips on the Timeline. Do not include the credits or audio in your selection.
8. Right-click any clip in the Timeline, and deselect Conform Lock Enabled. Doing so will disable the clips' lock on their media file paths, and prompt them to acknowledge all media that shares similar metadata and timecodes in the media pool.
9. In the File menu, choose Reconform from Media Storage.

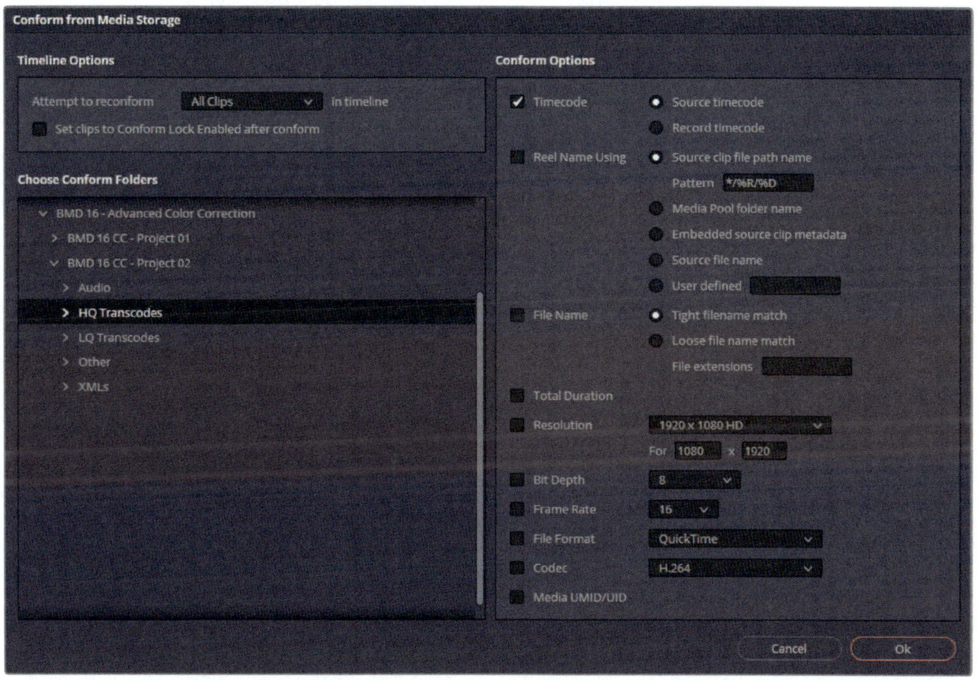

The Conform from Media Storage window allows you to refine the media that is being associated with the clips in the Timeline.

10 Under Timeline Options, choose “Attempt to reconform to Selected Clips in Timeline.”

11 Under Chose Conform Folders, select the BMD 16 CC - Project 02 > HQ Transcodes folder.

12 Under Conform Options, deselect Timecode.

13 Select File Name, and choose “Tight filename match.”

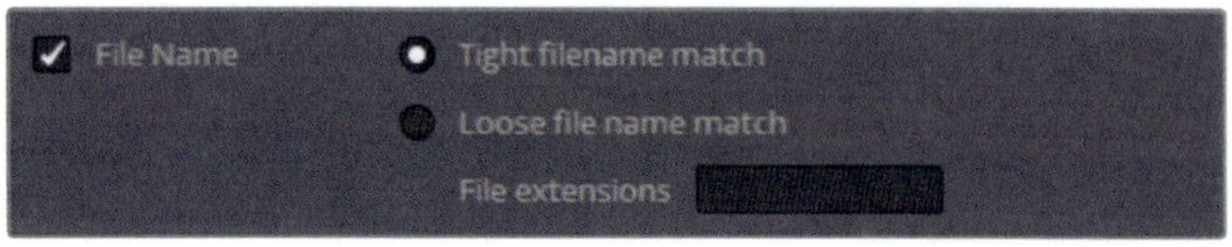

14 Click OK.

The HQ Transcodes bin is populated with the higher-quality clips that also replace the LQ clips on the Timeline.

However, this clip state might be difficult to see in the HQ Timeline because as the clips and Timeline appear exactly the same. You can adjust the appearance of the clips on the Timeline to verify that the link was successful.

15 In the HQ Transcodes bin, select all the newly imported clips.

16 Right-click one of them, and choose Clip Color > Orange. All the clips in the Timeline that were successfully switched to the higher-quality media will appear orange in the Timeline.

Before

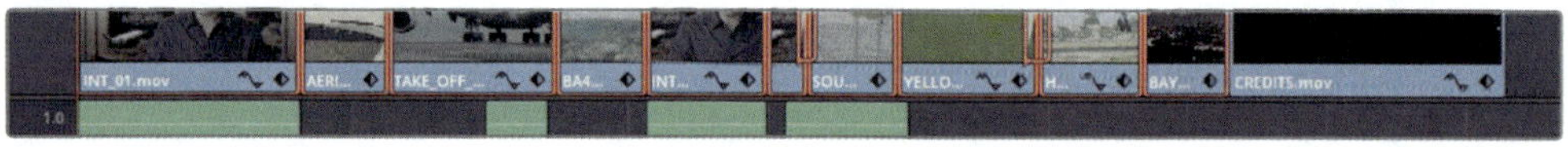

After

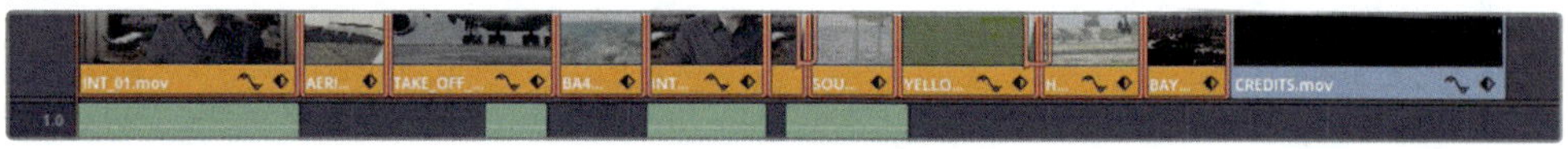

17 To lock the HQ clips to the Timeline, select them, right-click, and choose Conform Lock Enabled.

This method of changing file source locations gives you full control over the media used in the Timeline without the need to import additional XML files, or to change the file paths of the clips in the media pool. An important component of this workflow is a well-organized and consistently labeled file system, which is vital in all post-production workflows.

Having successfully imported and prepared the XML Timeline for grading, you can proceed with the knowledge that the Timeline is accurate, and that you are in control of your footage quality at all times. However, the media in this project is currently in a log-encoded color gamut that does not give an accurate visual reproduction of the hues and tonal range of the recorded images. The next set of steps will manage the log-encoded content to output to the more visually accessible and grade-friendly Rec.709 color gamut.

Maximizing the Dynamic Range

The grading potential of an image is determined primarily by its dynamic range, which is the range from its darkest point to its brightest point.

HD consumer and broadcast video cameras tend to record using a standard dynamic range based on the Rec.709 color standard. This standard ensures that the image looks as close to real life as possible, and displays as such on an HDTV or computer monitor. However, professional digital film cameras, such as the Blackmagic URSA Mini Pro, can capture a wider dynamic range by using a non-linear, or log gamma curve. This curve gives you greater flexibility for manipulating the brightness, contrast, and colors without distortion.

Ungraded video in log color gamut

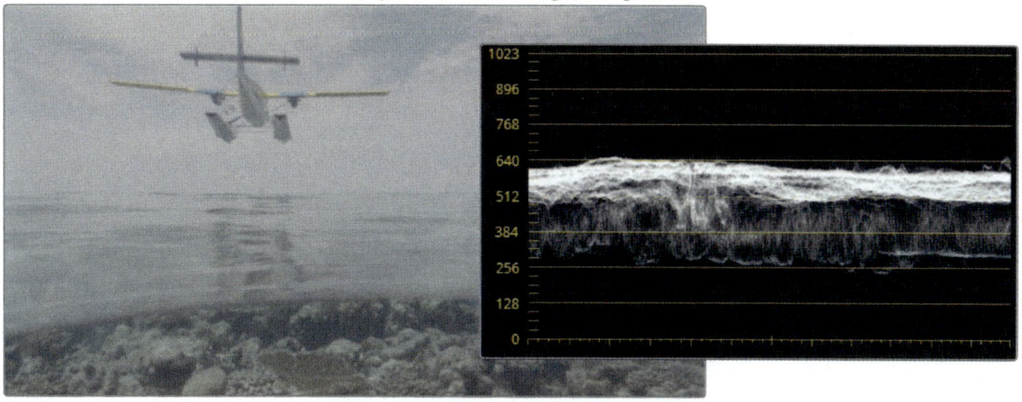

Ungraded video in Rec.709 gamma 2.4 color gamut

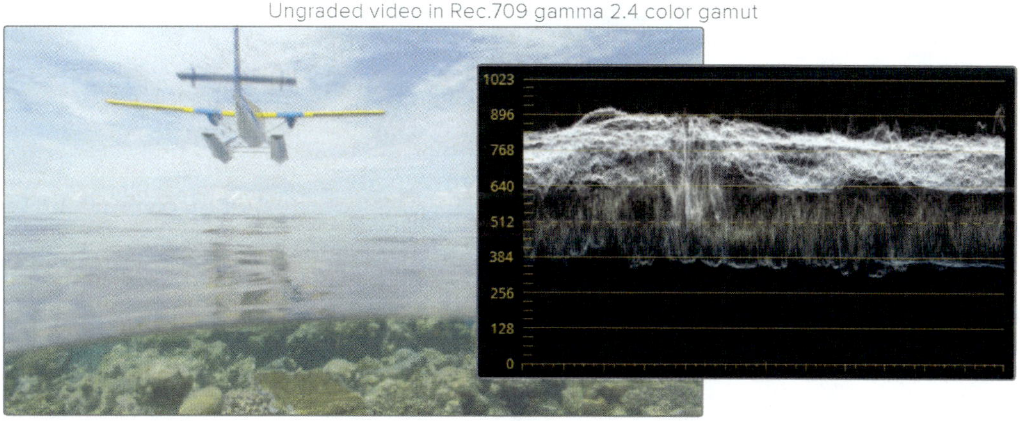

A by-product of encoding footage with a log gamma curve, however, is that footage initially appears flat and with low saturation when viewed on an HDTV or computer monitor.

Therefore, a colorist must first correct the log gamma curve so that it appears correctly on the display. This process is called a *display referred color management setup*. Because Resolve receives no direction on how the source media is meant to look, configuring that look is left to the colorist. This process often employs LUTs to convert from log to Rec.709 (assuming HD is the final output format).

However, DaVinci Resolve also includes a scene referred color management setup that allows the colorist to assign color profiles to media based on how that media was captured. Each clip's native color gamut and gamma curve are then converted to the desired output. The colorist no longer has to manage multiple LUTs for different sources, or manually convert each clip from log to Rec.709 using standard grading tools.

Choosing an Input Color Space

The DaVinci YRGB color management workflow begins by enabling it in the Project Settings and choosing an input color space.

1 Open the Project Settings by clicking the gear icon in the lower-right of the workspace.

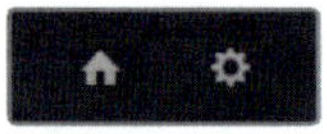

2 Click Color Management to the left.

3 In the Color Space & Transforms window, set the "Color science" menu to DaVinci YRGB Color Managed. Doing so will activate scene-referred color management and reveal the input and output color space options.

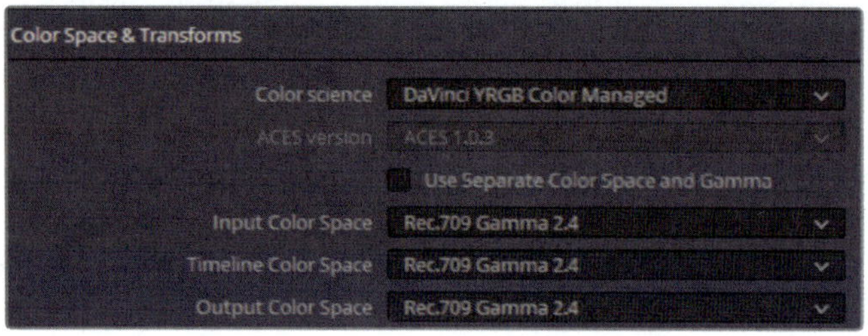

The three color space fields are responsible for the three stages of the DaVinci YRGB color-managed workflow and will define the way the color space of an image is processed and output. The Input Color space setting is based on the recording camera's gamut and gamma configuration.

4 In the Input Color Space menu, choose Blackmagic Design Film Gen 1. This identifies the camera model, data level, and software version that were used to record the footage in this Timeline.

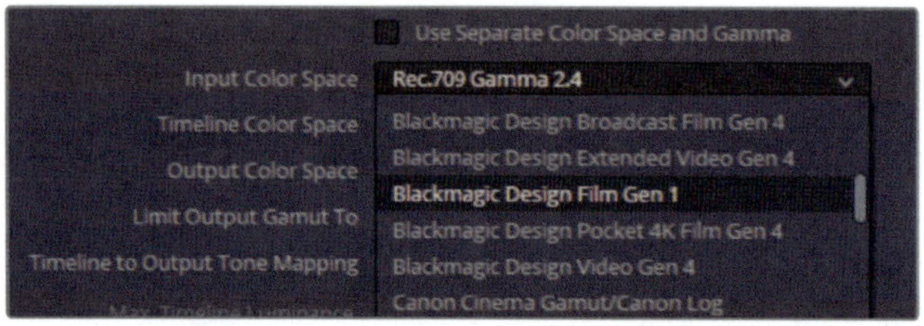

5 Leave the Timeline Color Space and the Output Color Space as Rec.709 Gamma 2.4.

6 Click Save to close the Project Settings.

Color management is set up in the project. However, you might not see an immediate change in your Timeline or Viewer because the media you have imported uses a default Rec.709 Gamma 2.4 input color space.

7 In the media pool, open the HQ transcodes bin.

8 Drag to select all the clips in the pool, or press Cmd-A (macOS) or Ctrl-A (Windows).

9 Right-click any of the selected clips, and choose Input Color Space > Project - Blackmagic Design Film Gen 1.

By setting the Input Color Space to Project, the media will now actively react to any changes you make in the Color Management tab of the Project Settings. The colors of the Timeline clips will shift as DaVinci YRGB color management is applied to the Color page Viewer. The gamma of every clip in the Timeline is translated from the Blackmagic Design log color space to Rec.709 with the HD standard 2.4 gamma curve. As a result, the clips will appear more vibrant and with more pronounced contrast.

DaVinci YRGB color management applies to all the clips in a project. If certain clips come from different sources from the rest of the Timeline, you can reassign their individual input color spaces through the media pool's contextual menu (or the Color page clip Timeline), which reflects the full list of color space options in the Project Settings.

The ability to assign individual input color spaces to clips can be extremely helpful when you are working on footage from multiple sources.

> **TIP** You could use a Smart Bin to filter clips based on their sources, and then select them in batches when changing their input color space settings.

DaVinci YRGB color management offers a structured, solid foundation for your primary and secondary grading stages. It does not remove the need to tweak the black point, white point, and saturation of your clips, but does provide a quicker and more color-accurate way to create a good starting point for grading.

> **TIP** If the image in your Viewer feels too flat when completing the exercises in this lesson, change the Output Color Space to Rec.709 Gamma 2.2, which is a more appropriate gamma curve for most standard computer monitors, or sRGB if you're using a Mac display.

When You Don't Know the Camera or Format

DaVinci YRGB color management operates at its best when you know and identify the correct input data. But identifying that data can be tricky when the origins of footage are unknown or forgotten, or when data details were not included during file transfer. You can derive some useful information by examining clip properties, but doing so usually will not provide information about the camera model or gamma range. You can acquire the most definitive information by directly contacting the production company's project manager, director of photography, or the camera operator and requesting the information. If all else fails, you can bypass DaVinci YRGB color management and manually normalize the clips.

Changing the Output Color Space

One of the most powerful aspects of using a color-managed workflow in DaVinci Resolve is that you can change the output color space at any time based on your final delivery requirements.

Doing so is particularly helpful when you need to output multiple masters to different destinations. You may want one master for Rec.709 HD, another for Rec.2020 UHD, and yet another for P3 digital cinema. Resolve manages the color transformations without the need to change anything on the Color page.

1 Open Project Settings > Color Management.

2 Set the Output Color Space menu to Rec.2020 Gamma 2.4.

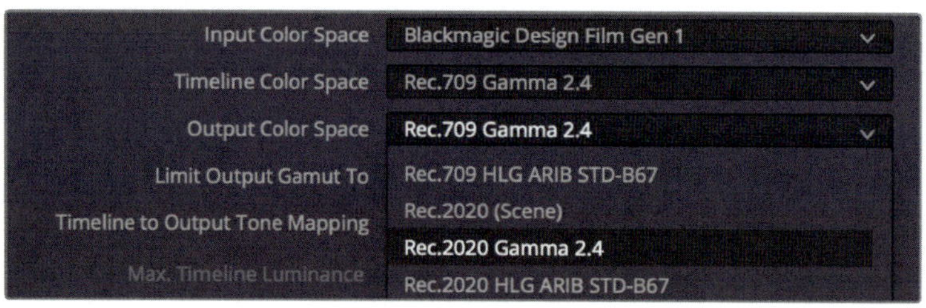

3 Click Save.

The color space is changed, and the Viewer reflects the updated results. On a standard computer monitor, the colors will now appear flat. However, if you had a calibrated UHD Rec.2020 display, the clips would look identical to their appearance under HD Rec.709. If you graded the media in the Timeline, the final colors would similarly be remapped to adhere to UHD Rec.2020 standards. So, you could instantly switch your Timeline grades between different deliverable standards.

Accurate Color Monitoring in DaVinci Resolve

Resolve was designed to work with industry-standard calibrated external displays connected via video output interfaces to enable critical color evaluation.

Most computer monitors are incapable of displaying the color gamut or gamma range required for broadcast and theatrical distribution. Additionally, most computer displays have their own color and contrast calibration as determined by the manufacturer, which is further altered by the workstation's operating system. For this reason, their color accuracy cannot be guaranteed to carry across after delivery, even when moving between different video players on the same machine.

Ideally, you should use an external monitor and video interface for all grading work. Alternatively, you could use a color calibration probe to analyze your computer display and generate a LUT that will remap the colors to the correct standard.

4. Open Project Settings > Color Management.
5. Set the Output Color Space menu back to the default Rec.709 Gamma 2.4.
6. Click Save.

TIP If you know in advance that you will be delivering content in multiple color gamut standards, consider starting your workflow at the widest gamut. For example, if delivering for web (Rec.709 Gamma 2.2), digital cinema projection (DCI-P3), and HDR broadcast (Rec.2100 ST2084), the best option would be to grade your project for HDR first. Then, duplicate the project and calibrate the Output Color Space to DCI-P3. Review the Timeline, make the necessary highlight adjustments to complete the cinema grade, and then remap the Output Color Space to Rec.709 for the web deliverable.

You can also change the gamma range separately from the color space by selecting "Use Separate Color space and Gamma" above the color space menus.

Separating the color space and gamma settings allows you to have full control over the chrominance and luminance processing of your footage. You can indicate gamma ranges that are not part of the standard preset selection of the color space menus.

Normalizing Exposure with Gamut Mapping

Another method of color management uses a ResolveFX effect that you may apply on a scene, Timeline, or node-by-node basis. The gamut mapping tool operates in the same way as the Color Management settings, but allows for much finer control over the individual behavior of the Timeline clips.

A common use for this tool is to reconfigure the brightness of highly exposed clips to better fit the SDR tonal range.

1 Enter the Color page.

2 Select clip 03 (AERIAL_SFO_02).

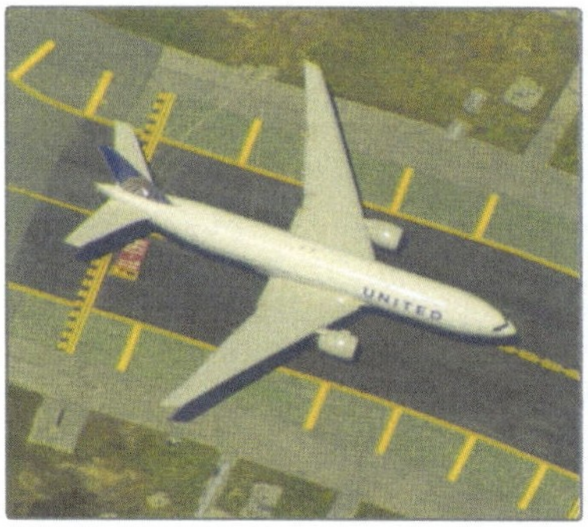

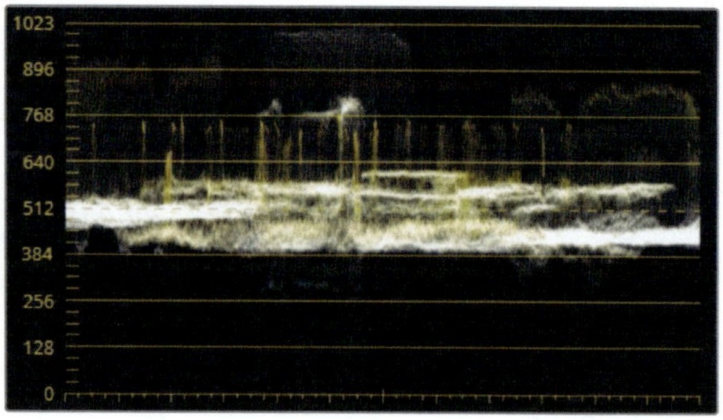

3 Use your mouse scroll wheel to zoom into the Viewer until the plane fills the Viewer.

This is a very bright video clip. In the scopes, you can see the plane's highlights touching the white point line at the top of the waveform scope. By reconfiguring the distribution of the tonal range and its trace, you can achieve a more realistic representation of this environment.

4 Label node 01 as **Gamut Map**.

5 Click the OpenFX button to open its panel.

6 Under ResolveFX Color, locate the Gamut Mapping effect, and drag it onto the Gamut Map node. It is currently reflecting the color management settings and outputting at Rec.709.

7 Change Tone Mapping Method to Luminance Mapping.

You reveal options to change the maximum input and output luminance values of the trace to remap the tonal range of the image. You can adjust the max. input luminance to indicate a wider spread of the tonal range than the waveform currently is displaying. The max. output luminance should reflect the nit range of your intended deliverable and grading monitor. In Rec.709 SDR, this range value is 100 nits.

8 Set Max. Input Luminance to 200.

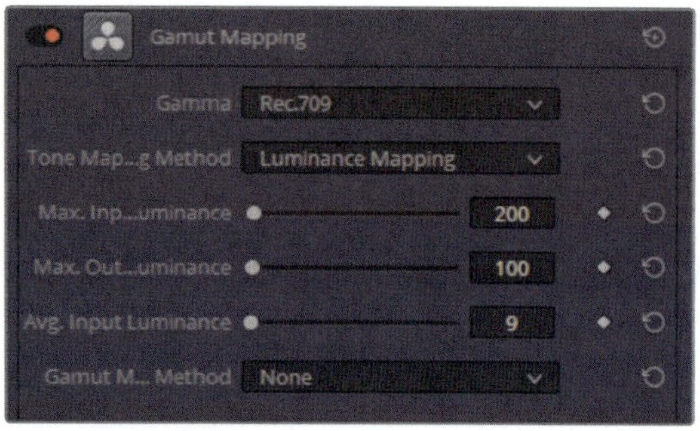

Gamut mapping will now assume that the clip's starting luminance range is double the permitted limit. This range is remapped down to 100 nits via the max. output luminance setting, thereby recovering the details in the airplane highlights.

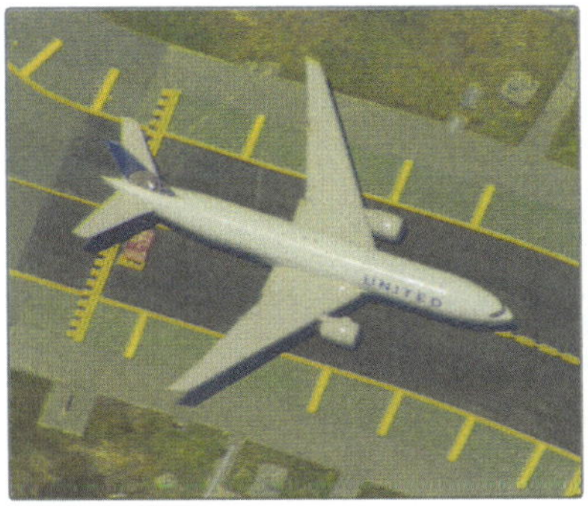

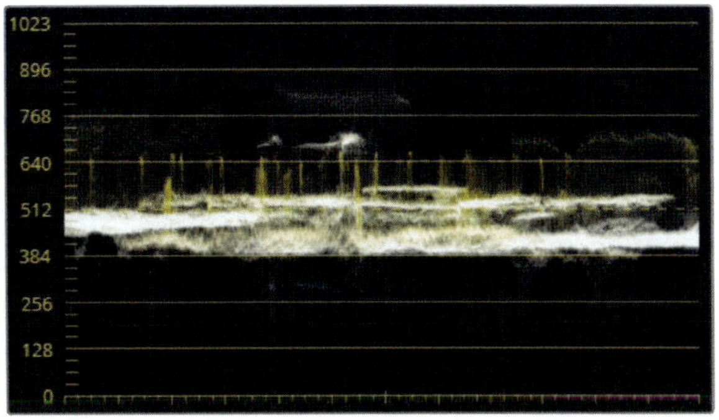

Additional controls in the Gamut Mapping settings allow you to activate Saturation Compression. This setting reduces saturation in light sources with a notable chromatic "ring."

You also can effectively use gamut mapping to address wide luminance issues in source media (such as over-exposed windows in interior scenes), and produce a workable starting point for the grade. To apply gamut mapping to an entire scene or Timeline, you can switch the node editor to group or Timeline mode before adding the effect. Group and Timeline grading are covered in Lesson 7 of this book

Understanding the Timeline Color Space

When utilizing color management, the Input Color Space of the video signal is first remapped to the Timeline Color Space which impacts the signal processing on a Timeline level and impacts the behaviour of the grading tools in the Color page.

The resulting signal is then remapped to the Output Color Space which affects its final appearance in the Viewer. This dual processing of the signal allows you to continue grading a project with the same grading tools, even when switching between different output standards.

In this exercise, you will compare how the grading controls are affected under different Timeline color spaces.

easyDCP Delivery

When grading with the intention of exporting to the easyDCP format, your choice of Timeline color space will determine the color management of the DCP, whether you have color management enabled or not.

Set the Timeline color space to Rec.709 Gamma 2.4 to render the DCP with the correct Rec.709 to XYZ matrix.

1 Click clip 01. The Timeline is currently color managed to output in the Rec.709 color space at a Gamma 2.4 range.

First, you will check how the change in the Timeline color space will affect an ungraded clip.

2 Open the Project Settings, and in Color Management, set the Timeline Color Space to Rec.709 (Scene).

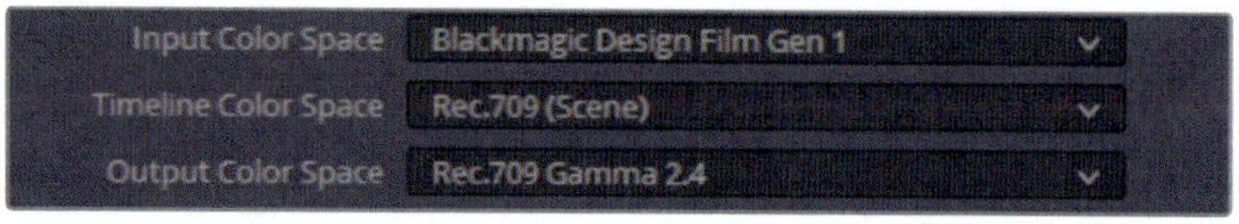

Rec.709 (Scene) refers to a distribution of the gamma curve meant to emulate the physical behavior of cathode ray tube (CRT) displays. This curve is mostly obsolete in the context of modern HDTV displays. In this exercise, however, it is used for demonstrative purposes.

3 Click the Project Settings interface header, and move the window to get a clear view of the Viewer on the Color page.

4 Alt-click Save to confirm the change.

This change did not impact the image in the Viewer because the project's output color space (Rec.709 with Gamma 2.4) remained unchanged, and also because the clip is not currently graded. The Timeline Color Space setting will affect only how the grading tools perform their function.

TIMELINE CS: REC.709 (SCENE) ungraded

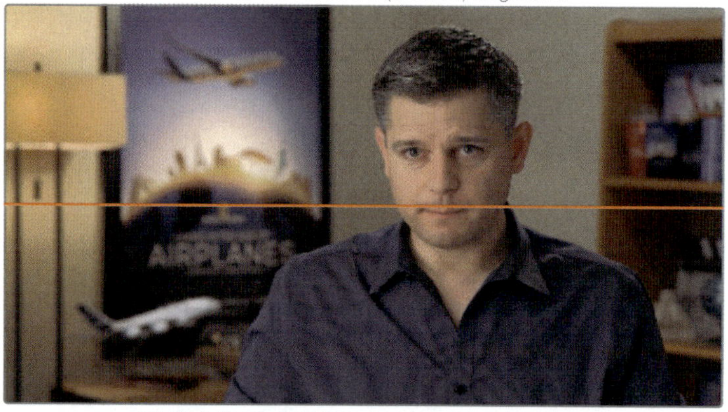

TIMELINE CS: REC.709 GAMMA 2.4 ungraded

5 Click Save to close the Project Settings window.

6 In the Curves palette, drag the master curve black point to the right until it is halfway to the second horizontal line in the graph.

7 Drag the master curve white point to the left until it is directly on the second horizontal line from the right.

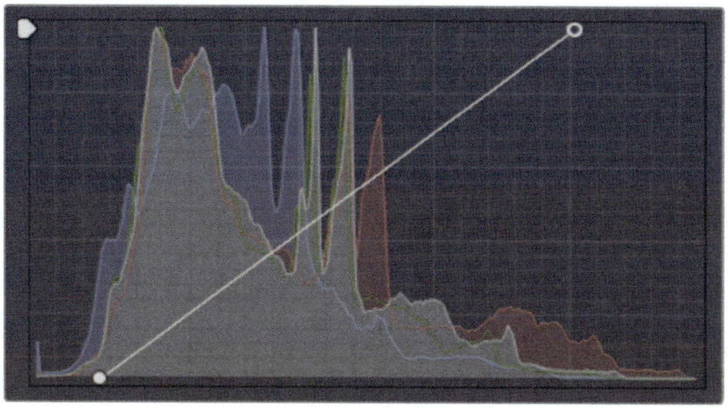

This adjustment results in an increase of the image contrast and saturation.

8 Right-click in the Viewer, and grab a still of the grade.

9 In the gallery, double-click under the still thumbnail, and enter the label *Rec Scene TCS*.

10 Return to the project settings, and change the Timeline Color Space back to Rec.709 Gamma 2.4.

11 Click Save to apply the change, and close the project settings window.

12 In the Gallery, double-click the Rec.Scene Timeline CS still to compare it side-by-side in the Viewer with the same curve adjustment done in a Gamma 2.4 Timeline color space.

13 Drag the wipe line to review the difference.

> **TIP** You can switch from a horizontal to a vertical wipe using the buttons in the upper-right corner of the Viewer, or by right-clicking and choosing Wipe Style > Vertical. Drag the wipe line to review the difference.

TIMELINE CS: REC.709 (SCENE) graded

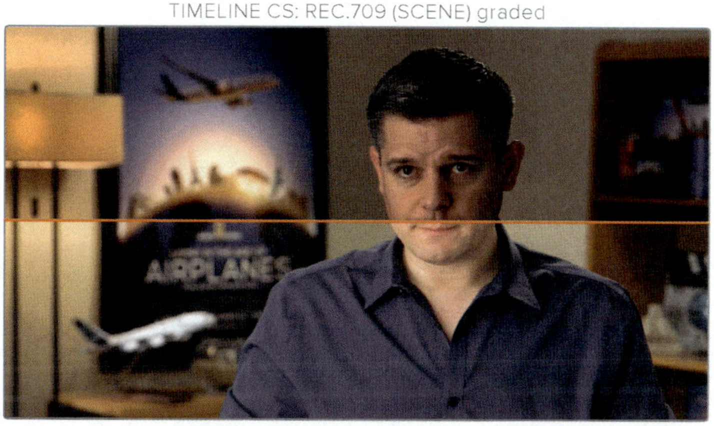

TIMELINE CS: REC.709 GAMMA 2.4 graded

Comparing the two shots shows a shift in the brightness and particularly in the shadows of the image. Though the output color space has remained the same, the standard at which the grading palettes are operating is changed.

For this reason, it is highly advisable not to change your Timeline color space after grading begins. Doing so could have a significant impact on the appearance of the luminance and colors in graded clips that you can only change manually or by resetting the Timeline color space to its initial standard.

14 In the upper-left corner of the Viewer, click the Image wipe button to turn off the wipe mode.

15 Right-click in the Node editor, and Reset All Grades and Nodes.

It is important to recognize that the Timeline Color Space setting defines the color gamut and dynamic range at the starting point of the grade. If you choose a narrow gamut/range in the Timeline Color Space, you will be unable to expand it to a wider standard in the Output Color Space without experiencing degradation of the video signal.

For example, let's say you were starting work on a project to be delivered in both HDR and SDR standards. The correct workflow would be to set both the Timeline and Output Color Spaces to an HDR gamut and dynamic range (such as Rec.2020) at the very start. After completing the grade, you would then switch the Output Color Space to SDR (such as Rec.709).

If uncertain, your safest option is to set your Timeline Color Space to match your Output Color Space at the start and leave it untouched for the remainder of your project.

NOTE You will continue to work on the Timeline created in this lesson over the next two lessons. If you would like to verify that your Timeline is correct, or are uncertain with the accuracy of your conforming, you may import **Project 02 – Age of Airplanes Trailer COMPLETED.drp** into the project manager and open the Airplanes - 03 HQ Ungraded Timeline. You can use this ungraded, conformed Timeline to complete the next two lessons in this book.

Lesson Review

1 During project migration, what is a translation error?

2 How do you appoint a video file as an offline reference movie?

3 When loading an XML file, why would you opt to "Ignore file extensions when matching"?

4 What does File > Reconform from Bins allow you to do?

5 Where do you activate DaVinci YRGB Color Management?

Answers

1. When inconsistencies exist in a reconstructed Timeline between programs
2. In Media storage, right-click the video file, and choose Add as Offline Reference Clip. Then, right-click the Timeline, and choose Timelines > Link Offline Reference Clip. Another method is to drag a video clip directly onto the source Viewer in the edit page when it is in Offline mode to assign the clip as a reference to the currently open Timeline.
3. To specify differently formatted versions of transcoded media (offline or online) to use in the Timeline reconstruction
4. Change the source of the media based on a different bin in the media pool.
5. In Project Settings > Color Management, set Color Science to DaVinci YRGB Color Managed.

Lesson 5

Mastering the Node Pipeline

The Node editor is a powerful component of the Color page that enables you to maintain precise control over the final appearance of images. With it, you may separate and target different stages of grading while ensuring an enhanced color output with minimum quality degradation. Additionally, the Node editor enables some truly complex secondary grading configurations, the foundations of which you will explore in this lesson.

Time

This lesson takes approximately 60 minutes to complete.

Goals

Understanding Node-based Compositing

Node-based compositing is different from the layer-based system familiar to many NLE editors. Unlike layers, in which the visuals are compounded based on their order in the layer stack, nodes process a single RGB signal, modifying it along the way.

As each node affects the image, it outputs the altered signal via an RGB link until the final RGB data reaches the output node of the Node editor. This output node presents the image in its final state to the Viewer, and determines how the media will look when rendered.

Nodes are capable of reusing information from previous nodes, substantially reducing the amount of processing power required to assemble and output a final image. This capability is particularly useful when working with keys, such as those generated by qualifiers and Power Windows.

The Anatomy of a Node

The Node graph is read from left to right. The RGB signal that constitutes the image begins at the leftmost green node—the RGB input—and travels through the links that connect the corrector nodes until it reaches the final node tree output to the right. The RGB signal must be uninterrupted for the node grades to be correctly compiled and output.

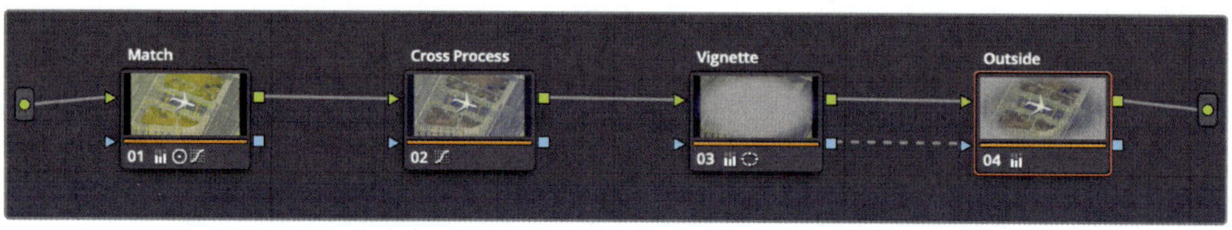

Standard corrector nodes have two inputs and two outputs.

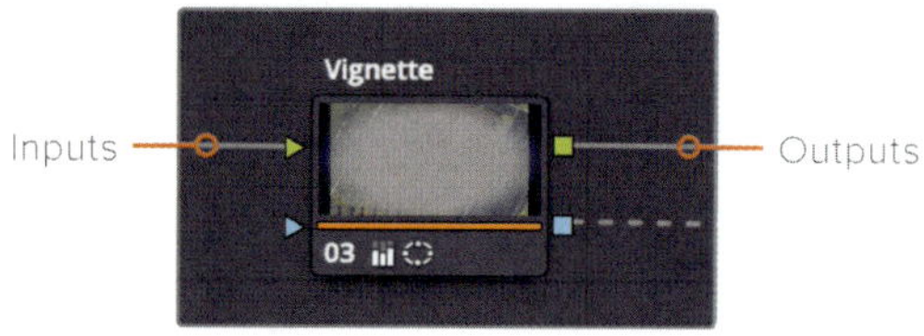

The green triangle and square shapes at the top of either side are the RGB inputs and outputs. These carry the pixel data of the image, which is manipulated within the node using the grading tools of the Color page. Corrector nodes can accept only one RGB input but can output multiple RGB signals to other nodes.

The blue shapes are the key inputs and outputs. These enable you to transfer the key data generated by the Power Windows and qualifiers (or external mattes) to be used by other nodes.

NOTE You can undo an action in DaVinci Resolve 16 by pressing Cmd-Z (macOS) or Ctrl-Z (Windows). The undo function is stacked to each clip in the Timeline. So, when you undo, only the changes from the selected clip are removed, and not from any other clips on the Timeline, even if you graded them more recently.

Understanding the Importance of Node Order

The RGB signal output of each node carries the full weight of its grade and directly affects the next node's interaction with it. The following set of exercises demonstrate how nodes impact one another.

Node Order Demos

The node structures of every exercise in this segment can be found in the "Node demos" album of the gallery in the Color page.

Influence of Color and Saturation Across Nodes

You can see how a node placed at an early pipeline stage influences the following nodes by removing its saturation and observing the results.

1. Open the Project 02 – Age of Airplanes Trailer project.
2. Enter the Color page.
3. Click clip 01 in the Airplanes – 01 HQ Timeline.
4. Label the first node **BW**.
5. Open the RGB Mixer palette, which is located next to the Color Wheel palette.
6. Select Monochrome (at the bottom of the palette) to turn the image black and white.

   The RGB mixer gives you full control over the strength of the individual RGB channels and is often used for tweaking black-and-white images to create an aesthetically pleasing balance of natural elements such as skin, sky, and trees.

7 Drag up the red output's R bar to increase the strength of the red channel in the image. This change will brighten the man's face against the background and create a good contrast.

8 Create a second node, and label it **Sepia**.

9 Open the Color Wheel palette, and drag the Offset color wheel toward orange-yellow to give the image a sepia tint.

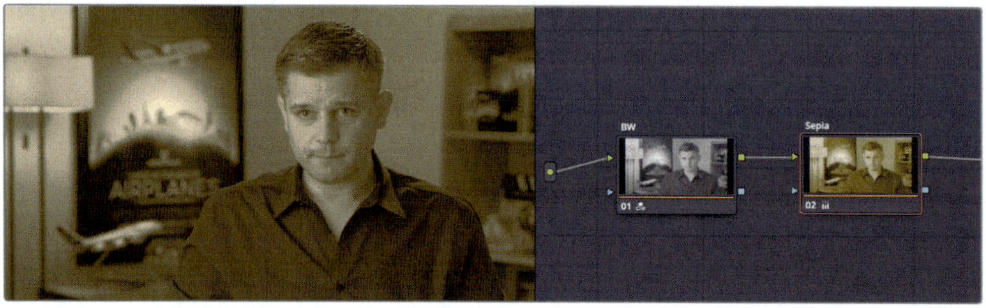

10 Click node 01 BW, and return to the RGB mixer palette.

11 Drag the blue output's B bar up and down to increase and decrease the strength of the blue channel in the image.

The effect on the final sepia grade shows that the luminance and contrast created in the first node continue to impact the image even after a second node dramatically changes its appearance.

For an even clearer visualization of how the node order impacts the grade, you can switch the order of the two nodes.

12 Click node 02 Sepia, and press E to extract it from the pipeline.

13 Drag the disconnected node onto the link in front of node 01 until a + (plus sign) appears.

TIP A quick way to switch the order of two nodes is to Cmd-drag (macOS) or Ctrl-drag (Windows) one node over another.

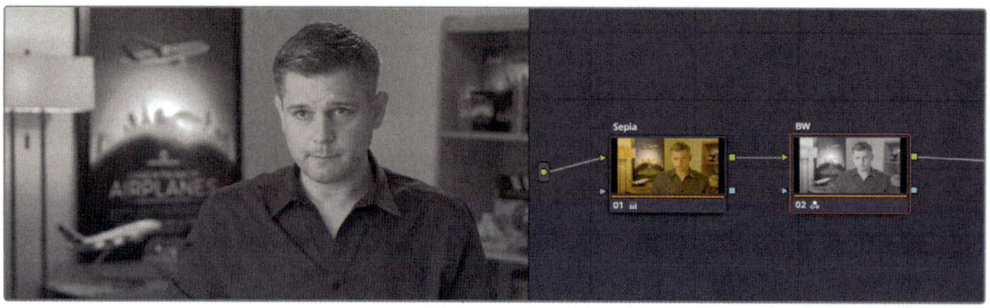

When reconnected, the image becomes black and white. Though the sepia grade is still performing its function in the first node, it is being completely overwritten by the BW node, which is turning the RGB signal monochromatic and sending it to the node tree output.

Adjusting Contrast and Luminance on Nodes

With a clearer understanding of the function of the RGB inputs and outputs, you can now check how mild adjustments to luminance and contrast can still have substantial impact on an image's signal quality.

1 Press Cmd-Home (macOs) or Ctrl-Home (Windows) to reset the grade in clip 01.

2 Label the first node **Lift**.

3 In the Color Wheel palette, drag the Lift master wheel to the left until it reaches -0.25.

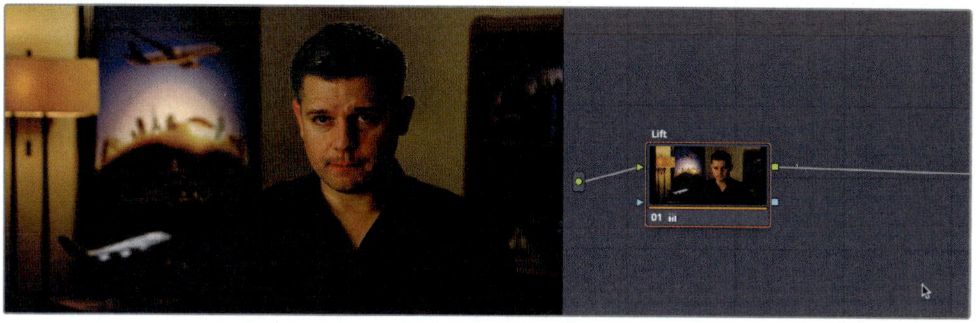

The clip will lose a great amount of detail in the shadows, and the bottom of the waveform trace will appear to be crushed against the black point.

4 Create a new node, and label it **Curves**.

You are going to attempt to restore the shadow data in this new node.

5 Open the curves palette, and ensure that the YRGB channels are linked.

6 Click the center of the curve to create a new control point, and drag it up to brighten the image.

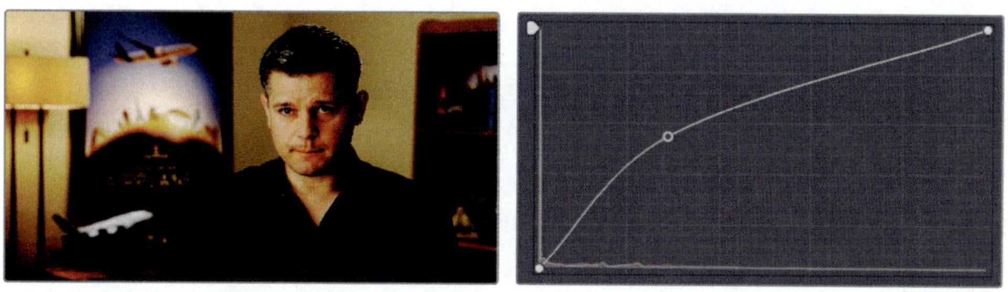

The clip is severely distorted. The fine detail that was contained in the shirt is crushed by the contrast, and the face becomes patchy and over-exposed. This demonstrates a "destructive" workflow in which the changes made in one node have clipped and restricted the RGB data used by the following nodes.

Thankfully, you cannot really destroy RGB data in the pipeline. By using the correct part of the curve, for example, you can fully restore the data of the original image.

7 Right-click the center control point on the curve to remove it.

8 Click node 01 Lift in the pipeline to review the appearance of the histogram trace in the curve palette graph.

9 Click node 02 Curves to compare the histogram trace in the same graph.

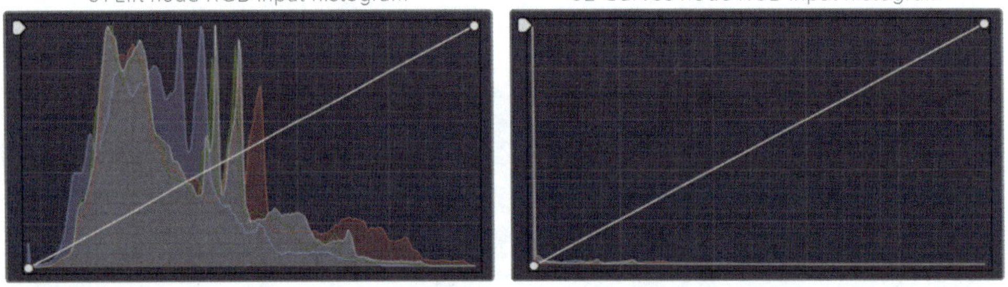

The histogram changes in response to the current node state of the video signal in the pipeline. When grading, such changes can be extremely useful for determining where to click on the graph to target specific luminance and chrominance ranges. The histogram readout in node 02 signifies that the majority of the data is crushed against the lower left of the graph, not the center.

10 Drag the black point of the Y curve upward along the left side of the curves graph. Stop dragging when you are just under the second horizontal line from the bottom.

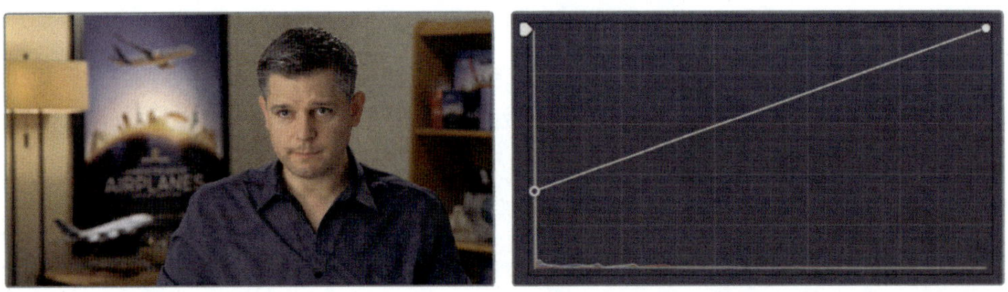

The black point of the curve is equivalent to the Lift master wheel, which is why you were able to retrieve the details that were crushed. By dragging the center of the curve, you were impacting the gamma range, which targets a very different range of luminance.

TIP You can set the curves palette histogram to react to your node adjustments as you are making them. To do so, open the curves palette options menu in the upper right of the palette, and choose Histograms > Output. The histogram now represents the outgoing RGB signal of the node instead of the input.

Though you were able to restore the image in this instance and continue using the previously crushed shadows, you can imagine how more subtle changes to the brightness and contrast of an image in early nodes could impact the quality of adjustments made to the shadows and highlights in later nodes.

It is important to keep in mind the potential of destructive grades. As a general rule, balancing, matching, and secondary grades should come before bold contrast adjustments and sweeping creative grades. It is far more acceptable to distort and crush data in final nodes because no other nodes rely on them for RGB info.

Impact of Dominance Color Grades on Surrounding Nodes

Another consideration when grading is choosing the order in which to apply color changes to an image. In this exercise, you are trying to create a clip with a distinct blue cast, while retaining control over the skin tone in a subject's face.

1. Reset the grade on clip 01.
2. To save time, the balance node for this clip was already created. Open the gallery, and ensure that the Stills albums button is enabled to show a List view of the available albums.

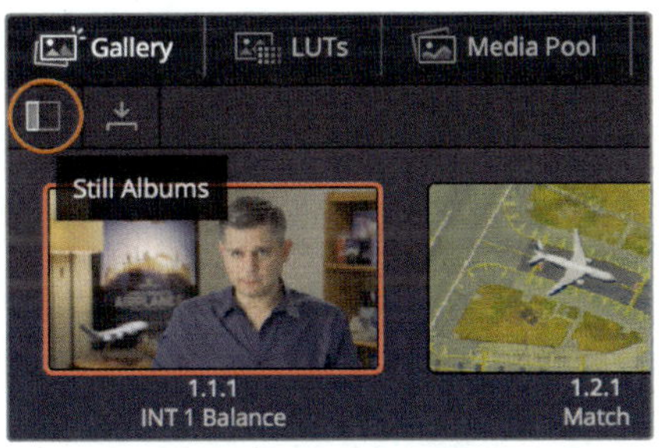

3. Open the Base grades album.
4. Right-click the INT 1 Balance still, and choose Apply Grade.
5. Create a new serial node called **Blue Look** (node 02).
6. In the Color Wheel palette, drag the Gain and Gamma wheels toward the blue-cyan range to cool down the image, and then counteract the blue dominance in the shadows by dragging the Lift wheel slightly toward red.
7. Use the Contrast and Pivot settings to refine the contrast and brighten the upper midtones of the image. Aim to create fine shadows on the man's shirt.

8 Finally, reduce the Saturation to 40 to remove the blue vibrancy and end up with a cold, desaturated image.

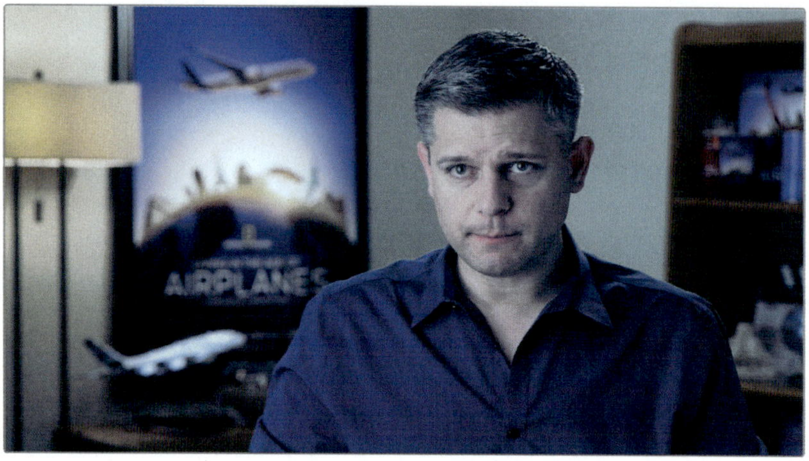

This look has a strong, purposeful design. It could effectively convey a somber mood or suggest a different point in time in a non-linear narrative. However, its impact on the speaker's skin tone reduces its effectiveness and could end up being tiring to the Viewer's eye.

9 Create a final node (node 3) called **Skin Tone**.

The man's face is close in hue to the color of the wall behind him, so using HSL curves might not be the most effective choice. A qualifier selection would give you a better chance of isolating the skin in this shot.

10 Open the Qualifier palette, and click the man's face to grab a sample.

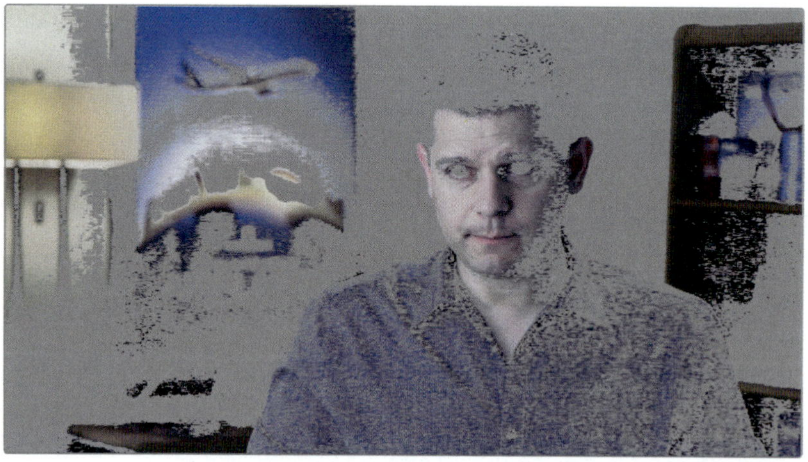

Due to the RGB signal passing through the Blue Look node, the qualifier is forced to work with a very cold, contrasted version of the man's skin. This is definitely not an ideal point in the Timeline to be keying skin or to be grading it.

11 Select the Skin Tone node, and press E to extract it from the pipeline.

12 Drag it onto the link between nodes 01 (Balance) and 02 (Blue Look).

13 Reset the qualifier on the Skin Tone node, and select the skin again. In the Qualifier palette, adjust the HSL and Matte Finesse controls to get the best extraction. Remember to turn on the Highlight mode in the Viewer to best observe the result of the selection.

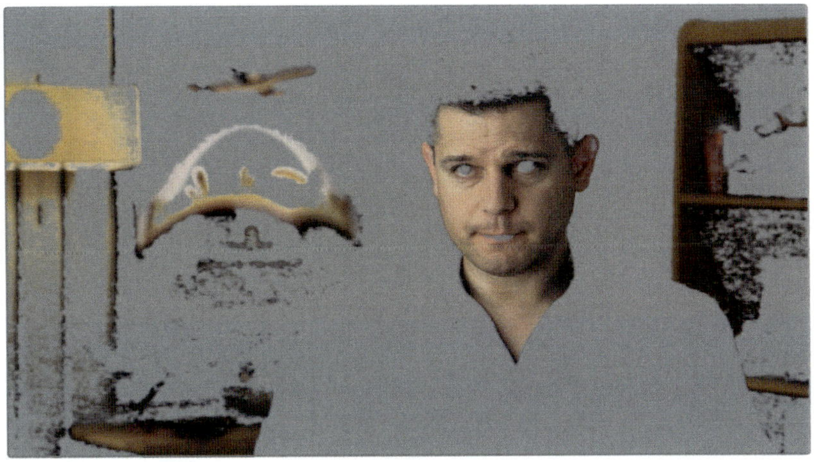

This time the qualifier gives you a much better result.

> **NOTE** The qualifier continues to be actively influenced by the nodes preceding it. Changing the hue or brightness of an earlier node at any point of the grading workflow will impact the selection (and quality) of the qualifier.

14 Use the Window palette to isolate and refine the selection of the man's face.

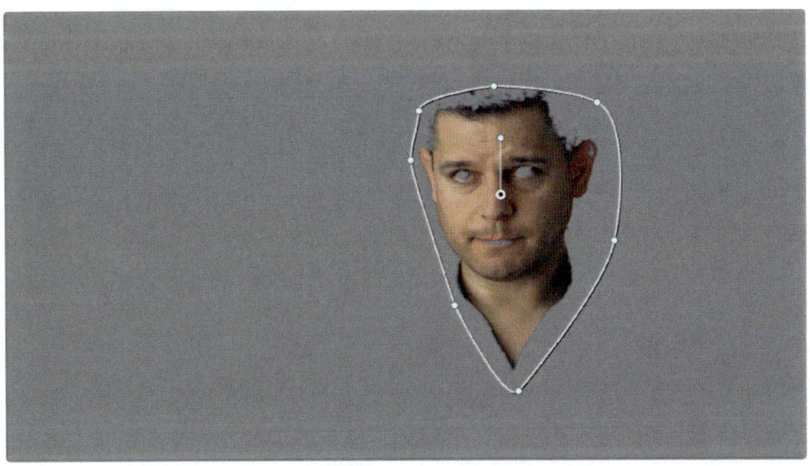

15 In the Viewer, turn off the Highlight mode.

16 Track the motion of his face in the Tracker palette, and then return to the start of the clip.

17 In the adjustment controls, raise the Sat value of node 03 Skin Tone to 55, and drag the Offset wheel slightly toward orange.

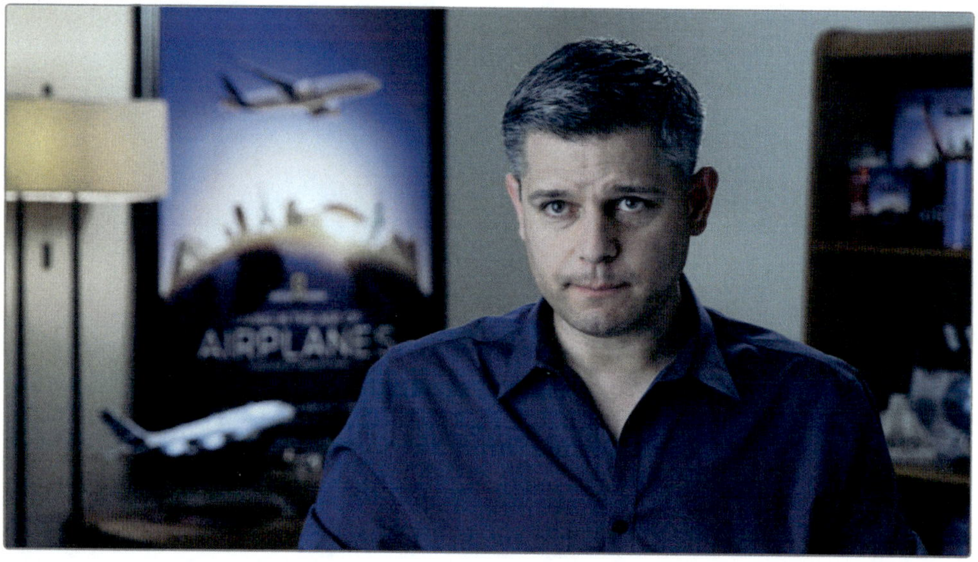

Overall, the resulting grade is much more acceptable. You were able to derive a clean qualifier key for the skin tone and adjust it to act as a visual contrast to the blue grade. However, because Blue Look is the final node to impact the image before the node tree output, you know that the original skin tone hues will always be tinted blue no matter how much you grade the Skin Tone node.

This exercise demonstrates how you might purposefully place of nodes based on your RGB needs. For example, when using a qualifier, you almost always want to process the ungraded or balanced version of the image, free of any severe color or contrast impact.

In the upcoming exercises, you will see examples of how you can derive primary and secondary grades from the same point in the node pipeline and recombine them with the help of Mixer nodes.

Creating Separate Processing Pipelines with a Parallel Mixer Node

Mixer nodes allow you to combine multiple nodes into a single RGB output. The two Mixer node types, Parallel and Layer, have identical structures but process the incoming node data differently.

The Parallel Mixer combines grades by blending them to an equal degree. The result appears similar to working on a linear node pipeline with the main difference being that nodes are able to extract RGB data from the same point in the node tree.

1. In Airplanes – 01 HQ Timeline, click clip 01.

   You will continue to work with the grade you constructed in the previous exercise. This time, the Blue Look and Skin Tone nodes will be placed alongside one another for the most optimal routing of the RGB signal between them.

2. Right-click node 02 Blue Look, and choose Add Node > Add Parallel, or press Option-P (macOS) or Alt-P (Windows), to add a Parallel Mixer node.

   A new Corrector node (node 05) is created, as well as a Parallel Mixer node that combines the RGB outputs of the two nodes before it.

3. To reuse the qualifier selection of the skin tone, you can select node 02 Skin Tone, and press Cmd-C (macOS) or Ctrl-C (Windows) to copy the node data.

4. Select node 05, and press Cmd-V (macOS) or Ctrl-V (Windows) to paste.

5. With the qualifier copied, you can delete the old node, 02 Skin Tone. For organizational purposes, you can rename the new node located under the Blue Look node to **Skin Tone**.

   You now have a node structure in which both the Blue Look and Skin Tone nodes are using the same RGB data from the Balance node. Their respective grades are then combined at equal strength in the Parallel Mixer node. The mixer sends out a single RGB link to the node tree output.

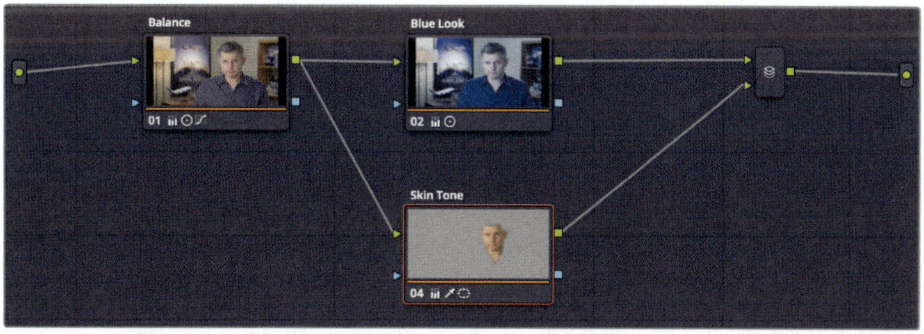

In the Viewer, you should notice only a subtle change to the skin tone. You no longer have a blue hue on the shadows of the man's face, and the overall color appears warmer. If the appearance is too dramatic, you can select the Skin Tone node and reduce the Sat value in the Color Wheel palette, or drag the Offset color wheel point closer to the center.

Skin tone adjustment using:

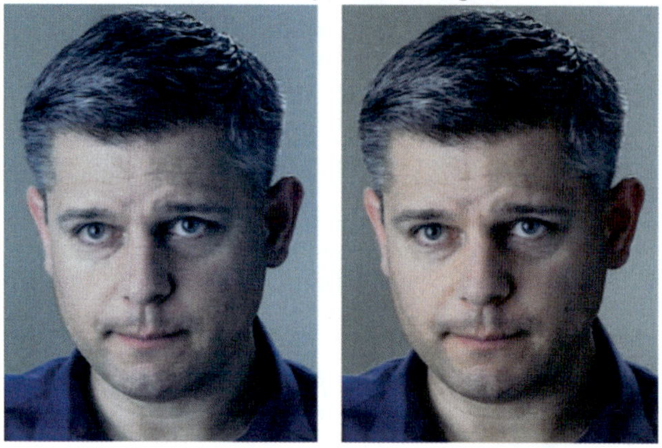

Linear nodes   Mixer nodes

The Parallel Mixer is perfect for performing organic and or natural-looking adjustments such as skin tone correction or hair work.

Morphing Mixer Nodes

An alternative to Parallel Mixer nodes is the Layer Mixer node. In the next few exercises, you will explore the differences between the two in more detail; but in the meantime, you will morph the current clip's Parallel Mixer into a Layer Mixer node to see the impact it will have on the image.

1 Click clip 01 on the Airplanes – 01 HQ Timeline.

2 In the Node editor, right-click the Parallel Mixer node, and choose "Morph into Layer Mixer Node."

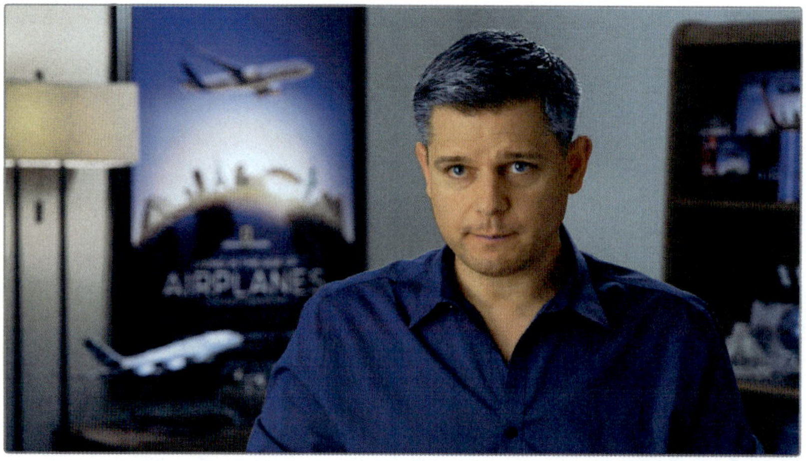

This change has a jarring effect on the image. The skin tone now appears far less realistic and the edge around the face is harsh and solid. This is because node 03 Skin Tone is being treated as an RGB image layer. The keyed face has 100% opacity and is overlaid onto the node 02 Blue Look image underneath.

In its current state, the grade is unusable. However, by adjusting to the opacity of the skin tone layer, you can still blend it into the Blue Look layer.

3 Select node 03 Skin Tone.

4 In the central palettes, open the Key mixer palette.

5 Enter the key Output gain as 0.5 to reduce the opacity of the skin tone node by half.

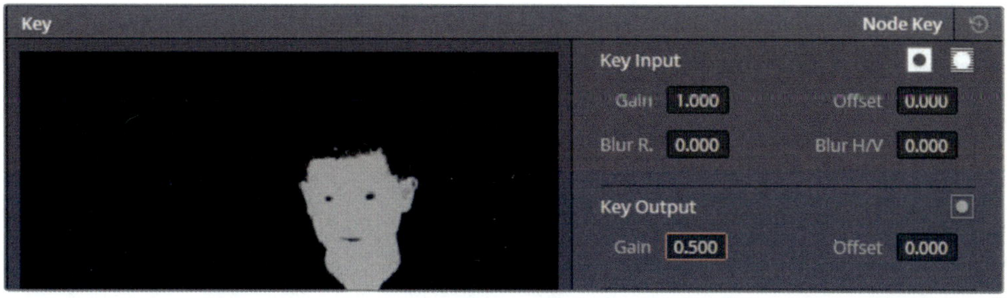

The face now blends much more naturally into the blue background node.

Both Parallel and layer Mixer nodes provide an easy option to morph them from one state to the other, so you can experiment with grade structure and find the optimal balance and blends of nodes.

Having switched between the two nodes and seeing how differently they affect an image, let's look more closely at how these mixers operate. Understanding their operations will help you understand when to choose one mixer over another.

Visualizing Mixer Nodes

A simple way to familiarize oneself with how mixers operate is to create a basic RGB graphic setup that will clearly display the relationship between the nodes.

First, you will need a plain grayscale background.

1 Enter the Edit page.

2 Open the Effects Library by clicking the button at the top of the page.

3 Inside Toolbox > Generators, locate the Grey Scale generator.

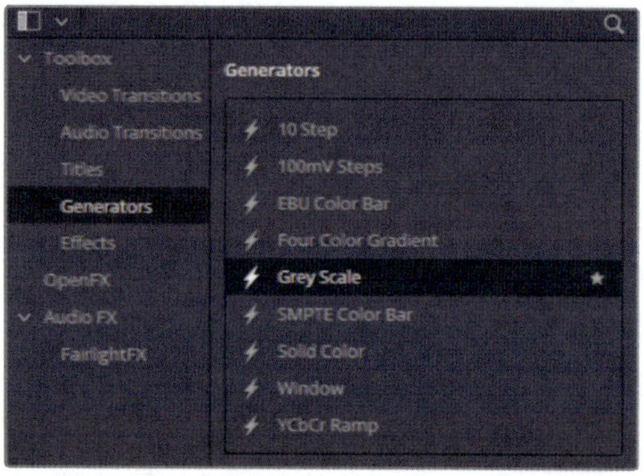

4 Drag the Grey Scale generator to the end of the Timeline.

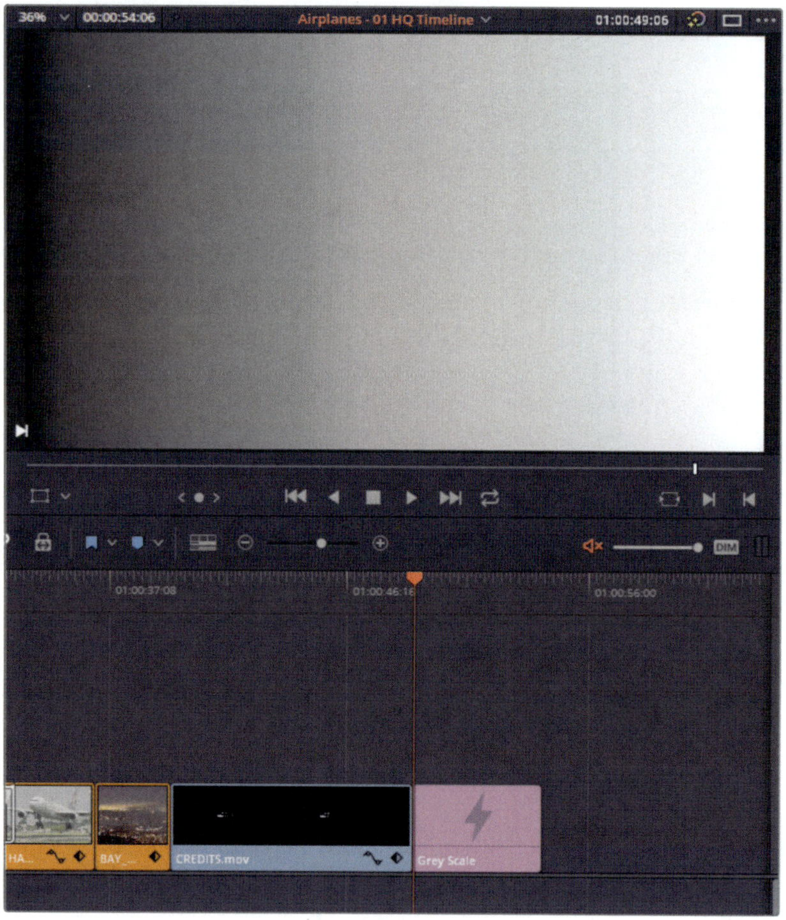

To work on the generator in the Color page, you first need to transform it into a compound clip, so it can take on video properties.

5 In the Timeline, right-click the generator, and choose New Compound Clip.

6 Name the compound clip **Grey Scale**.

7 Enter the Color page.

8 With the generator clip (clip 12) selected, create a new serial node.

9 Right-click node 02, and choose Add Node > Add Layer, or press Option-L (macOS) or Alt-L (Windows), to add a Layer Mixer node.

10 With node 02 selected, create another layer node to produce a stack of three layer nodes.

11 Label the nodes (from top to bottom) **Red**, **Green**, and **Blue**.

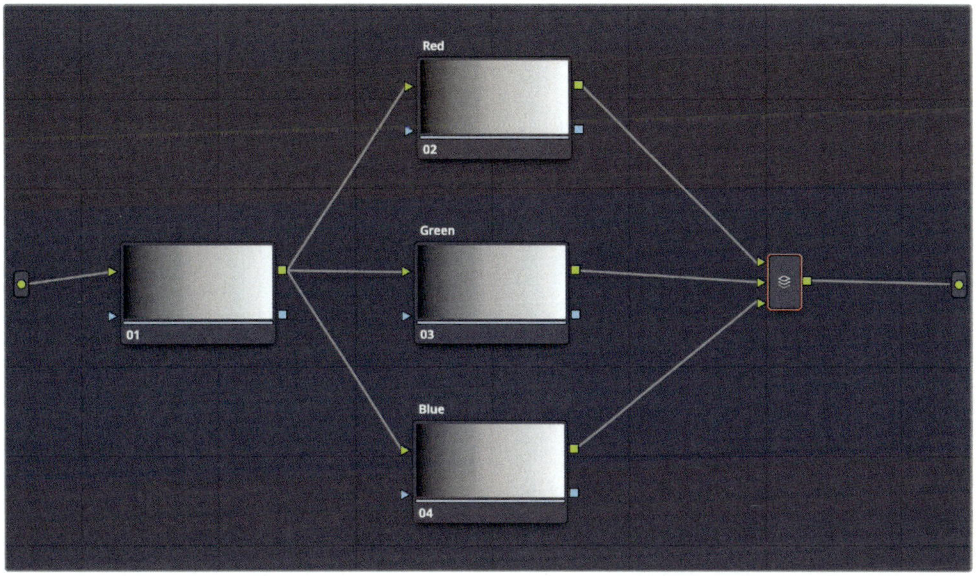

12 Select the Blue node at the bottom of the stack.

13 In the central palettes, open the Window palette, and click the circle button to create a circular window.

14 Open the RGB Mixer palette, and make the circle blue by dragging up the B bar of the blue channel.

15 Move the circle window to the lower-right of the Viewer. Your goal is to create three intersecting circles (red, green, and blue).

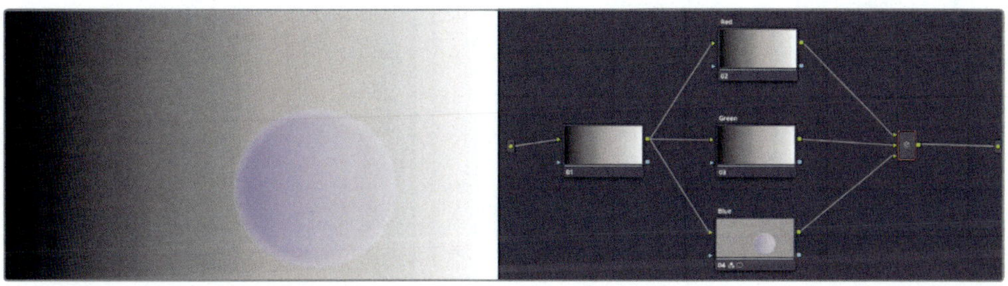

16 Select the Green node, and create a circle window in it.

17 In the RGB Mixer palette, make the circle green by dragging up the G bar of the green channel.

18 Move the Green node window to the lower-left of the Viewer.

19 Finally, create a red circle in the Red node. Turn it red using the RGB Mixer, and move it to the top.

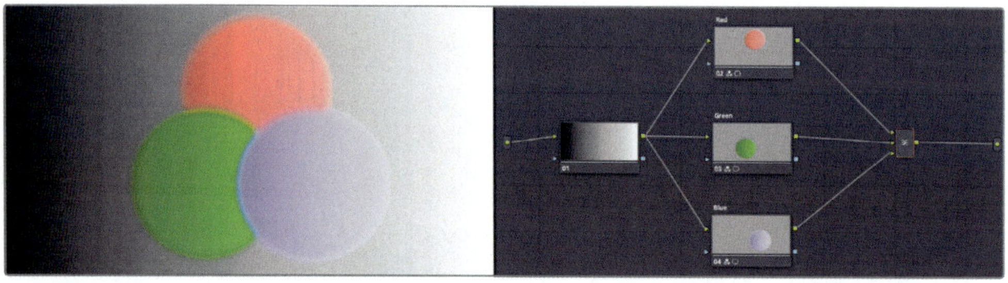

The results demonstrate how nodes interact when combined in a Layer Mixer node. Their behaviors are reminiscent of layer-based systems in which the upper RGB input of the Layer Mixer constitutes the lowest layer and is compounded by each subsequent RGB input. The default status of the nodes is to have full opacity until a Power Window or qualifier introduces transparency.

20 Right-click the Layer Mixer node, and hover your pointer over the options in the Composite Mode submenu.

Doing so will allow you to preview how the colors of the nodes will interact under the different hue and luminance blending methods. Note that all of the top nodes are blended until they reach the bottom layer (Red), which remains at full opacity.

21 Select Lighten to apply the Composite mode.

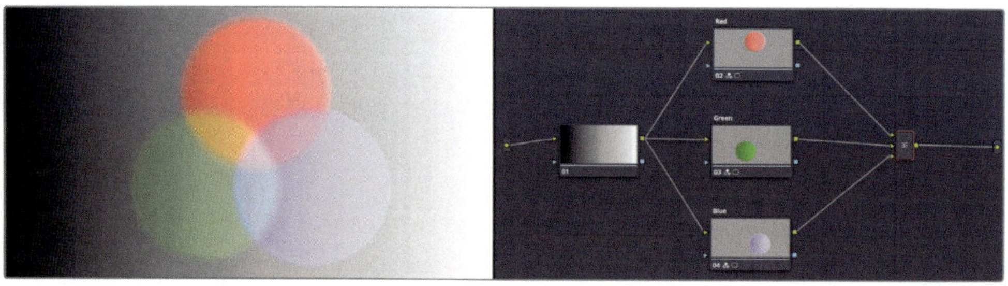

22 To remove the Blend mode, right-click the Layer Mixer node. Return to the Composite Mode submenu, and choose Normal.

Next, you'll change the order of the node layers.

23 Move your mouse pointer over the link between the Red node and the Layer Mixer to reveal the blue highlight. Drag the link to the bottom input of the Layer mixer to disconnect the Blue node from the Layer Mixer.

24 Drag the RGB output of the Blue node toward the top input of the Layer Mixer.

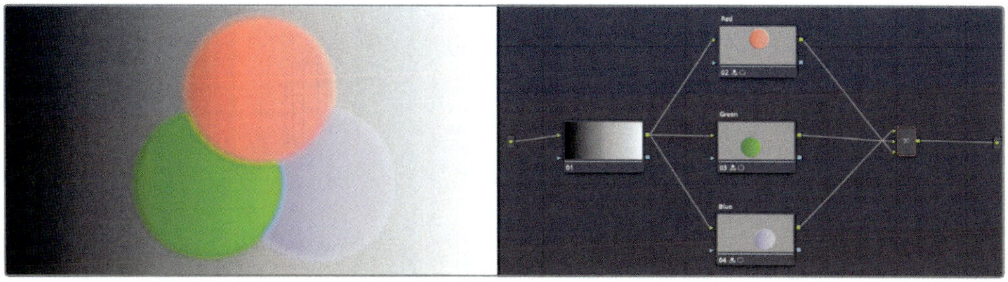

The red circle now overlaps the green and blue. This further demonstrates how the RGB input order in the Mixer node works. Additionally, it emphasizes that the physical location of the nodes in the Node editor has no impact on the grade and the final results in the Viewer.

25 To compare the interaction of the circles in the Parallel Mixer, right-click the Layer Mixer node, and choose Morph into Parallel Node.

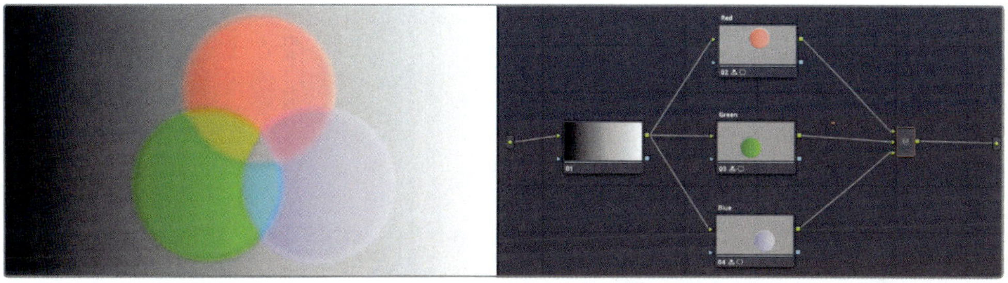

This operation changes the behavior of the three circles. Instead of treating the layers at full opacity, it adjusts their transparencies to show an equal amount of each. Unlike a blend mode, their luminance values are not targeted.

The composite blending options in Layer Mixer nodes can produce very dynamic looks. You can use them to emphasize some areas of your shots, or even to compile graphic design elements.

The Parallel Mixer is ideal for applying realistic-looking grades on nodes that are seamlessly blended into one another while deriving their RGB data from the same level in the node pipeline.

Compositing Effects with the Layer Mixer Node

In this exercise, you will use a Layer Mixer to construct an image that has several secondary grading needs. Unlike the interview example, the focus is not on seamlessly blending the colors of the image into each other, but to work on each distinct element separately.

1. Click clip 8 in Airplanes – 01 HQ Timeline.

   In the previous lesson, the reference Timeline indicated that the water in this clip needed to be turned blue.

2. In the Viewer, drag the playhead closer to the end of the clip to better see the plane against the water.

3. The end of clip 08 is in mid-dissolve with the following clip 09. To disable transitions and effects that are on the Timeline in the Edit page, click the Unmix button in the lower-left corner of the Viewer.

   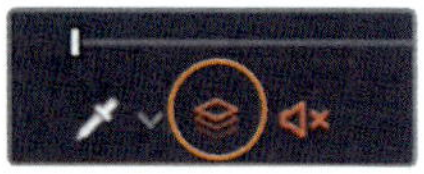

4. To bring up the reference video in the Color page, right-click the Viewer, and select Reference Mode > Offline. Doing so will adjust the Image Wipe mode to use the reference clip associated with the Timeline instead of using gallery stills.

5. In the upper-left corner of the Viewer, click the Image Wipe icon to compare the current clip to the one in the reference video.

   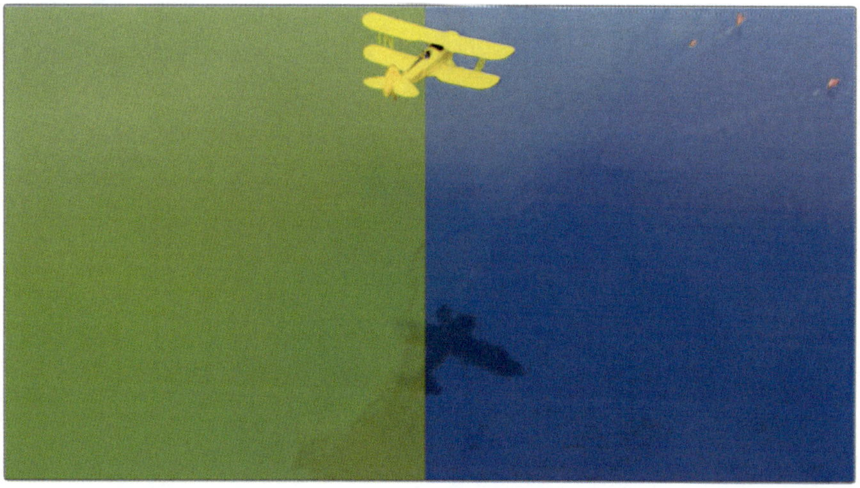

You have several ways to approach this secondary grade. You could use HSL curves or the qualifier, together with the RGB Mixer, wheels, or custom curves. When confronted with a specific grade problem, it is common to cycle through several options until you find the optimum grading solution. In this instance, you will use a combination of techniques, including the 3D qualifier and custom curves.

6 In the Gallery panel, from the "Base grades" album, apply the 1.8.1 Balance still to normalize the luminance of the clip on the first node.

7 Create a second node, and label it **Blue Water**. You will use this node to turn the image blue with focus on getting the correct blue hue in the water.

8 In the Custom curves palette, isolate the B channel, and drag its black point up the vertical plane until the water is a rich blue color.

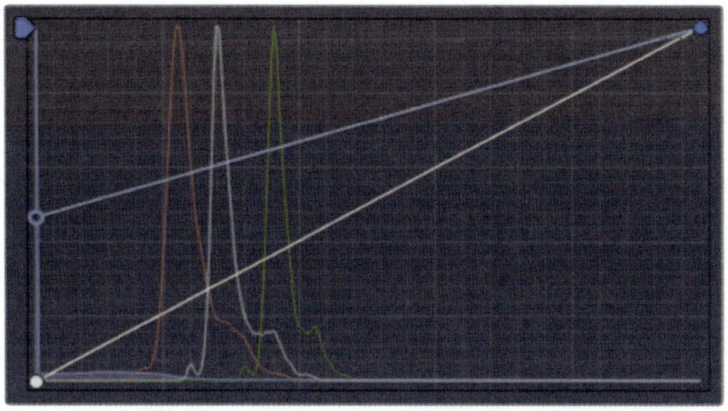

9 Lower the Gamma master wheel to control the brightness of the water.

10 Drag the Sat and Hue adjustment controls to produce the right water temperature.

Note that the plane will also be affected by these grade changes. That is acceptable because in subsequent layer nodes you will extract the plane and grade it separately.

11 Press Option-L (macOS) or Alt-L (Windows) to add a Layer Mixer and a new node (node 04). Label the new node **Yellow Plane**.

12 Open the Qualifier palette, and change the mode from HSL to 3D. This is the recommended qualifier mode for chroma key work due to its ability to intuitively predict hue and shadow fluctuations on green screens.

13 In the Viewer, drag the qualifier across the green water to make a selection. You can repeat this action as many times as necessary to build a reliable chromakey reference.

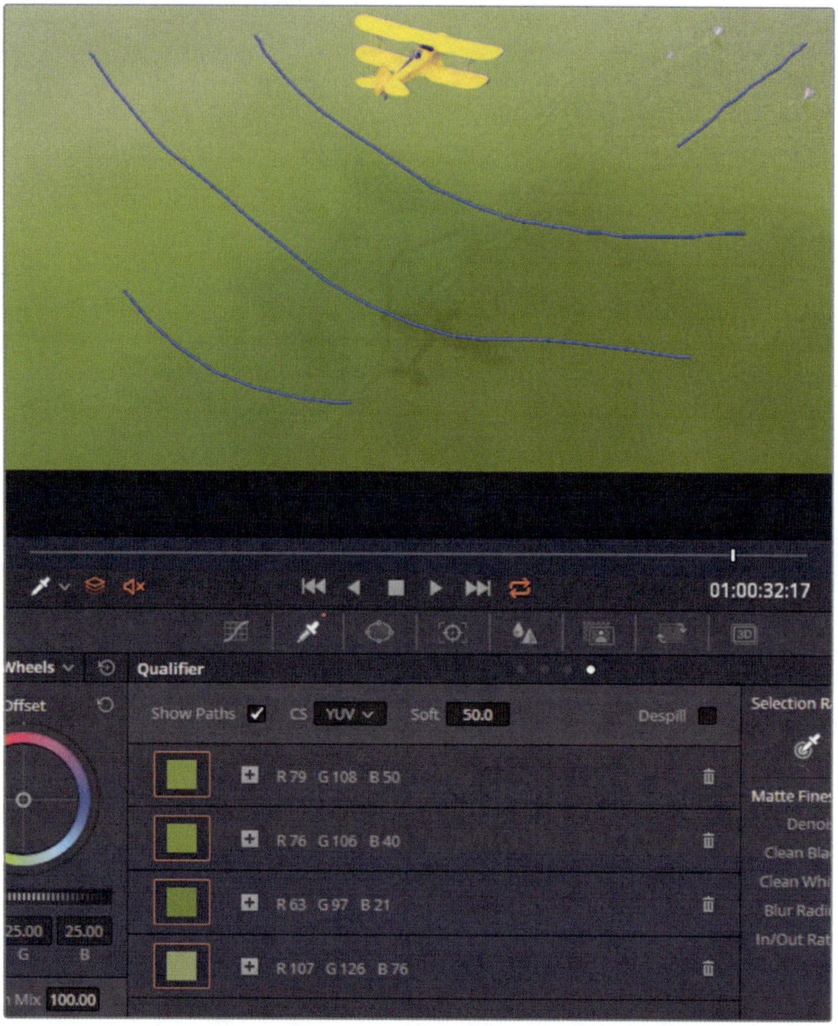

Every time you create a color sample, a swatch is placed in the 3D qualifier list to document the hues that are included in the selection.

14 When finished, in the Viewer, enable Highlight mode, and change it to represent the B/W mode.

15 Adjust the Matte Finesse controls to cover up any remaining unselected areas.

16 In the 3D qualifier window, click the Invert button to focus the extraction on the plane instead of the water.

17 In the Viewer, disable the Highlight mode.

18 In the Qualifier palette, deselect Show Paths to hide the selection lines.

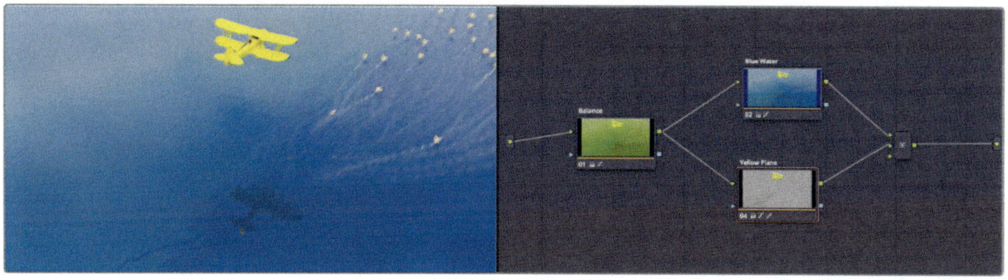

You have successfully extracted the plane and now have full control over its RGB values.

19 In the adjustment controls of the Color Wheel palette, decrease the saturation of the plane.

20 Create a gentle s-curve on the Y channel of the custom curves to enhance the contrast and detail on the plane.

Using Key Inputs and Outputs to Share Matte Data Across Nodes

The key inputs and outputs allow you to reuse node mattes and further adjust them in the receiving node.

In this exercise, you have not yet addressed a remaining component of the composite: the flamingos at the end of the clip. In the reference video, the flamingos in the upper-right corner of the shot are graded pink. In the current grade, the birds look desaturated and flat. Because you have already keyed-out the green water in the Yellow Plane node, it will be enough to reuse its key data and add a custom curve window to isolate the focus onto the birds in the corner.

1 In clip 08, click the Yellow Plane node.

2 Press Option-L (macOS) or Alt-L (Windows) to create a new layer node, and label it **Flamingos**.

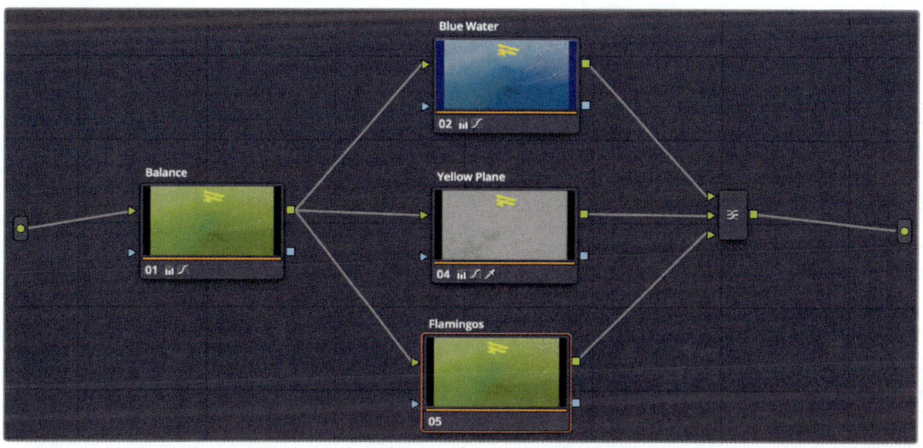

3 To reuse the matte data of the keyed Yellow Plane node, drag the key output square of the Plane node toward the key input triangle of the Flamingos node.

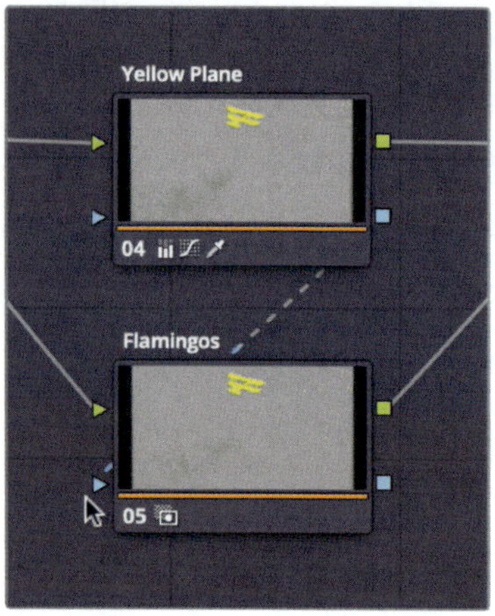

4 Scrub to the end of the video until you see the area that the flamingos occupy in the frame.

To isolate the matte to include just the birds, you can use a Custom curve window.

5 Open the Window palette, and click the curve window button. Label it **Flamingos Matte**.

6 Click around the flamingos in the image. When you're done, remember to click the first point last to close the loop and generate a shape.

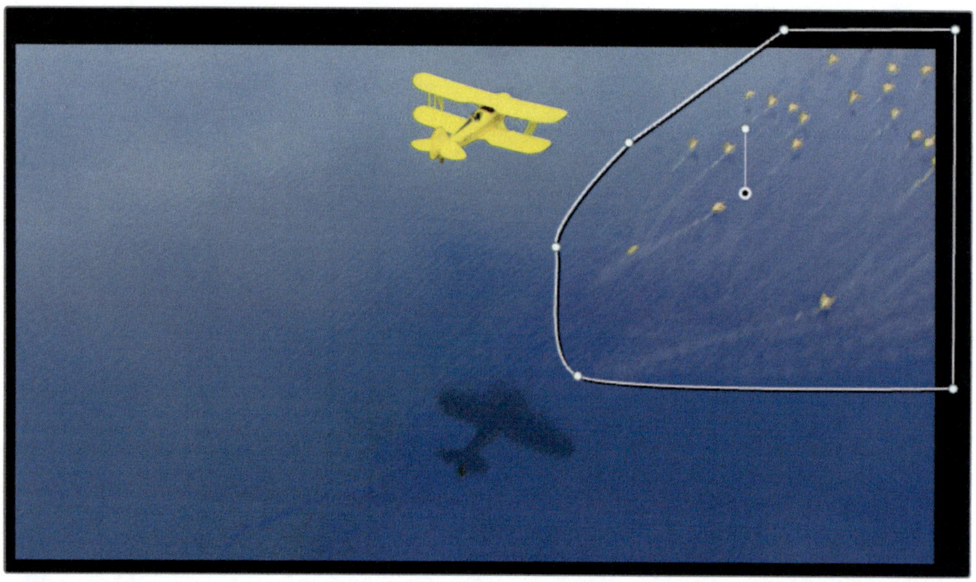

The birds appear in the shot only toward the end, so you will perform a rudimentary animation of the window across the screen. A simple way to animate windows in the Color page is by using the Frame mode of the Tracker palette.

7 Open the Tracker palette, and switch the mode to Frame.

8 Click the diamond-shape in the center of the keyframe controls in the upper-right corner of the Tracker graph.

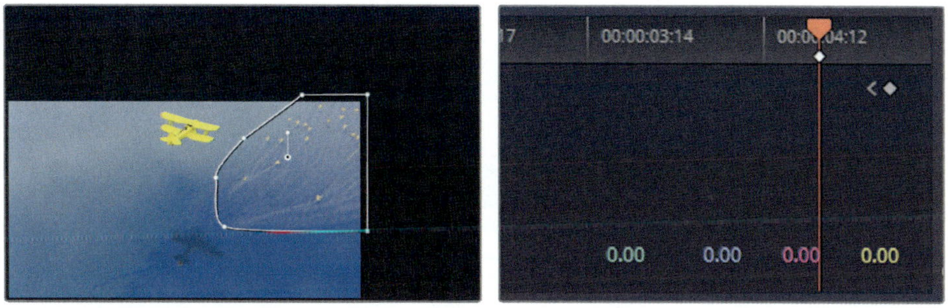

Doing so places the end keyframe for the curve window.

9 Drag the playhead left until the birds are off-screen, and drag the curve window after them in the Viewer. The Tracker graph automatically places a second keyframe, and an animation is generated between the two.

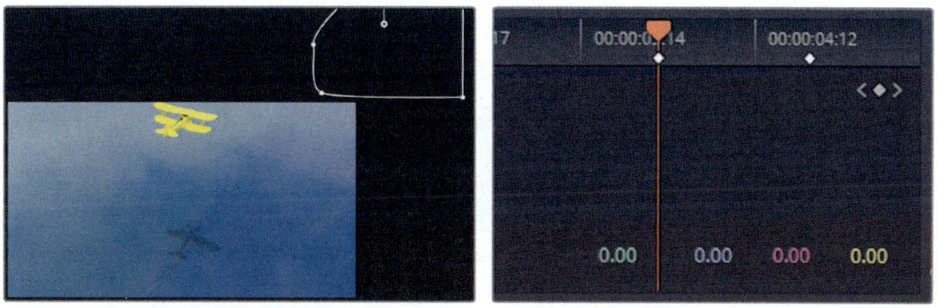

The Tracker graph reveals some additional frames at the end of the clip. This is the content of the clip used in the transition with clip 09.

10 Drag the playhead to the end of the tracker graph and further refine the shape and placement of the window.

Finally, there is also a default frame in the Tracker graph at the start of the clip.

11 Use the keyframe controls to jump to the start of the clip and move the window off-screen.

12 Scrub through the clip Timeline to ensure that the window is following the birds' movement.

You can now make the necessary grade adjustments to enhance the birds' pink color.

13 Drag the Gain master wheel left to darken the birds slightly.

14 Drag the Gain color wheel toward magenta to turn the birds pink.

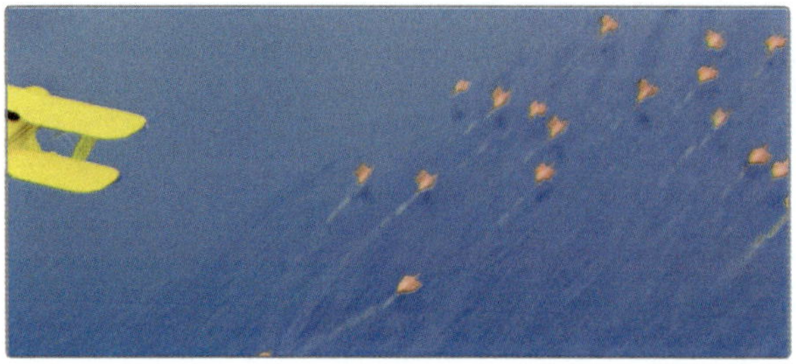

To simplify your pipeline and prepare it for further grading nodes, you can combine all the Layer Mixer nodes into a single compound node.

15 Drag in the Node editor to select all the nodes except the Balance node.

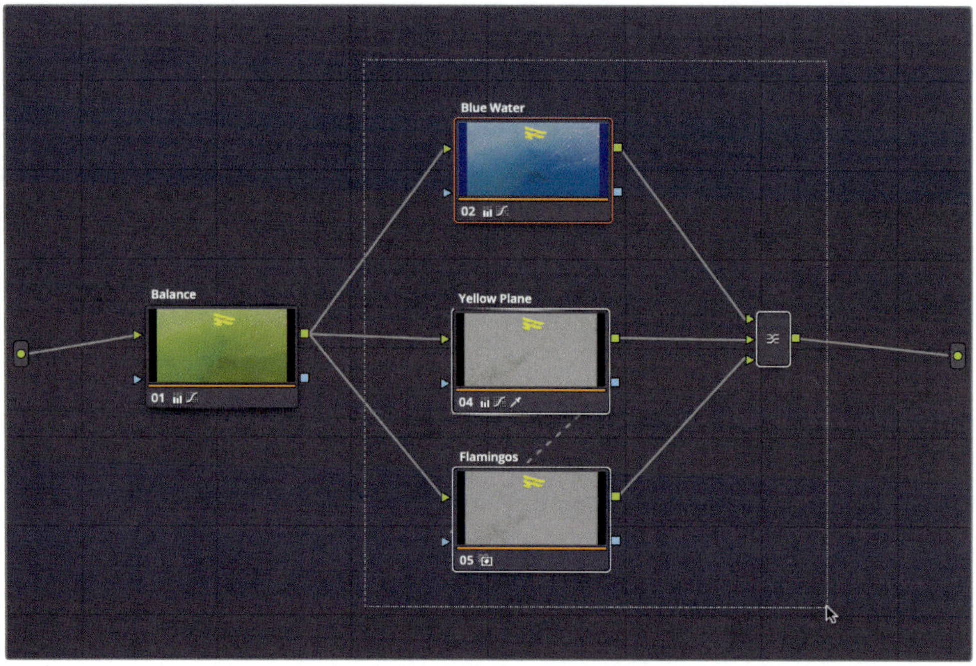

You now can press the Cmd-D (macOS) or Ctrl-D (Windows) to quickly bypass and evaluate the selected nodes without affecting the Balance node.

16 Right-click any selected node, and choose Create Compound Node.

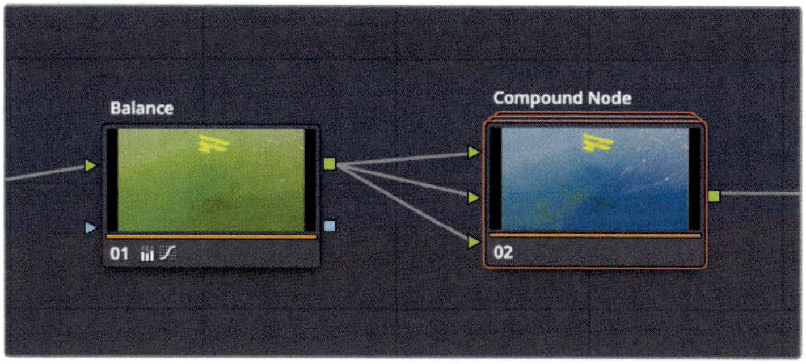

This step is an effective organizational tool when working on clips with large node tree structures. Additionally, you can still bypass the node to disable the color composites without affecting the Balance node.

You still have access to the original Layer mixer structure within the Compound node.

17 Right-click and choose Show Compound Node.

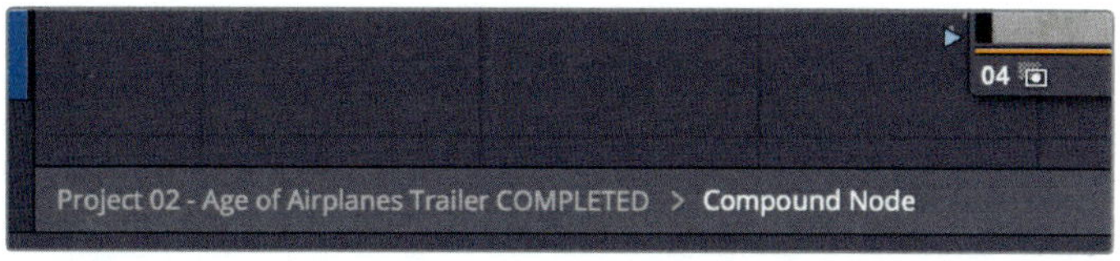

18 To navigate back to the main Node editor, click the project name Project 02 – Age of Airplanes Trailer link at the bottom of the Node editor.

19 If you want to return to the original node structure of the Compound node, right-click and choose Decompose Compound Node.

> TIP Another method for decluttering the Node editor is to hide node thumbnails. In the upper-right corner of the Node editor, click the options menu, and deselect Show Thumbnails. Doing so will collapse the nodes to just their labels, numbers, and palette icons.

Importing and using an External Matte

In their natural states, all tools that generate a selection (such as qualifiers and Power Windows) are actually just black-and-white visual guides that tell the image where it needs to be visible (white) and invisible (black). In post-production, these guides are called *mattes* (or *travelling mattes* when the matte is animated or generated using keyed live footage). You can see mattes in the Color page when the Viewer is set to Highlight mode and the Highlight B/W option is selected.

Because mattes fundamentally rely on this black-and-white graphic dynamic, any image or video that is black and white can technically be treated as a matte. This could even include outside media imported into Resolve that you can assign to a specific clip for selection purposes.

In this exercise, you will use an externally generated matte to perform a sky replacement in a tricky shot.

1. Click clip 07 on the Airplanes – 01 HQ Timeline.
2. From the Base grades album, apply the 1.7.1 Balance grade to the clip to neutralize its starting colors.

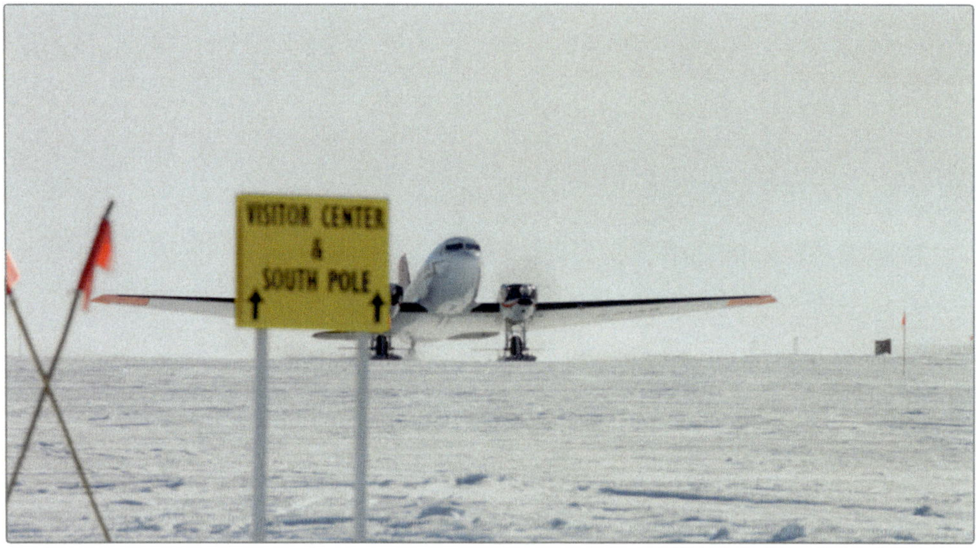

Selecting the sky in this image using standard keying tools is tricky because all of the elements are visually similar: the sky is almost purely white together with the snow on the ground, which is reflecting strongly onto the bottom of the airplane. Using the qualifier alone would produce a patchy selection.

To get an optimal result, you need to generate custom windows and track them to the environment to create a clean matte composite. Sometimes, this type of advanced keying work is delegated to a rotoscope artist or compositor while the colorist focuses on grading the media.

In this instance, a matte was already created for this video clip.

3. Enter the Media page.
4. In the Media storage panel, find the BMD 16 CC – Project 02 folder, and navigate to Other > Mattes.

   In Mattes, you will find the SOUTH_POLE_MATTE sequence folder. The matte image sequence in it will appear as a single video file.

NOTE To import individual stills from image sequences such as TIF, PNG, or DPX, click the options menu in the upper-right corner of the media storage panel, and choose Show Individual Frames.

5 Drag SOUTH_POLE_MATTE.png into the Graphics bin of the media pool.

6 Enter the Color page.

7 In the Node editor of clip 07, create a new serial node (node 02), and label it **Sky Removal**.

8 Click the media pool button at the top of the color page to open the media pool panel.

9 From the Graphics bin, drag SOUTH_POLE_MATTE.png into the Node editor.

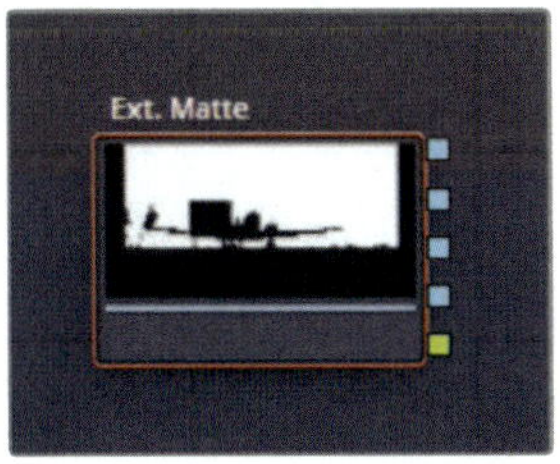

The matte PNG sequence appears in the Node editor within a dedicated Ext. Matte node. Notice that the node has no inputs but contains multiple outputs.

The uppermost blue square is the standard luminance, or Y, output. The three blue squares under it are RGB outputs that enable you to work on each channel of the image independently. The green square output at the bottom sends a standard RGB signal of the black-and-white matte.

10 Drag the uppermost key output to the Sky Removal node's key input.

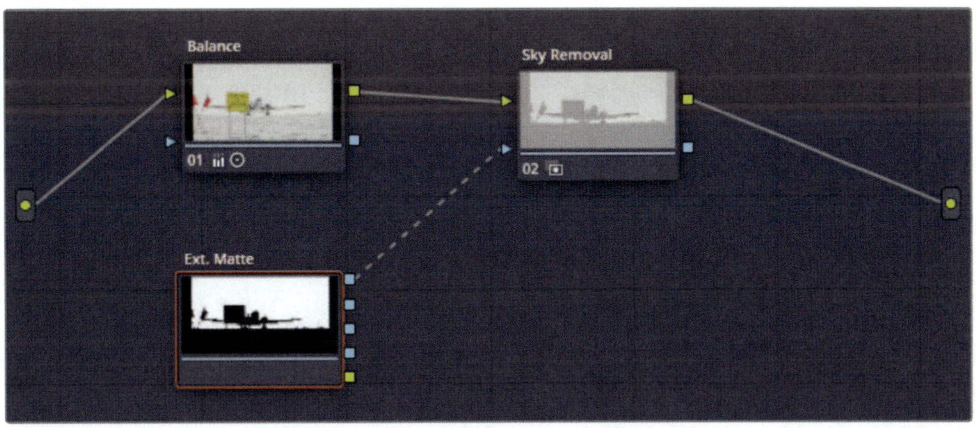

The key is immediately visible in the Sky Removal node thumbnail; however, it appears to be extracting the ground instead of the sky.

11 Select the Sky Removal node.

12 Open the Key palette, and in the key input section, click the Invert button.

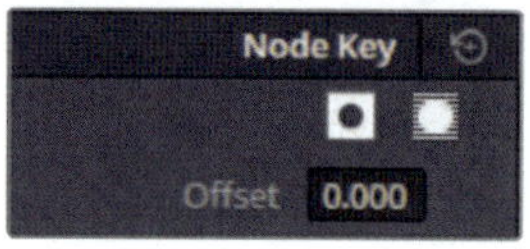

This workflow is frequently employed when the workload of a composite is broken up among multiple post-production departments. Though the Custom curve window can be extremely effective for rotoscoping, that activity might not be the best use of a colorist's time. Instead, the job could be handed over to a rotoscope or VFX artist who can generate an accurate travelling matte and export a black-and-white video or image sequence. The colorist can then use it to quickly extract a key in the Node editor and create the final grade or shot composite.

NOTE You can see the how the SOUTH_POLE_MATTE.png travelling matte was generated in the Fusion page of DaVinci Resolve.

Open Project 02 – Age of Airplanes Trailer COMPLETED.drp. Open the Airplanes – 01 HQ Timeline in the Color page, select the SOUTH_POLE clip, and enter the Fusion page. Click the Clips button in the interface toolbar at the top to reveal the Clips Timeline at the bottom of the page. Right-click clip 07, and choose MATTE > Load.

Doing so load the composition that was used to generate the black-and-white matte in this exercise. The workflow combined using keying tools on out-of-focus elements (such as the flags and sign) and vector masks on solid objects (such as the plane and ground).

Applying Transparency to Multiple Video Tracks

The following exercise will require a basic understanding of editing principles. Specifically, that a Timeline can contain multiple video or audio tracks in which you can stack media to occupy the same temporal point in the Timeline. Ordinarily, clips on upper tracks hide media on lower tracks unless transparency is introduced (which could be achieved using effects such as cropping, opacity reduction, or color blending). The Color page offers more advanced methods for incorporating transparency into clips and revealing lower video tracks in the Timeline.

1 Right-click in the Node editor, and choose Add Alpha Output.

A new output is added to the Node graph. You can use it to apply any key data in the node tree to the alpha channel of the clip.

2 Drag the key output of the Sky Removal node into the alpha output.

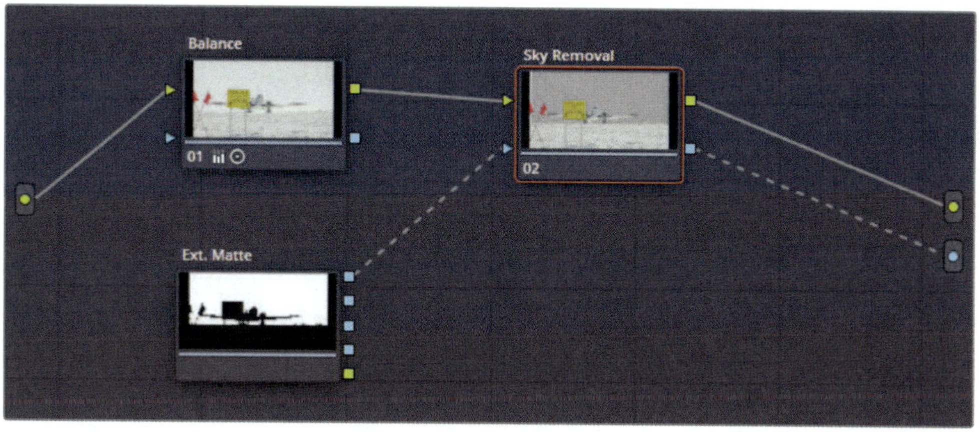

The key data is applied to the clip's alpha channel, thereby affecting its appearance in the Timeline and upon export. This behavior is different from the way the key data behaves when it is contained within the Node editor. In that context, it can be used only to determine which parts of the image are affected for grading (or effects) purposes.

3 Enter the Media page.

4 In the Other > Images subfolder of the Media storage, locate the Sky_Stock.jpg file, and drag it into the media pool's Graphics bin.

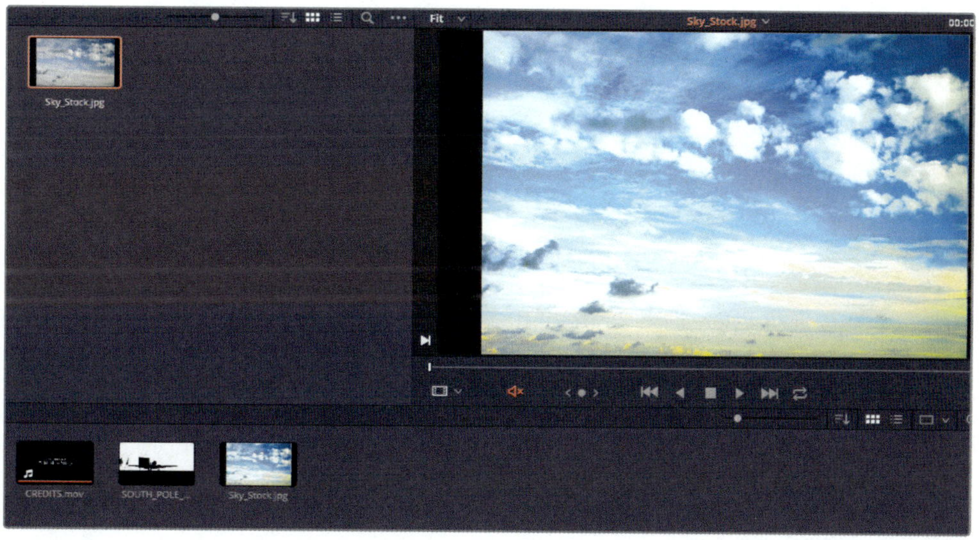

If the sky image's colors appear distorted in the Viewer, it is because they are impacted by the color management of the project.

5 In the media pool, right-click the image thumbnail, and choose Input Color space > Bypass.

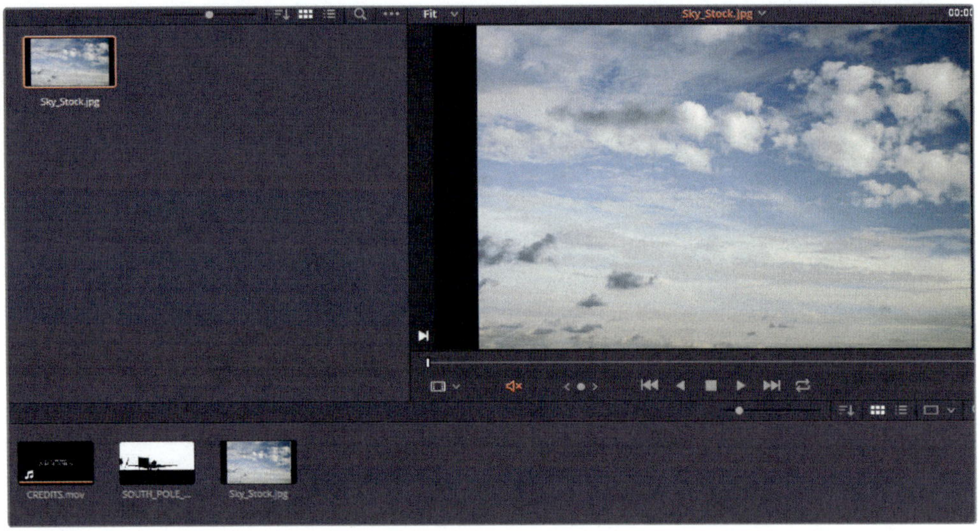

6 Enter the Edit page.

7 Drag the zoom slider, or press Cmd-+ (plus sign) in macOS or Ctrl-+ (plus sign) in Windows, to zoom in to the SOUTH_POLE clip.

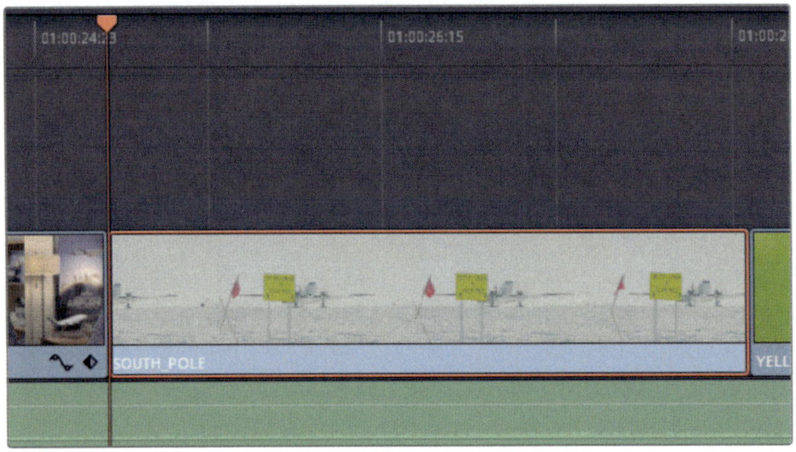

8 Drag the clip to video track 2. Doing so will create an empty space on the video track underneath.

9 With the clip still selected, press the X key to create an in/out selection equal to the clip's duration.

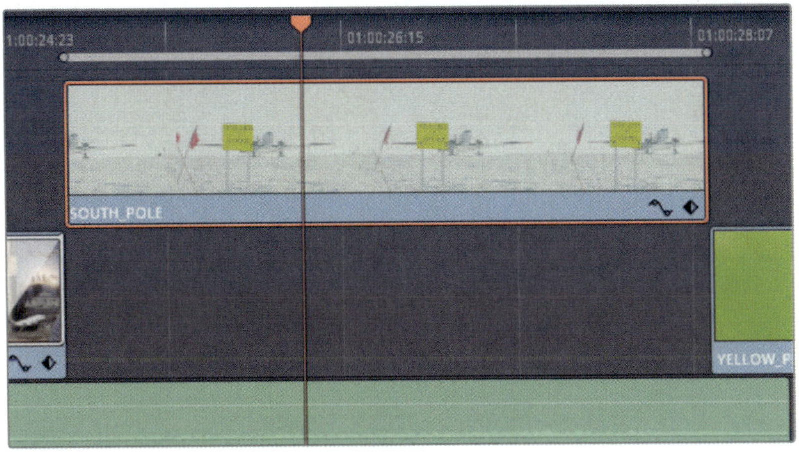

10 Drag Sky_Stock.jpg from the media pool into the Timeline Viewer. When the Viewer's edit controls appear, drag the image into Fit to Fill.

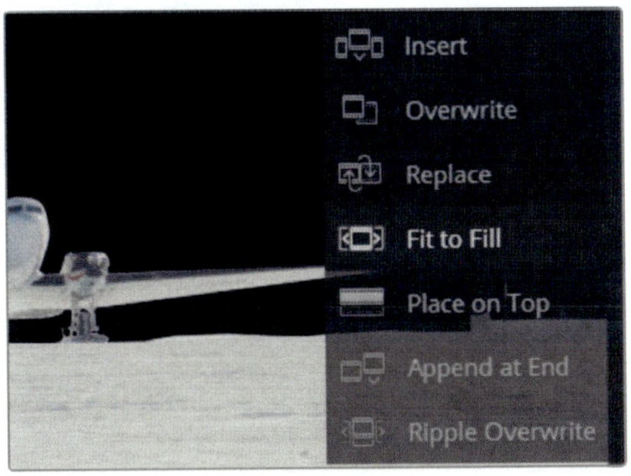

This action will fill the gap under the airplane clip with the still image of the sky based on the earlier in/out selection.

11 Press Option-X (macOS) or Alt-X (Windows) to reset the in/out points on the Timeline.

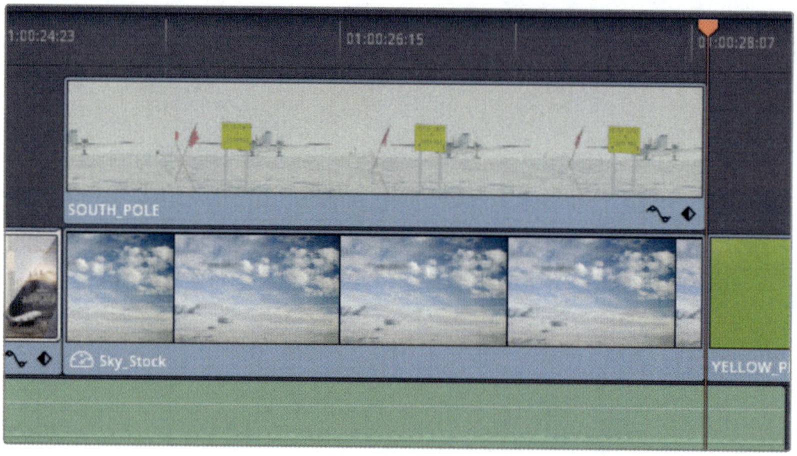

The end result will be a rough composite of the two images.

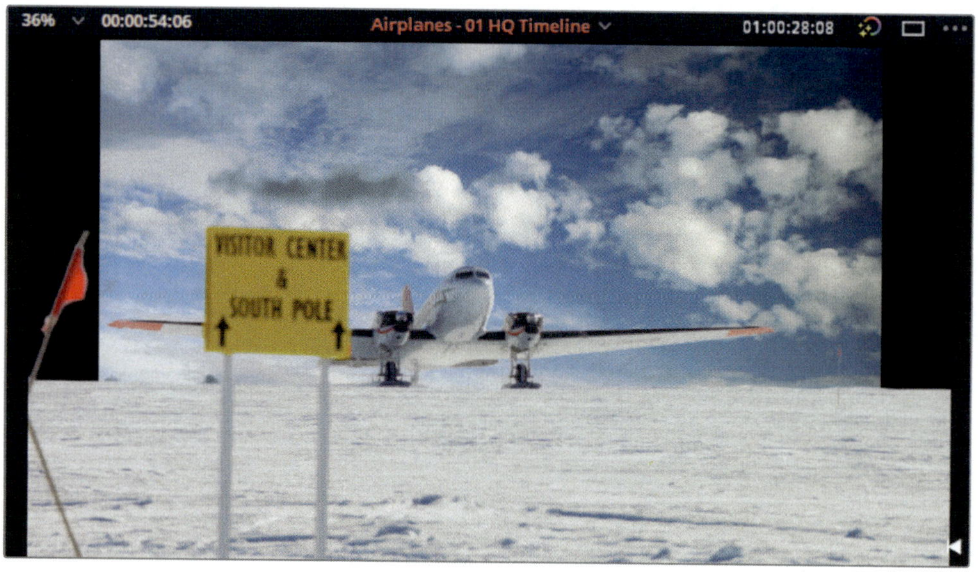

TIP By default, the duration of stills introduced into a Timeline is five seconds. If you wish to change this default value—for example, when you are working with photo-based time-lapses and wish your stills to be one frame long—you can enter DaVinci Resolve Preferences > User > Editing, and alter the standard still duration.

Image Processing Across DaVinci Resolve Pages

The layout of the pages at the bottom of the DaVinci Resolve interface represents the project workflow. Media is ingested (Media page), compiled into a Timeline (Cut and Edit pages), undergoes compositing (Fusion page); and is then graded (Color page), audio mixed (Fairlight page), and rendered (Deliver page).

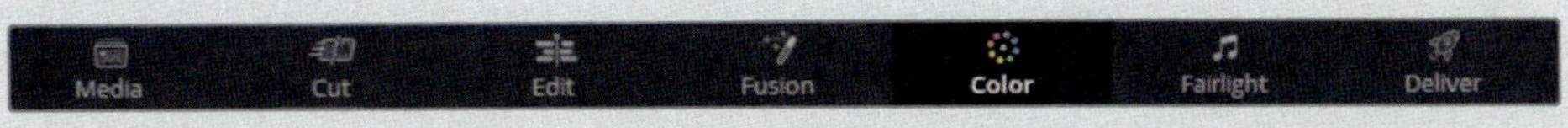

This order of operations also corresponds to the image-processing pipeline with some distinctions. The video signal of the source media in the Edit page flows to the Fusion page where it is processed and output to the Color page. However, if an effect (ResolveFX or OFX plug-in) is applied in the Edit page, it will NOT appear in the Fusion page, but will instead appear on the Color page. It is helpful to think of Edit page effects as being applied to the image data signal after it has left the Fusion page. To force an Edit page effect to be visible in the fusion page, you would need to turn the clip into a compound clip on the Timeline.

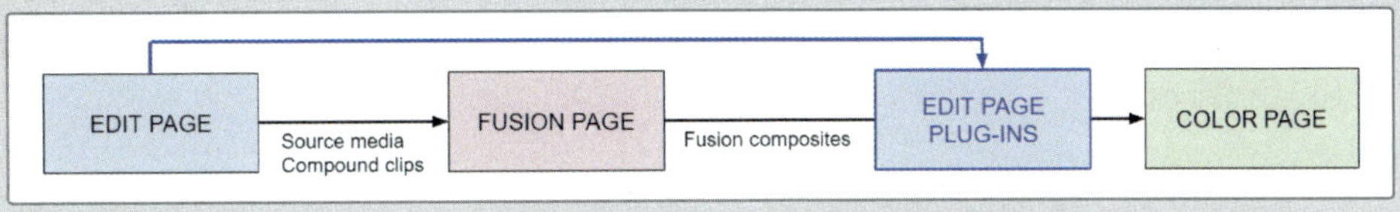

Finally, the Viewers on all three pages represent different stages of the video signal. The Edit page has two Viewers: the source Viewer shows the ungraded source video signal while the Timeline Viewer shows the signal after it is processed in the Fusion and Color pages. The Fusion page shows the ungraded video signal of a source or compound clip. The Color page shows all Edit and Fusion page effects, as well as the grading information.

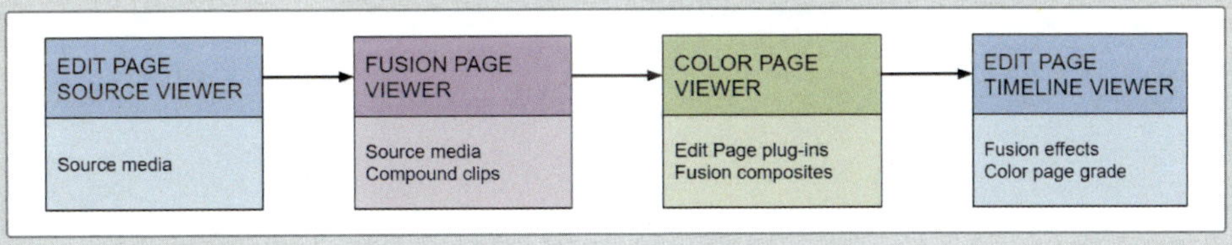

Creating a Finished Composite from Two Layers

Your next step is to clean up the placement, colors, and keys of both layers.

1 Enter the Color page.

> **TIP** If the sky is not visible behind the plane in the Viewer, click the unmix button in the lower-left of the Viewer to reenable visibility of edit page transitions, effects, and video layers.

2 In the Timeline, select the Sky_Stock image clip.

3 Open the Sizing palette, and adjust the Pan, Tilt, and Zoom values to fill the background with the sky image.

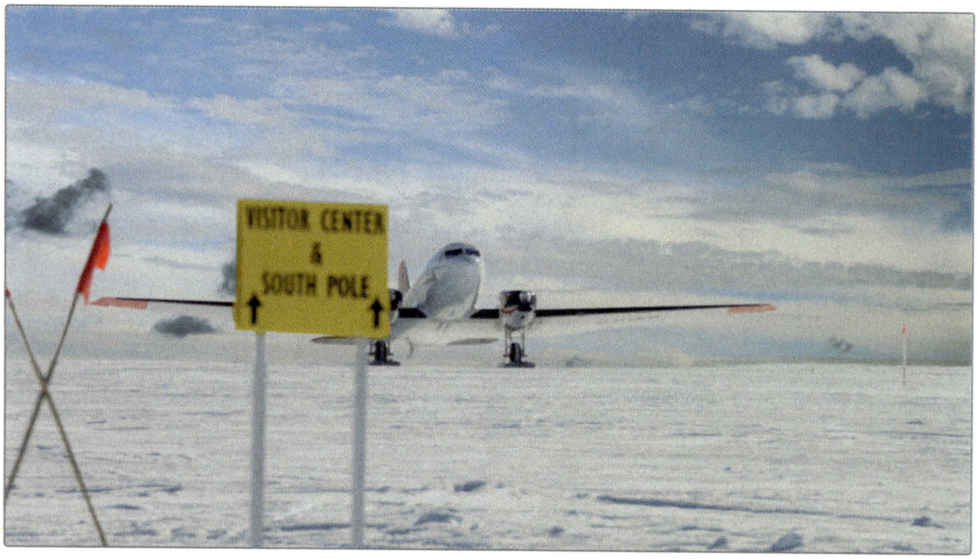

> **TIP** If an external matte does not match the timing of the action in a clip, you can adjust the matte timing in the Key palette. Select the Ext. Matte node, open the Key palette, and deselect lock matte. Doing so will reveal the Offset control with which you can offset the starting point of the matte.

Next, you will match the colors of the two layers to create a single neutral look for the environment.

4 Select the SOUTH_POLE clip (now identified as clip 08 in the Timeline).

5 Create a serial node after the Sky Removal node, and label it **Sky Match**. This node needn't interfere with the key output of the Sky Removal node that which continues to carry the necessary transparency data to the node tree output.

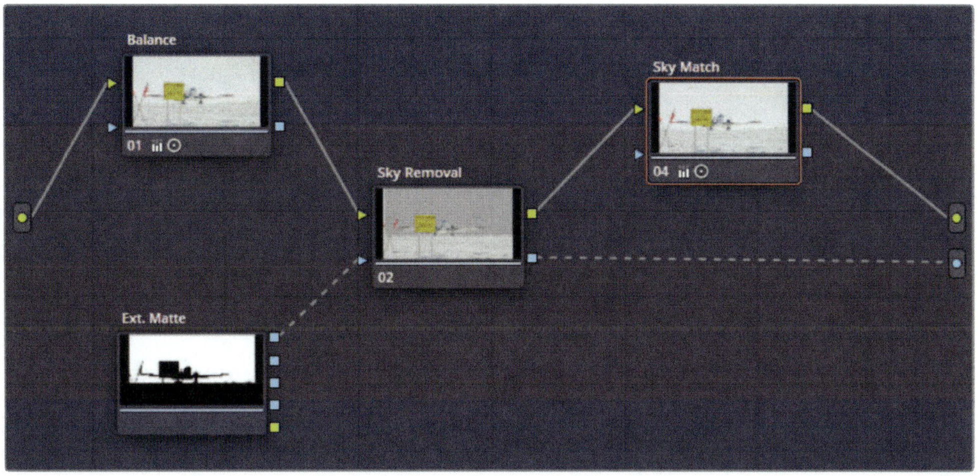

6 In the adjustment controls, increase the Contrast of the SOUTH_POLE plane footage, and drag the Offset wheel toward blue to cool it down.

You can make the sky look more realistic by blending it into the original video slightly. For that, you will need to adjust the matte key.

7 Click the Sky Removal node.

8 In the Key palette, drag the Key Output Offset to the right (0.300) to reintroduce some of the original sky into the composite.

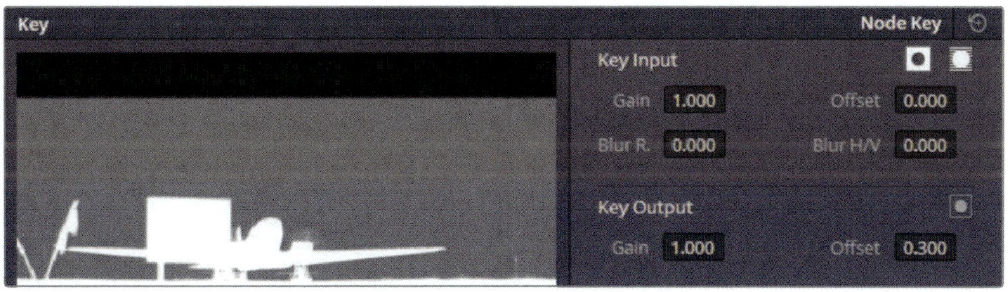

Performing a Match Move

Finally, you can match the movement of the sky to the pan of the camera in the plane shot.

1 With the Sky Match node selected, open the Window palette.

2 Create a circle window, and place it over the sign in the foreground to limit your grade to just the sign area. However, this is only a temporary window that is necessary for performing a track. You will disable it after the track data is extracted.

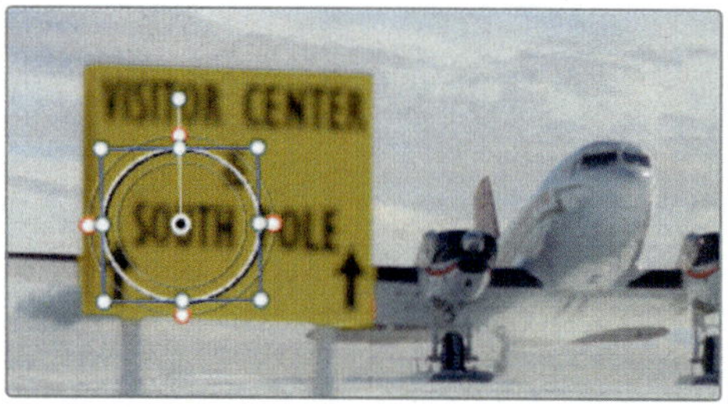

3 Open the Tracker palette.

4 Deselect the Tilt, Zoom, Rotate, and 3D parameters. This clip requires only a smooth track of the pan, so three-dimensional parameters will most likely interfere with the result.

5 Click analyze forward to perform a track of the camera pan.

6 When the track is complete, in the upper right of the palette, open the Tracker options menu, and choose Copy Track Data.

7 Go back to the Window palette, and click the circle button to disable it. The grade returns to the rest of your image and you now have the track data that you need to apply to the sky.

8 In the Timeline, click the Sky_Stock image clip.

9 Open the Tracker palette, and change the mode to Stabilizer.

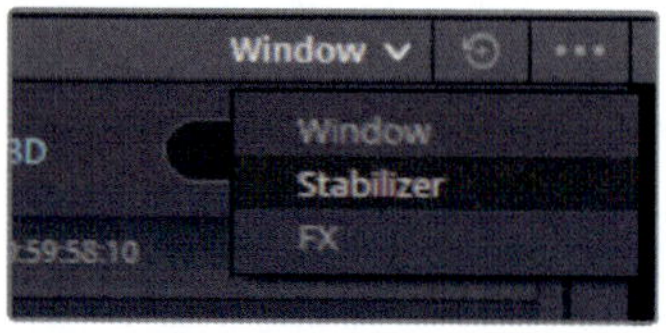

10 In the options menu of the Tracker palette, choose Classic Stabilizer. Doing so provides access to the Smooth and Strong controls of the stabilizer that are necessary for match moving.

11 Click the options menu of the Tracker palette again, and choose Paste Track Data.

You should see the Tracker graph fill up with the transform controls from the SOUTH_POLE clip track that you just generated and copied.

12 At the bottom of the palette, set Strong to -100 to invert the track data and apply it to the sky image, thereby creating the illusion of the sky moving with the foreground.

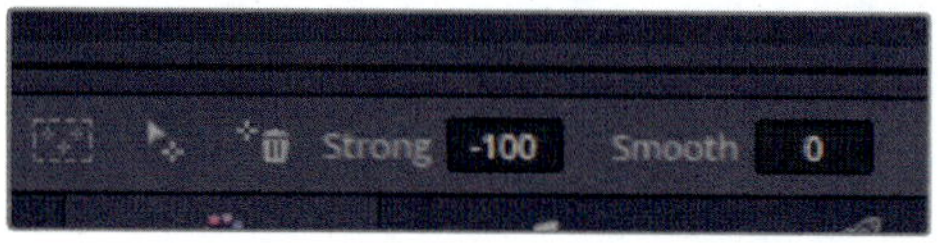

13 In the upper-right of the palette, click Stabilize to apply the tracking data. The sky is now tracked to the foreground image.

> **TIP** You can enter a Strong value of -95 to slightly offset the track on the background image, resulting in a more natural-looking parallax effect.

With the composite cleaned up, you can combine the two layers to continue treating them as a single clip.

14 Enter the Edit page.

15 Select both the SOUTH_POLE clip and the sky image underneath it.

16 Right-click either clip, and choose New Compound Clip. Name it **South Pole**.

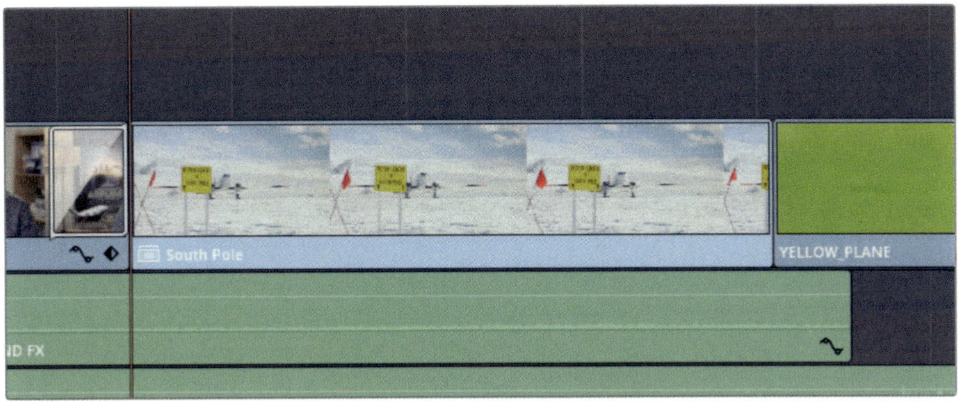

> **NOTE** Right-clicking a clip in the Timeline will also allow you to choose New Fusion Connect Clip. This choice will open Blackmagic Design's Fusion compositing software and allow you to assemble your image in a dedicated node-based compositing software. The link between the media will be live, and any changes applied in Fusion will translate to the clip in the Resolve Timeline.

17 Enter the Color page.

The South Pole clip has a blank node editor into which you can start applying a binding grade to make the composite truly look like a real image.

18 Label the first node **Look**, and tweak the colors to give the composite a colorful cyan look.

19 Create a second node called **Vignette**.

20 Open the Window palette. Instead of creating a new vignette from scratch, you can reuse the preset you saved in Lesson 3.

21 Click the options menu, and choose the Vignette preset.

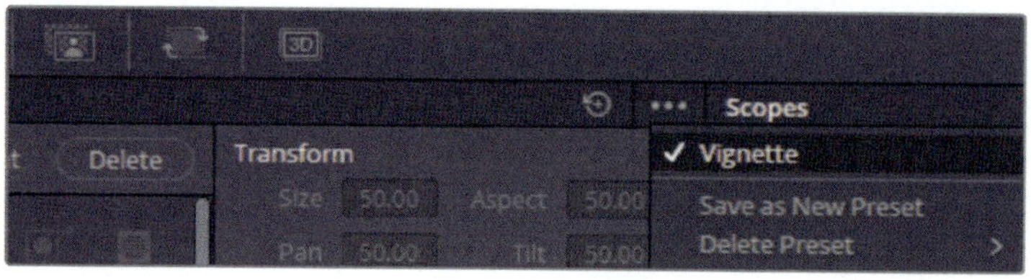

22 Use the Gamma master wheel to darken the edges of the frame.

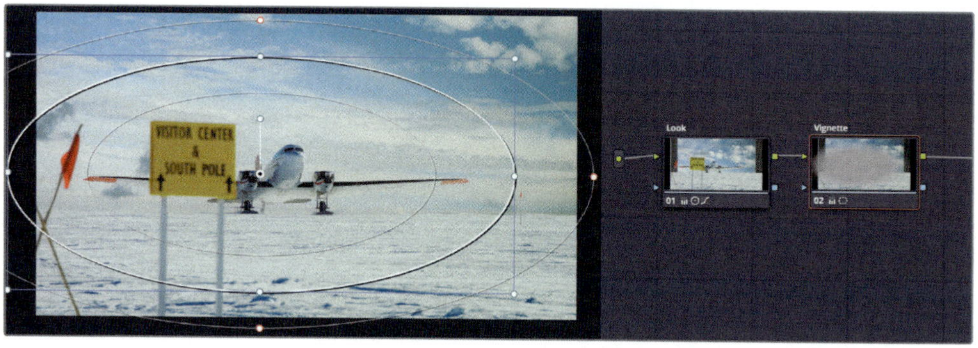

> **TIP** The two composited layers are still individually accessible by right-clicking the compound clip in the Edit page, and choosing Open in Timeline.

While extracting a portion of an image based on qualifier keys or mattes is generally straightforward, the real challenge is in assessing the end result and determining what you must do to achieve a realistic composite. It is helpful to write out a list of everything that looks unconvincing in the constructed image and address each item one at a time: shadows, color match, scaling, positioning, and so on.

The exercises in this lesson gave you an overview of the potential of the node editor. Though you've practiced a variety of possible workflows, there is ultimately no single correct way to utilize nodes in grading. Continue to practice using nodes for more advanced grading and you will soon arrive at your own preferred style. Above all, aim for the dual goals of workflow efficiency and the preservation of image quality.

Self-guided Exercise

Complete the following exercise in the Airplanes – 01 HQ Timeline to test your understanding of the tools and workflows covered in this lesson.

Clip 05—Find the external matte for this clip in the Project 02 – Age of Airplanes Trailer folder, and use it to retain the color of the poster in the background while making the rest of the image black and white.

When finished, combine the background and poster nodes via a Layer Mixer node and experiment with the blending modes to find more dramatic or subtle ways of integrating the colors of the poster into the black-and-white image.

When you've completed this exercise, you can open and view the Project 02 – Age of Airplanes Trailer COMPLETED.drp to compare your node construction on this clip with a finished version of the project.

Lesson Review

1 Can a Corrector node have multiple RGB inputs?

2 What are the blue symbols on either side of a node?

3 True or False? A node key can be connected to the input of a node that is in the same parallel or layer mixer stack.

4 In the Key palette, what does the Key Output Gain affect?

5 True or False? You can add additional RGB inputs to Mixer nodes.

Answers

1. No. A Corrector node can have only a single RGB input, though it can have multiple RGB (and key) outputs.
2. Key input and output
3. True. A node output (both RGB and key) can be linked to any other input further down the pipeline, as well as to other nodes in a mixer stack.
4. Opacity of the selected node
5. True. Right-click a mixer node to add more inputs.

Lesson 6

Managing Grades Across Clips and Timelines

Grading a film or video project requires a considerable level of attention to detail and the use of a variety of tools throughout both primary and secondary stages. However, once a look is established, a project often makes repeated use of existing grades that propagate throughout the Timeline. An obvious example of this is when you are working on multiple clips that come from the same source file, or clips used from different takes of the same shot.

DaVinci Resolve 16 includes a wide variety of workflows that help reproduce and refine grades across clips. These include a straightforward copy and paste, extraction of individual nodes for isolated adjustments, and even the migration of grades across different Timelines. In this lesson, you'll examine the variety of workflows you will need to efficiently copy and manage grades within a single project and beyond.

Time

This lesson takes approximately 45 minutes to complete.

Goals

Copying Grades from Clips and Stills

When copying grade data across clips or stills, you copy the entire node pipeline of the original clip. This pipeline includes all primary grading adjustments, secondary selections, mixers, external keys, and compound nodes. Because secondary selections, such as the qualifier and Power Windows, tend to be specific to the clip they were generated on, you need to double-check and adjust their accuracy before continuing with your grade.

In the previous lesson, you applied a grade from a still in the gallery. You can perform the same action using current clips in your Timeline.

1. Open Project 02 - Age of Airplanes Trailer.
2. Enter the Color page.
3. In the Airplanes - 01 HQ Timeline, click clip 05. Selected clips are always the target when copying grading data.
4. Right-click clip 01, and choose Apply Grade.

   The node pipeline from the first interview clip is copied to the selected clip 05, overwriting any previous nodes. The clip-specific face tracking in the Skin Tone node (04) was not migrated, which gives you the opportunity to perform a new track to the new face motion in clip 05. However, if you ever do want to retain the original track data when copying grades, in the Tracker palette options menu, you can choose Copy Track Data and Paste Track Data across clips.

   Another useful tip when copying grades between clips and stills is to use your middle mouse button, if available.
5. Click clip 04.
6. In the Gallery, open the Base Grades album.
7. Middle-click the 1.4.1. Balance still.

   This simple motion transfers the still's balance grade to clip 04.

> **TIP** Press = (equals sign) to apply the grade prior to your selected clip. Press – (minus) to apply the grade from two clips prior. This second keyboard shortcut is ideal for scenes shot on two cameras or for interviews in which you need to frequently reuse the grade from two cuts previous.

In the next exercise, you will build upon the grade in clip 04 and start to experiment with different looks using local versions.

Working with Local Versions

Versions enable you to associate multiple grades with a single clip in a Timeline. You can use versions to preserve a grade at earlier stages of the grading process, or when creating a series of shot-grading options to share with a creative supervisor for selection and approval. Each version remains intact and can be recalled when needed. Versions are easily accessible in the contextual menu of each clip and can be created, deleted, bypassed, and switched between local and remote.

In this exercise, you will begin by creating a new grade on a clip, and then apply preexisting grades from the Gallery to quickly build up a set of local versions.

1 In the Airplanes - 01 HQ Timeline, continue to work on clip 04.

2 For a better representation of the clip's content, drag the playhead to the middle of the clip where the plane is in view.

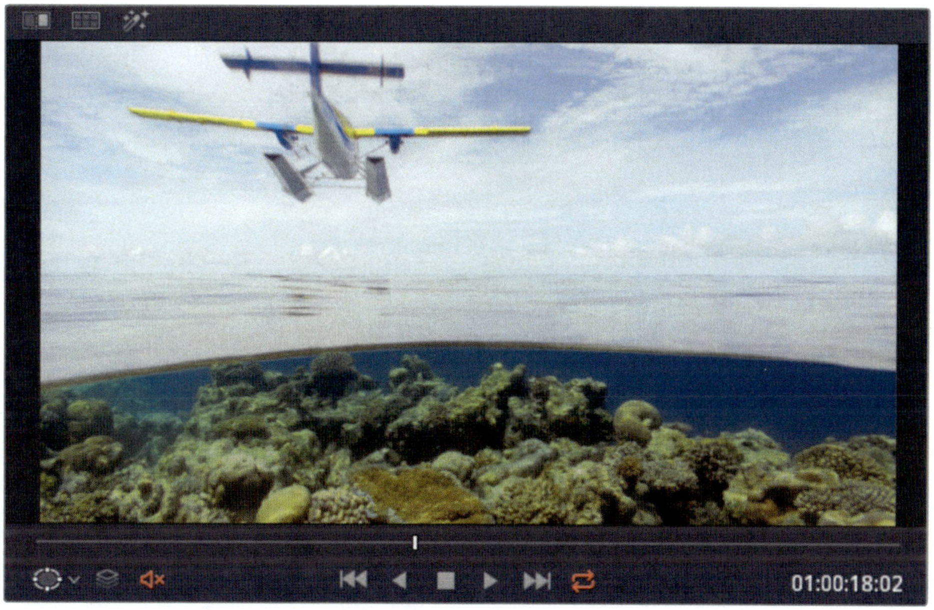

3 Create a second node labelled **Cross Process**.

4 Open the Custom curves palette. To create a cross-process look, you will want to push opposing complementary colors into the image highlights and shadows. This tends to result in a retro film camera look.

5 Click the YRGB link to ungang the channels.

6 Isolate the blue channel, and drag the black point up to turn the shadows blue. Then drag the white point down to turn the highlights yellow.

7 Isolate the red channel, and create control points in its lower and upper midtones. Drag them into an s-curve, thereby pushing cyan into the shadows and red into the highlights.

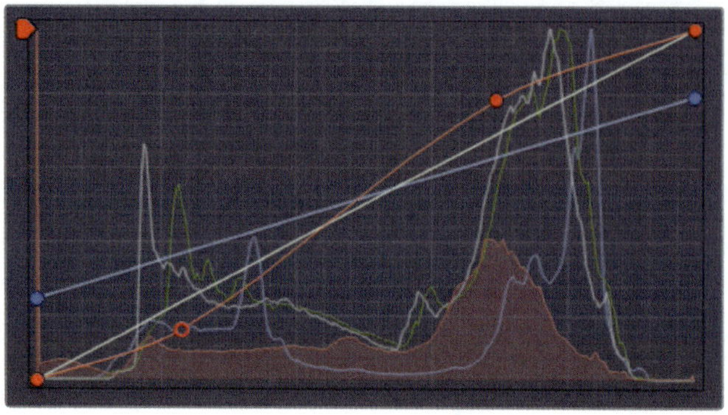

8 Create a new serial node 03, and label it **Contrast**.

9 In the adjustment controls of the Color Wheel palette, increase the contrast of the image (1.200), and use the pivot to reduce the strong exposure in the sky (0.600).

You have now successfully created the first look for this shot. By default, every clip begins as Local Version 1. You can rename the version to identify a specific look or purpose of a grade.

10 In the Timeline, right-click the clip 04 thumbnail, and under Local Versions, choose Version 1 > Rename.

11 Enter the name **Cross process**, and click OK.

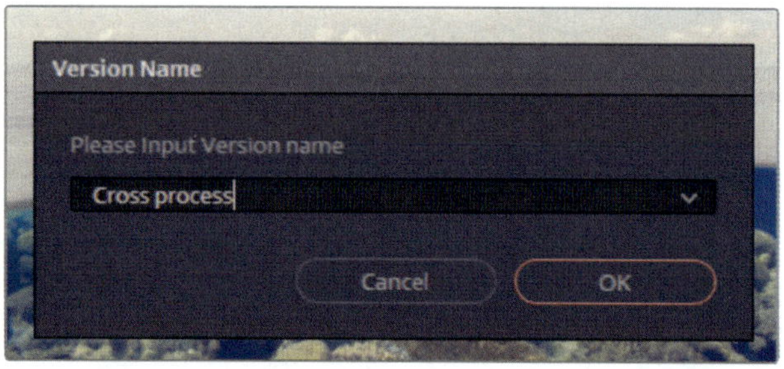

You will be applying several variants of grades on this clip. Each variant will be designated as a new local version. To save time, you will use the preexisting grades in the Clip 04 grades album of the gallery.

12 Right-click clip 04, and choose Local Versions > Create New Version. Enter the name **Bleach bypass**.

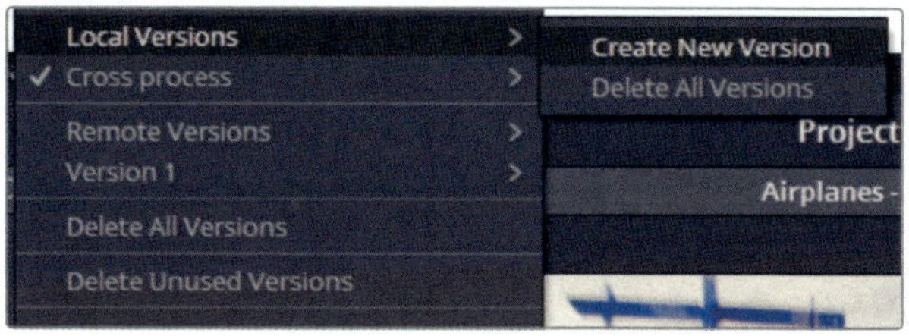

13 Reset the cross process grade by choosing Color > Reset All Grades and Nodes, or press Cmd-Home (macOS) or Ctrl-Home (Windows).

This is a necessary step if you want to start with a fresh clip every time you design a new look. Otherwise, you can continue tweaking the image using the previous grade's settings.

14 In the Clip 04 grades album, middle-click the Bleach bypass still to apply the grade.

> **TIP** When you hover over the stills in the Gallery, a preview of their grades will appear over the clip in the Viewer. To disable or change Live Preview behavior, click the three dot options menu in the upper-right corner of the Gallery. Click Live Preview to disable it, or move your mouse pointer over Hover Scrub Preview to choose if the image will scrub in the Viewer and Thumbnail, Thumbnail only, or neither.

15 To make another version, right-click the clip again, and choose Local Versions > Create New Version. Enter the name **Simple pop**.

You could reset the grade again, but because you are simply overwriting the current grade with the still grade, that will not be necessary.

16 In the Clip 04 grades album, middle-click the Simple Pop still to apply the grade.

> **TIP** Press Cmd-Y (macOS) or Ctrl-Y (Windows) to create a new version in a clip.

17 Right-click clip 04, and choose Local Versions > Create New Version. Enter the name **Navy blue**.

18 In the Clip 04 grades album, middle-click the Navy blue still to apply the grade.

Having created a series of versions, you can now compare them in the Viewer using a split-screen display.

19 At the top of the Viewer, between the Image Wipe and Highlight buttons, click the Split Screen button.

20 In the upper-right corner of the Viewer, choose Version.

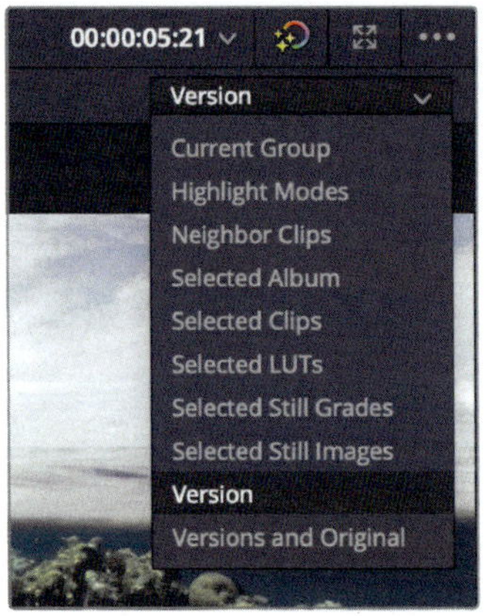

The split-screen view is enabled, displaying all four grades in a grid in the Viewer.

Comparing the versions might be difficult at the moment because they have been scaled-down to fit into the small Viewer window. You can resize the Viewer for full-screen playback and optimal viewing.

21 Choose Workspace > Viewer Mode > Cinema Viewer, or press Cmd-F (macOS) or Ctrl-F (Windows).

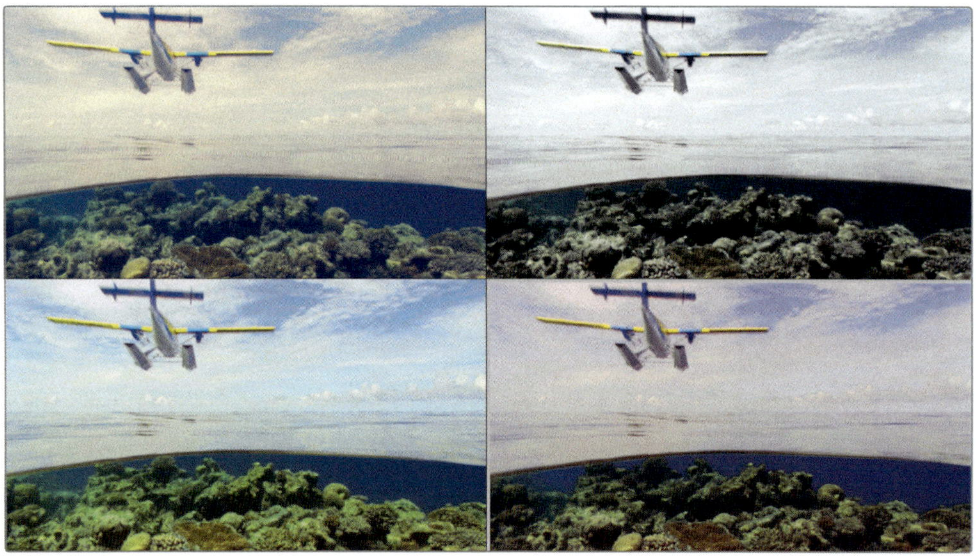

In the next few exercises, you will apply the cross process look to other clips in the Timeline.

22 In the upper-left corner of the split-screen view, double-click the Cross process version to select it.

23 Press Esc to exit the full-screen mode.

24 Right-click in the Viewer, and choose Split Screen > On/Off to disable the split-screen view, or click the Split Screen button above the Viewer.

TIP Press Cmd-B or Cmd-N (macOS), or Ctrl-B or Ctrl-N (Windows) to cycle through the versions of a clip in the Viewer.

Remote Versions

In the contextual menu, under the Local Versions options, you may have noticed a similar section for Remote Versions. This area offers another method of retaining multiple grades in a clip.

Remote versions are different from local versions in two ways: first, when a clip is graded within a remote version, its grade affects all other Timeline clips that were derived from the same source clip; and second, the grade appears on all subsequent uses of the source clip in all other Timelines of the active project (provided that the clips in those Timelines are also using remote versions).

One popular application for remote version grading is for a DIT (digital imaging technician) using master Timeline workflows. Upon ingesting, you can place all the media on a remote Timeline and apply preliminary grading to the clips. When you eventually create a cut in the Edit page or migrate an editor's Timeline, those remote grades automatically transfer to the new Timeline. In short, local version grades are applied on a Timeline basis, whereas remote versions are applied on a project basis.

Appending Grades and Nodes

In the previous exercise, you applied stills grades to a clip by choosing the Apply Grade contextual menu option, or pressing the middle button of your mouse. Doing so overwrites the existing grade on a clip and replaces it with the entire node tree of the copied grade. At times, you will want to apply just portions of a node tree, or add the node tree after a clip has undergone balancing or matching.

The following exercises will show you how to be selective in copying grade nodes.

1 Click clip 02 on the Airplanes – 01 HQ Timeline. You will be applying the cross process grade to this clip.

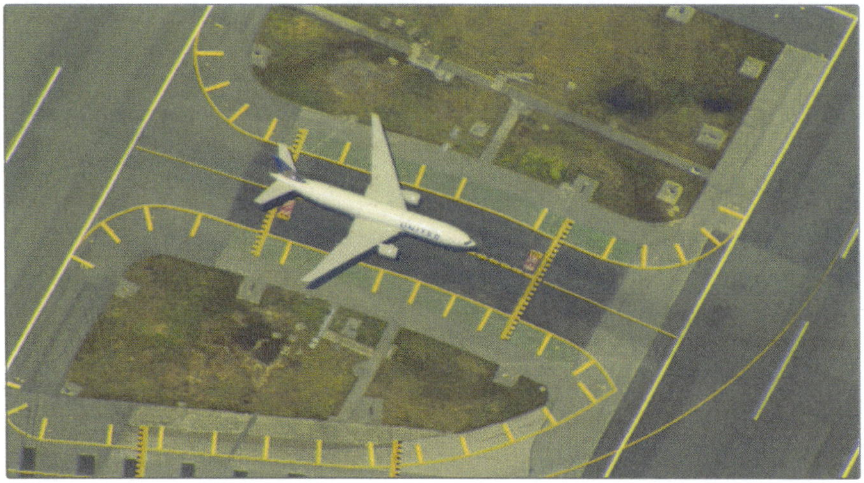

Clip 02 had its gamut remapped, but is currently unbalanced with a strong yellow tint. You could normalize and balance it, but that would not necessarily optimize it for the cross process grade. As you learned in Lesson 2, clips must be matched to share grade data accurately. Without matching, grading tools will behave unpredictably and the differences between the clips will continue to be obvious.

A match was already prepared for this exercise.

2 Open the Base grades album, and apply the 1.2.1. Match still to the clip. To more closely match 04, the highlights are neutralized, and the contrast increased.

3 Open the Clip 04 grades album.

A cross process grade is already prepared and stored in the gallery. If you directly apply the cross process still from the gallery, it will overwrite the base grade (gamut map and match nodes) that you just applied to the clip. Instead, you will append the cross process grade to the current node graph.

4 Right-click the 1.4.1 Cross process still, and choose Append Node graph.

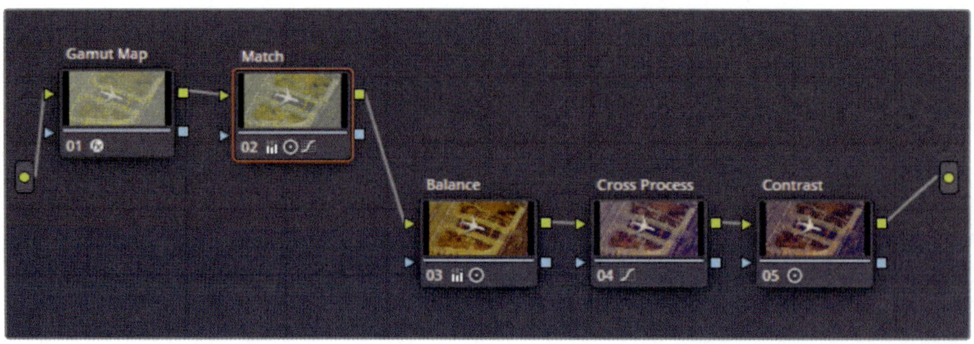

TIP You can also drag a still from the gallery onto a connection line in the node graph to append it to an existing grade.

Clip 02 now has its original gamut map and match nodes followed by the cross process pipeline. However, the grade still does not look right. By appending the grade, you added all the nodes from the original cross process grade, included the original Balance node that was created specifically for clip 04. That node does not work in the context of clip 02 and should be deleted.

5 Select node 03 Balance, and press the Delete or Backspace key.

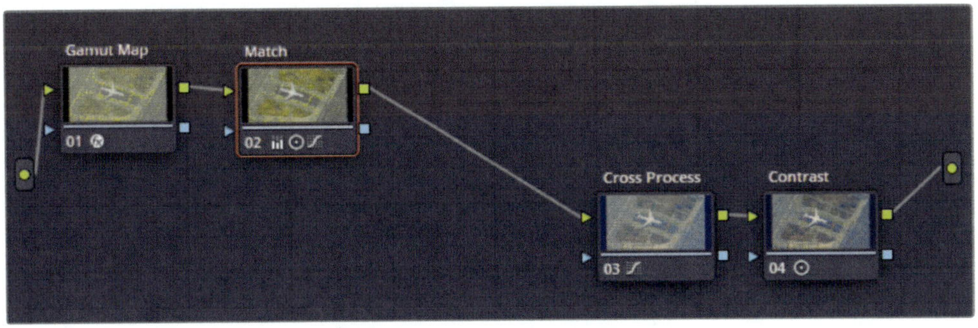

You now have a clean cross process look on the second airplane shot that more closely resembles the one in clip 04. You'll apply this same look to a third shot, but without the Balance or Contrast nodes.

Copying Individual Nodes from a Still

So far, you have used all of the the grading data stored within stills. You copied and appended the entire node pipeline to the Node editor, and tweaked the nodes based on the clips' needs.

However, you also have access to a still's node graph while it is still in the gallery. This ability allows you to apply very specific adjustments from a saved grade.

1 Click clip 03 on Airplanes – 01 HQ Timeline.

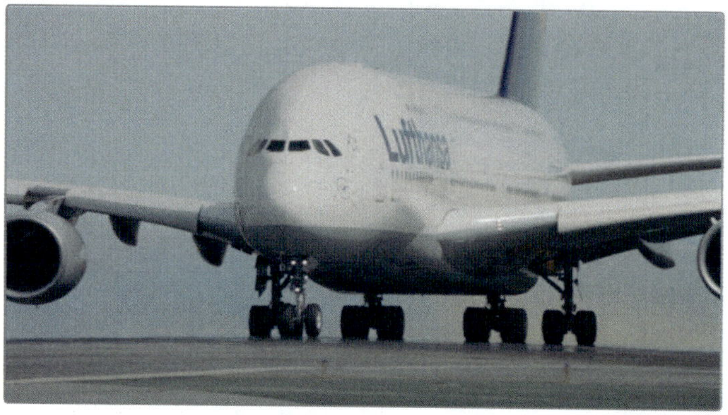

This clip looks relatively neutral but is distinctly different from the starting looks of clips 02 and 04. As in the previous exercise, you will apply a match still to prepare it for the cross process look.

2 Open the Base grades album, and apply the 1.3.1. Match and Contrast still to the clip.

Doing so significantly alters the look of the clip but is vital for ensuring a good base for the incoming grade. The Match node is there to mimic the yellow tint of clip 02, while the Contrast node addresses the stark difference in location and shot angle to more closely match the final luminance ranges of clips 02 and 04.

You can now proceed to apply the cross process grade. Because the clip is balanced and already has correct contrast, you need only to transfer the Cross Process node itself.

3 Open the Clip 04 grades album, right-click the 1.4.1 Cross process still, and choose Display Node Graph.

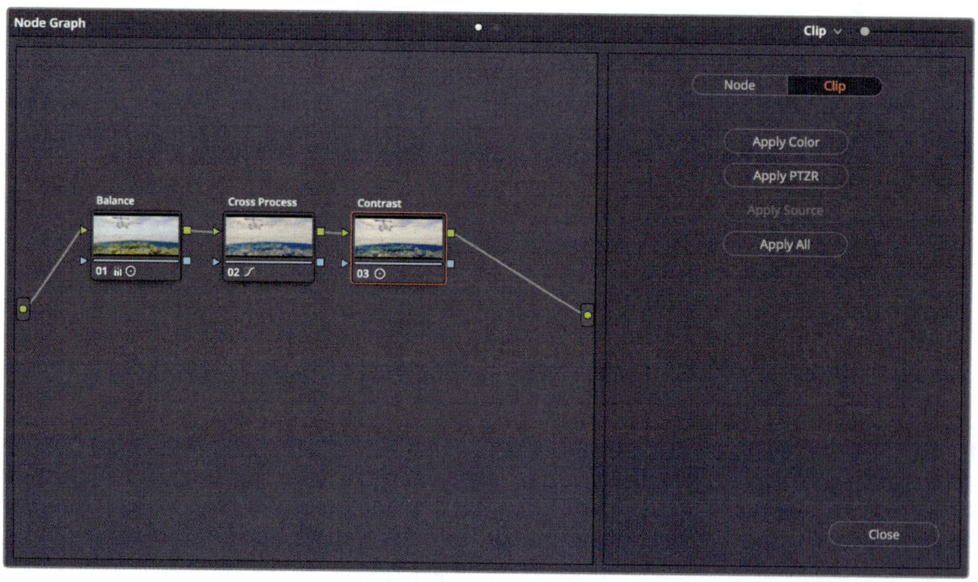

The node graph appears in a separate window with the node pipeline of the grade as it appeared in the node editor when the still was generated. To the right of the window, a tabbed interface allows you to apply only the color or sizing adjustments of the node graph (PTZR: pan, tilt, zoom, rotation). A button at the top allows you to switch to a node-based refinement of the parameters that you will include during copying.

4 From the still's node graph window, drag node 02 cross process to the Node editor of clip 03. While holding down the mouse button, position the pointer over the connection link between node 01, Match and node 02, Contrast.

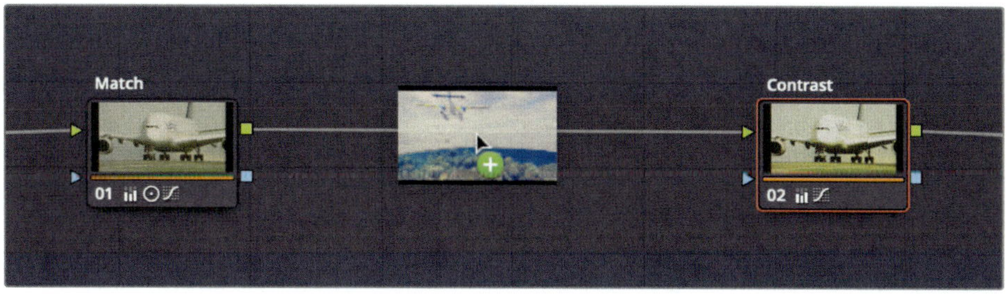

A + (plus sign) will appear over the link to signify that you can release the mouse button and attach the Cross Process node between Match and Contrast.

5 In the still's node graph window, click Close.

Having access to the node structure of every still facilitates cleaner, more precise workflows. You separate the primary balance and match nodes from the contrast and creative look nodes, and copy only what is necessary for every new clip grade. As with all grading, you should tweak and refine the grades to ensure maximum visual quality and similarity.

Using Shared Nodes Across Multiple Clips

As mentioned previously, color grading is often an iterative process. After establishing an initial grade, you will often return to earlier nodes to make additional tweaks. When unifying a look across multiple clips, minor adjustments can become extremely time consuming as you manually copy node data between clips, each with its own individual node structure.

DaVinci Resolve provides several tools and techniques to simplify this tweaking process as much as possible. Among those tools are shared nodes that allow you to link and lock a single node across multiple clips. In this exercise, you will create a Shared node across three clips and change their collective look with a single adjustment.

1 Click clip 02 on Airplanes – 01 HQ Timeline.

2 In the Node editor, right-click node 02 Cross Process, and choose Save as Shared Node.

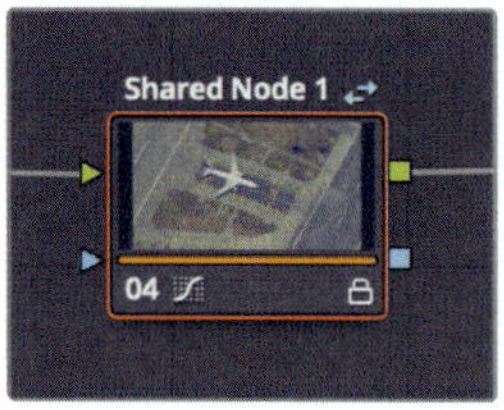

The node now features a pair of blue arrows to indicate its status as a Shared node. Additionally, an icon in the lower-right corner shows that the node is locked.

3 By default, the node is renamed to Shared Node 1. Right-click and choose Node Label to rename the node to **Cross Look**.

Before making changes to this grade, let's assign the shared node to clips 03 and 04.

4 Click clip 03.

5 In the Node editor, right-click node 02 Cross Process, and choose Add Node > Cross Look.

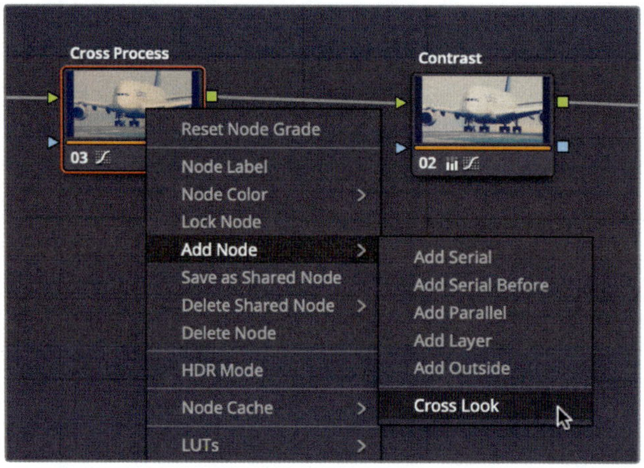

The Cross Look shared node is added after node 03, thereby doubling the effect of the cross process grade.

6 Select node 03 Cross Process, and press Backspace to remove it.

7 Click clip 04, and repeat steps 5 and 6 to replace its existing cross process node with the shared node. The three clips now share the Cross Look node.

8 While still on clip 04, right-click the shared node (03 Cross Look), and choose Lock Node to disable the lock.

9 In the Custom curves palette, ensure that the channels are unganged.

10 Right-click the two s-curve points on the red channel to delete them.

11 Drag the black point of the Y channel right to darken the shadows of the image.

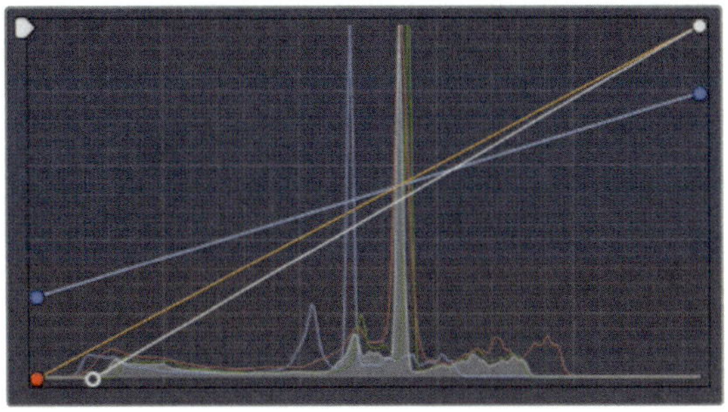

Doing so has the effect of reducing the colorful cross process look while maintaining a similar retro film appearance.

12 Click clips 02 and 03 to verify that the adjustment was copied to these clips.

13 Right-click the shared node on any of the clips, and choose Lock Node to prevent accidental changes.

Let's now add a vignette to a new node on all three clips.

14 In the Node editor, select the last node on clip 02, and press Option-S (macOS) or Alt-S (Windows) to add a new node.

15 Right-click node 05, and choose Save as Shared Node.

16 Label node 05 as **Vignette**, and unlock it.

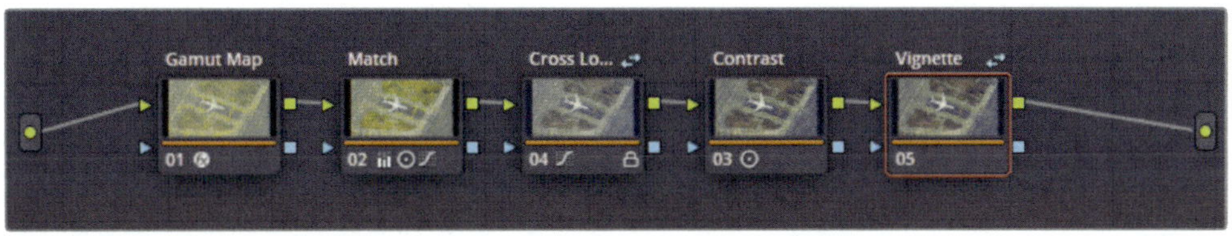

17 Open the Window palette, and apply the Vignette preset.

18 Drag down the Gamma master wheel to darken the edges of the frame.

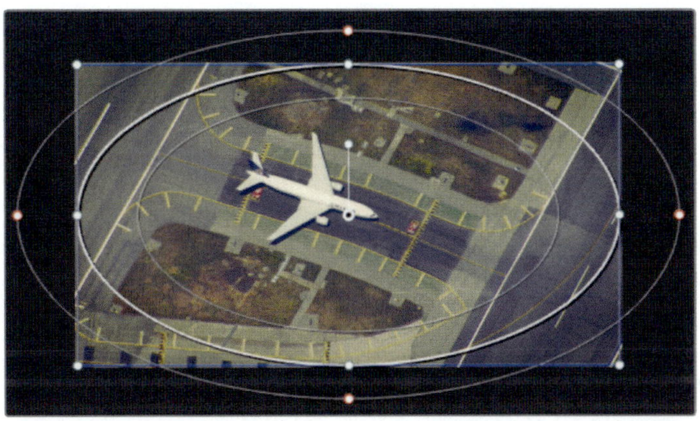

19 With clip 02 still selected in the Timeline, Shift-click clip 04 to select clips 02, 03, and 04 sequentially. The selection is indicated by a red highlight in the Timeline.

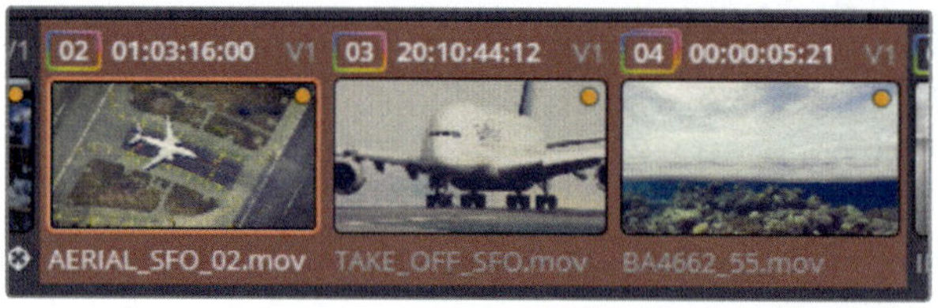

20 Choose Color > Append Node to Selected Clips.

Doing so adds the selected Vignette node to the end of the pipeline of all the selected clips on the Timeline. This action is often used to copy a look across multiple clips, but it can be even more effective when appending a shared node, which you can continue to use for future adjustments.

Shared nodes behave similarly to regular Corrector nodes, which makes them easy to use across a variety of grading and organizational workflows. You can copy and paste shared nodes using keyboard shortcuts, retain them when switching between versions, and even save them in the pipelines of Gallery stills.

TIP You can create an ungraded (but fully labeled) node pipeline and save it as a still to use as a template for future grades. Shared nodes can be preemptively included in preset pipelines to ensure that creative grades are automatically applied across all clips when grading.

Saving Grades for Other Projects

The stills contained in the gallery albums of the Color page will ordinarily be accessible only in the project. A different kind of gallery album, the PowerGrade, makes stills accessible to all other projects generated by the same user (and within the same database) on a workstation.

1 In the Still Albums list of the Gallery, open the Clip 04 grades album.

2 Drag the **Bleach bypass** still to the PowerGrade 1 album at the bottom of the list.

3 Click the PowerGrade 1 album to view its contents. The Bleach bypass will now appear in the PowerGrade 1 album of all the projects you create on your current workstation.

The Gallery panel also has additional features contained in its expanded version.

4 In the upper-right corner of the Gallery, click the Gallery View button.

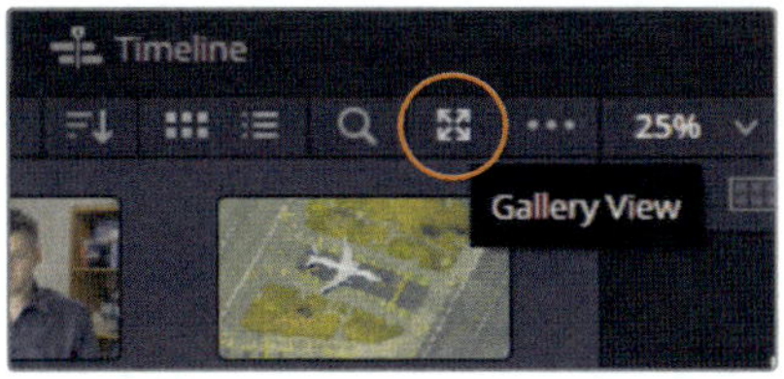

A separate window opens displaying the full contents of the gallery.

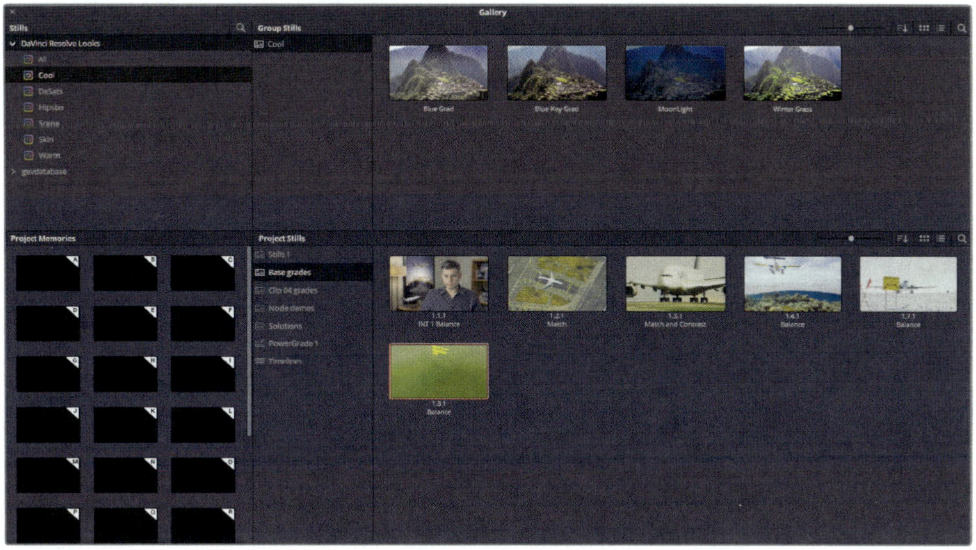

The Stills panel in the upper-left features a collection of DaVinci Resolve looks and provides access to stills from other databases and projects on the same workstation. The Group Stills panel next to it displays the stills associated with the album that is currently selected.

At the bottom is the current project's gallery panel, and to the left is the Project Memories panel in which you can designate shortcuts to frequently used stills.

TIP To save a still as a memory, drag it from the gallery onto one of the memory slots. You can apply these memories to clips on the Timeline using shortcuts that correspond to the letter of the memory as expressed numerically. For example, memory B will have the shortcut Cmd-2 (macOS) or Ctrl-2 (Windows).

5 In the lower-half of the full Gallery window, select the PowerGrade 1 album.

6 In the DaVinci Resolve Looks list, select the Skin album, and drag the Diffused still into the Powergrade 1 album in the Project Stills window below.

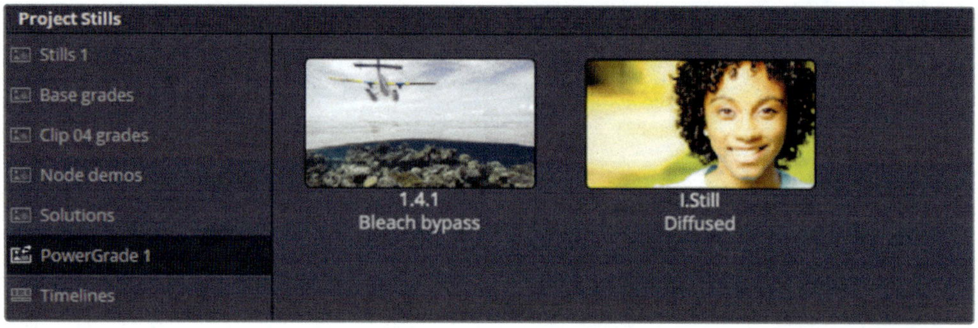

You've now moved one of the preset stills into the Gallery and will be able to apply it to the current project.

7 Close the Gallery view.

8 In Airplanes – 01 HQ Timeline, choose the South Pole compound clip 07.

9 Right-click and create a new local version called **Diffused**.

10 Right-click the Diffused still, and choose Apply Grade.

> **TIP** You can double-click a PowerGrade still to apply the grade to a selected clip on the Timeline.

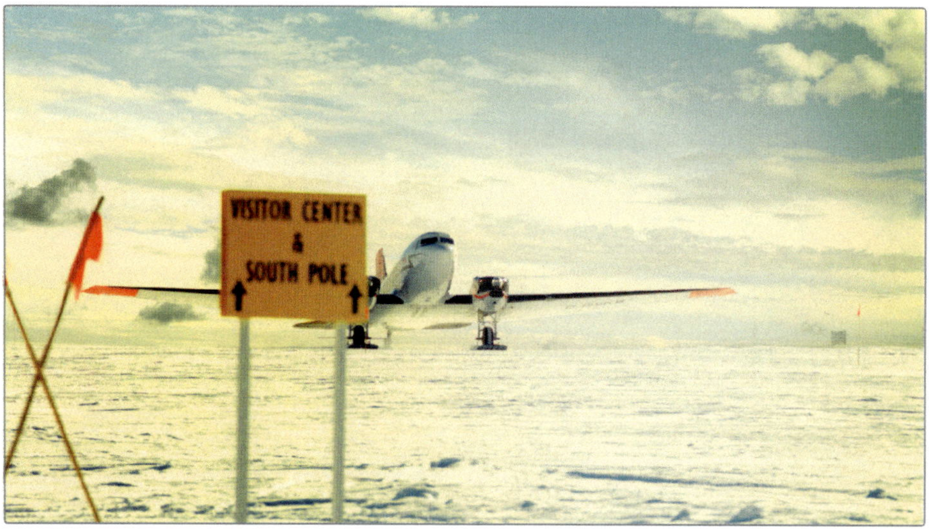

Outside of using databases and PowerGrade albums, you can also share grades across different workstations by exporting them from the gallery.

11 In the Gallery, open the Clip 04 grades album, and right-click the 1.4.1. Cross process still.

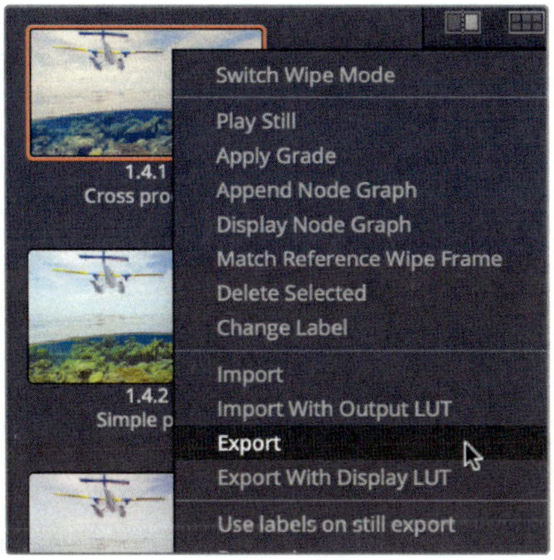

12 In the pop-up menu, choose Export.

The still's visual and grading information is exported and contained in two files. The DPX file format is an image format used for comparison and review. The DRX file contains the node tree and grading data. You need both files to migrate stills with grade information.

13 Indicate a location on your workstation, create one folder for the two files, and label it **Airport cross process**. Click Export.

14 Open a file browser on your computer, and locate the two files.

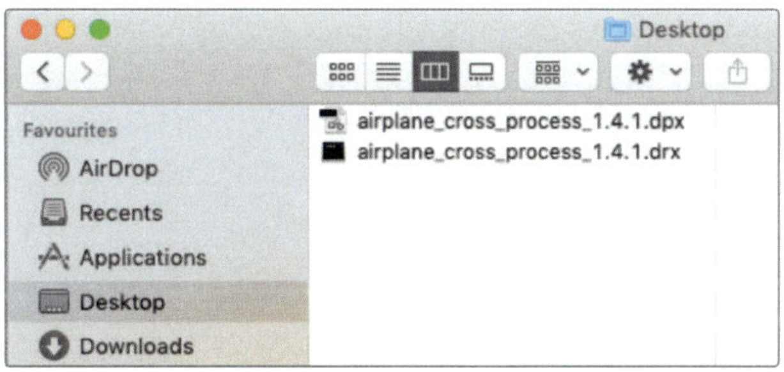

You can share the DPX file as you would any regular image file without the need for Resolve. The DRX file is a DaVinci Resolve exchange file used to carry the grading parameters for the shot and can only be used together with the DPX. To import a grade into a new Resolve project, both files must be located in the same folder or directory.

Let's import a grade that was created for one of the clips on the Timeline.

15 Return to the Color page, and in the Gallery, open the PowerGrade 1 album.

16 Right-click and choose Import.

17 In the file browser, locate the BMD 16 CC – Project 02 folder, and navigate to Other > Stills.

18 Select Punchy film_1.9.1.dpx, and click Import.

Note that only the DPX file is visible in the Resolve file browser, even though the DRX file is located in the same folder. The DRX file is bound to the DPX and its grading data will be included in the still upon import.

19 Apply the Punchy film grade to clip 09 (HAWAIIAN_LANDING) in the Timeline.

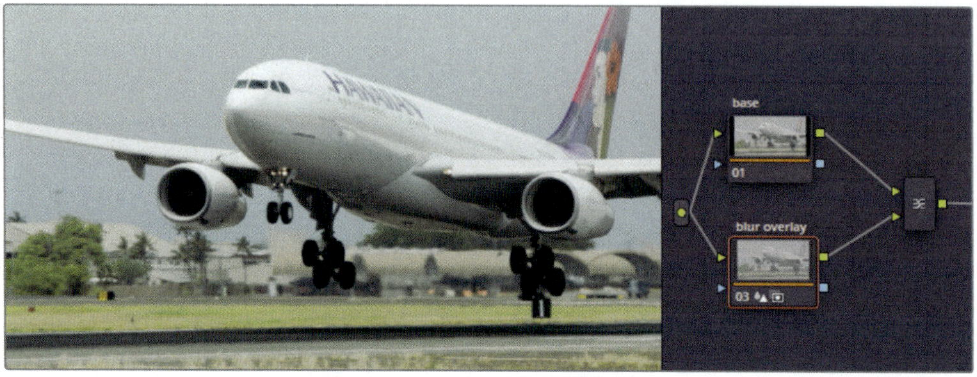

NOTE Selecting "Export with Display LUT" will export the DPX and DRX files in a format that is supported by monitoring applications. You can upload these files to camera Viewers or monitor displays.

Here are some additional options for working with the Gallery and stills that many colorists employ for organizational and practical purposes:

- **Right-click in the Viewer, and choose Grab All Stills.** Doing so will generate a still for each clip in the Timeline (either from the first or middle frame) and place them in the media pool. Colorists use this option to keep track of their grade process over time (day 1, day 2, and so on) or separate the stills into pass bins (balance, match, secondary, and so on).
- **Right-click in the Gallery, and choose One Still Per Scene.** This choice will restrict the number of stills you generate from any given clip to a single still. This popular option is for colorists who frequently grab stills of their clips while grading and do not want their Galleries to become cluttered with thumbnails.

Copying Timeline Grades using ColorTrace

ColorTrace is a feature in DaVinci Resolve that enables the transfer of grading information from one Timeline to another. It is a much faster and more organized method of copying mass grade data than using stills.

One scenario in which you may use ColorTrace is when multiple project types use the same source materials (film, trailer, teaser, behind-the-scenes, and so on). Another scenario is when an editor creates changes in a Timeline that a colorist has already begun grading. In both cases, a major task would usually await the colorist: a still would need to be created for each clip in the old Timeline and then carefully re-applied to each corresponding clip on the new Timeline. This job is full of error potential because an overworked colorist might have to generate, organize, and retrack dozens (or hundreds) of stills in the Gallery.

ColorTrace bypasses all that by presenting two Timelines side-by-side and helping the colorist identify where their common media is located. The colorist then needs only to confirm (or deny) that the media is correct, and the transference of grading data is instantaneous.

1 Enter the Edit page, and in the media pool, open the Timelines bin.
2 Choose File > Import Timeline > Import AAF, EDL, XML.
3 Navigate to the Project 02 – Age of Airplanes Trailer folder, open the XML subfolder, and select Airplanes – 02 Color trace Timeline.xml. Click Open to import it.
4 In the Load XML window, deselect the option to Automatically import source clips into the media pool, and click OK.

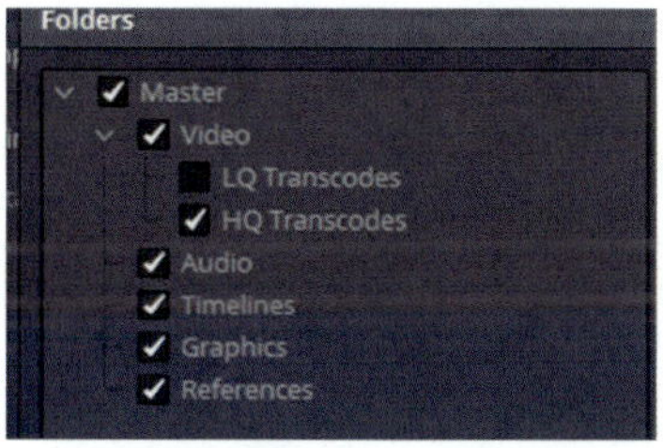

A pop-up window will prompt you to indicate the bins where the Timeline's media are contained.

5 Expand the bin structure, and deselect the LQ Transcodes bin to ensure that the media is linked only to the high-quality versions of the clips. Click OK.

NOTE If any media does not appear on the Timeline, it is possible that the corresponding HQ clip is not in the media pool. Enter the Media page, and drag any remaining clips from the Media storage HQ Transcodes folder into the media pool HQ Transcodes bin. Remember to set the Input Color Space to Project to ensure they are correctly remapped.

The Airplanes - 02 Color Trace edit will appear in the Timeline panel of the Edit page. The orange color of the clips informs you that they are from the HQ Transcodes bin.

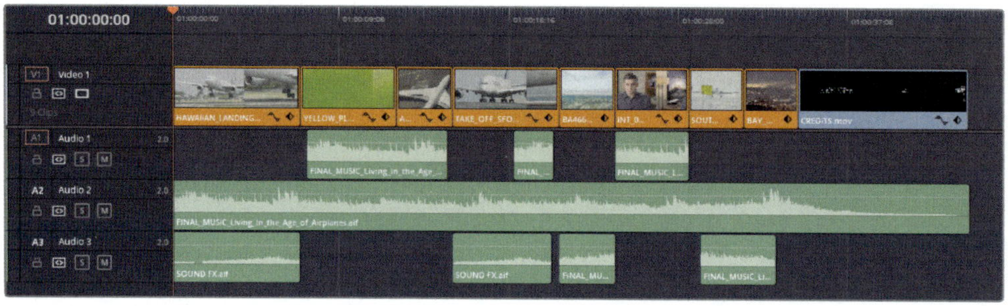

6 Enter the Color page to check the grade status of the clips.

None of the grades applied to the Airplanes – 01 HQ Timeline were transferred.

7 Return to the Edit page.

8 In the media pool, right-click the Airplane – 02 Color Trace Timeline, and choose Timelines > ColorTrace > ColorTrace from Timeline.

9 In the ColorTrace Setup window, expand the Local Database folder and locate Airplanes – 01 HQ Timeline.

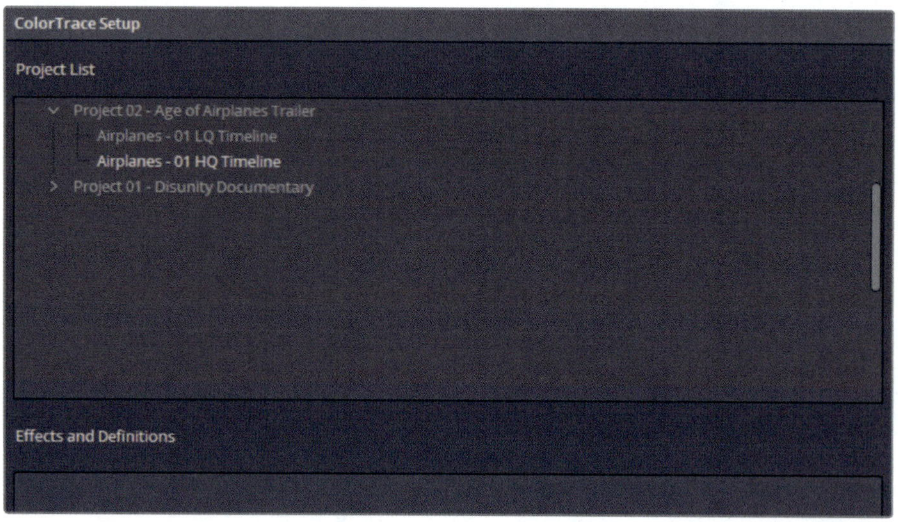

Effects and Definitions

The Effects and Definitions panel underneath the Project list enables you to define a set of naming conventions for clips in the Timeline with names that were changed since the original Timeline versions.

An example is applying this feature in VFX workflows. Assume that the original filenames of two Timeline clips were car.mov and sky.mov. Both clips were sent to the VFX department for some compositing work. The VFX department returns the finished composites under the names car_vfx.mov and sky_vfx. mov, and they are inserted into a new version of the Timeline. When ColorTrace is used to transfer the grading data from the original Timeline, the two VFX clips are not recognized due to their new filenames. By entering *_vfx* in the Effects and Definitions panel, Resolve can exempt the suffix when associating the media between the Timelines.

10 Select the HQ Timeline, and click Continue to proceed to the ColorTrace interface.

At the top of the interface, you'll find options to switch between the Automatic and Manual modes of the feature.

Automatic attempts to locate the same clips used in both Timelines based on source name, regardless of any change in position or trim.

Manual allows you to identify matched clips by selecting them yourself. Using this method, you can assign grades when the original filenames or metadata were changed between edits.

The bottom of the interface provides additional information and control over the copy parameters. To the left is a table that compares the metadata of the source and target clips, which is useful when comparing the file paths of two clips to ensure that they are derived from the same take. To the right is a list of criteria that will be included or removed during the grade transfer.

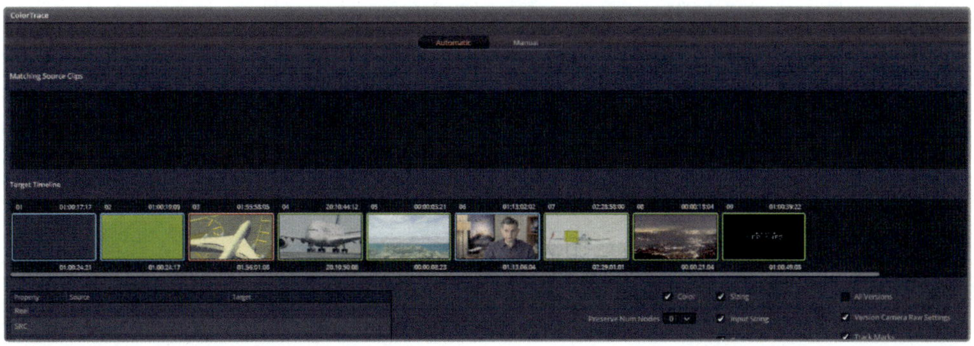

The clips in the Target Timeline have colored outlines that indicate the grade match status of the clips:

- **Red**—No match was found.
- **Blue**—Multiple potential matches were found.
- **Green**—A match was found.

You will need to review the Target Timeline to ensure that the matches are accurate.

> **TIP** Select Hide Matched Clips at the bottom of the interface to remove all clips that are already matched in the Timeline. Doing so will allow you to focus on the clips with no matches or conflicting matches.

11 Clip 01 on the Target Timeline has a blue outline. Select it to see which clips are proposed as possible options in the Matching Source Clips list above it.

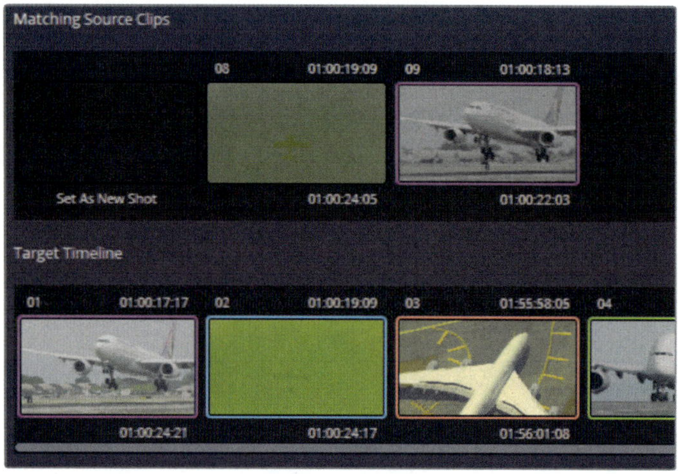

Clip 01 clearly corresponds to the clip numbered as 09 in the source clips window.

12 Double-click clip 09 to confirm the match. Both clips' outlines will turn magenta to confirm the selection.

13 Clip 02 also has a blue outline. Select it, and double-click the corresponding clip 08 above to confirm the correct match.

14 Clip 03 has a red outline and offers no options in the Matching Source Clips list. You will address this clip manually after first confirming the automatic matches.

> **NOTE** You can choose Set As New Shot to identify clips with no links to the original Timeline. They will appear ungraded after the ColorTrace is performed.

15 Clip 06 has a blue outline. Click it to reveal two identical-looking clips.

Check the metadata in the lower-left columns to verify that both clips come from the same source. The REC timecode of source clip 06 is nearer to the timecode of the target clip. Usually, this implies that the same trimmed media is in different versions of an edit.

16 In the source timeline, double-click clip 06. Both the source and Timeline clip outlines should turn magenta.

17 At the bottom of the window, click Copy Grade to confirm the copying of grade data between the green and magenta clips.

18 To resolve the red clips, at the top of the window, click the Manual tab.

19 In the Target Timeline, select clip 03.

The source Timeline does not feature this clip. However, it is extremely similar to clip 02, which features a wider version of the same shot.

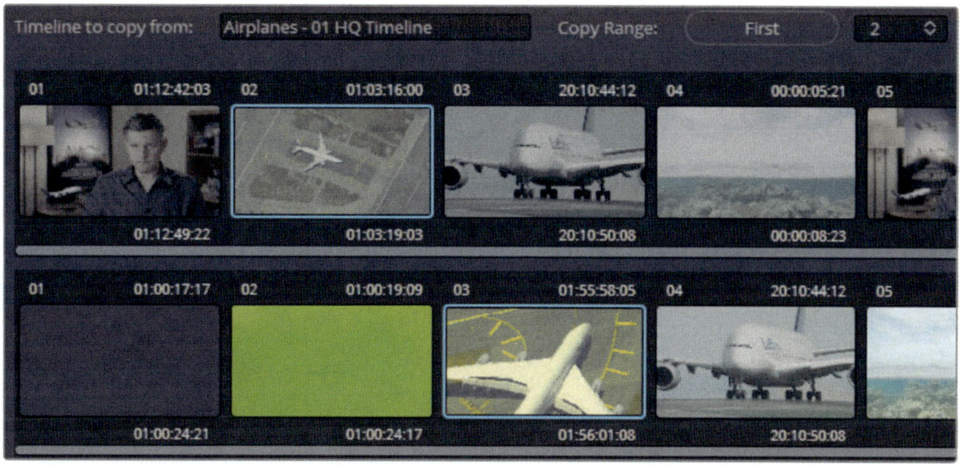

20 In the source Timeline, select clip 02, and click Paste to confirm the grade transfer.

The grade has also failed to migrate from the SOUTH_POLE clip because it was composited with another layer and turned into a compound clip.

21 In the target timeline, select clip 07, and manually paste the grade from clip 07 of the source Timeline.

22 Click Done, and exit the ColorTrace interface.

23 Enter the Color page to verify that all the clips that were graded in the 01 HQ Timeline were successfully copied to the 02 Color Trace Timeline.

Just as migrating Timelines requires confirmation, the ColorTrace function also calls for some manual review to ensure that all grades have transferred correctly. Regardless, ColorTrace still substantially reduces your workload by managing the majority of the color transference process.

Copying Grades using the Timelines Album

One of the quickest ways to transfer a grade between clips in different Timelines is by using the Timelines albums in the Gallery.

In the previous exercise, one clip in the Airplanes – 02 Color Trace Timeline remained ungraded because its counterpart in the 01 HQ Timeline was also ungraded. In this exercise, you will perform a quick grade on the remaining clip and transfer it to the original Timeline.

1 In the Airplanes – 02 Color Trace Timeline, click clip 08.
2 In the Custom curves palette, ungang the channels, and adjust the Y curve to increase the contrast in the nighttime-lapse footage.
3 Switch to the red channel, and create an S-curve to add cyan to the lower midtones of the image.

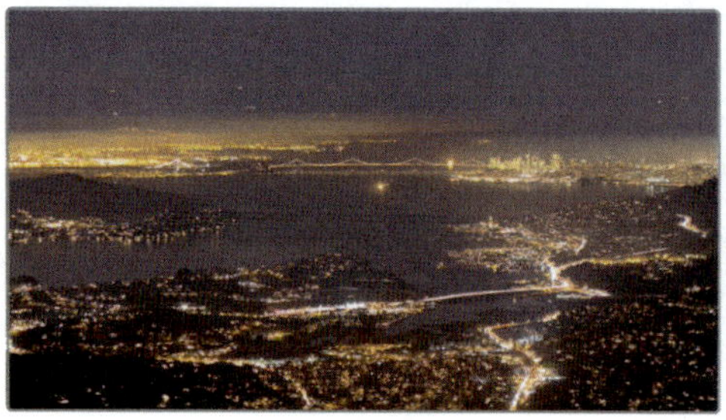

Before

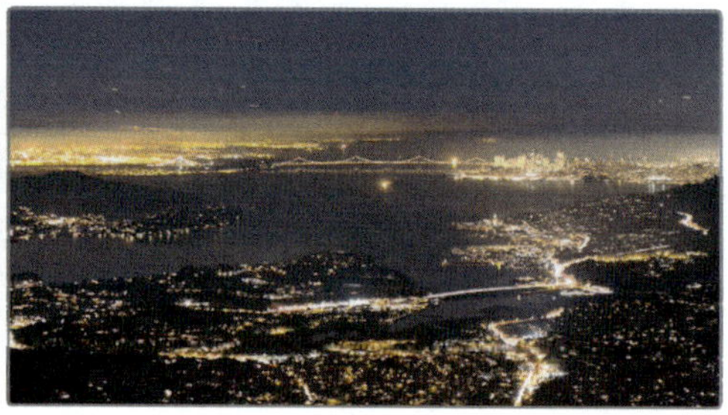

After

4 Use the pop-up menu above the Viewer to return to the Airplanes – 01 HQ Timeline.
5 In the gallery panel, click the Timelines album.
6 Use the upper pop-up menu to switch the gallery to the Airplanes – 02 Color Trace Timeline stills.

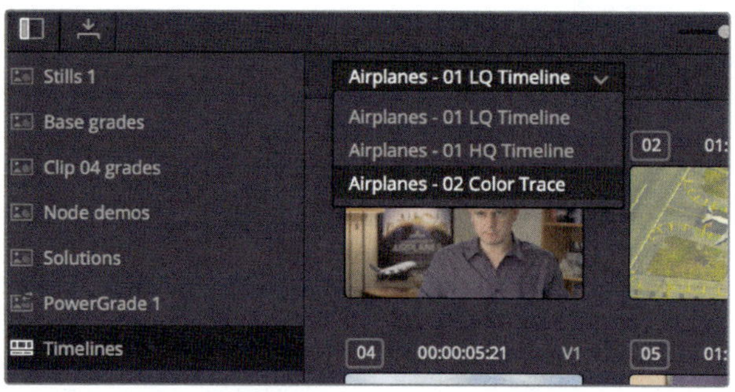

The Gallery now displays the current state of all the clips in the 02 Color Trace Timeline. Note that even the ungraded credits clip is included. This behavior helps you keep track of both graded and ungraded clips in various Timelines.

7 In the Airplanes – 01 HQ Timeline, select clip 10.

8 In the Gallery, middle-click clip 08 to transfer the cyan night sky look.

All the clips in the Airplanes – 01 HQ Timeline are now graded.

The exercises in this lesson presented a broader list of options for grade setup and duplication. When copying grade data, it is important to consider your needs on a project-by-project basis. In most cases, a combination of one or more of these copying methods is ideal; in other cases, a mix of methods could be less efficient than employing a more broad-based solution such as remote versions or ColorTrace.

Lesson Review

1. How do you create a new local version of a grade?
2. Which shortcut resets a clip's entire grade?
3. How can you access stills saved in other projects and databases on the workstation?
4. How do you copy just one node from the node tree of a still in the gallery?
5. Yes or no? You can create keyboard shortcuts for your favorite grades and stills.

Answers

1 Right-click and choose Local Versions > Create New Version, or press Cmd-Y (macOS) or Ctrl-Y (Windows).

2 Cmd-Home (macOS) or Ctrl-Home (Windows)

3 Click the Gallery View button to access the expanded gallery.

4 Right-click the still, and choose Display Node Graph. Then drag the necessary node into the node editor of the active clip.

5 Yes, in the form of Project Memories

Part 3: Optimizing the Grading Workflow

Lessons

- Using Groups
- Adjusting Image Properties
- Working with RAW media
- Project Delivery

Welcome to Part 3 of Color Correction with DaVinci Resolve 16. This section covers more advanced node-based grading workflows and looks under the hood of the many Resolve processes that manipulate and render image data. As usual, the emphasis will be on image-processing efficiency as you adopt group grading workflows, set up RAW materials, and deliver the final project.

Project File Location

You will find the content for this section in the folder BMD 16 CC - Project 03. Continue to follow the instructions at the start of every lesson to find the necessary folder, project, and Timeline. If you have not downloaded the third set of content files, return to the Getting Started section in this book for more information.

Lesson 7

Using Groups

In this lesson, you will focus on an organizational feature of the Color page that enables clip grouping based on shared visual criteria.

Although generating and organizing groups is incredibly simple, they open up a new grading workflow within the Color page. In addition to applying group-wide grades via the Node editor, the grouping feature allows Timeline filtering based on group name, and the activation of a split screen to compare clips in the same group.

Time

This lesson takes approximately 60 minutes to complete.

Goals

Preparing Media Using Scene Cut Detection

Your final video project in this book involves a single, self-contained video file. Placing the video file directly into a Timeline in DaVinci Resolve 16 would result in it being treated as a single clip, and all grading changes would affect it uniformly. To avoid this situation, you can place cuts throughout the Timeline to separate the individual shots and allow for content-specific grading. Unfortunately, doing this manually is time-consuming.

Fortunately, the Scene Cut Detection feature in Resolve performs the heavy lifting for you. It can analyze edited video files prior to import to divide their content into subclips and facilitate clip-by-clip grading.

1 Open DaVinci Resolve 16.
2 In the project manager, click the New Project button, and enter the name **Project 03 - The Long Work Day Commercial**.
3 Right-click in the bin list next to the media pool, and choose Add Bin. Label this new bin, **Video**.
4 In the Media storage library of the Media page, locate the BMD 16 CC - Project 03 folder.
5 In the folder, right-click the Project 03 - The Long Work Day SCD.mov file, and choose Scene Cut Detection.

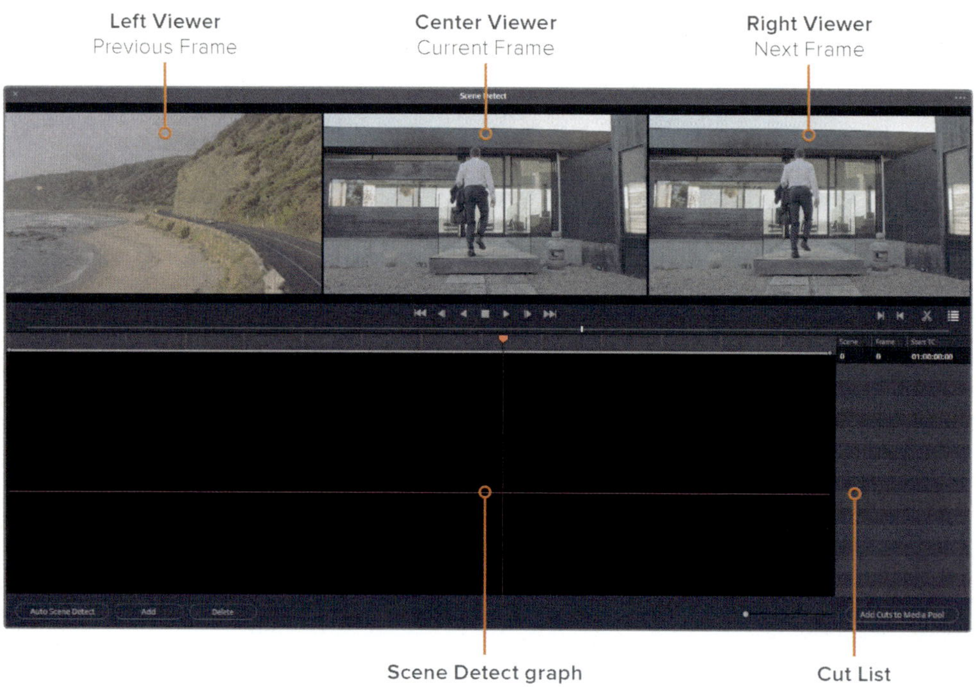

The Scene Detect window appears. You will use this interface to run the edit analysis and import the resulting subclips. At the top of the window, three Viewers display the current frame (middle), the previous frame (left), and the following frame (right). Below the Viewers, the Scene Detect Graph displays the location of the video's cut points after the analysis. To the right, the Cut List identifies the cuts and their timecodes.

6 In the lower-left corner of the window, click Auto Scene Detect.

As the analysis is run, the assumed edit points are marked with green lines in the Scene Detect Graph and their timecodes are recorded in the Cut List.

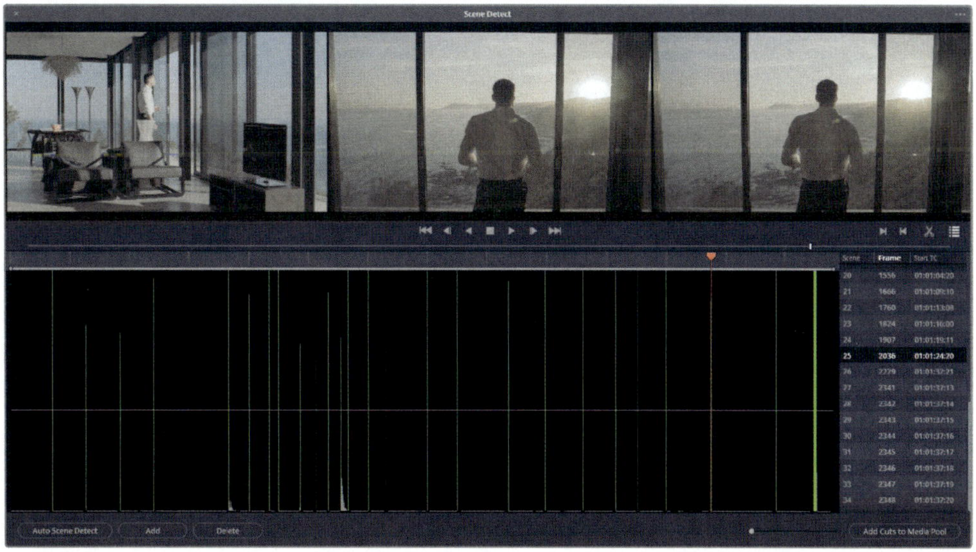

TIP The height of the green cut lines indicates Resolve's level of confidence that a cut was correctly identified in that location. Cuts that fall under the magenta confidence line are omitted from the cut list and appear gray on the graph.

When a video has many jump cuts and whip pans, the scene detection might place many cuts beneath this confidence line. To include less confident cuts in the final Cut List, drag down the magenta line until the edit lines turn green.

7 To review the edits, scrub through the Timeline by dragging the orange playhead, or click inside the Cut List, and press the Up and Down Arrow keys to navigate and verify the cut points.

TIP You can also press P (previous) and N (next) to jump between cut points.

A correctly identified cut will display a unique image in the left Viewer, followed by two similar images in the next two Viewers.

8 Navigate through the edits in the Cut List until you reach scene 12.

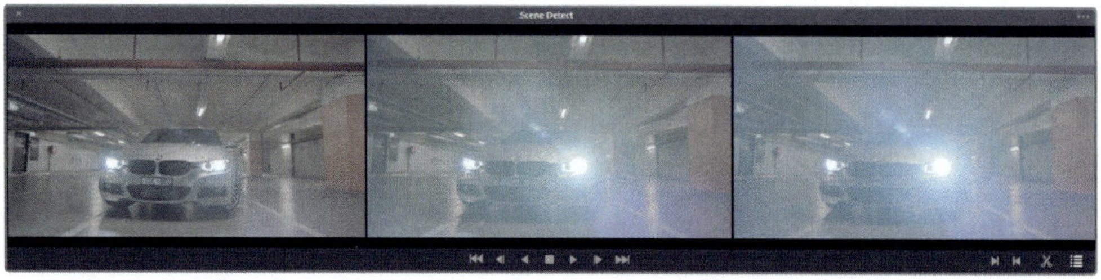

Although Resolve detected a cut here, this is actually part of the same take. The false detection happened due to a headlight-caused lens flare that created enough of a visual change in the frame to make Resolve identify it as the start of a new shot.

9 With the cut already selected, in the lower left of the scene cut detection window, click Delete to remove it.

TIP You can also press the + (plus) and minus - (minus) keys on your keyboard to add and delete cuts, respectively.

10 Press the Down Arrow key to continue navigating through the Cut List and ensure that all cuts are correctly located.

Toward the end of the Timeline, you will find a large cluster of cut points. Dissolves and transitions are prone to misidentification and may be identified as a series of rapid cuts.

11 Drag the playhead in front of this cluster, and press I to create an In point in the Scene Detect graph.

TIP Drag the scroll bar under the scene cut graph to zoom in on the cut points, if necessary.

12 Drag the playhead after the cut cluster, and press O to place an Out point.

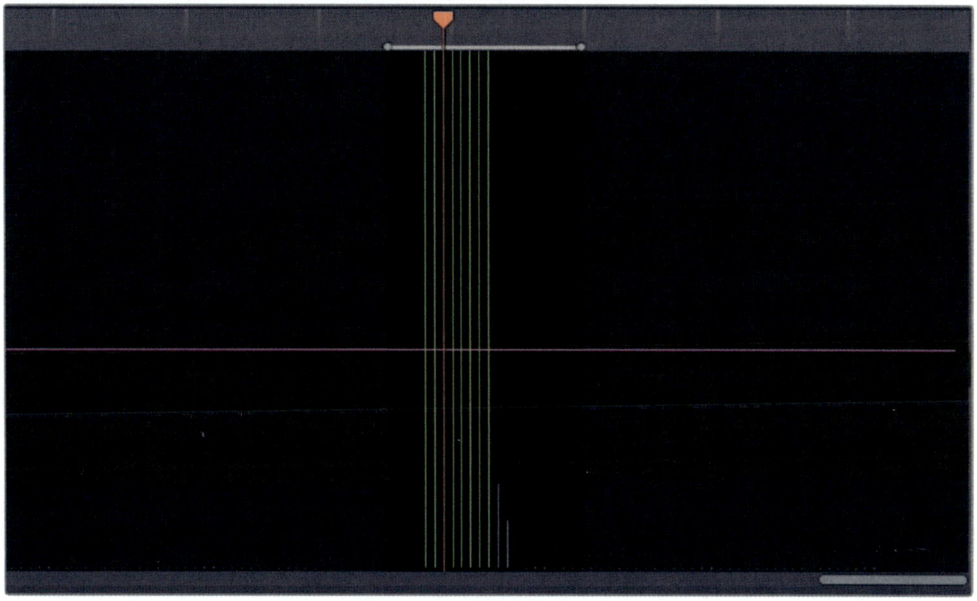

13 Under the right Viewer, click the scissors icon to delete this batch of false cut points.

14 Ensure that no other cut points from the transition area remain. If some are still present, drag the mouse over them and press Delete.

15 Press the Left and Right Arrow keys to move through the video frame-by-frame and identify the exact cut point between the last clip and the solid white color matte at the end of the Timeline.

16 Click Add to add the edit to the Cut List. A green line appears under your playhead to indicate an edit point. A new item also appears on the Cut List with the frame number (2352) and start timecode (01:01:38:00) of the cut.

You have now addressed all the issues on this Timeline. At this point, you should have 26 scenes in your Cut List.

17 In the lower-right corner, click Add Cuts to Media Pool.

TIP When working on longer films, or with edits featuring jump cuts, reviewing scene cut detection can become a time-consuming (and fatiguing) process. You may choose to break up the task into several sessions, saving your progress as you go.

You can save a scene cut in progress by accessing the options menu in the upper-right of the window, and choosing Save Scene Cut. In the same options menu, you can also open a previously saved scene cut file.

18 If a dialogue box appears to inform you that your Project Settings don't match the clips' frame rates and video formats, click Change to adjust the project Timeline to accommodate your media.

19 Close the Scene Cut Detection interface.

The commercial will now appear in your media pool as a series of clips in the Video bin.

Before you can start grading your cut media, you will first place it in a Timeline. To ensure that the clips fill the Timeline in the correct order, you will organize your media pool by clip timecode.

20 Switch to List view by click the List view button in the upper-right of the media pool.

21 Click the Start TC column title to sort the clips by their start timecodes.

File Name	Reel Name	Start TC	End TC	Duration	Frames	Type	Resolution
Project 3 - The Long Work Day SCD.mov		01:00:00:00	01:00:05:00	00:00:05:00	120	Video	1920x1080
Project 3 - The Long Work Day SCD.mov		01:00:05:00	01:00:09:01	00:00:04:01	97	Video	1920x1080
Project 3 - The Long Work Day SCD.mov		01:00:09:01	01:00:13:07	00:00:04:06	102	Video	1920x1080
Project 3 - The Long Work Day SCD.mov		01:00:13:07	01:00:17:08	00:00:04:01	97	Video	1920x1080

The clips are now ready to be placed into a Timeline.

22 Enter the Edit page.

23 Select all the media in the Video bin by selecting one clip, and pressing Cmd-A (macOS) or Ctrl-A (Windows).

24 Right-click any of the selected clips, and choose Create New Timeline Using Selected Clips.

25 Name the new Timeline **Project 03 - The Long Work Day**, and click Create.

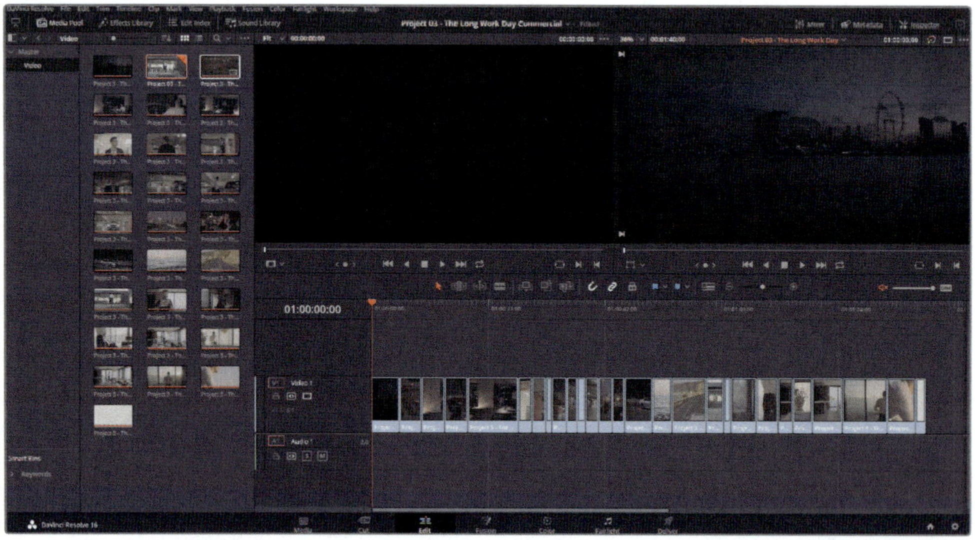

A new Timeline appears on the Edit page populated with the 27 selected clips in the media pool.

26 In the media pool, create a Timelines bin, and place the Timeline into it.

TIP Another method for importing self-contained video files using the Scene Cut Detection tool is to not directly import the created subclips, but to save the EDL file of the scene cut results (in the options menu in the upper-right). Then, import the EDL into the media pool by right-clicking and choosing Timelines > Import > Pre-conformed EDL. This method will also produce a Timeline full of cuts; but additionally, it will retain their trim points. This technique allows you to apply dissolves between the clips, as needed.

You would ordinarily use this method of flattened video migration when working with remote clients that do not have access to servers or fast internet connections. Additionally, this workflow is often necessary when working on older projects in which the original media no longer exists and only the master export file is available. In both cases, it is crucial to use the highest-quality codec and file format possible; and to avoid overlaid text, effects, or transitions that cannot be disabled in the flattened video file.

Setting Up Color Management with Tone Mapping

As in the previous project, you will use color management to remap the color space and gamma of the clips in the Timeline prior to grading. In this exercise, you will look at a few additional features for more accurate tonal mapping.

1 Enter the Color page.

2 Press the Up and Down Arrow keys to travel along the Timeline and review the clips in the Project 03 - The Long Work Day timeline.

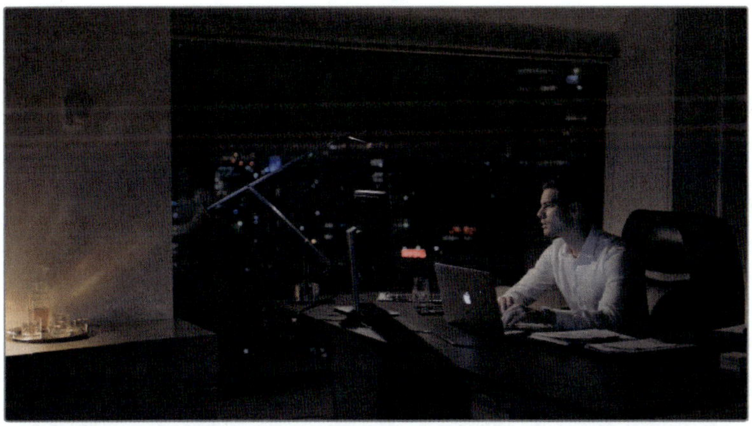

The footage appears flat and desaturated, which is indicative of a log color space. This indicates that you have access to a wide dynamic range within the image, but currently have a poor starting point for your grade.

3 Open the Project Settings, and navigate to the Color Management tab.

4 Set Color Science to DaVinci YRGB Color Managed.

5 Set Input Color Space as Blackmagic Design 4.6K Film Gen 1.

6 Leave the Timeline and Output Color Spaces as Rec.709 Gamma 2.4.

7 Click Save to exit the Project Settings.

The clips appear unchanged because their individual input color spaces are set to Rec.709 Gamma 2.4. Video media always adopts the Timeline color space of a project upon the moment of import. You need to change the input color space to reflect the active project settings.

8 Press Cmd-A (macOS) or Ctrl-A (Windows) to select all clips.

9 Right-click any clip, and choose Input Color Space > Project - Blackmagic Design 4.6K Film Gen 1.

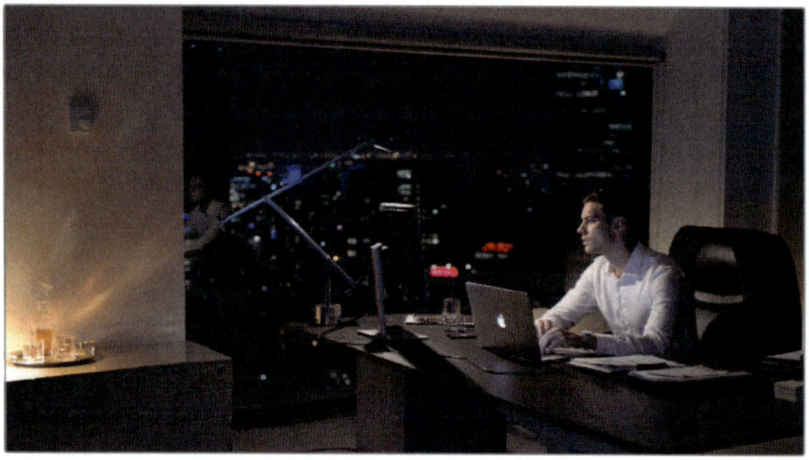

The appearance of the clips in the Timeline is dramatically improved. Colors appear naturally saturated and the highlights are raised.

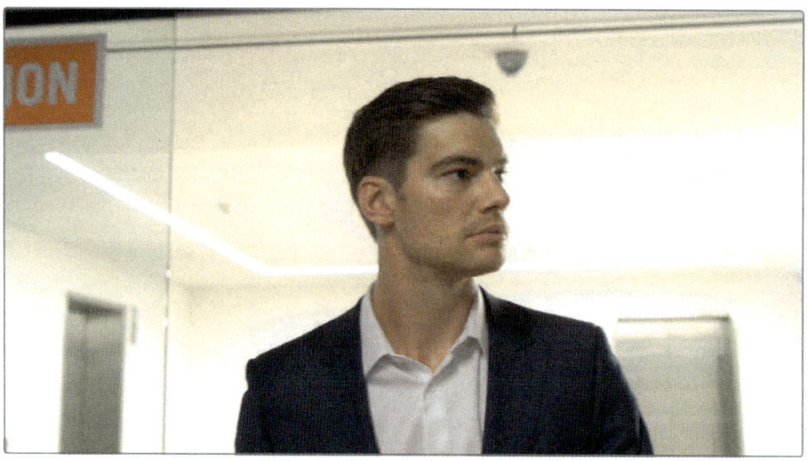

However, as you navigate to scenes with dramatic light sources, you might feel that the highlights are now too extreme. This can happen with footage that is captured on a camera with a very wide dynamic range that preserves several f-stops of data within the video signal. In the previous project, you used the Gamut Mapping node to address this problem. In this project, you will apply a project-wide tonal adjustment to all the clips.

10 Open the Project Settings, and navigate to the Color Management tab.

11 Use the pop-up menu next to Set Timeline to Output Tone Mapping to Luminance Mapping. Doing so will reveal a field into which you can enter a nit value.

A *nit* is a measurement of brightness that describes the luminance value of monitors and displays. When working with footage that has a wide dynamic range, you can use a customized curve operation to precisely map the video luminance to a default SDR display range of 100 nits.

12 The Max. Timeline Luminance refers to the luminance range of the source media. To take into account its wide dynamic range, enter the value as **300** nits.

13 Click Save to exit the Project Settings.

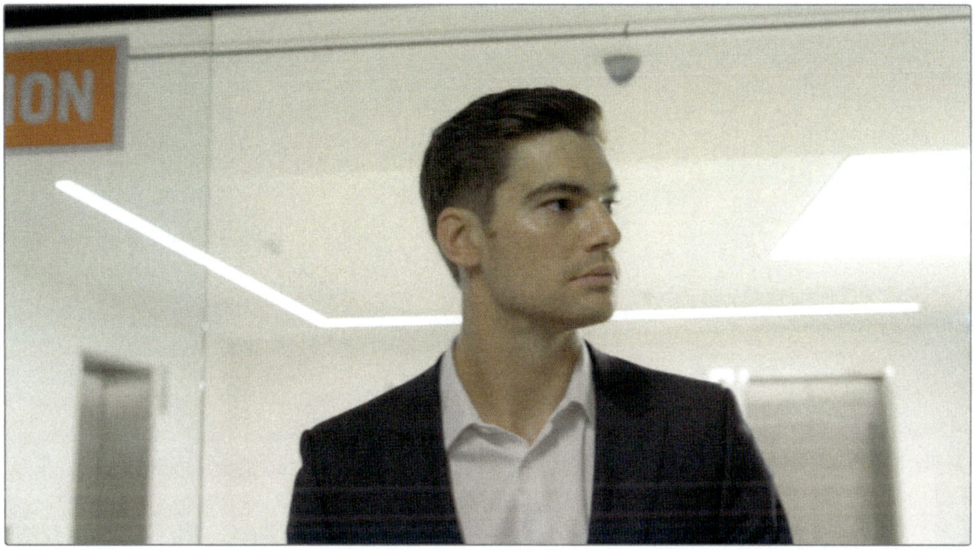

This luminance value will substantially improve the appearance of highlights in the Timeline. The color management operation now takes into account the increased luminance values in the original footage (specified as 300 nits) and applies a more appropriate curve to unpack them within the 100 nit project range.

TIP In footage with a wide dynamic range, the light sources appear over-saturated after color management. You can use the Timeline to Output Gamut Mapping controls in Project Settings to remap saturation in the same way as you remapped luminance. Adjust the Saturation Max. to reduce the maximum saturation value on the Timeline, and lower the Saturation Knee to set the image level at which saturation mapping begins.

14 Select clip 01 on the Project 03 – The Long Work Day timeline.

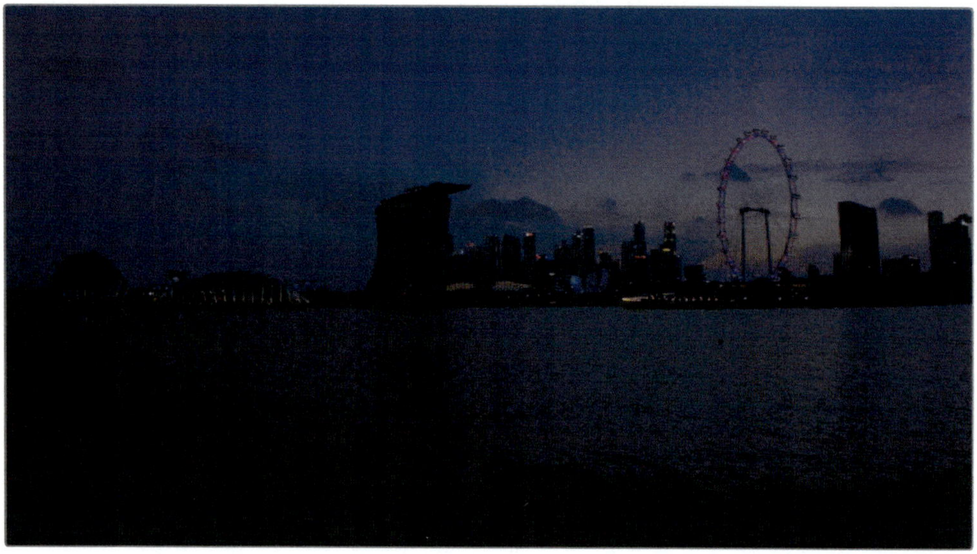

The clip appears much darker, noisier, and more saturated than the rest of the footage because this clip was captured on a different camera than the rest of the media. The project-wide color management utilizes an input color space that does not correspond to this clip's source gamut, so its colors are incorrectly remapped and distorted.

15 Right-click clip 01, and choose Input Color space > Blackmagic Design 4K Film Gen 1.

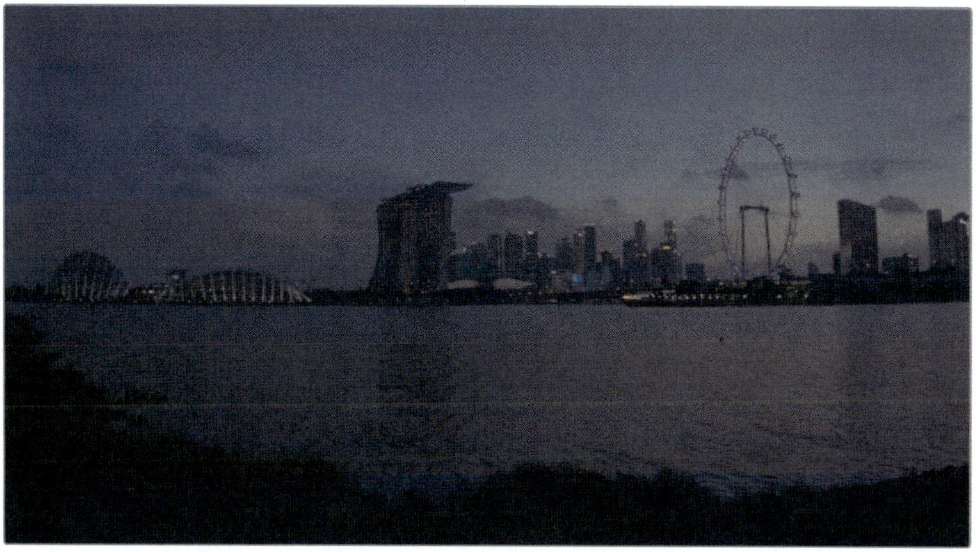

Doing so corrects the remapping operation to use the input color space of the camera used to capture this clip. In situations when you are uncertain of a clip's origin, it is best to set the Input Color Space to Bypass.

Creating a Group

When incorporating groups to a grading workflow, your first task is to choose a grouping strategy for your Timeline. Depending on the project, you can base groups on locations, scenes, color temperature, shot size, or any criteria of your choice.

In the commercial project in this lesson, you will create groups to differentiate between scenes based on their locations and times of day.

1 Click clip 06, and Shift-click clip 13 to select the eight consecutive garage clips in the Timeline.

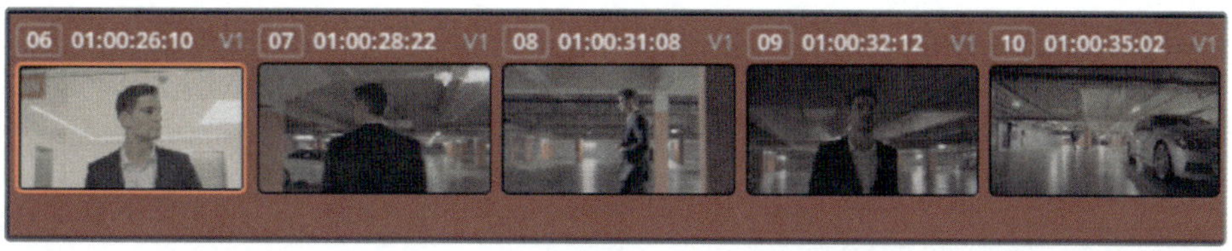

2 Right-click any of the highlighted clips, and choose Add into Current Group.

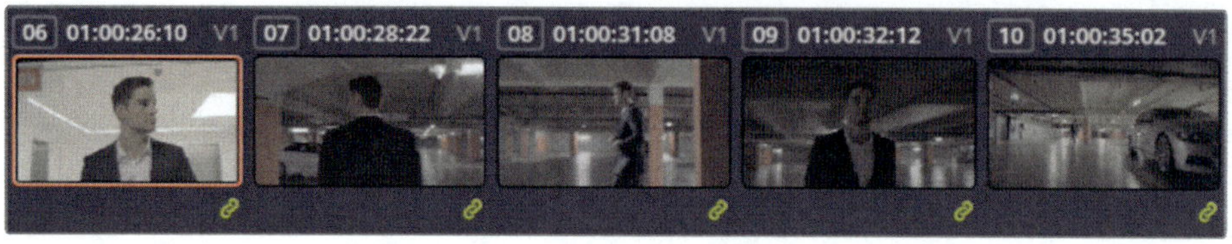

A green link symbol appears in the lower-right corner of the clips to indicate their group relationship.

3 Right-click any of the grouped clips, and choose Groups > Group 1 > Rename.

4 Enter the group name **Garage**. These clips will now be linked when you start utilizing the group-level Node editor in later exercises.

Upon closer inspection, it appears that clip 13, the highway shot, does not belong in this scene and should not be included in this group.

5 Right-click clip 13, and choose Remove from Group.

You can also use groups for filtering purposes.

6 In the Timeline, Cmd-click (macOS) or Ctrl-click (Windows) clips 02 and 13.

7 Right-click one of them, and choose Add into a New Group.

8 Enter the group name **Highway**.

The link symbols on the Garage group disappear and are now visible only in the Highway group. From now on, the green link symbols will appear only when a grouped clip is selected.

The two Highway clips are relatively far apart on the Timeline, so matching them could be tedious if you have to constantly navigate up and down the Timeline to compare them.

9 Choose Clips > Grouped > Highway.

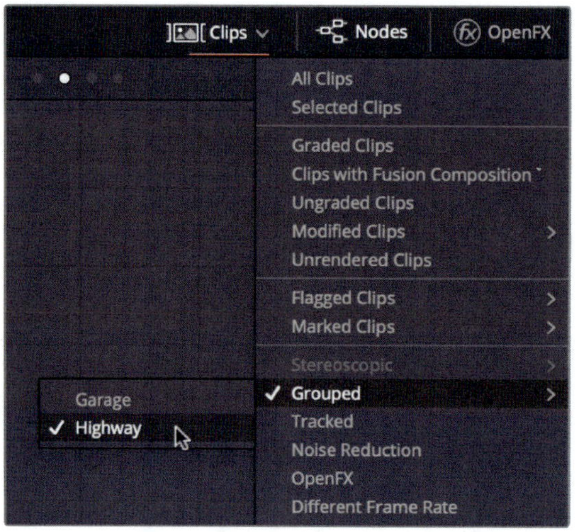

The two highway clips are now located side-by-side and you can quickly assess and match them by pressing the Up and Down Arrow keys.

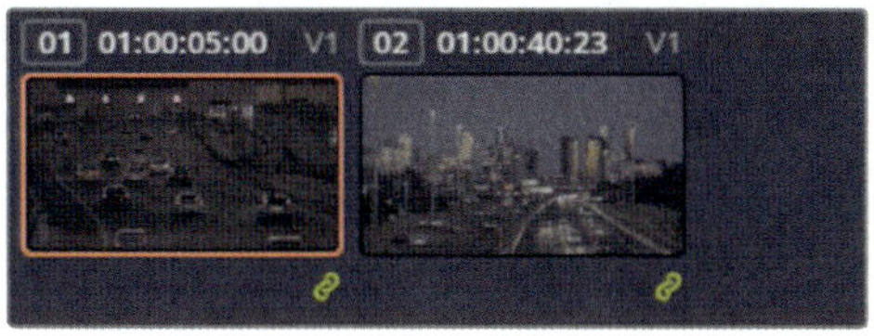

10 Select Clips > All Clips to remove the Timeline filter.

You'll need to create one more group to prepare for the exercises in this lesson.

11 Scroll down the Timeline, select clips 19 to 26, and add them to a new group called **Home**.

Adopting Groups in a Classic Color Grading Workflow

With your clips sorted into groups, you can now choose the modes in which their grading will be targeted—from individual adjustments to group-wide uniform changes. Doing so will enable a much faster and more precise workflow in which you'll no longer need to duplicate and reapply grades to individual clips. By reducing this duplication of effort, you'll also have less chance that mistakes will creep into your workflow. Instead of readjusting specific nodes on multiple clips or keeping track of dozens of stills, you may tweak a group grade to amend all of a scene's clips at once.

The following figure shows how the classic color grading workflow, previously expressed as a node tree structure in Lesson 1, can be translated into group-based node structures.

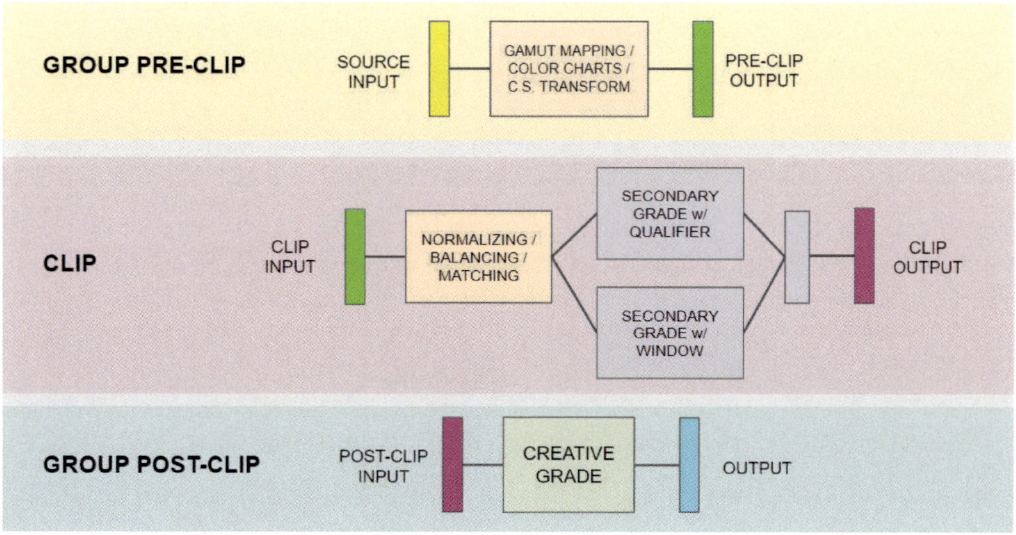

The following is a list of available grading modes in the Node editor and their relationships to the traditional grading workflow:

- **Group pre-clip** permits you to apply preparatory grading adjustments such as gamut mapping, color chart auto-correction, or color space transform (the OpenFX equivalent of using color management in the Project Settings). At this stage, you can also normalize footage with common luminance ranges and address obvious tint or temperature issues in the dailies.
- **Clip** mode enables you to address the individual needs of each clip in a group, including normalization, balancing, matching, and secondary grade adjustments.
- **Group post-clip** is best utilized for creative scene grading. By this stage, your clips should be matched, and their individual secondary requirements met. Matching these clips ensures that the creative grade is uniformly applied, and requires only minimal tweaking on a clip-by-clip level.
- **Timeline** will affect every clip on the active Timeline of your project. Color correction and creative grading is not recommended at this stage, but you could use this mode to implement artificial grain and film effects, apply vignettes to short form projects, or remap the color space of the Timeline via Color Space Transform FX.

This breakdown suggests the order in which to address and process visual data, but you should not see it as a strict order of grading operations. As with any standard grading workflow, it is entirely acceptable (and expected) to jump between group levels to make adjustments throughout the grading process. Note that the output of earlier modes is the direct input of later modes (that is, the pre-clip output leads to the clip input). It is therefore helpful to think of the group modes as being one long pipeline.

Applying Base Grades at Pre-Clip Group Level

In the pre-clip group level, you can make adjustments that will affect the individual clip-level RGB input video signals of all the clips in the group.

It is important to keep in mind that all the clips in a group are affected by these changes, so you must avoid focusing too strongly on achieving a perfectly neutral appearance in any single shot. Instead, pick a key shot that is representative of most of the footage in the group and apply the necessary grades, LUTs, or ResolveFX to establish a good starting point for matching at the next grading stage.

Using a Color Chart to Balance a Group

One method for normalizing the tonal range and balance in a sequence of clips is to use the calibration charts that were captured at the start of the scene shoot. Calibration charts allow for automated balancing that gives you a much more accurate output than regular auto-balancing due to their reliable luminance ranges and meticulously designed color swatches.

1. Change the Clips Timeline filter to display only the clips in the Home group.

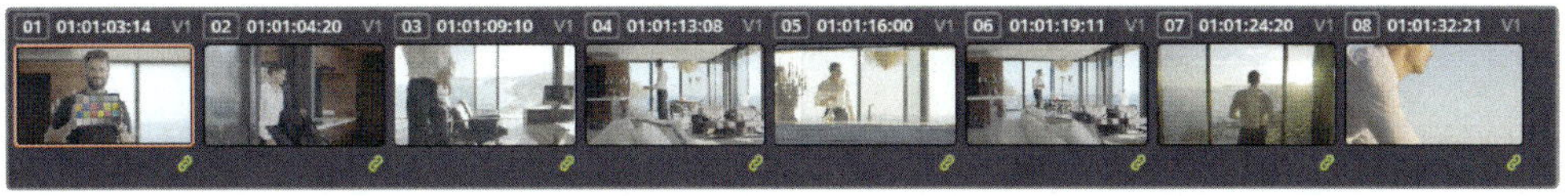

   These clips feature a color checker clip that you can use to quickly calibrate the group's color space and gamma. A shot of the color checker is usually captured at the start of every new scene, light change, or location during filming to facilitate the quick normalization of clips in that sequence.

2. In the pop-up menu at the top of the Node editor, switch to Group Pre-Clip mode. All the adjustments you are about to make will be applied to the whole group.

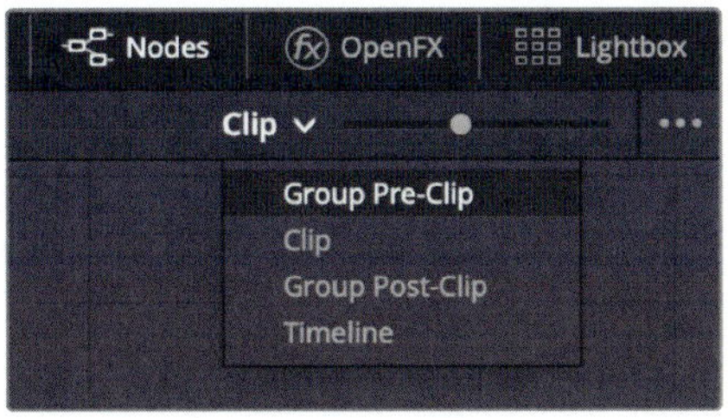

3. In the Home group Timeline, click clip 01.
4. Label node 01 as **Color Match**.
5. In the left palettes of the Color page, open the Color Match palette.

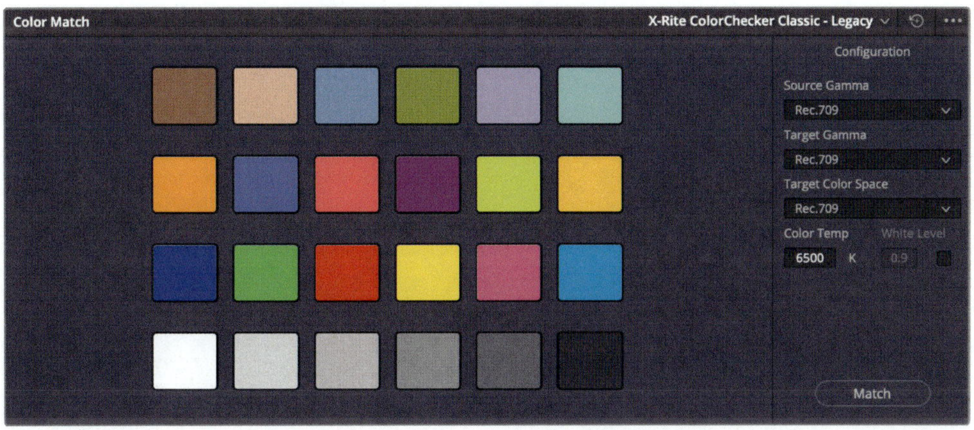

6 In the pop-up menu in the lower-left of the Viewer, choose the Color Chart tool.

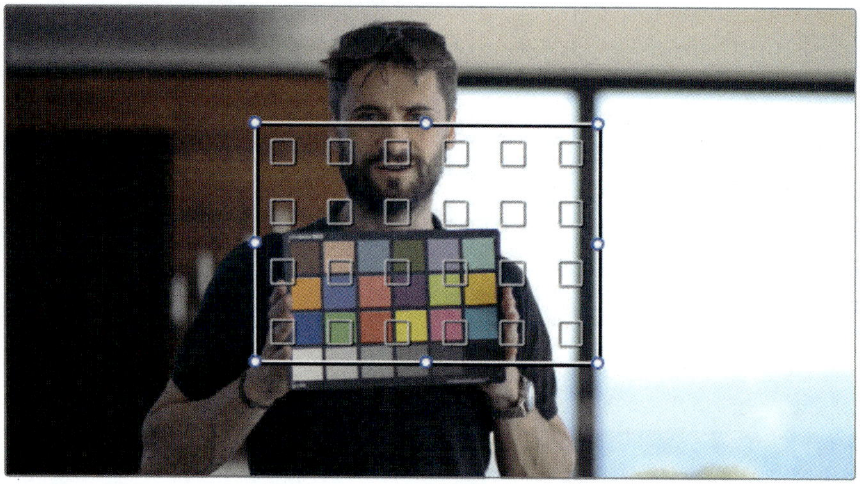

7 Drag the corners of the color chart interface to the corners of the color checker chart in the image. Ensure that the small squares in the middle of the color chart outline are filled with the colors they are meant to be analyzing. Any interference with the black chart borders or the man's fingers will affect the quality of this analysis.

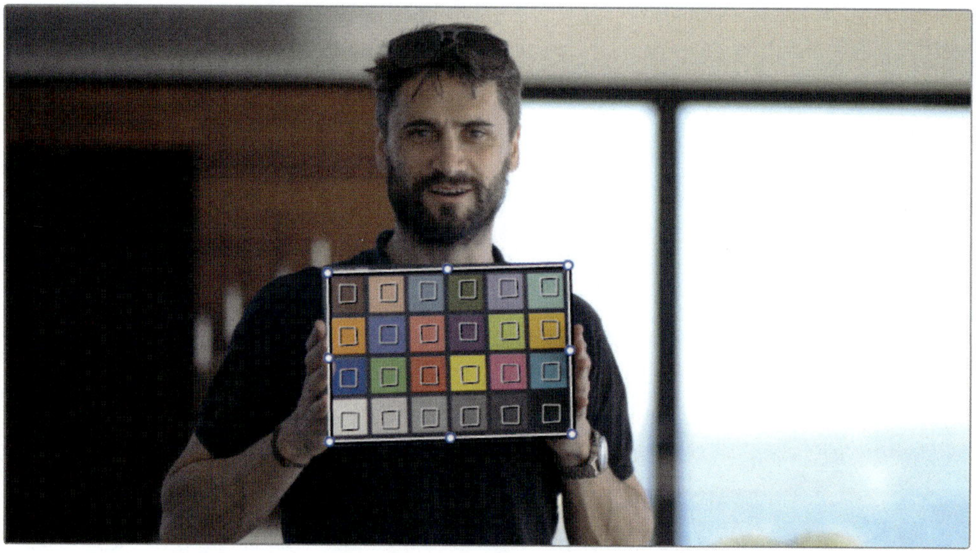

8 At the top of the Color Match palette, verify that X-Rite ColorChecker Classic - Legacy is chosen. This selection is based on the version and type of color checker chart in use.

9 Set the Source Gamma to Gamma 2.4.

The RGB signal of the image is processed after its colors are remapped by the color management feature of the Project Settings. Gamma 2.4 is the gamma level indicated as the Output Color space in the color management of the project.

10 Change the Target Gamma to Gamma 2.4 to retain the same gamma range as the rest of your color-managed Timeline while still balancing the colors of the sequence.

11 At the bottom of the Color Match palette, click Match. You will see a slight shift in color, most notably in the skin of the man, as the clip is balanced according to the chart.

The rest of the clips in the Timeline have now adopted the automated color balance.

You've created a better starting point for all the clips in the scene while retaining the full gamma range and color quality to perform individual balancing, matching and creative grading down the line.

TIP When working on a project that utilizes conversion LUTs, the pre-clip group level is the stage at which the LUTs are applied.

Making Clip-Specific Adjustments at the Clip Group Level

By default, the standard Node editor applies grade changes on a clip-by-clip basis. It is the ideal way to match footage and make secondary amendments. When working with groups, you continue to have access to the Node editor in Clip mode.

Matching Shots at the Clip Group Level

Before you can apply a creative grade to a group of clips, it is important to ensure that all of those clips match in terms of tint, temperature, and luminance level distribution.

1 Filter the Timeline to show only the Garage group clips.

2 Switch the Node editor to Clip mode.

3 Select clip 01. At first glance, the shot appears to be substantially brighter than the other clips in the scene.

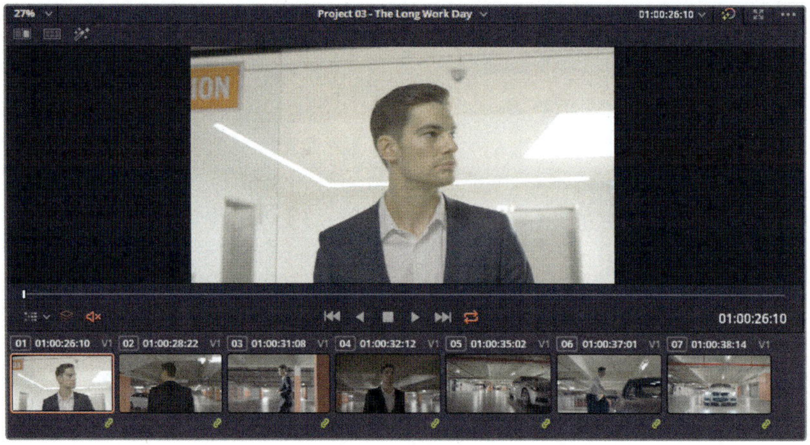

4 Drag the Viewer playhead to the end of clip 1.

After the man enters the garage, the shot appears to be exposed similarly to others in the sequence and will not require aggressive matching.

5 By default, thumbnail images in the Timeline represent the first frame of a clip. Drag within the thumbnail of a clip to change the frame represented in the thumbnail.

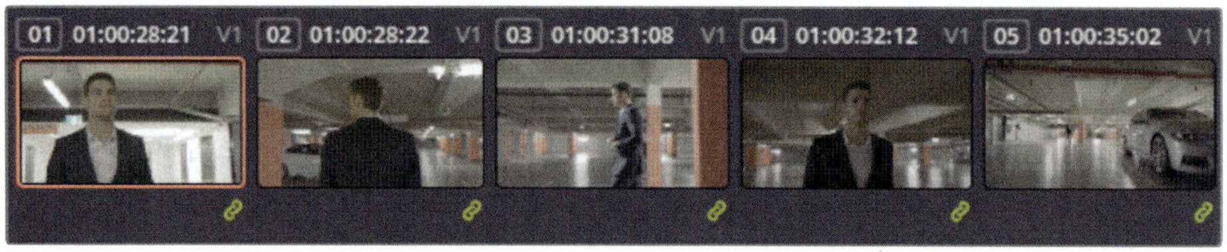

When comparing and balancing clips, remember that the first frame is not always the most reliable choice for matching, and you should always play through the entire clip before making a grading decision. In this case, you can leave clip 01 as it is.

6 Select clip 04. This shot is definitely darker than the rest of the sequence.

7 Right-click clip 05, and choose Wipe Timeline Clip to enable the Wipe mode in the Viewer.

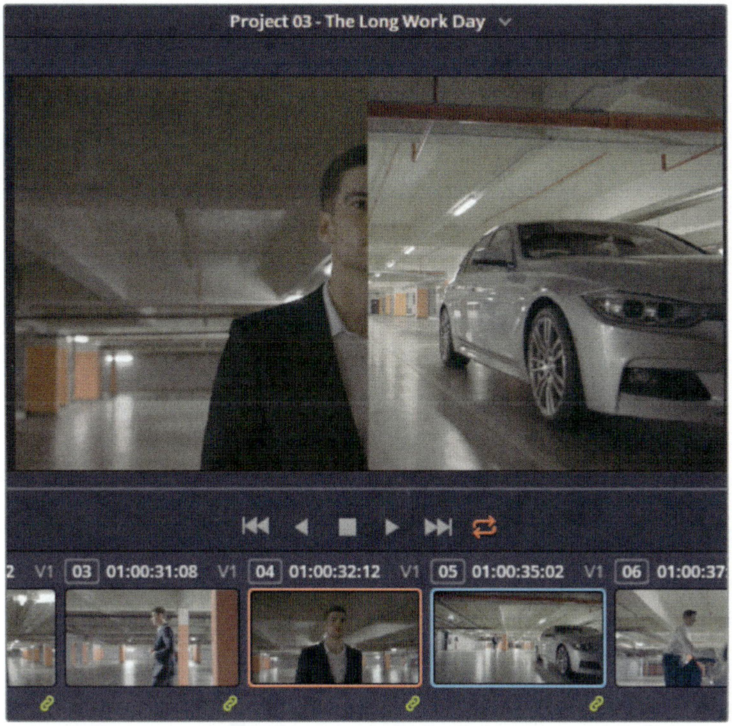

8 Open the Sizing palette in Reference Sizing mode, and pan and zoom clip 05 to more clearly see the man in the wide shot.

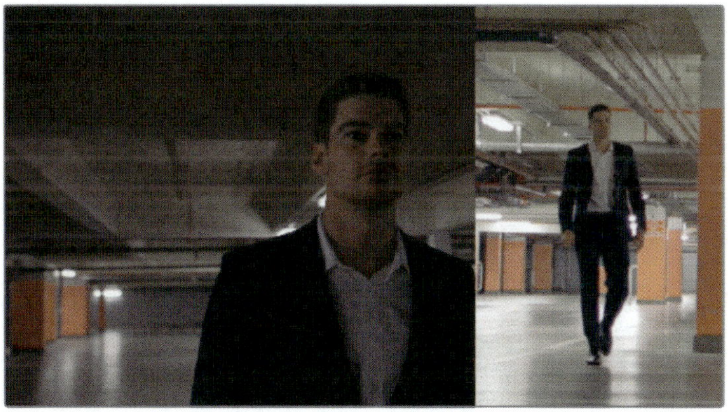

9 Press Option-F (macOS) or Alt-F (Windows) to expand the Viewer and get a better view of the differences between the clips.

10 Open the waveform scope (in RGB mode with Colorize enabled) to view a graphic representation of the chrominance differences between the clips. Just as in the Viewer, the waveform is split along the wipe line.

11 Label node 01 in clip 04 as **Match**.

12 Drag the Gain master wheel up to brighten the highlights and upper midtones of the image. Keep an eye on matching the floor, walls, and lights to the reference image.

13 Drag the Lift master wheel down slightly to create a matching balance with the shadows and lower midtones in the reference waveform.

14 Clip 04 has a significant green tint in its shadows. Drag the Lift wheel toward magenta/blue until the tint in the man's suit is neutralized.

When the suit begins to match the one in the reference, the remainder of the room will start to look too magenta. You can counteract this by targeting the tonal range of the dark walls and ceiling (gamma) and precisely adjusting the color imbalance using Primaries Bars.

15 Switch the Color Wheels palette mode to Primaries Bars.

16 Drag up the green Gamma bar to remove magenta from the midtones of the image.

17 Lower the blue Gamma bar to bring warmth back into the lights in the ceiling.

18 Raise the Y Gamma bar to brighten to overall image.

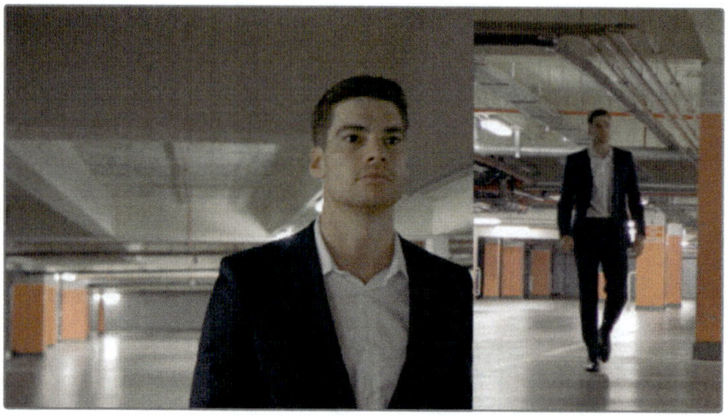

The waveforms don't match. Are the clips really color matched?

When matching clips using waveforms, your goal is not always to make the waveforms look identical. Rather, it is to use the reference waveform as a guide to inform the overall spread of the luminance data, the heights of the brightest parts of the image, and the depths of the shadows.

In this example, clip 04 will always have a waveform that is concentrated at the bottom of the graph because it features a mid-close-up of the man and his dark suit.

In clip 05, the suit occupies a very small part of the shot and appears in the waveform as a small dip to the shadows—the depths of which are now matched. Likewise, the lights in both waveforms follow a similar trajectory.

Lastly, the overall waveform in clip 04 is spread out to a similar distance to clip 05. Bypass the grade in clip 04 to compare how compressed the waveform used to look.

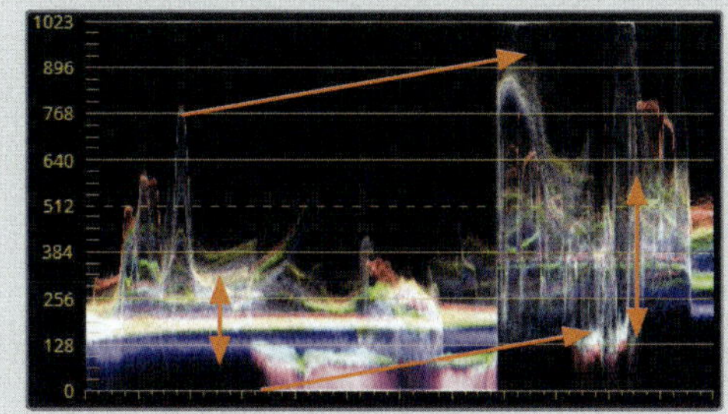

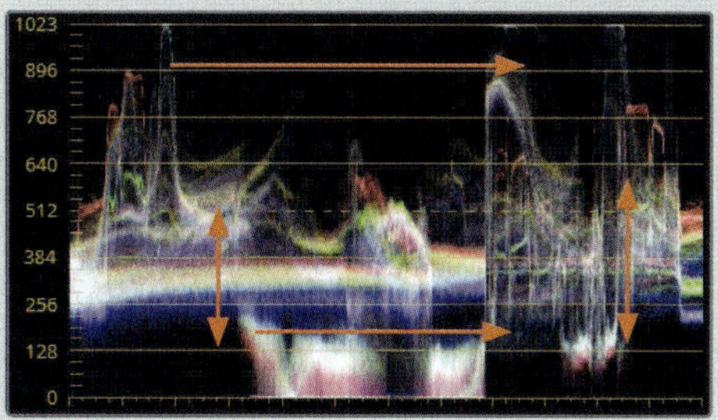

19 Press Option-F (macOS) or Alt-F (Windows) to exit the Enhanced Viewer mode but leave the Wipe mode on.

20 Reset the Reference Sizing mode of the Sizing palette, and drag the wipe line to the center of the Viewer.

21 Click clip 07.

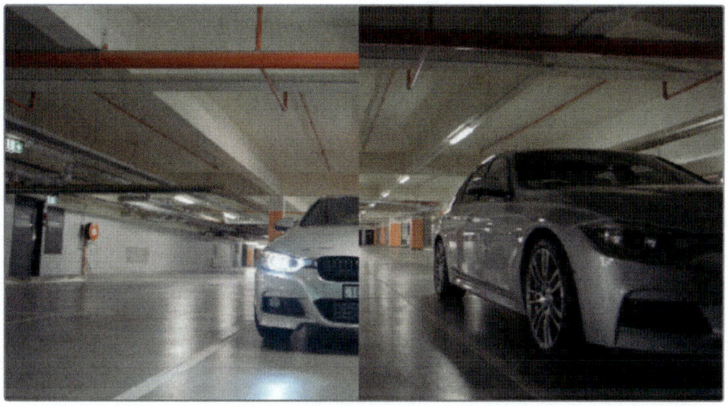

The clip colors are already a good match for the rest of the Timeline, but the shot is too bright overall which will affect the quality of the post-clip grade.

22 Label node 01 as **Match**.

23 Drag the Offset master wheel left to darken the shadows to the same level as the reference clip. A good reference to watch as you adjust the image luminance is the garage ceiling, which should match in all shots.

Intermediary Matching Between Clips

At times, you will want to grade shots to show a gradual change in color or temperature between clips. Doing so is not strictly a color match; but rather, an intermediary grade designed to transition between clips with different looks without jarring a viewer's perception of the scene.

In this exercise, two clips captured at sunrise are intercut with media captured later in the day. You will match the daylight clip between them, and then grade the preceding clip to suggest a natural change in sunlight from the first half of the Timeline to the second.

1 Cmd-click (macOS) or Ctrl-click (Windows) clips 04 to 07 to select them.

2 In the Viewer, enable Split Screen mode.

3 In the pop-up menu in the upper-right of the Viewer, choose Selected Clips.

4 Press Option-F (macOS) or Alt-F (Windows) to expand the Viewer.

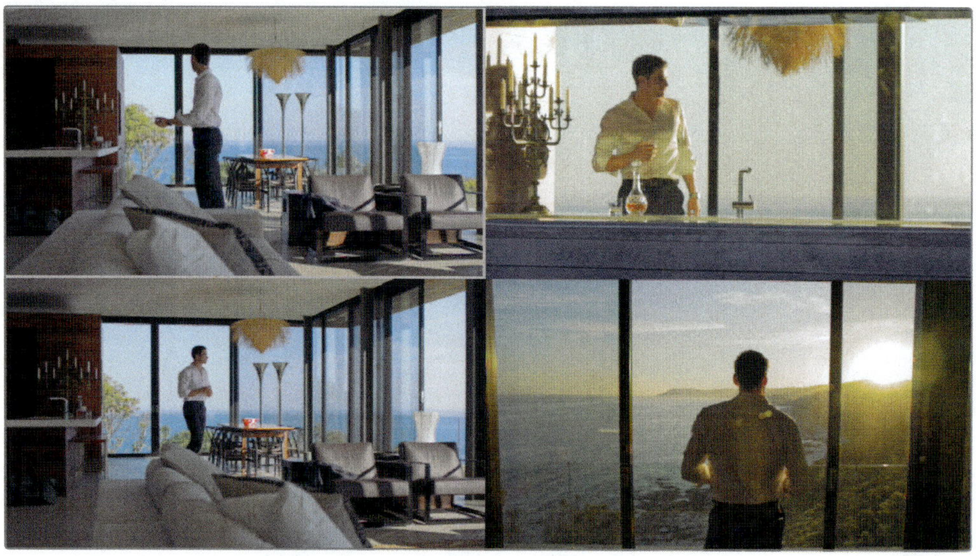

5 In the split screen Viewer, ensure that clip 06 (lower-left) is selected.

6 Open the Node editor and label node 01 as **Match**.

7 Drag the Gain wheel toward yellow until the color of the sky matches the skies in the surrounding clips.

8 Reduce the contrast in the adjustment controls until the window frames and furniture shadows have the same low contrast as the surrounding sunrise clips.

9 To reduce the resulting orange cast in the room, open the Lum Vs Sat curve, and reduce the saturation of the brightest parts of the image.

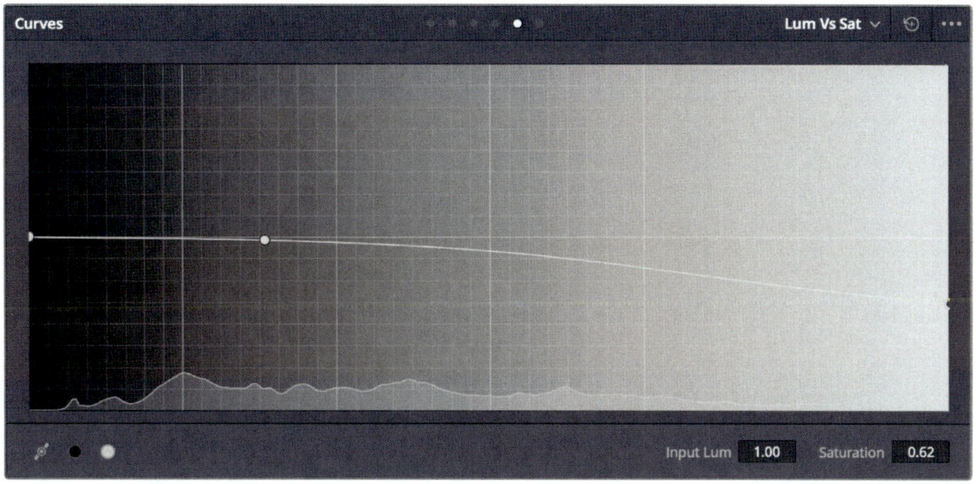

10 Finally, to match the hue of the water, open the Hue vs Hue curve and adjust the cyan area to be a cooler blue shade.

11 Copy the Match node grade of clip 06 into the first node of clip 04.

To ensure a smooth transition between clips 03 and 05, you will want to reduce the severity of the grade in clip 04.

12 Open the Key palette, and change the Key Output Gain to 0.600. The grade intensity is halved, and the original colors of the image now show through for a smooth transition between the first and second halves of the scene.

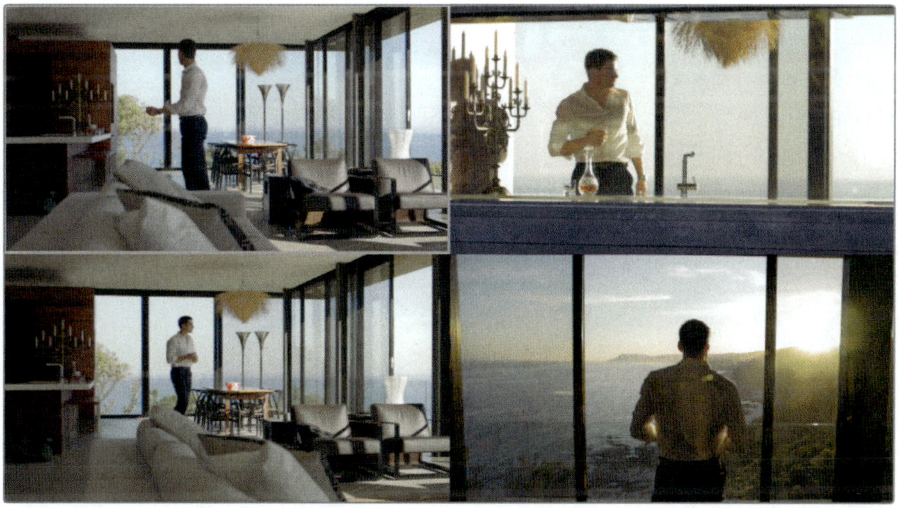

13 Press Option-F (macOS) or Alt-F (Windows) to exit the Enhanced Viewer mode.

14 Exit the split screen Viewer.

Creating a Unifying Look Using the Post-Clip Group Level

When you achieve a color consistency in the clips within your groups, you are ready to move on to the final post-clip group level in which you will design and apply creative grades on a scene-by-scene basis. At this stage, other members of the creative process, such as the director and director of photography, usually get involved to discuss the aesthetic needs of the film.

Applying a Post-Clip Grade with an External Reference

In this exercise, you will work with a reference image that a client has shared with you. You will import it into the gallery and treat it as a still for visual comparison.

1 Filter the Timeline to show only the Garage group clips.

2 Switch the Node editor to Group Post-clip mode.

3 Click clip 07. This is the key shot you will use to grade the rest of the group.

4 To import an external reference image, right-click in the Gallery, and choose Import.

5 In your file browser, navigate to the BMD 16 CC - Project 03 folder, and open the References subfolder.

   If you do not see any images in the folder, ensure that your browser window is specified to identify all files as opposed to just the default .dpx format files.

6 Select the FK_Bridge_Reference.png image, and click Import.

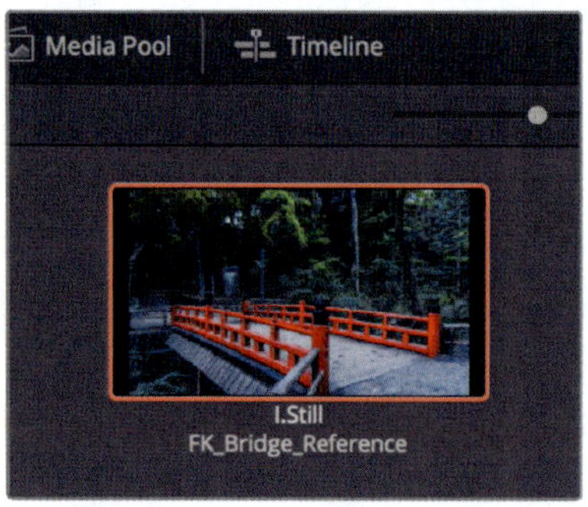

7 Double-click the still to wipe it in the Viewer.

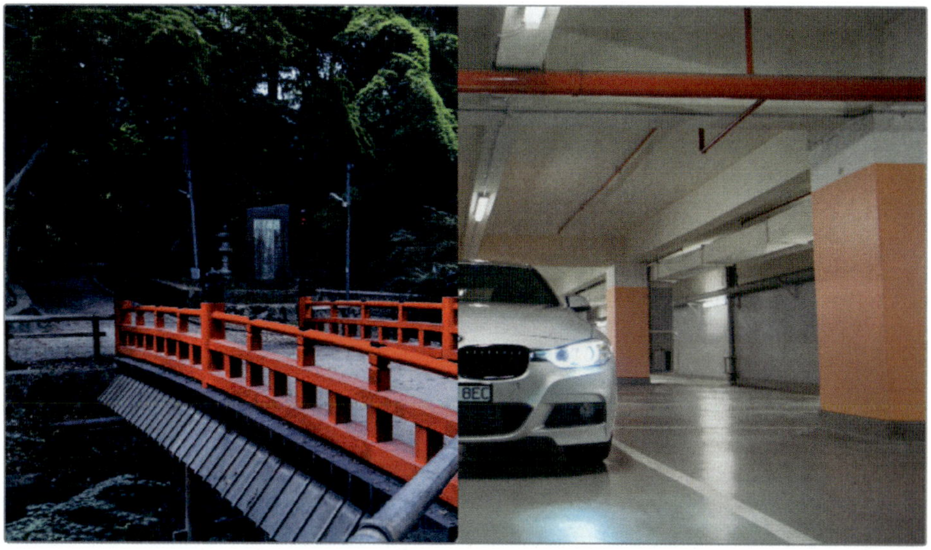

Clients often use visual references from photographs, art, or even existing films/TV shows to communicate their desired looks for a project. In this case, the highly-stylized reference image points toward a scene with cool, dark shadows and vibrant midtones.

First, let's match the contrast and cold look of the reference shot.

8 Label node 01 as **Dark Blue**.

9 In the Custom Curves palette, drag the master curve black point across the bottom of the graph until the shadow under the car is almost pitch black.

10 Shape the master curve into an S-curve to add contrast to the midtones, while bringing some intensity into the lights within the image.

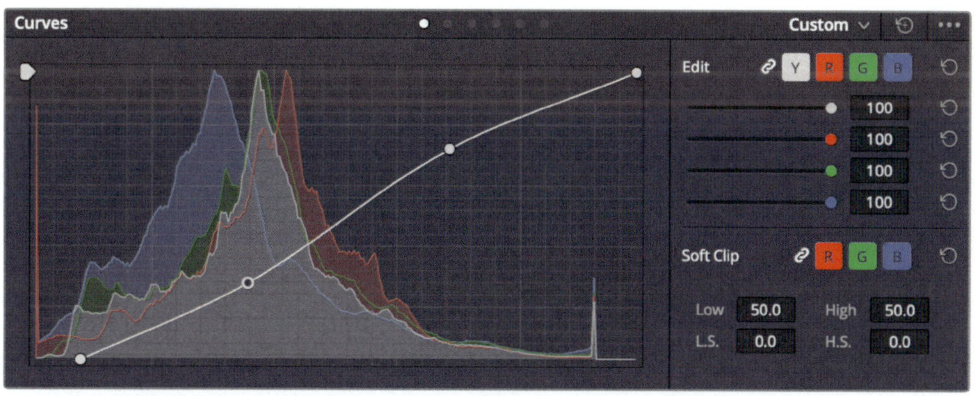

11 Drag the Offset wheel toward cyan to create a strong blue tone.

12 Drag the Lift wheel toward red to undo some of the coolness in the shadows and make them slightly more neutral.

13 Drag the Gamma wheel toward magenta to reduce the green tint in the image and create a soft pink definition in the back of the garage compared to the blue foreground.

You can address the over-saturated blue headlight reflections on the floor in the Lum vs Sat curve of the Curves editor.

14 Click the white swatch under the curve graph to generate an anchor next to the rightmost point of the saturation graph. The area between the two points represents the most saturated parts of the frame.

15 Drag down the rightmost point until the reflections are not overly saturated. You'll notice that the area immediately around the reflections is not affected as strongly.

16 Drag the anchor point left to expand the region you are targeting. If necessary, click the curve to create a new adjustment point, and drag it down until the edges of the reflection are no longer saturated. Keep an eye on the other colors in the image to ensure that you are not desaturating any prominent elements such as the columns or the hood of the car.

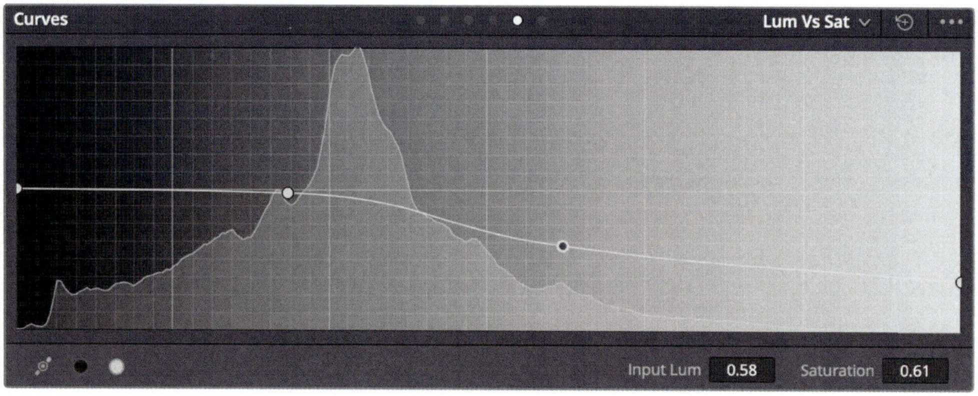

The overall temperature and tonal range of the scene is complete. You can now place a second node to enhance the garage's red columns and pipes.

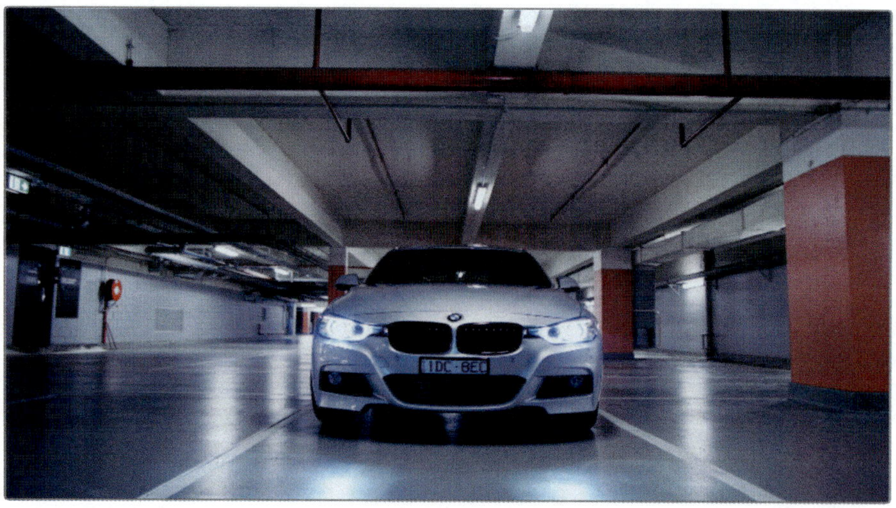

It's not common to create secondary grades in post-clip group node graphs; but when the scenes have a consistent color scheme, it can work.

You will get a better secondary grade result if you use the original RGB signal of the clip instead of the RGB signal coming out of the heavily-graded and contrasted Dark Blue node.

17 Create a new Parallel Mixer node, and label it **Red Pipes**.

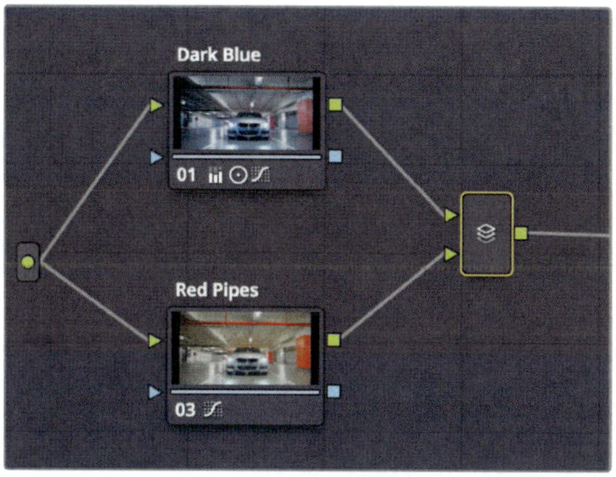

18 In the HSL curves, open the Hue vs Sat HSL curve.

19 Click the red swatch at the bottom of the palette, and increase the Sat by 50%. Doing so enhances the reds in the image, but also makes them a little distracting due to their unnatural brightness.

20 In the Hue vs Lum HSL curve, click the red swatch, and reduce the Lum by 50%. This darkens the red colors and matches them more closely to their environment.

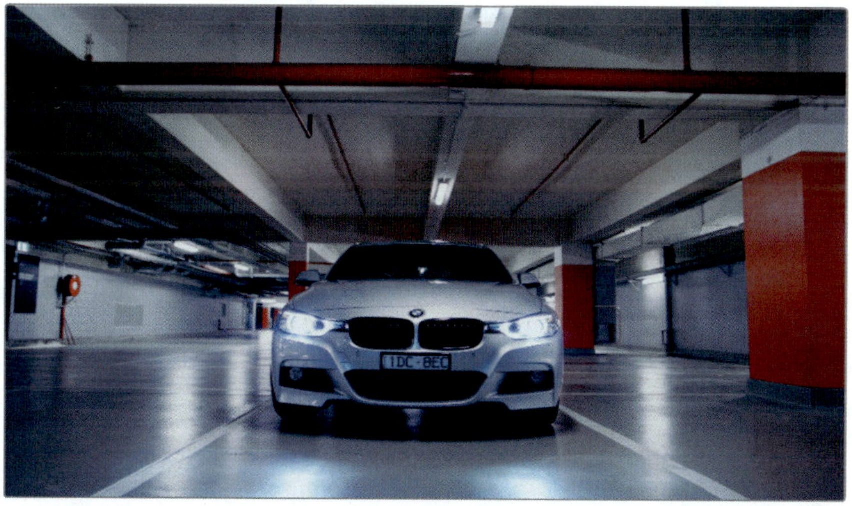

TIP To bypass the entire node tree within a specific level grade, press Option-D (macOS) or Alt-D (Windows). Doing so will leave your other node levels intact so you can assess the changes you have made within the current clip level.

Adjusting Clips After a Post-Clip Grade

Occasionally, a post-clip grade will emphasize or reveal inconsistencies in the clips which will result in mismatched grades. In such cases, you will need to return to Clip mode in the Node editor to make further adjustments.

In this exercise, you will return to the Clip mode to apply an effect to the key shot, and then fix a discrepancy that was revealed in one of the shots on the Timeline.

1. With clip 07 still selected, return the Node editor to Clip mode. You will be applying an effect to the final clip to make the headlights more dramatic.
2. Create a second node, and label it **Headlights**.
3. Open the Open FX panel.
4. Find the ResolveFX Light category, and drag the Aperture Diffraction effect onto the Headlights node.

   The result is an optical effect that mimics the diffraction of light. The settings in the OpenFX panel allow you to refine the pattern, intensity, and color of the effect.

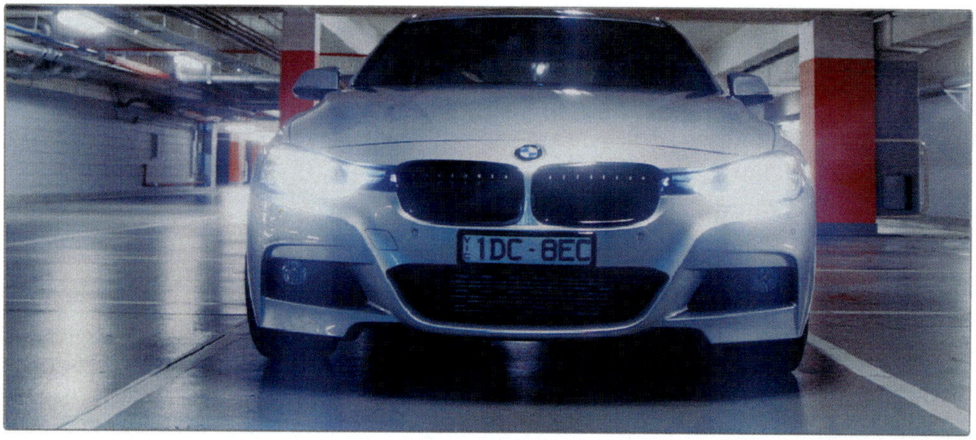

5 Under Aperture Controls, change the Iris Shape to Square.

> **TIP** In the Output category of the Aperture Diffraction settings, change Select Output to Diffraction Patterns Alone to get a clearer view of the light patterns as you adjust the settings. Change the output back to Final Composite to see the final result.

6 Under Compositing Controls, increase the Brightness to 0.600.

7 Increase the Colorize value to 0.300, and use the swatch underneath to change the color to magenta.

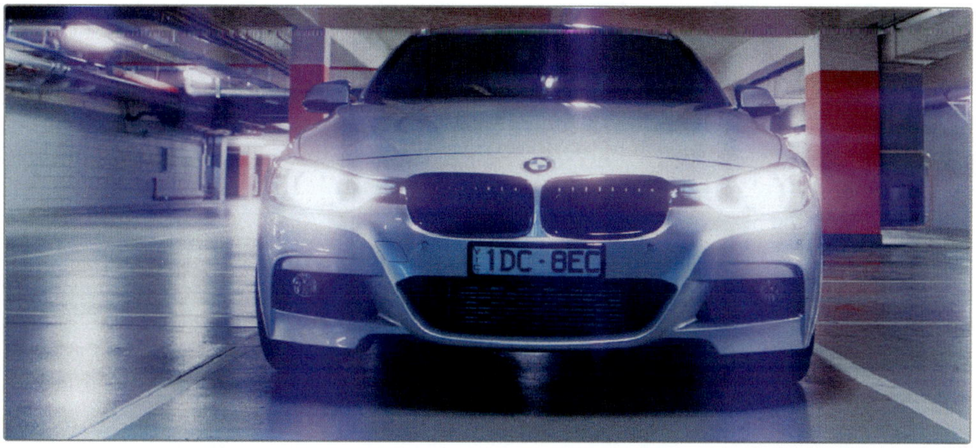

This simple effect dramatizes the final shot of the sequence as the car drives away. A variety of light-based effects in the Open FX panel enable you to stylize your shots and make features "pop" in subtle or exaggerated ways.

Next, you will check the remainder of the garage sequence to ensure that all shots match.

8 Navigate through the clip Timeline, and check the other clips for consistency.

You can see that the upper midtones in clip 06 are substantially bluer when compared to the environments in clips 05 and 07. Clip 06 is also fairly dark which is making it difficult to see the actor's face.

9 Click clip 06. Use the Enable the Wipe Timeline contextual menu to compare it to clip 07.

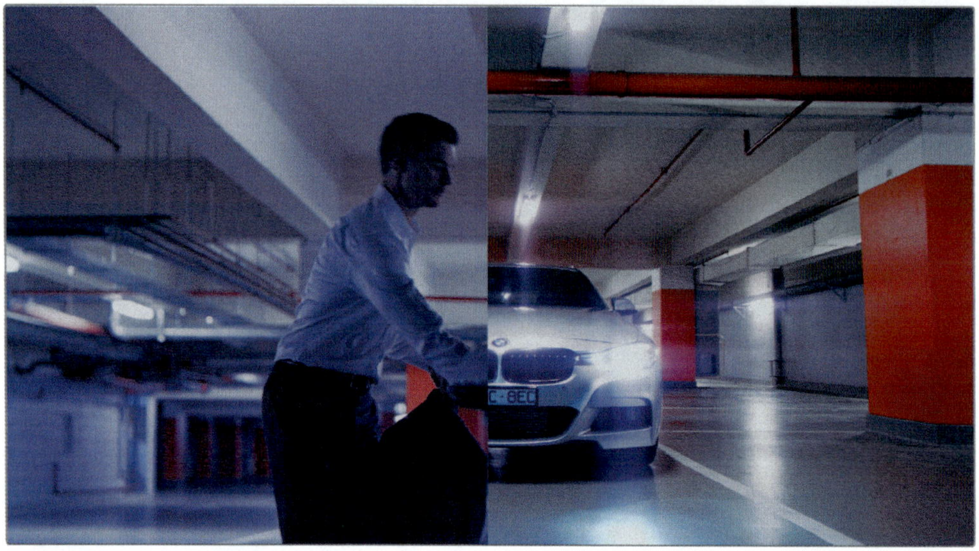

10 Change the Node editor to Clip mode.

11 Label node 01 as **Match**.

12 Drag the Offset wheel slightly toward orange to remove the blue dominance in clip 06, and in the adjustment controls, increase the contrast slightly.

13 In the Custom curves, isolate the lower midtones of the Y curve, and drag the curve upward to brighten up the man's face.

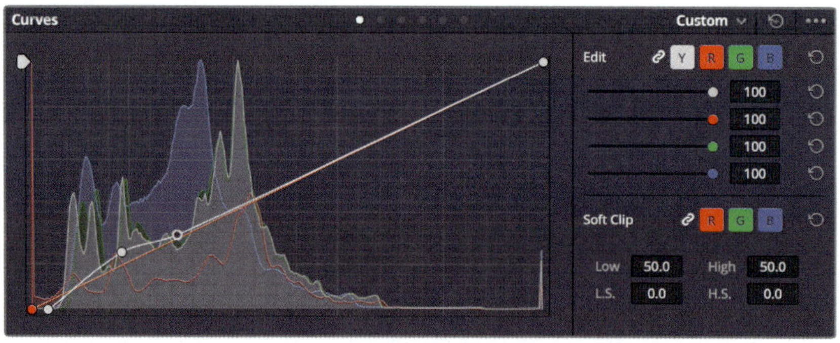

TIP The histograms in the Curves palette graph can be extremely helpful for determining the presence of dominant colors in different tonal ranges of the image. Use these histograms to guide the creation of adjustment controls and anchors.

The overall blue dominance of the shot is reduced, and the man's face is more clearly visible.

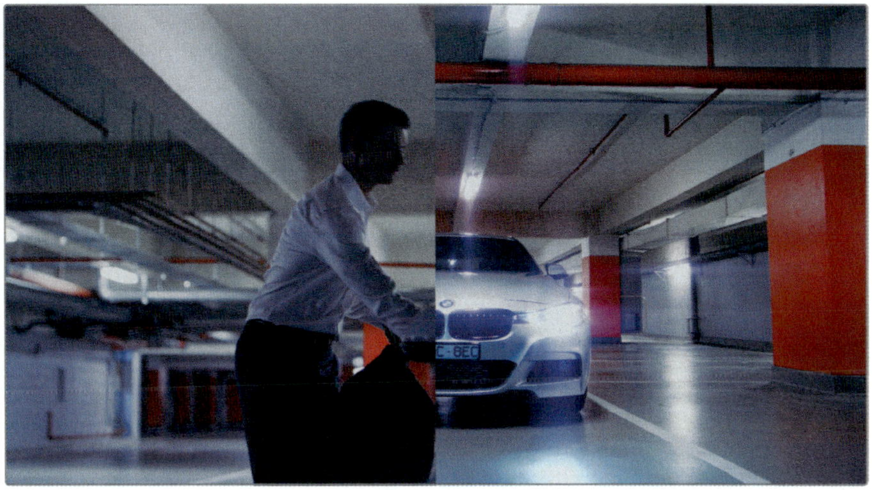

14 Disable Wipe mode in the Viewer.

The convenience of the group grading workflow is that no single stage or node is permanent. It is easy to jump between the different stages and tweak them as required, all while seeing the final output in the Viewer.

Applying Timeline Level Grades and Effects

The Timeline level is available in the Node editor whether you use a groups workflow or not. As the name implies, adjustments made at this level affect every Timeline clip uniformly. This functionality can sometimes be useful for image property applications such as custom blanking, color space transforming, gamut mapping, adding a vignette, or inserting film grain/analog video effects. It is not as strongly advised for grading purposes, but you can apply it to great effect in short video projects with consistent base colors.

In this exercise, you will apply an analogue video look to your entire project, followed by the data burn-in details that will make it easier to keep track of timecodes and clip names during the feedback stage of post-production.

Apply an Analogue Video Look to an Entire Timeline

Artificial film grain and analogue video artifacts are occasionally added to digital media for a variety of reasons. In some cases, the film needs to look outdated as a component of the storyline (such as flashbacks, home movies, found footage, and so on). Film grain and damage can also add realism to shots with artificially imposed elements or CGI graphics by making them appear to have been captured on tape or a celluloid film camera. Finally, film grain and damage is also an aesthetic choice made by many filmmakers.

> **NOTE** This exercise requires DaVinci Resolve Studio 16 to complete.

1. Turn off the Timeline filter to show all clips.
2. Switch the Node editor to Timeline mode.

   By default, the Node editor appears without a node 01, which acts as a useful reminder that this stage of the grading workflow is optional and can cause significant repercussions in the appearance of the entire Timeline.
3. Press Option-S (macOS) or Alt-S (Windows) to create a new serial node that will already be connected to the RGB input and node tree outputs.

   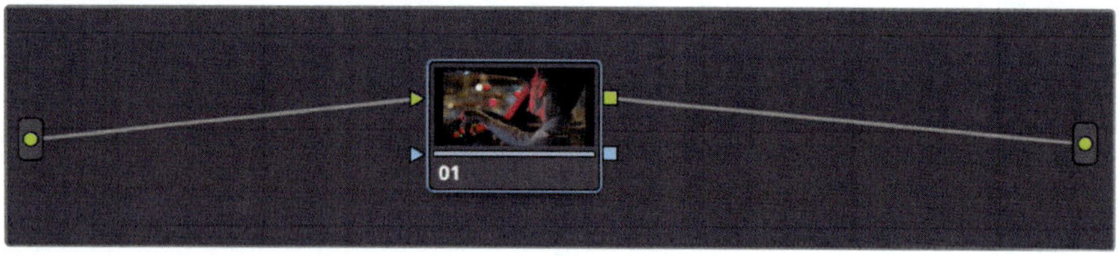

   The blue outline around the node is another visual reminder that you are not in any of the standard grading node levels.
4. Label node 01 as **VHS**.
5. Open the OpenFX panel.
6. Find the ResolveFX Texture category, and drag the Analog Damage effect onto node 01.

7 Press Shift-F to expand the Viewer and improve access to the Analog Damage panel settings.

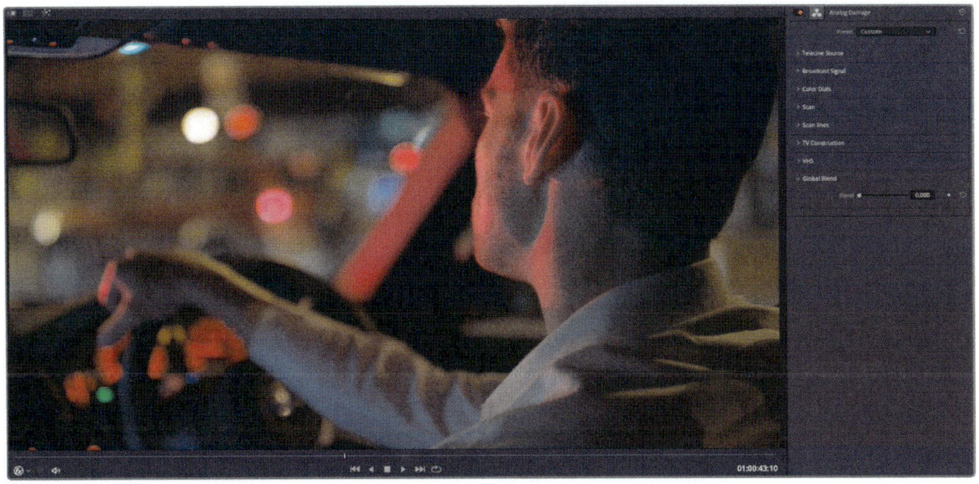

The top of the panel features a preset pop-up menu with a collection of common analog looks—early B&W television, transmission technologies from the 70s/80s, VHS, and so on. Beneath, individual parameter controls enable you to adjust a wide variety of damage components such as vignetting, noise, scan lines, chromatic aberration, jitter, and screen curvature.

8 Set the preset to Old VHS.

9 To remove the visible frame on the left, open the Scan category. Adjust the H-Shift to 0.050.

10 To remove the horizontal black lines running throughout the sequence as it plays, reset V-Hold to 0.000.

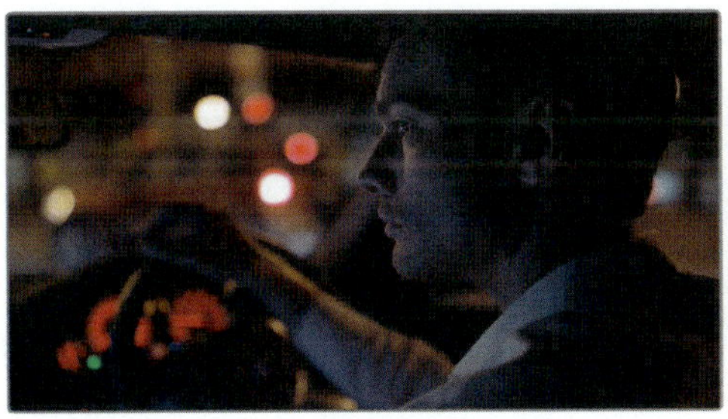

Before

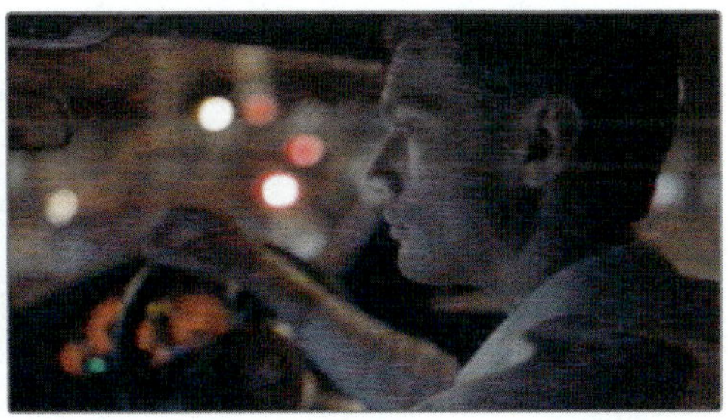

After

11 Click play to review the result. All the clips on the Timeline are affected by the VHS look. Press Shift-F to exit the full screen Viewer.

12 Before moving onto the next exercise, bypass the VHS node. The Analog Damage effect is processor-intensive, so it is a good idea to disable it until you are ready to export the project.

TIP The Film Grain FX in the ResolveFX Texture category can similarly be applied to achieve the look of celluloid film on digital footage. It comes with a variety of film stock presets (8mm, 16mm, 35mm) as well as a collection of grain parameters for optimal customization on a Timeline or clip-by-clip basis.

Adding Data Burn-in to the Viewer and Final Video

Another common feature applied on a Timeline basis is data burn-in which overlays a timecode, clip data, or any number of designated text metadata over the Viewer. It works independently from the Node editor and you can use it in-program for editorial purposes, as well as for the final delivery of the video.

1 Choose Workspace > Data Burn-In.

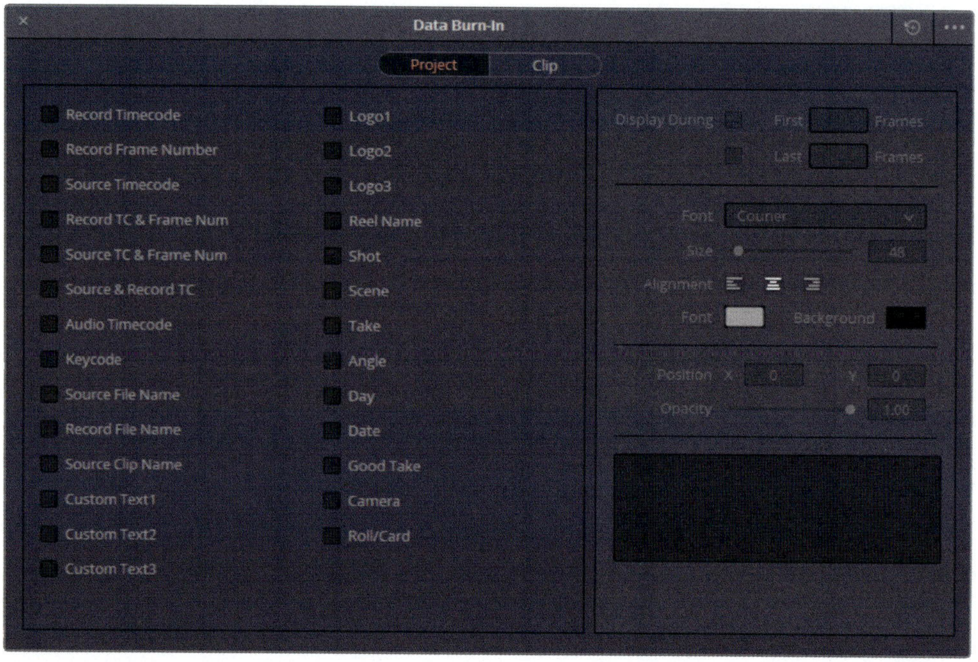

The left side of the Data Burn-In window features a wide selection of data options that you can superimpose over the video. The right side of the interface changes depending on the option you have selected and allows you to adjust the placement of text, font, color and so on.

The Project and Clip buttons at the top of the Data Burn-In window allow you to apply the data on a Timeline or clip basis. This choice can be useful when you are trying to leave comments for specific clips—for example, when communicating with the audio or VFX department about the requirements of specific shots.

2 Select Record Timecode to display the Timeline's timecode on the video.

3 Select Source Clip Name to display the name of each clip as it plays in the video. Note that in this case, because all the clips are sourced from a single flattened video file, they will all have the same source clip name.

4 Select Custom Text1, and in the Custom Output Text field, type **The Long Work Day version 1.1**.

> **TIP** To apply a watermark over a video, use one of the Logo options in the Data Burn-In interface. You can import a custom image/logo file and adjust its opacity using the transform controls.

5 Close the Data Burn-In window.

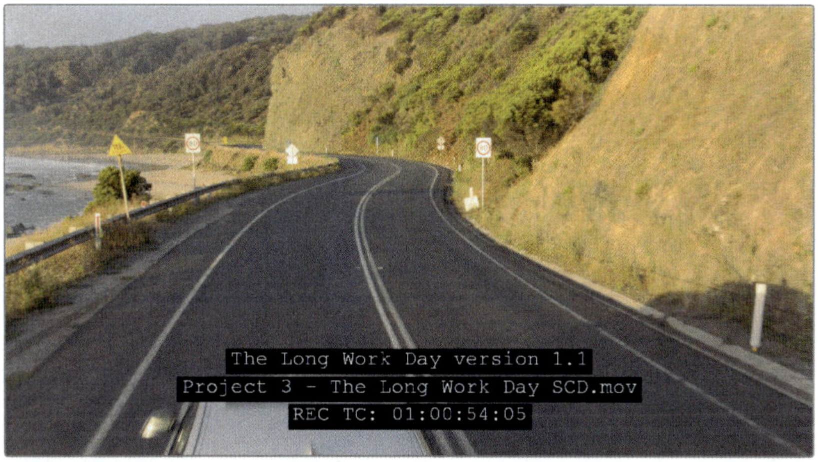

Data Burn-In options can be extremely useful for inserting quick and accurate communications between departments and clients. Instead of describing clips visually, exact clip source names can be used in feedback. Likewise, the precise timecodes ensure that your collaborators are not using the general timecodes of their video players (which usually lack frame data).

> **NOTE** The Data Burn-In windows includes fields such as Reel Name, Shot, Take, and many others that display the information entered into those respective fields in the Metadata panel of the Media page.

By combining the knowledge you gained in previous exercises with the group-driven workflow of this lesson, you can design extremely efficient project workflows that clearly divide and allocate the purposes of each group level and node.

Self-guided Exercise

Complete the following self-guided exercises in the Project 03 - The Long Work Day timeline to get more practice with groups, primary and secondary grading, and creative grade construction.

Home Group

- Create a post-clip group grade on the Home group. Import the GC_Island_Reference.png image from the BMD 16 CC - Project 03 > References subfolder into the Gallery as a reference. Aim to create a bright, warm, saturated look with a bit of contrast. Use HSL curves to emphasize the blue color of the sky and water outside the windows.

Highway Group

- Match the two clips in the Highway group. Pay particular attention to the color of the road in both shots.

Office Group

- Add clips 03-05 to a new group called **Office**.
- Perform pre-clip group grades in the Office group. Aim to get a good luminance range that preserves detail in the midtones while reducing the overly bright light sources in the room.
- Use the final clip (clip 03 in the filtered Timeline) as the key shot for matching clips 01 and 02. Pay attention to the contrast and create a similar cyan shadow range on all three clips.
- Perform secondary grading on clips 01 and 03 to address the red saturation in the lights. If you find it difficult to adjust the saturation without affecting the rest of the image, use windows to isolate the grade.
- Perform post-clip group grades in the Office group. Aim for an overall cyan look in the lower midtones of the image while maintaining neutral shadows and a red tint in the image gain. Return to Clip mode in the Node editor to tweak any inconsistencies revealed in the group grade.

Morning Group

- Add clips 16-18 to a new group called **Morning**.
- Perform pre-clip group grades in the Morning group. Ensure a good tonal range while still preserving the look of the bright sunrise.
- Perform contrast and color matching on the clips the Morning group. Make the sunset in clip 01 (in the filtered Timeline) look warmer to match the sunset in clip 02. Reduce the green and blue hues in the shadows of clip 03 to better match the preceding clips in the sequence.
- Perform a post-clip group grade in the Morning group. Aim for a yellow-and-orange sunrise look. Return to Clip mode in the Node editor to tweak any inconsistencies in the group grade.

When you've completed this exercise, open the Project 03 - The Long Work Day Commercial COMPLETED.drp and review the finished Lesson 7 Timeline to compare it with your work.

Lesson Review

1 True or False? A clip can belong to more than one group.
2 Which group level is ideal for performing shot matching?
3 True or False? Placing clips into groups allows you to bypass the normalizing/balancing stages of the grading workflow.
4 Which tool (and palette) can you use to quickly and accurately calibrate the starting colors and gamma of a group of clips in a scene?
5 How is Data Burn-In enabled?

Answers

1 False. A clip can have only one pre-clip and post-clip Node editor mode. Adding a clip to a group will remove it from any previous group that it was in.

2 Clip mode

3 False. If the clips in a group do not match each other, their differences will continue to be evident when a group grade is applied.

4 A color chart and the Color Match palette

5 Workspace > Data Burn-In

Lesson 8

Adjusting Image Properties

Though image colors tend to be a primary concern of the colorist, you can also make many transformative changes to footage to better accommodate the narrative and aesthetic output of a project. Such changes can include alterations to the scaling and positioning of the frame, noise reduction, and keyframing grades to change over time.

Applying such changes can impact the speed at which your computer is able to render and play the clips. For this reason, it is helpful to leverage the multiple caching methods in Resolve to ensure the quickest render on a clip and node basis, using both automatic (smart) and manual (user) methods.

Time

This lesson takes approximately 70 minutes to complete.

Goals

Understanding Timeline Resolutions and Sizing Palette Modes

In the following set of exercises, you will address the variety of ways in which you can impact the frame of your project in DaVinci Resolve 16. Specifically, you will change the project resolution, reframe individual shots, and sample portions of an image at the node level.

Changing Timeline Resolutions

In this exercise, you will change the project resolution to evaluate how doing so will impact the image quality and secondary grades of the clips in your Timeline.

> **TIP** To disable the group grades while working on this clip, enter the Group Pre-Clip node editor and press Opt-D. Repeat for Group Post-Clip and return to the Clip node editor.

1. In the Color page, apply blue flags to clips 1, 5, and 15, the clips you will focus on in this lesson.
2. Use the Clips filter to display only the blue-flagged clips.
3. In the filtered Timeline, select clip 02.

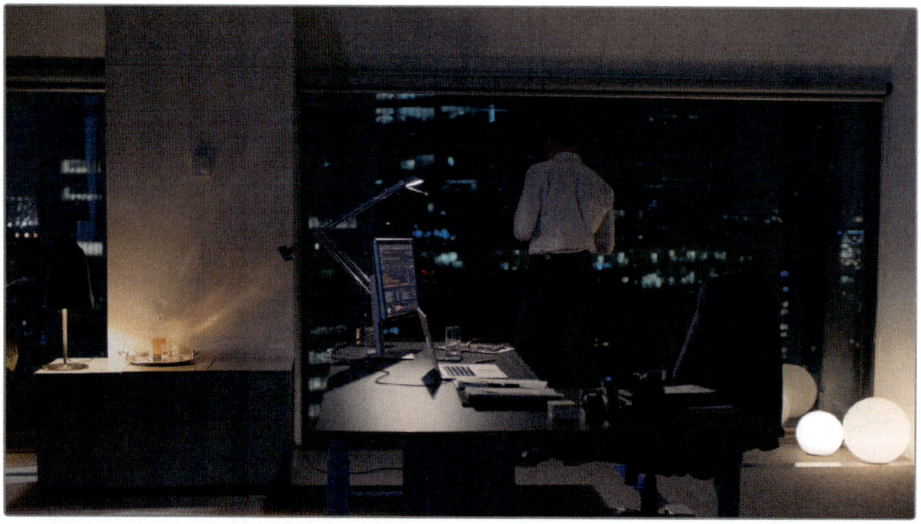

4. Create a new node called **Vignette**.
5. In the Window palette, apply the Vignette preset. Reposition and resize it to focus on the man at the window.

6 Drag the Gamma master wheel to the left to darken the edges of the frame. Drag the Lift wheel toward blue/cyan to give the room a cool look.

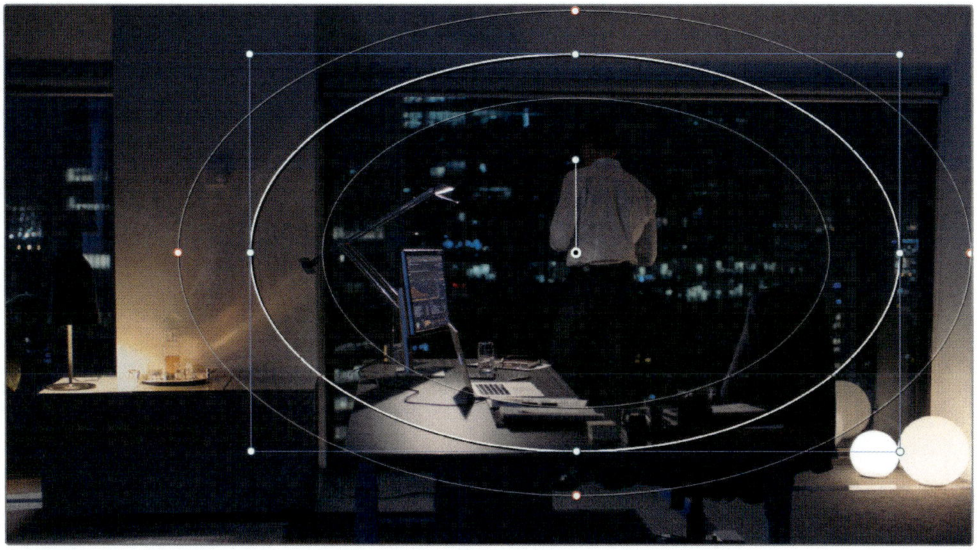

7 Open the Project Settings, and enter the Master Settings tab.

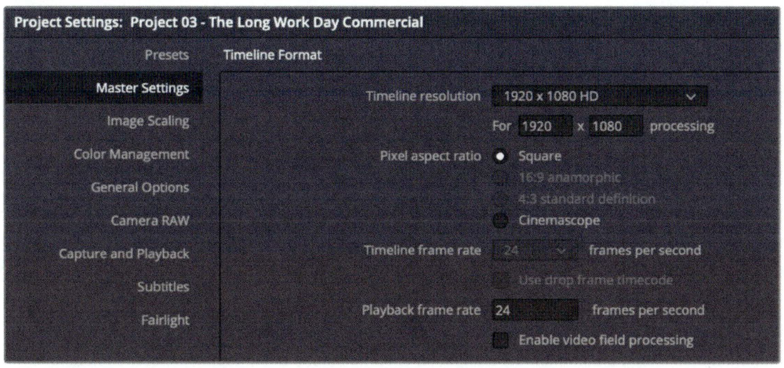

8 Change the Timeline resolution to 3840 x 2160 Ultra HD which is a 1.77:1 aspect ratio 4K resolution with the same aspect ratio as 1920 x 1080 HD.

TIP When rescaling media to a higher resolution (for example, converting 720p content to a 1080p Timeline, or 1080p to a 4K Timeline), you can activate a high-quality upscaling feature called Super Scale. To do so, right-click a low-resolution clip (in the Media, Edit, or Color pages), and choose Clip Attributes. In the Video tab, in the Super Scale pop-up menu, choose 2x (or higher) to double the resolution. Doing so will substantially improve the method by which the image is upscaled in higher-resolution projects. However, this is a processor-intensive operation that may compromise real-time playback.

9 Click Save to exit the Project Settings.

10 If the video appears zoomed in, press Shift-Z to fit the video frame to the Viewer panel.

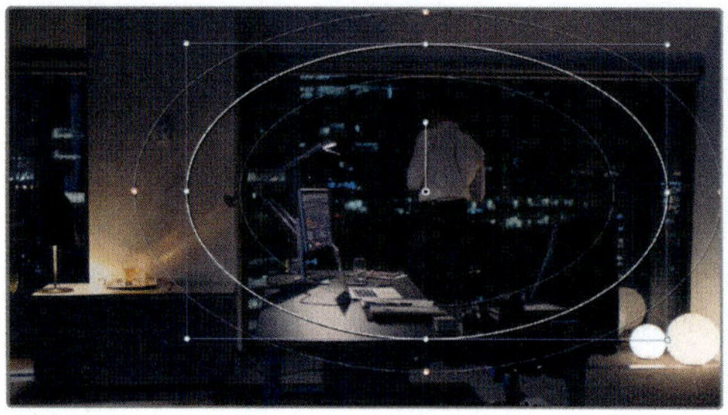

1920 x 1080

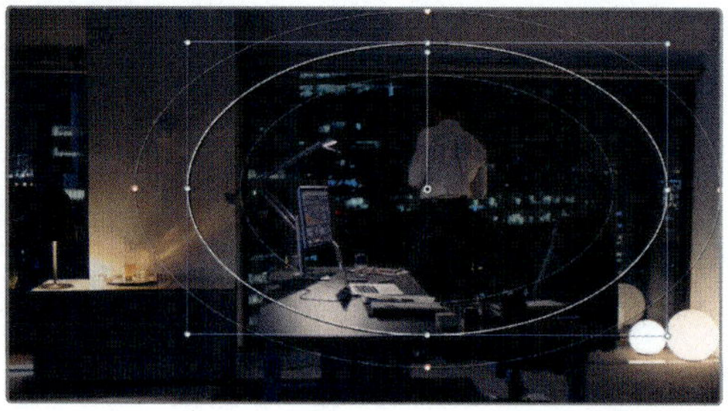

3840 x 2160

Compare the difference between the two resolutions. Note that the clip's frame and positioning in the Viewer has not changed. Additionally, the Power Window is rescaled to the new resolution while maintaining the placement in relation to the media clip.

This behavior is one of the most invaluable features of Resolve when grading and applying effects. The program is resolution independent, which allows you to change the frame size and aspect ratio of a project without affecting the positions of clips, images, secondary grades, effects, and generators created on the Edit or Color pages.

11 Delete the Vignette node.

4K to 1080p to 4K Workflow

Switching the Timeline resolution is an effective method for optimizing workstation performance during your editing stage. Doing so can ensure that clips are rendered and played in real time without lag and without altering the quality of the final film. A common workflow for 4K footage is to set the Timeline to 2K or 1920 x 1080 during the editing process, and then reset it to 4K prior to rendering. Alternatively, you can permanently set the Timeline to 1920 x 1080, and (in the Master settings or the Deliver page Render settings) set the Output Scaling to 4K to restore the full resolution during rendering.

The Proxy mode will continue to affect your image regardless of resolution. So, if you are reducing your Timeline resolution for faster playback during editing or preliminary grading, consider turning off the Proxy mode in the Playback menu to prevent further reduction of image quality in the Viewer.

Also, be aware that the grading potential, as well as the accuracy, of key-dependent secondary grading tools (such as the qualifier) is reduced at a lower image resolution. Therefore, you are advised to change the Timeline to the full media resolution before grading.

Reframing Individual Clips

The Sizing palette becomes an increasingly versatile tool when you take advantage of its sizing modes. These modes allow you to switch the sizing focus from clips to entire Timelines, or to individual nodes. In this exercise, you will rescale and reposition clips on an individual and Timeline basis.

1. Enter the Project Settings, and reset the Timeline resolution to 1920 x 1080 HD.
2. In the blue flag-filtered Timeline, click clip 03.

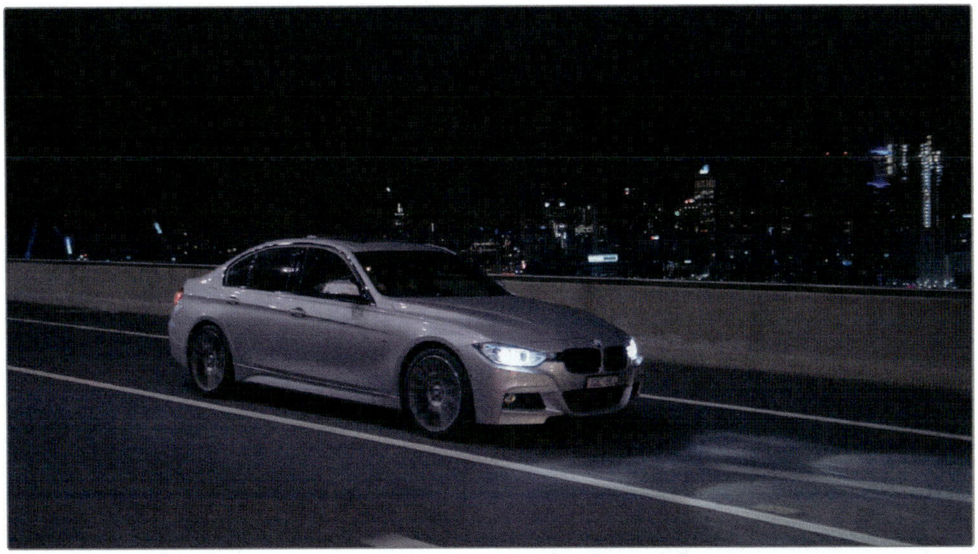

3. Enter the Sizing palette, and set the Zoom value to 1.500 to scale up the image.
4. Return to clip 02.

   Notice that clip 02 was not affected by the reframing of clip 03. In fact, every clip in the Timeline, with the exception of clip 03, has remained unchanged because clip 03 was changed at the clip level (Input Sizing) in the Sizing palette.
5. Return to clip 03, and reset the Sizing palette.

   It is necessary to remove filters when applying changes that affect the whole Timeline.
6. Use the Clips filter to display All Clips.
7. In the upper-right of the Sizing palette, in the pop-up menu, choose Output Sizing.
8. Enter the Zoom as 1.500 again.
9. Click the other clips in the Timeline to verify that they were altered by the change in scale.

   Sometimes, rescaling makes sense on a Timeline-wide basis, such as when appropriating media to a different resolution or aspect ratio. However, reframing tends to be much more specific as to the visual content of each shot.

10 Use the Clips filter to display only the blue-flagged clips.

Let's reframe shots 02 and 03 based on content.

11 Change the Sizing palette mode to Input Sizing.

12 In clip 03, change the Pan to 45.00, and the Tilt to 50.00.

13 In clip 02, change the Pan to 90.00, and the Tilt to -25.00.

14 Switch between the clips to verify that they retain their Output Sizing zoom, but have adopted different pan and tilt values.

NOTE Output sizing is also commonly used to adapt footage with a different aspect ratio to a certain standard—for example 4K DCI will appear to have horizontal blanking in a 4K UHD Timeline. Output sizing can be used to quickly fill the frame of the video.

These changes used two modes (Input and Output) of the Sizing palette. Previously, you rescaled and reframed a wiped still using the Reference Sizing mode.

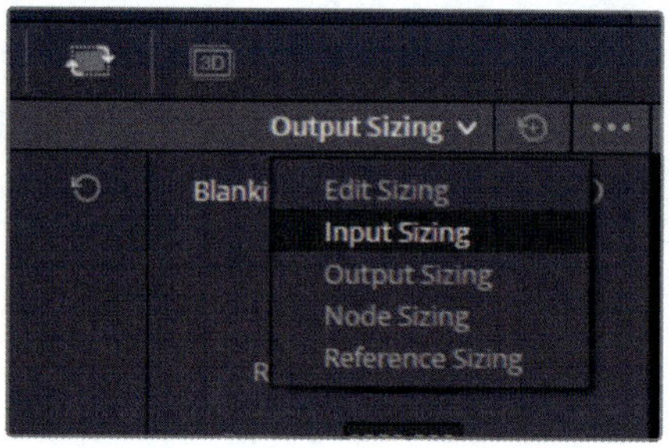

The full list of sizing modes and their impact on the image is as follows:

- **Edit Sizing** reflects the transform changes applied to a clip in the inspector of the Edit page.
- **Input Sizing** reflects the sizing changes made to a clip in the Color page. It targets clips on the same level as Edit Sizing, but isolates the function to the Color page.
- **Output Sizing** applies to the entire Timeline.
- **Node Sizing** applies to the selected node in the Node editor.
- **Reference Sizing** applies to the reference movie or still that is visible in the Viewer's wipe mode.

TIP To apply blanking to your Timeline, click Timeline > Output Blanking, and choose an aspect ratio. This method preserves the original video resolution while permitting you to change the project aspect ratio.

Custom Resolutions and Aspect Ratios

Under the Timeline resolution presets of the Project Settings, you may enter a custom resolution that will result in a non-standard video resolution at the aspect ratio of your choosing. Be aware that changing the aspect ratio or resolution to a non-industry standard value could mean that it may not be playable on some projectors or video players. When outputting to equipment that only recognizes standard video formats, it is a safer option to use a common (preset) resolution and apply custom blanking to change the aspect ratio.

Sampling Visual Data with Node Sizing

The ability to change an image's sizing data at the node level permits some interesting creative and practical application. You could clone an image to display multiple versions of it within the Viewer, or perform visual repair by sampling portions of the image for cover-up work.

In the following exercise, you will use node sizing to produce a creative layered look.

1. Reset the Input and Output sizing data from the previous exercise.
2. In the blue flag-filtered Timeline, click clip 03.
3. Label node 01 as **Base**.
4. Create a new serial node called **Backplate**.

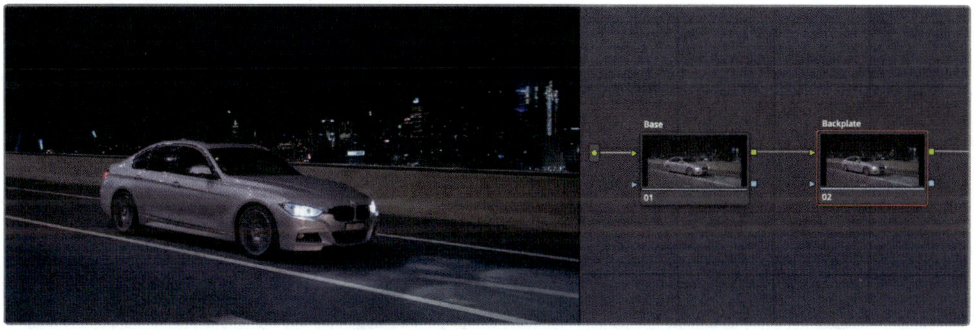

5. Press Option-L (macOS) or Alt-L (Windows) to create a Layer Mixer node.
6. Rename the new node (node 04) that is connected to the Layer Mixer as **Crop** and select it.
7. Open the Window palette.
8. Activate a linear window, and reposition the corners to capture the front half of the car.

9 Change all the Softness values to 0.00 to give the window a sharp edge.

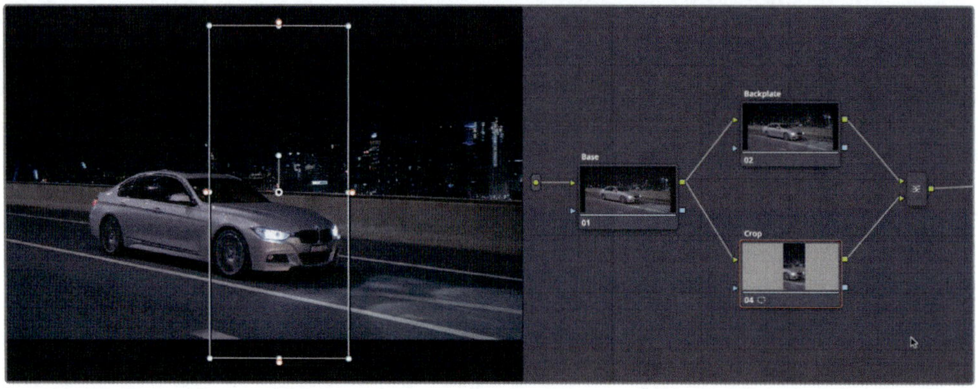

10 Open the Sizing palette, and set it to Node Sizing mode. From now on, all changes to the Sizing palette will affect only the 04 Crop node.

11 Change the Zoom to 2.0 to scale up the linear window and its contents.

The backplate remains unchanged.

12 Pan the window (375.000) until you can no longer see the backplate to the right of the Viewer.

13 Tilt the window upward (300.000) to see more of the road in the scaled-up node.

14 Select the Backplate node.

15 In the Sizing palette, pan the image left (-300.000) to place the car in the left-half of the Viewer.

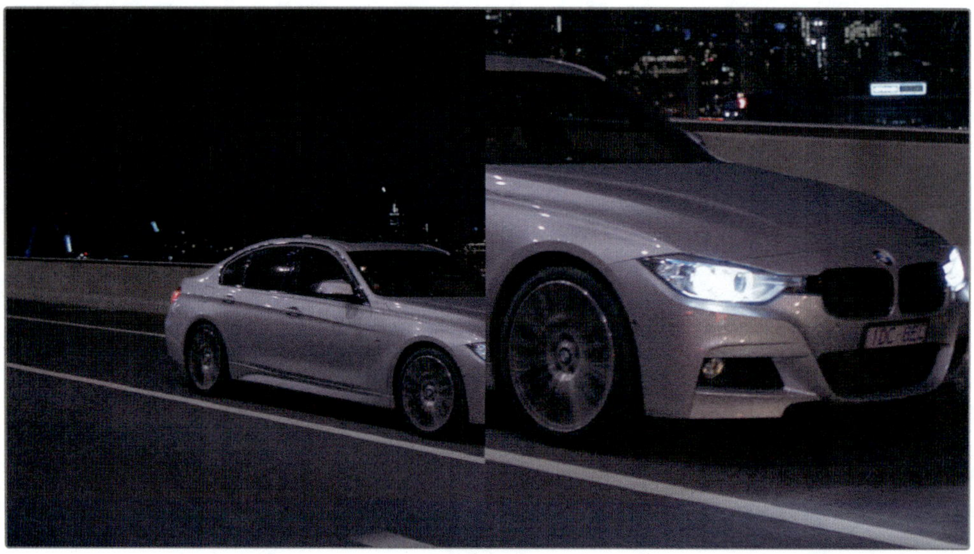

16 Reselect the Crop node to begin grading the car close-up.

17 Drag the Offset wheel toward blue to give the shot a cool metallic look.

18 Drag the Lift wheel toward red to slightly offset the blue in the shadows.

19 Increase the contrast and adjust the pivot of the image until it is significantly lighter than the original, but still contains pitch-black shadows and metallic highlights. Adjust the Offset master wheel, if necessary.

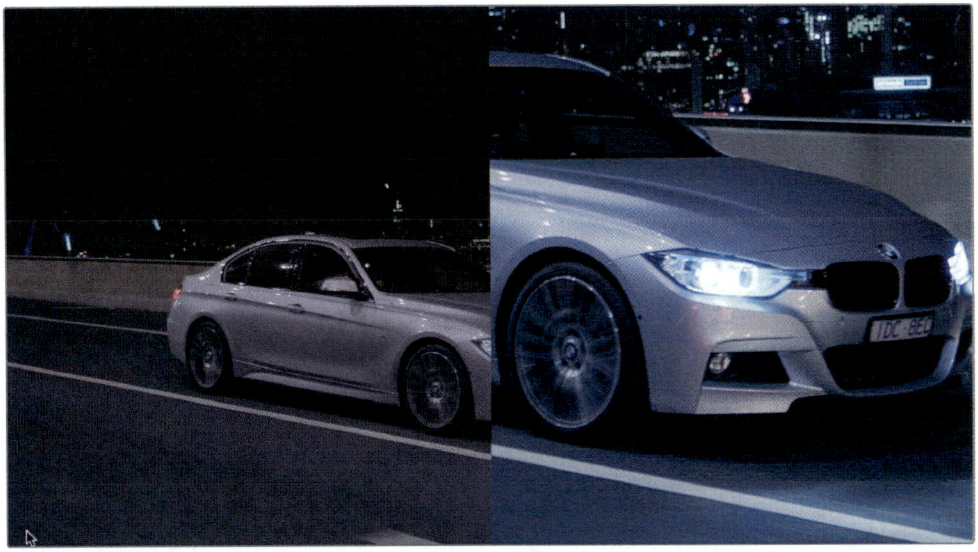

20 Play the clip to display the two versions of the footage simultaneously.

In layer-based compositing systems, this effect would be possible only by creating a second video track, duplicating the clip over itself, and applying a crop tool. Due to its less efficient method of reusing video data, layer-based compositing tends to be more processor-intensive. Nodes provide a much cleaner approach to the duplication and resampling of RGB signals.

NOTE You can combine node sizing with group node levels to adjust sizing data on multiple clips at once. This technique is particularly effective because resizing tends to preserve maximum video quality when performed on the Edit or Input level of the Sizing palette.

This technique is often used in HD projects incorporating 4K footage that can be zoomed up to 200% (on a 1080p Timeline) before visual quality is noticeably degraded. In contrast, HD footage can only be scaled 110-120% past its native resolution before the image will visibly soften.

Creating Cover-ups with Patch Replacer ResolveFX

You can also use node sizing for more practical compositing solutions, such as sampling a portion of the video to cover up an undesirable artifact. This type of painting or cover-up work is often used to fix continuity errors, conceal visible booms, and improve set design.

In this exercise, you will use the advanced Patch Replacer ResolveFX to quickly perform cover-up work and automatically adjust the grade of the sampled area to match the destination.

> **NOTE** DaVinci Resolve Studio 16 is required to complete the following exercise.

1. In the blue flag-filtered Timeline, click clip 02.

   This is a visually interesting shot with good set design and a great choice of location. However, one minor element is distracting from the luxurious office: the wall thermostat. Your aim is to remove the thermostat by covering it with a sample of a portion of the wall.

2. Create a new serial node and label it **Coverup**.
3. Open the Open FX panel.
4. From the ResolveFX Revival category, drag the Patch Replacer effect onto the Coverup node.

   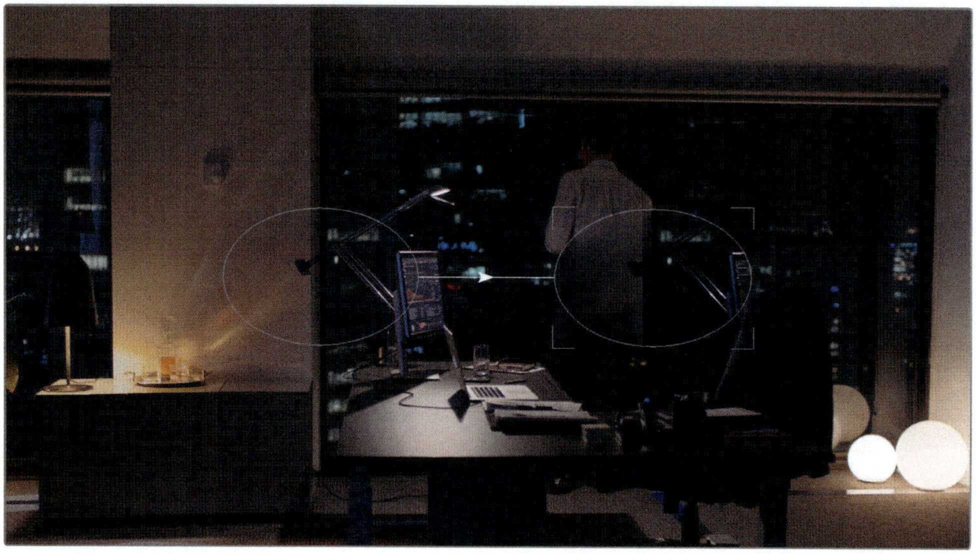

   Two oval outlines appear in the Viewer. The left oval represents the source patch, which is actively sampling the portion of the video under it. The right oval with the four corners is the target patch that is receiving visual data from the source and actively grading it to match its surroundings.

5 Drag the target patch over the wall, and resize it to outline the thermostat and its shadow.

6 Drag the source patch over an empty area of the wall near the target.

7 If necessary, zoom in on the Viewer to refine the placements.

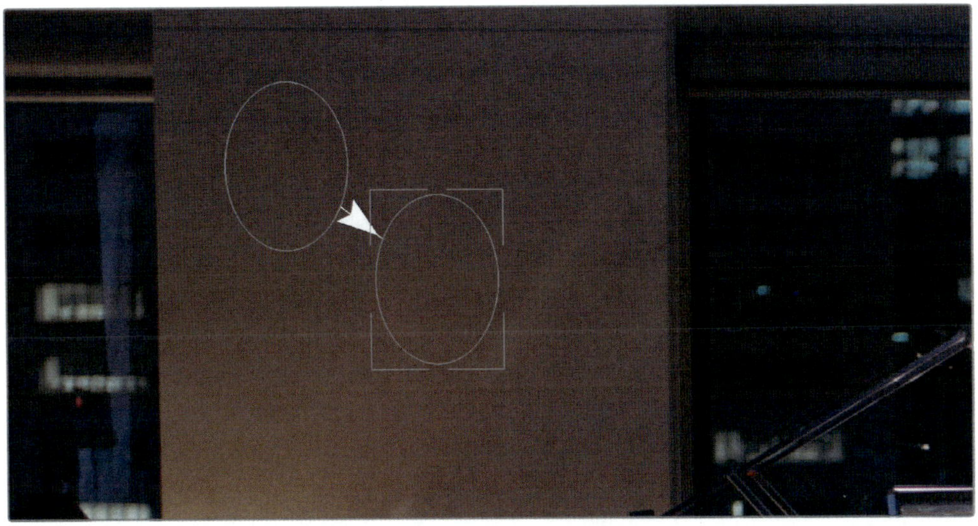

TIP To navigate inside the Viewer after zooming in, hold down your middle mouse button and drag in the Viewer. If you do not have a middle mouse button, you can Shift-Option-drag (macOS) or Shift-Alt-drag (Windows) to move horizontally and vertically within the Viewer.

The cover-up is successful, but only on the first frame of the clip. As soon as you play the video, the thermostat is revealed from behind the cover-up node. To complete the composite, you will need to track the effect to the camera movement.

8 Press Shift-Z to fit the video frame to the Viewer panel.

9 Open the Tracker palette, and in the upper-right pop-up menu, change its mode to FX.

To perform motion tracking, you will need to specify a tracking point. Ideally, you will want to identify the element you are covering up or a trackable area that is on the same plane as that element. In the case of this clip, the original thermostat is an ideal tracking point.

10 Click the Coverup node name to bypass that node, and reveal the thermostat under the patches.

11 In the lower-left corner of the Tracker palette, click the add tracker point button.

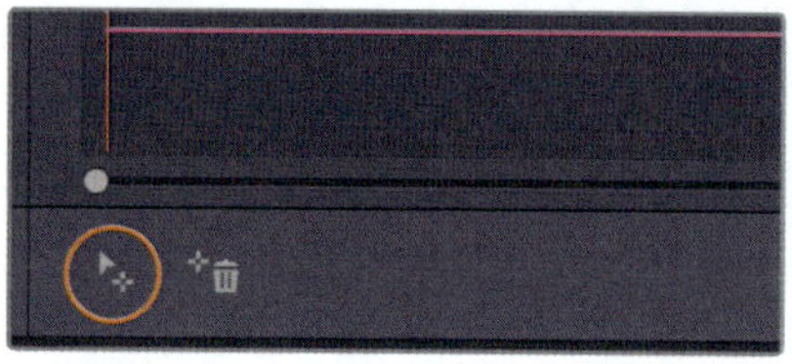

Blue crosshairs appear in the center of the frame. These crosshairs indicate the area of the image that will be analyzed for tracking.

12 Drag the crosshairs over the thermostat on the wall.

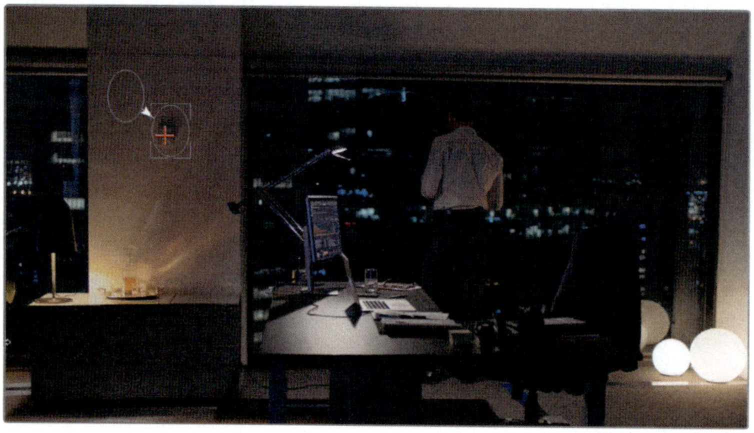

The crosshairs turn red when the default position is altered.

13 In the Tracker palette, click the Track Forward button to perform the track analysis.

14 After tracking is completed, click the Coverup node name to see the patches.

15 If necessary, in the lower-left corner of the Viewer, turn off the on-screen controls to hide the patch and tracking point outlines.

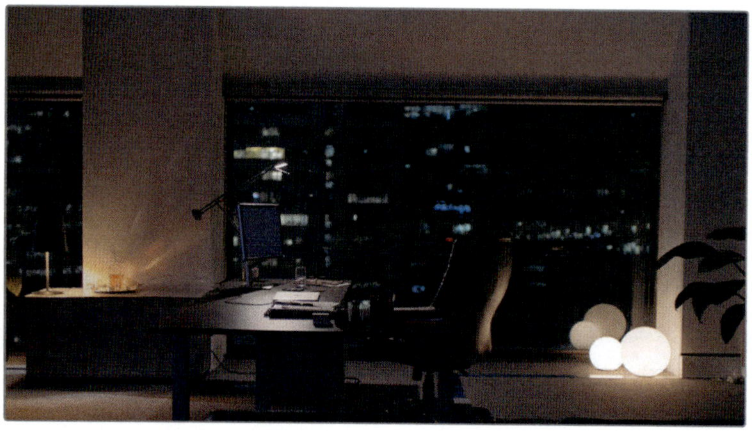

16 Play the clip to check the accuracy of the cover-up. Make further adjustments to the size and placement of the source and target patches, if necessary.

The result is a clean cover-up of the wall that is ready for further editing and grading.

> **TIP** You can also perform this type of cover-up effect using node sizing. With a Backplate node in place, create a Layer node, and use a Power Window to sample a clean portion of the video. In the Sizing palette, move the Layer node over the portion of the image you want to cover up. In the case of moving camera shots, begin the workflow by tracking the video with the standard window tracker before moving the Power Window over the sample area.

Node-based cover-ups are frequently employed to address the aesthetic needs of a scene or to resolve issues that were not noticed during the shoot (for example, removal of visible set equipment or covering spots on actors' faces). These workflows tend to work best on footage with little movement and good sample areas.

> **TIP** Another tool that you can use for cover-up work is the Object Removal effect (also in the ResolveFX Revival category). Whereas the Patch Replacer samples data from the current video frame, Object Removal uses the data from surrounding frames to cover up a moving object. To remove an object, first draw a Power Window around it and track it through the shot. Then, drag the Object Removal FX node onto that node. Right-click the node and choose Use OFX Alpha to connect the tracked window key to the FX node. Click Scene Analysis in the OpenFX Settings and wait. If the object you're removing is moving but the camera is locked, enable Assume No Motion. If enough visual data is available, the object will be successfully removed.

Using Keyframing

To understand keyframing, you need only to grasp the concept that you need just two keyframes to create any animation. And those keyframes need to communicate just two things to the program: their points in time and their values. By placing the keyframes at different points in the Timeline, you indicate the length of time through which the change occurs; and by giving those keyframes individual values, you specify the nature of the change.

Animating Position Values with Dynamic Keyframes

Dynamic keyframes uniformly adjust parameter values across frames which creates the effect of smooth change over time. In this exercise, you will animate the transform values and the color grade of a clip to imitate a camera move and sunrise effect.

1 Select clip 01 on the Project 03 - The Long Work Day timeline.

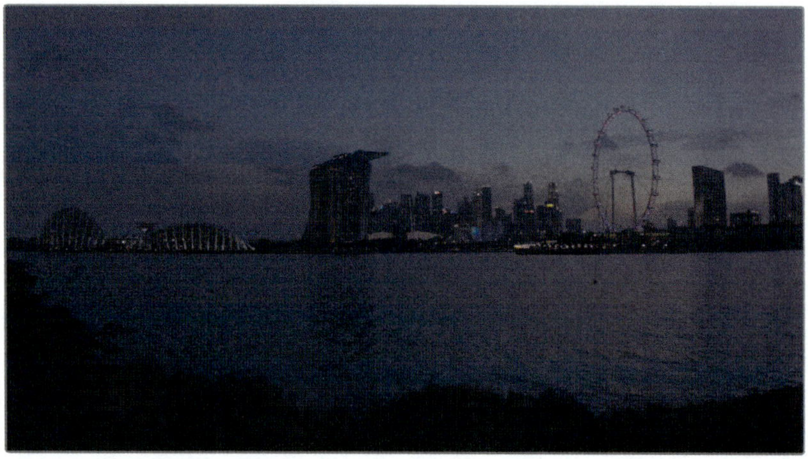

This video was captured late in the evening and appears very dark. Before you can begin grading it creatively, you should expand its luminance range to take advantage of the colors and contrast.

2 Label node 01 as **Balance**.

3 Drag the Gain master wheel to the right (2.10) to increase the waveform spread and overall brightness of the image. Some noise issues are revealed in the low-light conditions. You will resolve these after the grade is completed.

The clip is a locked establishing shot. Even though it was captured in real-time, it has a time lapse feel to it. In the next few exercises, you will introduce animation to the shot to imitate the fast passage of time in the environment.

Your first goal is to create a pan-and-zoom movement starting from the wide shot and ending on the city skyline.

4 To the right of the palettes in the Color page, open the Keyframes editor.

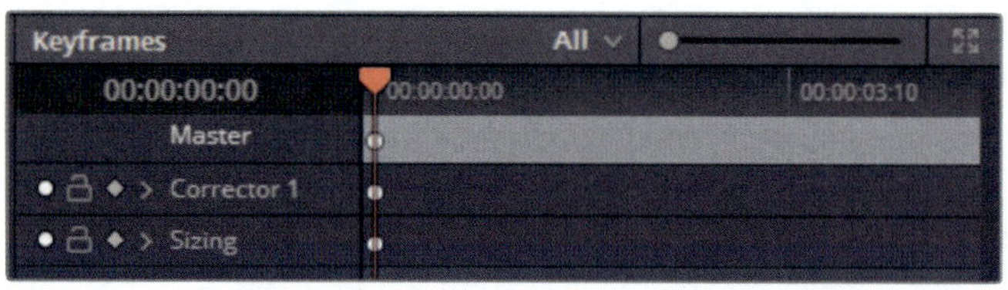

The palette currently includes animation controls in two categories: the individual controls of node 01 (Corrector 1) and the Sizing value of the overall clip.

5 Create a new serial node and label it **Sunrise**. Corrector 2 appears in the list of the Keyframes palette.

Each new node you create will receive its own corrector header in the Keyframes editor.

6 To prepare to animate the motion in the image, expand the Sizing category.

7 Click the diamond-shaped keyframe symbol next to Input Sizing to activate animation in that palette.

8 While on the first frame of the clip, right-click the circular keyframe next to Input Sizing, and choose Add Dynamic Keyframe.

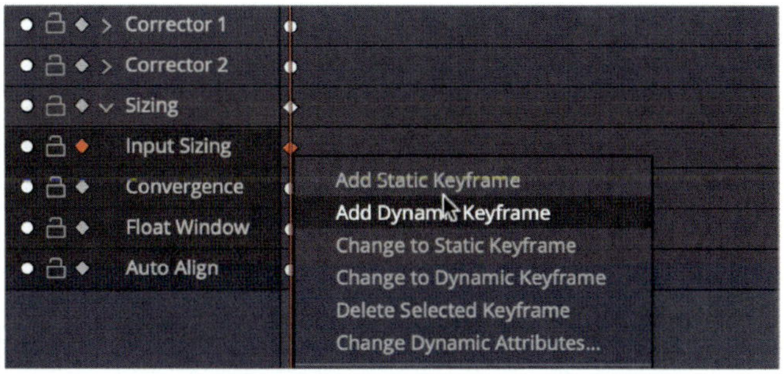

The circular keyframe becomes diamond-shaped.

9 Drag the playhead to the end of the clip duration in the Keyframes Timeline.

10 With the Sizing palette in Input Sizing mode, change the Zoom to 1.500, the Pan to -400.000, and the Tilt to -200.000.

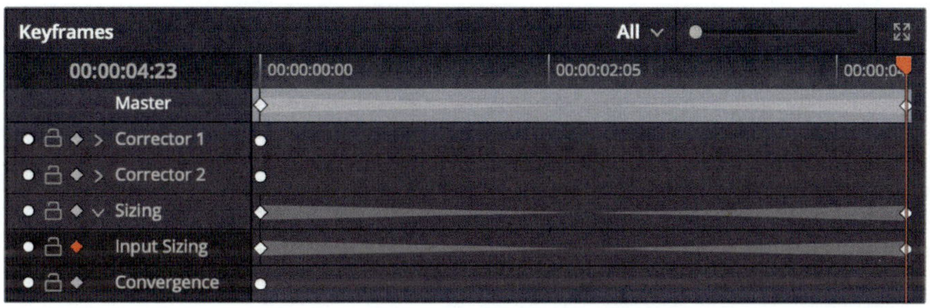

Two new dynamic keyframes are automatically added to the keyframes Timeline—one for the Input Sizing parameter, and one for the general Sizing header in which it is contained. Additionally, two dimmed triangles indicate that a dynamic animation was generated.

11 Play the clip to watch the animation in action. The shot begins with a wide view of the city and then quickly zooms in on the skyline in the distance.

TIP If you click the Loop button in the Viewer playback controls, the playhead will play the same clip over and over instead of continuing through the entire Timeline.

Changing Color Values Over Time with Dynamic Keyframes

Next, to animate the color values of the clip, you'll directly target the keyframe controls within the nodes.

1 In the blue flag-filtered Timeline, drag the playhead to the first frame of clip 01.

> **TIP** You can click the expand button in the upper-right corner of the Keyframes editor to increase the interface size. Doing so will move all other palettes to the left of the Color page, thereby giving you more room to focus on keyframing.

2 Select node 02 Sunrise.

To imitate the look of the sun rising, you will first need to create a pre-dawn look.

3 Drag the Gamma master wheel to the left to darken the midtone ranges of the image, and then drag the Gamma color wheel toward blue to cool the temperature of the shot.

4 Accentuate the shadows and details in the skyline by increasing the Contrast in the adjustment controls.

5 Finally, reduce saturation to 30.00 to imitate the reduced perception of color in dark environments.

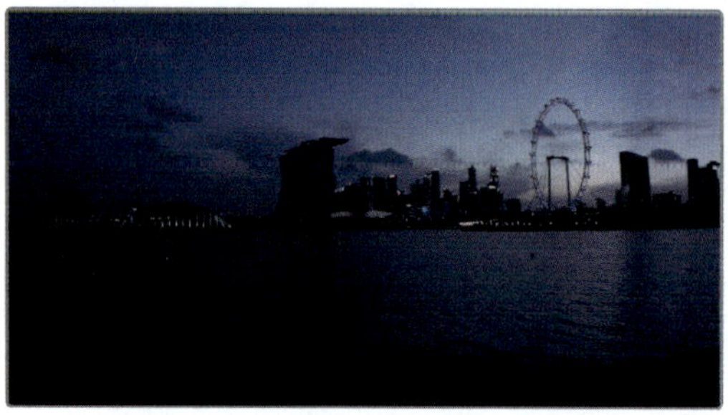

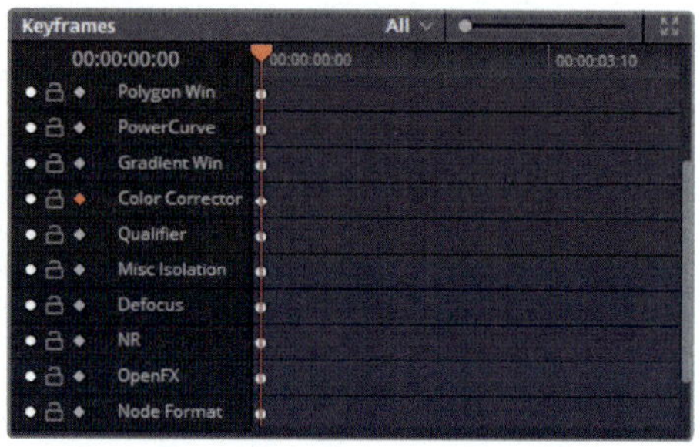

6 In the Keyframes palette, expand Corrector 2.

7 Click the keyframe symbol next to Color corrector to activate keyframing.

8 Right-click in the Keyframes Timeline, and choose Add Dynamic Keyframe.

9 Drag the playhead to the last frame of the clip.

10 To imitate sunrise, drag the Gain and Offset master wheels to the right to brighten up the image.

11 Drag the Gamma and Gain color wheels toward yellow and orange to warm up the image.

12 Return the Saturation to 50.0 to more accurately represent the colors.

> **TIP** Press the [(left bracket) and] (right bracket) keys to navigate between keyframes in the Keyframes palette. This shortcut can save you time when comparing the different stages of an animation.

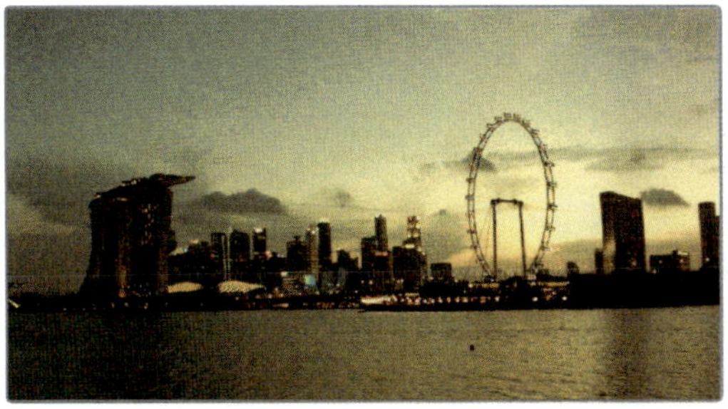

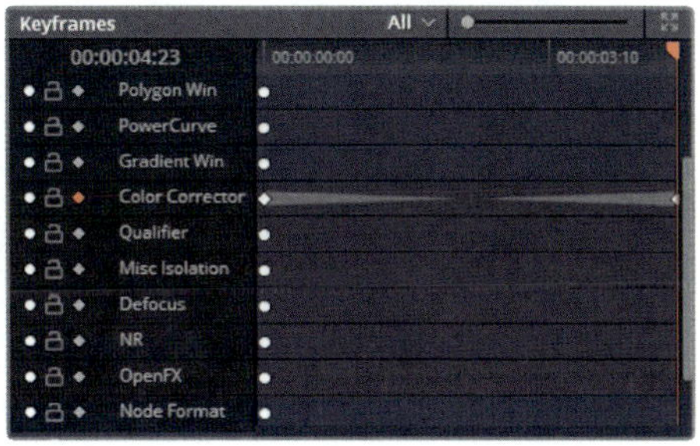

13 Play the clip to see the colors animate over time.

A common reason for keyframing color grades is to address color temperature fluctuation. Shoots in which the camera operator frequently maneuvers from indoor to outdoor locations (documentaries, wedding videography, and so on) benefit greatly from these types of animated grade workflows.

> **TIP** OpenFX can also be keyframed. When an effect is added directly to a pipeline, it will appear under its own name in the master list of the Keyframes palette. When an effect is dragged onto a corrector node, it will appear in the list under the appropriate corrector header.

Applying Dynamic Attributes

Though the animation in this example was successful, the zoom still appears a little artificial due to the linear nature of the animation. In this exercise, you will simulate a more realistic camera zoom by altering the animation speed and style using dynamic attributes.

1 With clip 01 still selected, select and right-click the first keyframe in the Input Sizing parameter.

2 Choose Change Dynamic Attributes.

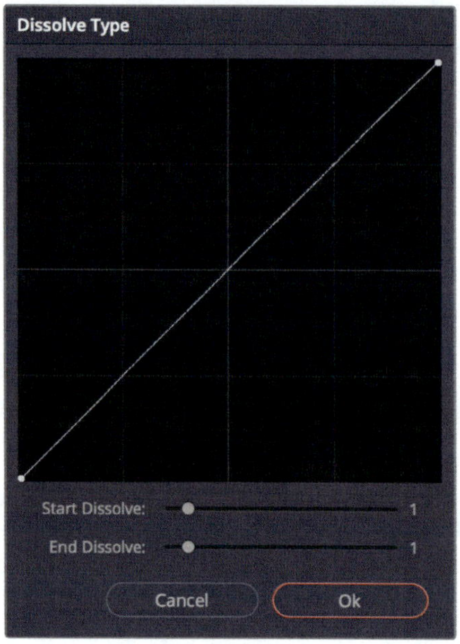

The dynamic attributes pop-up interface controls the behavior of the animation from the currently selected frame to the next frame.

3 Set the Start Dissolve value to 2. The almost-horizontal shape of the line at the start indicates that change will be slow and gradual, before it accelerates and finishes in a linear fashion.

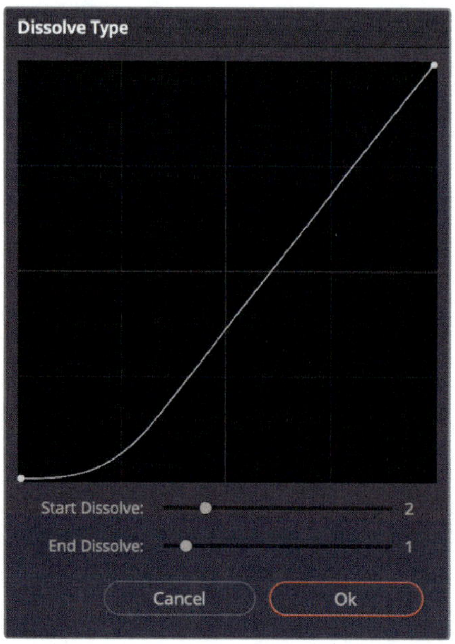

4 Click OK to confirm the change.

5 Play the clip and note the slow start to the animation. This move makes the simulated zooming effect more realistic.

Using Static Keyframes

When creating a new keyframe in the editor, the alternative to dynamic keyframes is static keyframes. Static keyframes do not animate the change between values. Instead, they abruptly change the value when the playhead reaches that keyframe.

You can combine static and dynamic keyframes within a single animation, such as when a change needs to be gradual, but to abruptly appear/disappear at the start or end of the animation—for example, with a lightbulb that lights up abruptly and then gradually increases in brightness and temperature.

Mastering keyframe animation can take some getting used to; but in time, and with consistent practice, generating keyframes and creating changes can become a common and frequently utilized part of your grading workflow.

Applying Noise Reduction

Resolve's noise reduction feature runs on a powerful video engine that is able to distinguish noise from environmental data by performing a temporal analysis of the video frames. This feature enables a strong reduction of noise while preserving a high level of detail in the subjects of the image. Applying the additional spatial method of noise reduction further cleans up the image by analyzing and removing repeating noise patterns.

NOTE DaVinci Resolve Studio is required to complete the following exercise.

1 In the blue flag-filtered Project 03 - The Long Work Day timeline, click clip 01.

2 Drag the playhead to the last frame of the clip to see it at its brightest.

Due to the low-light conditions in which this footage was captured, the brightening of the gamma and gain has revealed digital noise in the shadows and midtones.

3 For a better view of the noise detail in the image, change the Viewer Zoom to 200%.

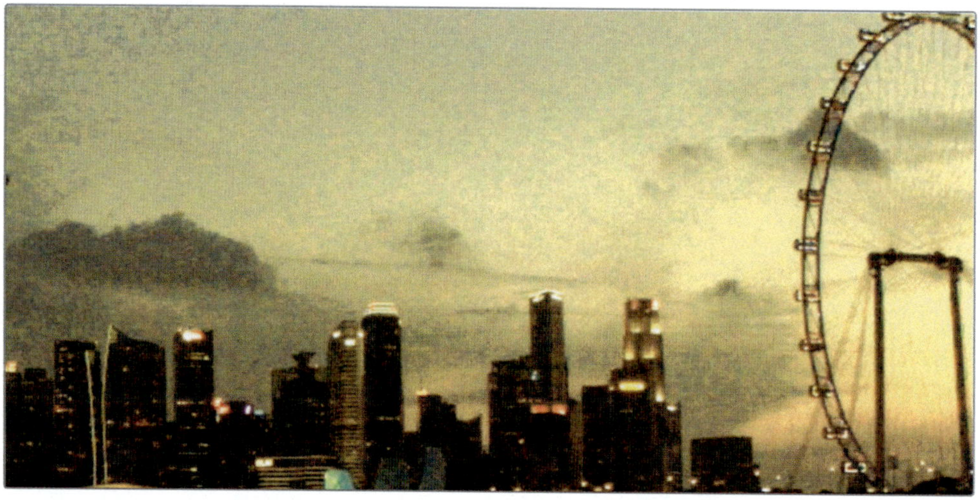

4 Create a new serial node after Balance (node 03) and label it **Denoise**.

5 Open the Motion Effects palette.

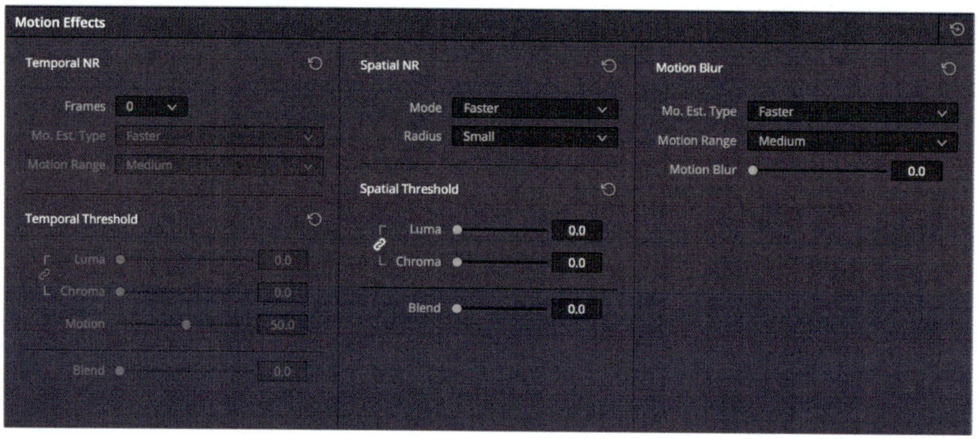

This palette is divided into three control areas:

- **Temporal NR** analyses the video across several frames to detect moving subjects and backgrounds. It excludes moving elements from the most aggressive noise reduction processing to prevent unwanted blurring of vital information.
- **Spatial NR** softens high-frequency noise while retaining the data in levels of high detail. This tool is extremely effective for reducing fine-grain noise that Temporal NR missed.
- **Motion Blur** is not a noise-reduction tool, but uses the same analytical engine to produce its results. This tool helps make action shots more dynamic by allowing you to add motion blur to moving subjects.

6. Under Temporal NR, you will first need to choose the number of frames that will be averaged to separate the detail from noise. For this shot, which features no camera movement or moving subjects, an analysis of 2 frames is sufficient.

   The higher the number, the more accurate the analysis will be, but at the expense of extra processing time. However, a higher analysis rate could also produce artifacts in shots with overlapping moving subjects.

   The Mo. Est. Type (Motion Estimation Type) setting enables you to indicate the method used to detect motion in the image. A setting of Faster prioritizes speed of output over quality, whereas Better produces a finer result at the expense of extra processing time. Choosing None bypasses the motion detection feature and applies noise reduction to the entire image.

7. For clip 01, choose Better.

   Motion Range allows you to indicate the speed at which the subjects are moving to exclude areas with motion blur from the noise reduction effect.

8. Clip 01 has almost no motion, so Small is a good choice.

   The Temporal Threshold controls how aggressively noise reduction is applied to luma and chroma levels. By default, these options are linked; but if the image has monochromatic noise (or vice versa), it is advisable to unlink the two parameters and target the luma directly.

   This is the setting that will activate noise reduction in the image, so you can begin by entering any number, and then dragging left or right to increase or decrease the effect.

9. Enter 5.0 as the starting Threshold.

   To see how much the Temporal NR is affecting the image, you can use the Highlight tool to assess the pixel difference.

10. In the Viewer, enable Highlight mode.

11. In the upper-right of the Viewer, click the A/B icon to activate the Difference mode.

    The patterns you see in the Viewer show the amount of noise that was removed from the original image.

12. Drag the Thresholds to the right to increase the intensity of the noise reduction.

13. Stop adjusting when you start to recognize the outlines of objects on the horizon indicating that the noise reduction has become so aggressive that it is now removing legitimate visual information. Drag the Threshold left (10.0) until only noise remains.

Good noise reduction

Noise reduction too aggressive

The Motion value acts as a pivot for the point at which moving objects are excluded from noise reduction based on the motion controls. A lower value excludes larger areas of the image, whereas higher numbers assume less motion and target more of the image.

14 Very little motion occurs in the image, so a high Motion value of 60.0 is appropriate.

The Blend value allows you to blend the original image into the noise-reduced version. This adjustment can be helpful when the noise reduction is too aggressive and areas of the image take on a plastic appearance.

15 Leave Blend unchanged for this clip.

16 Disable the Highlight view, and toggle the Grade Bypass to compare the image before and after the Temporal NR.

The noise reduction is substantial. However, you still have room for improvement by reducing the more generic noise patterns in the image.

> **NOTE** Because Temporal NR is designed to carefully avoid applying noise reduction to moving elements in a shot, it is best applied to locked-off images. In a shot with a quick pan or handheld camera motion, every element will be moving which defeats the purpose of the Temporal NR analysis.

17 Under Spatial NR, set the reduction Mode to Enhanced.

As with Motion Estimation Type, this setting is responsible for determining the speed/quality of the final output; though, in this case, Faster, Better and Enhanced refer to different analysis algorithms. Choosing Enhanced will produce a substantially improved output.

The Radius value indicates the area of the image that is analyzed to determine the noise type within the frame. The larger the area, the more accurate the analysis will be at the expense of processing speed.

18 For more subtle noise types, as in this image, a Radius setting of Medium is enough for a successful analysis.

As with the Temporal NR, the Luma and Chroma Threshold settings determine the intensity of the Spatial NR.

19 Change the Luma and Chroma Threshold settings to 40.0 to see a further reduction in the remaining image noise. As you did previously, use the Highlight tool to ensure that the details in the image are not too strongly affected.

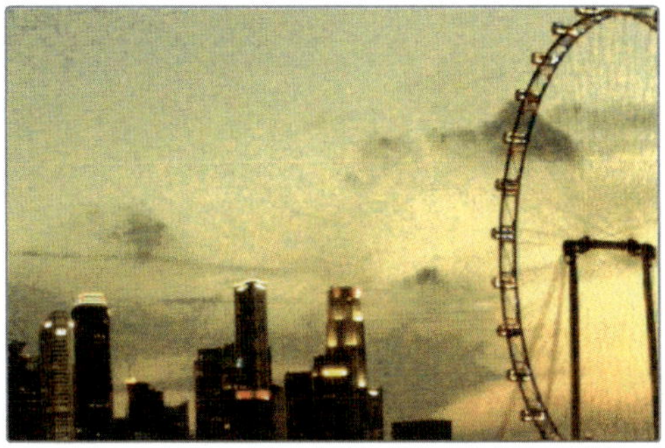

Before noise reduction

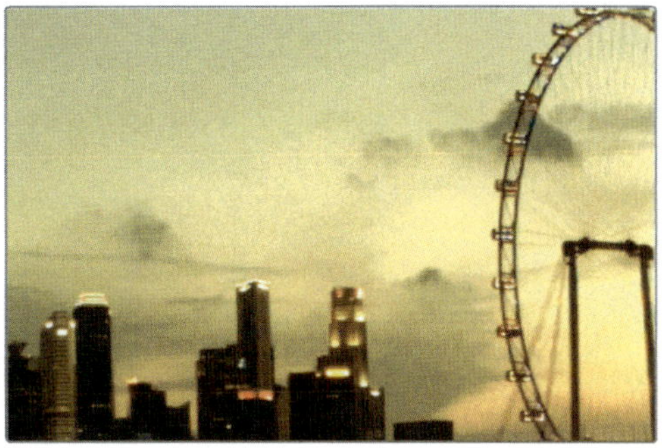

After noise reduction

20 Press Cmd-D (macOS) or Ctrl-D (Windows) to bypass the Denoise node and compare the image before and after noise reduction. Pay particular attention to the preservation of the fine detail in the image—the Ferris wheel spokes and the windows in the buildings of the skyline.

Before moving on, it would be worthwhile to check whether changing the location of the Denoise node could improve the noise reduction.

21 Select the Denoise node, and press E to extract it from the pipeline.

22 Drag the Denoise node to the link between the RGB input and node 01 (Balance). Doing so will perform noise reduction on the original RGB signal before any grading or animation takes place.

In this instance, the change softens the impact of the noise reduction and gives a better visual output.

23 Bypass the Denoise node before moving to the next exercise.

It is always advisable to use a dedicated node for noise reduction. After the noise is reduced to a satisfactory level, you can disable the Denoise node before proceeding with the rest of the grading process. Deactivating the Noise Reduction node will reduce the amount of processing and caching that the software will need to perform for playback.

Where Should You Place the Noise Reduction Node?

Applying NR at the start of the node tree is advisable because it analyses and uses the original RGB data to reduce noise. However, this placement may potentially impact the precision of key-based selection methods (HSL curves, qualifier).

Applying noise reduction at the end of the node tree can avoid this issue (if it is present), but can also produce a slightly less detailed image. When unsure, change the position of the NR node in the Node editor until you find the optimal position.

Optimizing Performance with Render Cache

Almost anyone who has done graphic-intensive work on a computer will be familiar with the frustration of experiencing lag when the workstation is incapable of processing the data in real time.

DaVinci Resolve offers a variety of methods for improving workstation performance. For example, by using Optimized Media, or any transcoded media workflows, you can change the size and quality of the footage to ensure faster playback during editing.

Another powerful method for increasing playback speed is allowing Resolve to render your footage while the application is otherwise inactive. You can then play the cached media without the need to actively render effects-heavy clips.

Understanding Source and Sequence Caching

The process of rendering footage in the background, or generating a cache, in Resolve can be enabled on a variety of levels. In the following exercises, you will enable smart caching in your project and observe two early caching levels: source and sequence.

1. Enter the Edit page.
2. Choose Playback > Render Cache > Smart.

   By using the Smart Cache option, you are leaving it up to the software to choose which media or nodes are computationally intensive and require caching.

   The first level at which caching takes place is the source. When in Smart Cache mode, it is generated for processor-intensive video formats such as H.264 and RAW. The Project 03 - The Long Work Day timeline is using media in an intermediary codec (DNxHR) that is already optimized for editing; therefore, the program is able to play it in real time without performing source caching.

   After the source cache, a sequence cache is generated in the Edit page when additional effects such as transitions, titles, or generators are applied to clips in the Timeline.
3. In the Edit page, open the Effects Library palette.
4. In the Titles folder under Toolbox, locate the Text title generator.
5. Drag the title generator onto video track 2, and extend its length to cover the first five clips of the Timeline.
6. In the upper-right of the Edit page, open the inspector palette.

7 Click inside the text box under the Rich Text heading, and enter the project name **The Long Work Day**.

A red line appears over the Timeline to indicate that a cache is being generated for all the media under the title tool.

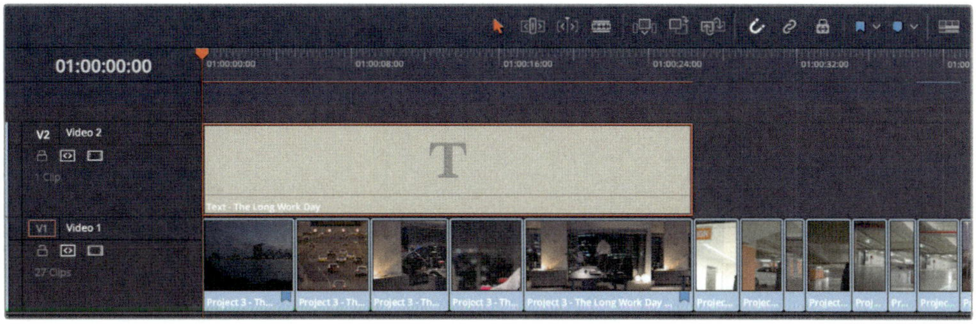

When the rendering process is complete, the line turns blue.

Generating a Node Cache

The node cache appears in the Node editor of the Color page after the application of grades and effects. Like the source cache, when Smart Cache is enabled, rendering occurs only when Resolve deems the processes to be intensive.

1 Enter the Color page.
2 Change the Timeline filter to show All Clips.
3 At the top of the page, click the Timeline button to view the Timeline Ruler in the Color page and see your video tracks and cache processes.

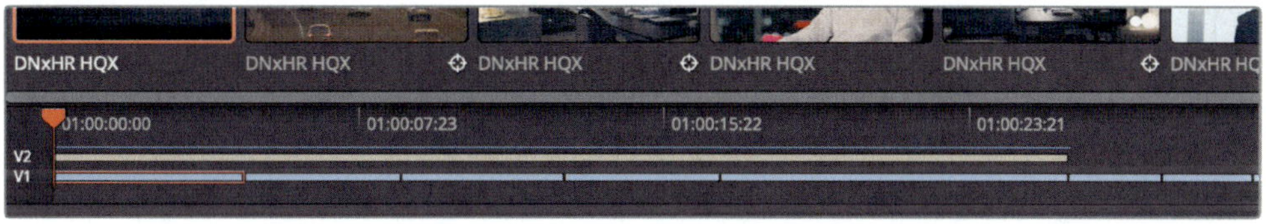

4 Note that the sequence cache over the title generator is still active. Because you do not need to see or cache the titles during your grading work, you can disable them by clicking V2 on the Timeline Ruler.
5 Click clip 01.
6 The Denoise node was bypassed in a previous exercise. Click the Denoise node name to activate it.

The timecode above the clip thumbnail will turn red to indicate that it is in the process of caching. The node name and number will turn red in the Node editor for the same reason.

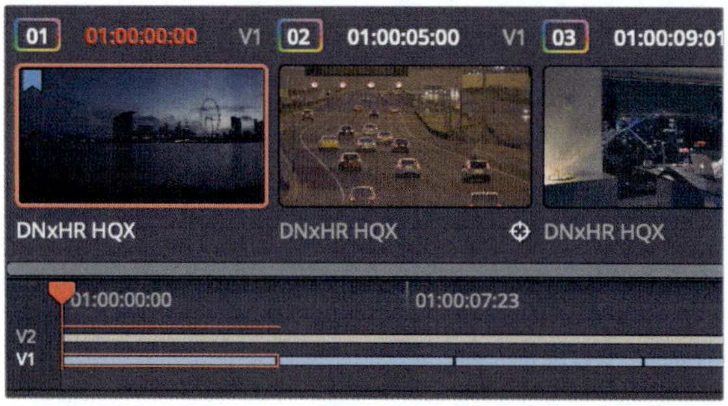

The cache line on the Timeline Ruler will eventually turn blue as caching is completed.

7 Create a serial node after the Sunrise node, and label it **BW** (node 04).

8 In the adjustment controls, drag the Sat value to 0.

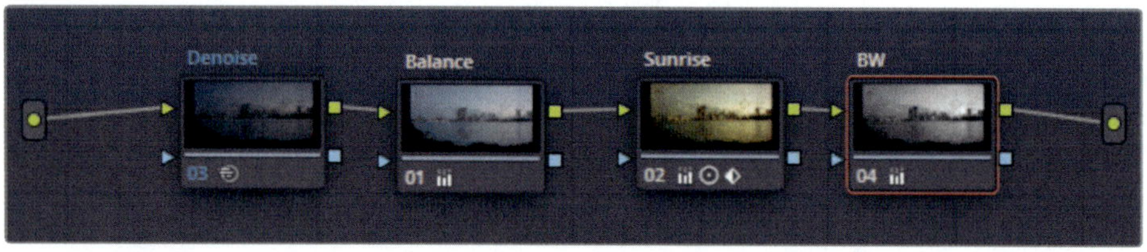

Your image retains its sunrise animation, though it is now displayed in only black and white. The BW node did not turn red and will not require caching because the standard color grading controls are usually not intensive enough to disrupt clip playback.

Adding the BW node has not enacted a re-cache of the Denoise node because the denoising is not affected by the changes made in the BW node. If you follow the path of the RGB signal, it is denoised before it is desaturated, and so the same denoised version of the cache can continue to be used.

9 Click the Denoise node, and press E to extract it.

10 Drag the node over the connector at the end of the pipeline to place it after the BW node.

The Denoise node turns red as it re-caches the new RGB signal.

11 After the Denoise node turns blue, click the BW node, and adjust the Contrast in either direction.

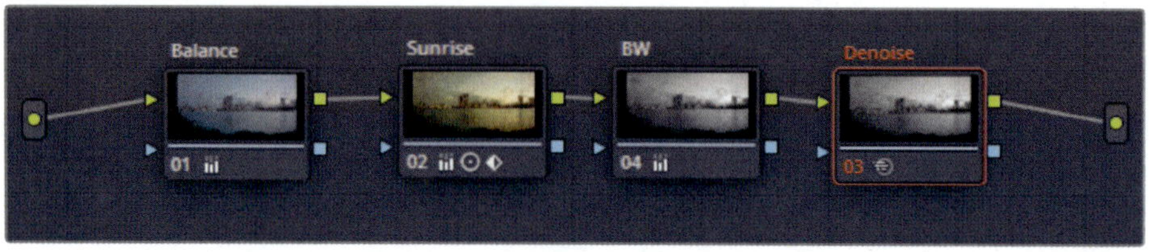

This time, the change prompts the Denoise node to turn red and require a new cache. The BW change affected the RGB input of the Denoise node, which has to perform a new render using the new RGB signal.

Utilizing User Cache Modes

As you have seen, the decision to render clips on every level of the workflow is made within the background processes of the software. Smart Cache allows you to continue to focus on your project while Resolve detects when rendering is necessary to enable faster playback.

However, at times, you might want to control which clips are rendered. For that, you can enable User Cache that will not perform any media rendering until you specifically tell it to do so.

1. Choose Playback > Render Cache > User.

   The blue highlights on clip 01 and the Denoise node disappear when automated caching is disabled. From now on, all caching will occur only on your command.

   Some colorists prefer to work in this mode when they do not want background caching to occur throughout a project. One reason may be because they are using RAW media and want to cache only those clips that they are actively working on instead of the entire Timeline.

2. Click clip 01.
3. Right-click the Denoise node, and choose Node Cache > On. Once again, caching is performed and the node name turns blue.

> **TIP** When working on a larger project, you could use the Clips filter to isolate clips with noise reduction and manually cache them to avoid enabling Smart Cache.

In addition to selecting individual nodes in User Cache mode, you can manually render a clip's entire node tree.

4. Right-click clip 05, and choose Render Cache Color Output.

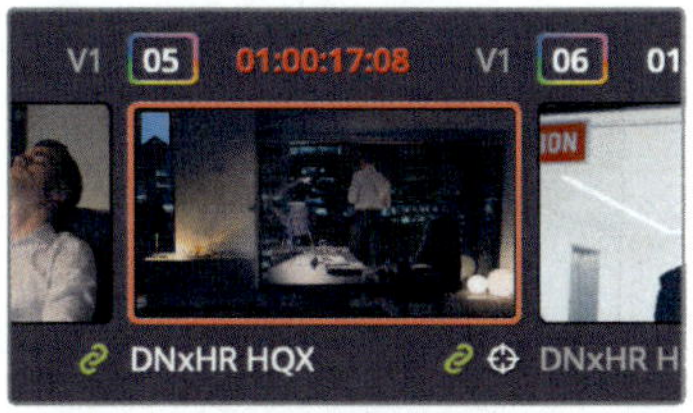

The clip's timecode turns red in the Timeline while the nodes remain white. In this scenario, the entire node pipeline is cached, which results in even faster playback when compared to rendering individual nodes. However, it also means that making changes to *any* of the nodes in the pipeline will require that the entire clip be re-cached.

5 In the clip 05 Node editor, add a new serial node called **Magenta Look**.

6 Drag the Offset color wheel toward magenta to add color to the clip.

Although the process of adding color to the clip is not processor intensive, the clip immediately turns red in the Timeline because a new cache is generated for the entire pipeline.

Configuring Cache Quality

When you play media in the Viewers of the Edit and Color pages, you can see the playback frame rate in the GPU status indicator in the upper-left of the Viewer.

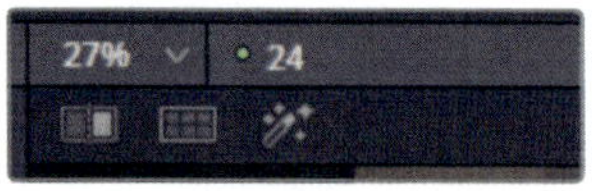

A green light indicates that the media is playing in real time. A red light indicates lag, with the numerical value displaying the actual frame rate. Caching should result in the GPU status indicator displaying a green light during playback. If it does not, you should consider lowering the proxy mode resolution or reducing the quality of the cache for faster review.

1 Open Project Settings, and click the Master settings tab.

2 Scroll down until you see the Optimized Media and Render Cache section.

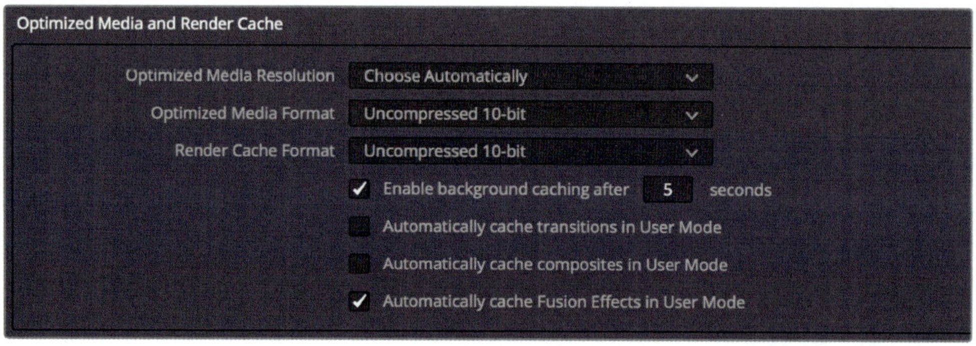

The Render Cache Format field allows you to set up the quality and format of your cache data.

Lowering the cache quality will reduce your cache file size and prevent your hard drive from filling up too quickly with cached data. However, this setting will lower the visual quality of the rendered media in your Viewer. You should avoid reducing cache quality if precision of color, luminance, and key data is important.

Inversely, raising the cache quality will ensure a faithful reproduction of your image data, but at the expense of producing very large rendered files.

3 Set the Render Cache Format to one of the full quantization formats (444 or 4444) in preparation for the upcoming lessons.

Beneath the Render Cache Format menu are a few checkbox options.

You can specify the amount of time that needs to pass before background caching begins in Smart Cache mode. By default, the interval is five seconds, but you can increase it if you prefer to tweak your settings at a leisurely pace when grading.

Additionally, you can enable automated transition and composite rendering when in User mode, which will mimic the behavior of Smart Cache mode.

4 Select "Automatically cache transitions in User Mode".

5 Click Save to exit the Project Settings.

Clearing a Cache

Wherever clips are cached (in the Edit page, Color page, or in individual nodes), a copy of the visual cache data is stored on your disc drive. Eventually, it might be necessary to remove this data to make room for more caching or to delete unnecessary materials from older projects.

1 Choose Playback > Delete Render Cache > Unused.

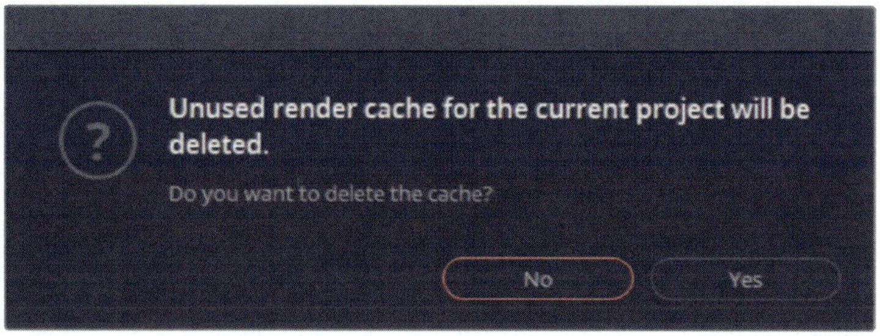

A prompt will ask you to confirm that you want to delete the unused cache.

2 Click Yes. The media in the Timeline remains rendered, while all previous cache versions of the clips are removed.

Other options for deleting the render cache allow you to delete all cached media or selected clips on the Timeline. It is important to remember that no actual media is affected by clearing a cache; and even if you accidentally delete a cache that is currently used in your project, it will be regenerated when it is next needed.

TIP Occasionally, you might come across a graphic anomaly in which the Viewer in the Color page is outputting visual data that does not match the changes you made to a clip. For example, a Media Offline message appears when you are certain the media is connected. Clearing the render cache will remove the program's memory of the clip render and force it to re-render the clip correctly.

NOTE Cached media is placed in the folder specified in the Project Settings under the Working Folders of the Master settings. By default, the Cache folder is located on the first media storage location (Preferences > System) of your database; but to optimize playback, you may want to redirect it to a drive other than the one that contains the Resolve application and your project files.

Proxies and offline media are vital for a clean editing workflow; but their use is discouraged for the grading process because they do not offer an accurate representation of the image when colors are graded (or when qualifier selections are made). For this reason, the render cache is the recommended optimization method.

Self-guided Exercises

Complete the following exercises in the unfiltered Project 03 - The Long Work Day timeline to test your understanding of the tools and workflows covered in this lesson.

Clip 02—Use node sizing to cover up the speed limit signs at the top of the frame.

Clip 08—Use dynamic and static keyframes together with the Highlights master wheel to flicker the lights in the garage.

Clip 15—Generate a node before the base node and apply noise reduction.

When you've completed this exercise, you can open the Project 03 - The Long Work Day Commercial COMPLETED.drp and review the Lesson 8 Timeline to compare your work with this finalized version.

Lesson Review

1 True or False? If you change the Timeline resolution of a project, you will need to go over your secondary grade nodes and manually resize all the Power Windows to fit the new resolution.

2 Where can you animate the sizing and color properties of a clip?

3 What are dynamic keyframes?

4 True or False? Noise reduction should be applied only to node 01 of any clip.

5 Would adding a vignette to a clip cause Smart Cache to render the clip?

Answers

1. False. DaVinci Resolve is resolution independent, so all secondary tools automatically resize themselves to fit a new project resolution.
2. Keyframes palette
3. Keyframes that gradually change a value between two points in time
4. False. Noise reduction can be applied to any node in the pipeline, based on necessity.
5. No. Primary and secondary grading tools are not considered processor intensive enough to prompt a Smart Cache render. However, if you were in User Cache mode and the clip was set to Render Cache Color Output, any change, including a vignette, would trigger a re-cache.

Lesson 9

Setting up RAW Projects

RAW media refers to a variety of still and video formats in which visual data is captured as an unprocessed video signal. In its initial state, RAW media does not have any visual properties. It is only through a processing method called *debayering*, that you are able to assign a color space and gamma to the image to view it on a monitor. RAW media has far greater grading potential due to its wide dynamic range and uncompressed approach to pixel data.

In this lesson, you will work with Blackmagic RAW (.braw) clips. Blackmagic RAW offers the same grading latitude as other RAW standards with the additional benefit of GPU-acceleration and partial debayering, which results in dramatically smaller file sizes and faster playback.

Time

This lesson takes approximately 30 minutes to complete.

Goals

Adjusting RAW Settings at the Project Level

The color management exercises you completed in Lesson 4 demonstrated how you can configure a project's color space and gamma to set up the starting point of a grade. Debayering RAW footage works on a similar premise, though it is a far more essential part of the grading process. Without it, the RAW media cannot be displayed in the Viewer.

RAW format sensors are defined by their ability to record the radiometric properties of light. Rather than representing a set of pixels with hard color data, RAW formats record the light intensity of a scene within the geometry of the sensor's individual photoreceptive elements, or *photo sites*.

Each photo site has a filter that allows the capture of only one channel of color (with green captured at double the frequency of red and blue). Together, the filtered signals make up the Bayer filter mosaic that contains all the data necessary to recreate a digital image.

For this reason, RAW files are sometimes referred to as *digital negatives*: visual information that contains a wide dynamic range that remains unviewable until it is processed. Debayering (also known as *demosaicing*) allows you to appoint values to the radiometric signals and produce a visible image in a designated color gamut and resolution.

Determining Whether Clips Are RAW

You can generally recognize the RAW video file formats supported by DaVinci Resolve 16 by their file extensions (.ari, .braw, .cin, .dng, .crm, .rmf, .nef, .r3d, .vrw, and others). Additionally, you can check the codec and file type of any clip in the Metadata panel of the Media page or the clip attributes in the contextual menu.

Another quick way to verify whether footage is RAW is to place it on the Timeline, and open the Camera RAW palette in the Color page. If a selected clip is in a RAW format, the palette becomes active and displays options for the Decode Quality and Decode Using fields. If the clip is not RAW, the Camera RAW palette is dimmed and inactive.

In this lesson, you will work with Blackmagic RAW media. This RAW format is unique in that it undergoes partial debayering in the camera hardware, which results in much smaller file sizes and its storage as a single video clip (as opposed to image sequences). This format allows for much faster playback, media management, and file transfer compared to traditional RAW formats.

NOTE The exercises in this lesson build on the tools and skills you learned in the previous sections of the book. If you skipped ahead to this lesson, you may need to review Lessons 1, 3, and 5 to gain a better understanding of primary and secondary grading and the Node editor.

1 Open DaVinci Resolve 16.
2 Create a new project, and name it **Blackmagic RAW Project**.
3 In the Media page, create two bins in the Media pool – **Media** and **Timelines**.
4 In the Media storage library, locate the BMD 16 CC - Project 03 folder, and enter the Blackmagic RAW subfolder.
5 Open the Media folder, and drag the three RAW clips into the media bin.

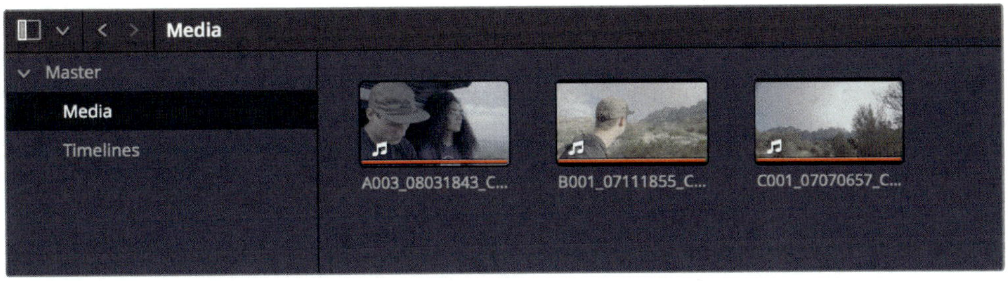

6 Enter the Edit page.
7 Select the three Blackmagic RAW clips. Right-click one of them, and choose Create New Timeline Using Selected Clips.
8 Name the Timeline **Blackmagic RAW Timeline**, and place it in the Timelines bin.

   The newly generated Timeline contains the three Blackmagic RAW clips in the order they were sorted in the media pool.

9 Enter the Color page.

NOTE If Smart Cache is enabled in your project, the Blackmagic RAW clips will immediately begin the caching process. Unlike the media you've used in the previous lessons, RAW formats are not intermediary codecs and need constant debayering and caching.

In previous lessons, you used color management to configure the visual starting point for your footage. You will similarly use the Camera RAW section of the Project Settings to determine how your RAW video content is processed.

10 Open Project Settings, and enter the Camera RAW section.

   These parameters affect the debayering of RAW footage on a project-wide basis.

11 Set RAW Profile to Blackmagic RAW.

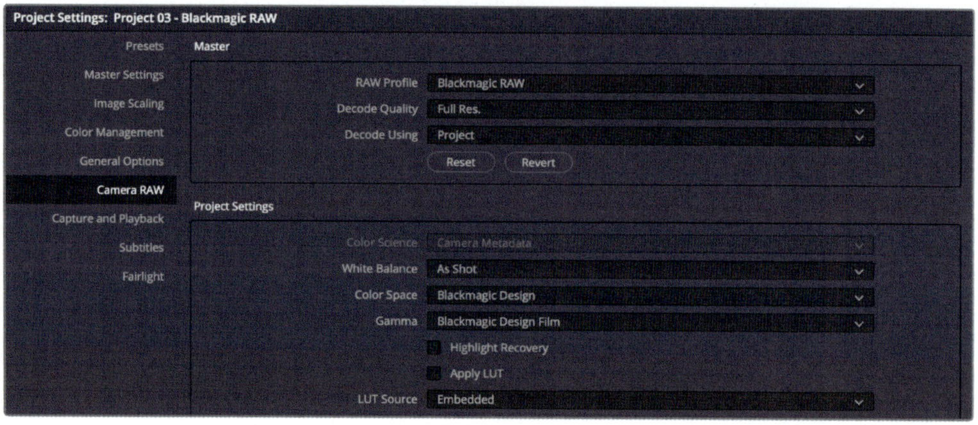

The Decode Quality is set to Full Res. (full resolution) by default, so the RAW media is debayered at the Timeline resolution specified in the Master Settings. Changing the quality to Half or Quarter will substantially reduce the amount of processing required to play the footage (at the expense of the visual quality within the Viewer/monitor), but is a viable option for slower systems.

The Decode Using field allows you to specify how the color gamut of the RAW signal is debayered. By default, it is set to Camera Metadata, which is the color gamut set by the camera operator when capturing the media. Changing it to Blackmagic RAW Default will prompt it to use any associated sidecar files that contain additional information such as ISO, white balance, color temperature, contrast, and many others. Setting the decode method to Project will reveal the fully customizable project and camera metadata settings at the bottom of the window.

NOTE DaVinci Resolve automatically detects the source of all supported RAW formats. Changes to the Project Settings will have an immediate effect on RAW clips in the media pool and Timeline, even when working with multiple RAW profiles.

Also, Camera RAW settings will impact only the RAW media in your project. Non-RAW clips remain unaffected.

12 Leave Decode Using set to Camera Metadata (default), and click Save to exit the Project Settings.

13 In the Blackmagic RAW Timeline, click clip 01 (A003).

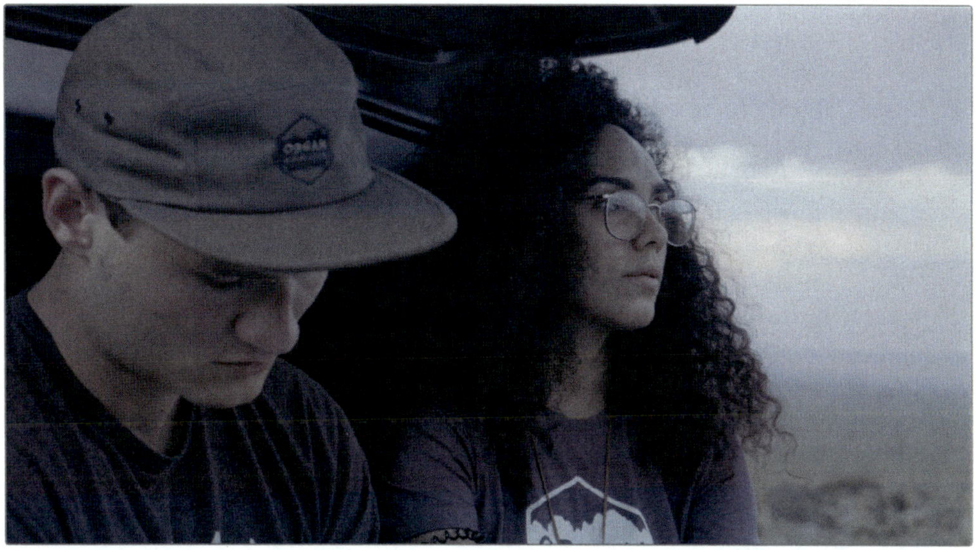

In this clip, the camera operator had the camera set to capture media in the log color space. He likely had a viewing LUT loaded in the viewfinder or field monitor to see the colors and contrast more accurately, but this has not travelled with the RAW clips. If you had access to that particular LUT, you could import it and apply it to the clip as a reference for the grade.

> **TIP** To import LUTs into Resolve, open the Project Settings, and enter the Color Management tab. In the Lookup Tables pop-up menus, click Open LUT Folder. Drag your LUT into the Resolve LUT folder, and in the Project Settings, click Update Lists.
>
> The imported LUT will become available in the LUT panel of the Color page, and in every clip and node contextual menu.

When using log as a starting point, it is especially important to normalize and saturate the media to achieve a neutral starting point, thereby mimicking the Rec. 709 color space.

14 With node 01 (*Normal*) selected, drag the Lift (1.15) and Gamma (0.06) master wheels to spread the waveform and brighten the clip.

15 Raise Saturation (80.00) to bring out the clip's natural colors.

The clip now has a satisfactory starting point using the original colors in the scene. You will use a separate corrector node to enhance the details in the image.

16 Create a new node 02 (**Contrast**), and make an s-curve in the Curve Editor. Aim to give the image rich shadows while preserving detail in the woman's hair.

17 On the second page of the adjustment controls, increase Midtone Detail (20.00) to further sharpen the features on the couple's faces and clothes.

You can use secondary nodes to manipulate the original colors and to target the wide dynamic range.

18 Create a new node 03 (**Shirts**), and adjust the Hue vs Hue curve to turn the cold blue shirts/sky to a warmer cyan.

19 Adjust the Hue vs Sat curve to desaturate the shirts, thereby giving the scene a more stylistic look.

Finally, you can target and enhance the sunset in the background.

20 Create a new parallel node (**Sky**), and activate a gradient window to select the sky on the ride side of the frame.

21 In the adjustment controls, adjust Contrast and Pivot to reveal the finer cloud detail in the background.

22 Switch to the second page of the adjustment controls, and increase Color Boost (15.00) to emphasise the dramatic sunset colors.

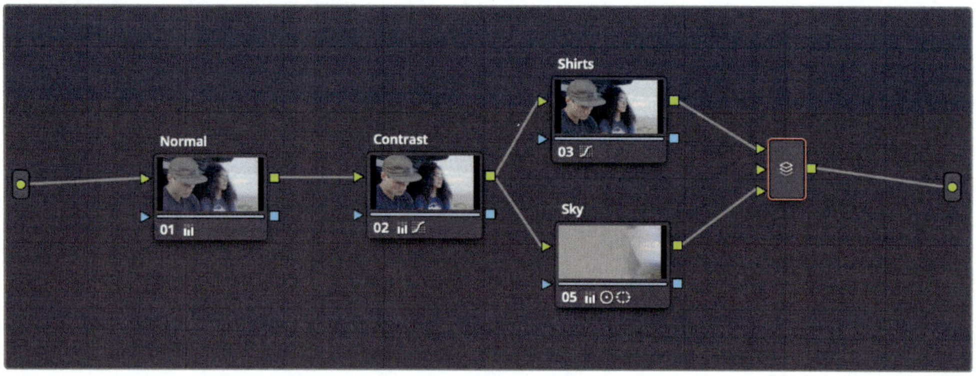

In many cases, grading RAW media is no different than grading non-RAW media. The wide dynamic range demands increased attention and handling; but, as you have seen in this exercise, the primary and secondary tools and workflow remain the same.

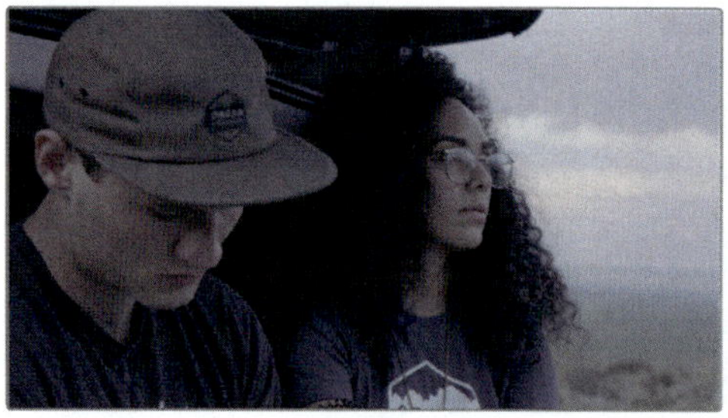

Before

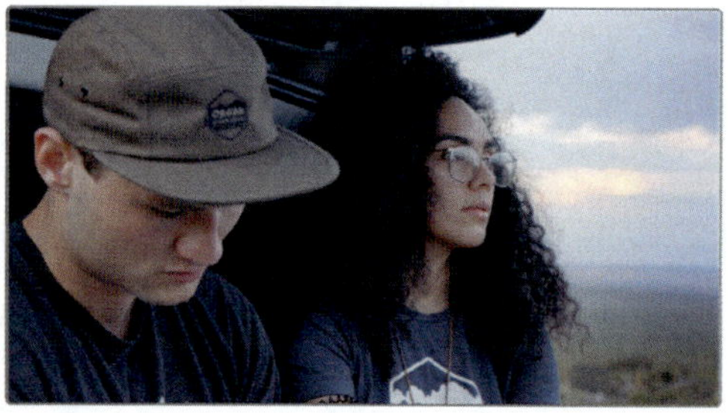

After

Adjusting RAW Settings at the Clip Level

You will often want to set up RAW media to address the individual needs of clips. Using the Camera RAW palette in the Color page allows you to tweak on a clip-by-clip basis.

1 Click clip 02 (B001).

2 In the left palettes of the Color page, open the Camera RAW palette.

3 Set Decode Using to Clip. Doing so will disassociate it from the Project Settings and allow you to individually adjust the RAW settings on the clip.

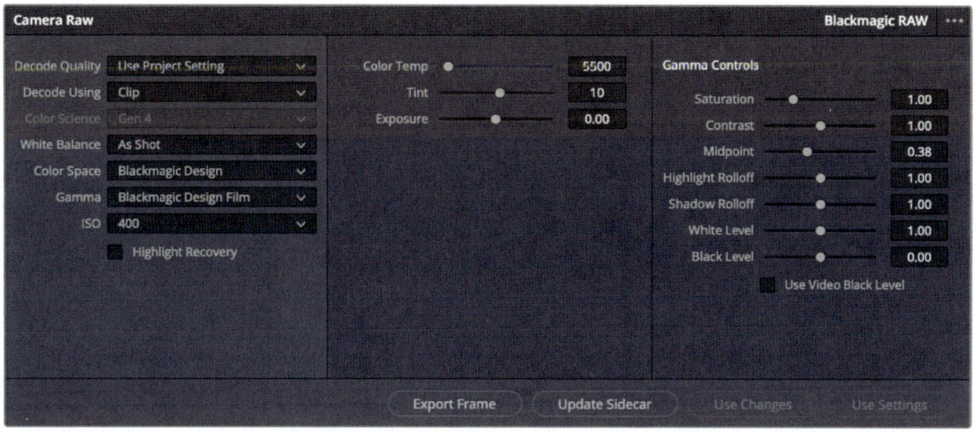

The Camera RAW palette gives you access to a variety of color and detail adjustments that you can apply to the visual data of the image during debayering. The debayer level affects images before they enter the RGB input node of the Node editor.

4 Set the Color Space to Rec.709.

The saturation is adjusted to accommodate the new color space; however, the luminance (gamma) is still displayed with the Blackmagic Design Film log-encoded gamma curve.

The gamma can be adjusted in the pop-up menu under the color space controls. BMD Video applies a Rec.709-like gamma curve to standard dynamic range (SDR) media for HD/UHD displays. BMD Extended Video takes into account media with a wide dynamic range (such as RAW) and carefully rolls off the highlights to be viewable in an SDR monitor.

5 Set the Gamma to BMD Extended Video.

It is now possible to adjust some of the camera settings used during recording.

6 Change the ISO to 200.

Though the image has already been captured, you can adjust the sensor sensitivity to better accommodate the starting point of your grade to the luminance in the scene. This is a feature unique to RAW media workflows.

7 Change the ISO back to 400.

8 Decrease the exposure by one f-stop (-1.00).

9 Drag the playhead across the clip to verify that the adjustments are satisfactory on all planes of the environment (the man's skin, the hill in the foreground, the mountains, and the clouds in the sky). Leave the playhead on the last frame of the clip.

The settings on the right side of the Camera RAW palette offer advanced gamma controls. Highlight and Shadow Rolloff allow you to selectively lighten or darken those respective tonal ranges while maintaining a smooth blend in relation to the midtones. The white and black levels act as gain and lift adjusters. The Use Video Black Level checkbox adds a pedestal to accommodate video data levels (64-940).

10 Drag the Highlight Rolloff left (0.30) to better preserve the highlights and details in the clouds.

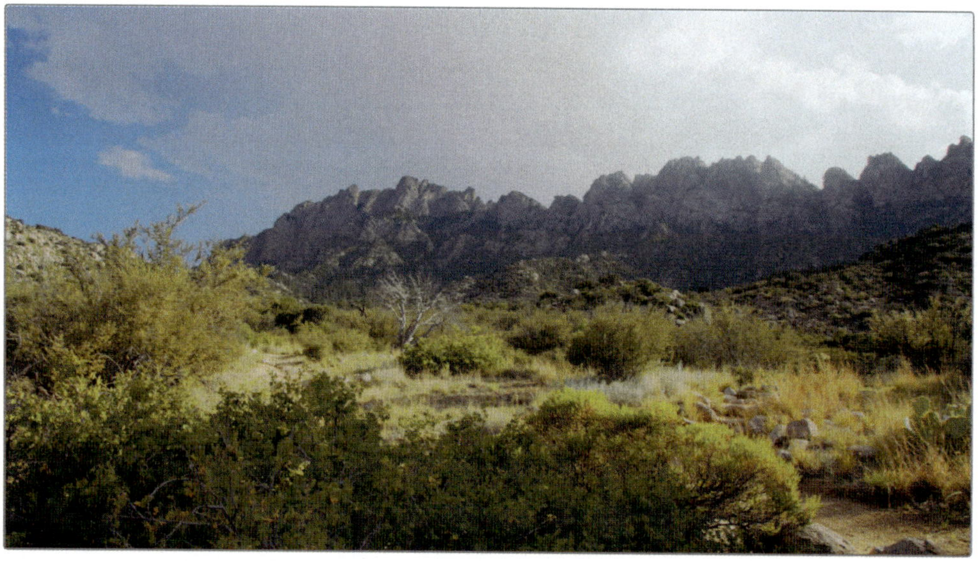

TIP To copy Camera RAW settings (such as Color Space and Gamma) across multiple clips on the Timeline, Shift-click to select a sequence of clips, and click Use Settings to apply the current clip's Camera RAW settings.

If you need to adjust multiple clips on the Timeline after setting up their individual RAW parameters (for example, to increase the Color Boost of a sequence without overwriting the unique ISO and Exposure settings of each clip), Shift-click to select the clips, and click Use Changes to copy only the altered parameter.

With the clip successfully set up, you can begin grading in the Node editor as usual.

11 Label node 01 as **Normal**.

In this case, you can leave the normalization node untouched. The setup in the Camera RAW palette has addressed all of the clip's immediate luminance needs. Regardless, the labelled node is good to keep in the pipeline to give you the option of making tonal adjustments should later grades reveal subtle highlight/shadow issues.

12 Create a new serial node (02) and label it **Contrast**.

13 Adjust the contrast (1.2) to reveal the fine details in the mountain range.

14 To avoid overexposing the man's skin at the start of the clip, draw a linear window around the right side of the frame (isolating the mountain) with a strong Soft 1 edge (18.00), and then track it to the camera pan.

The track does not have to be too accurate—you are simply concealing the division between the contrasted plane on the right and the un-contrasted area with the man on the left.

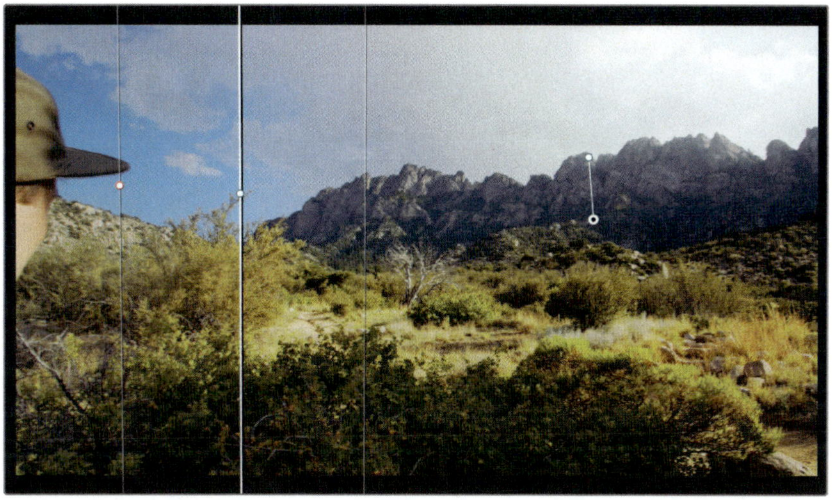

So far, the contrast looks great on the mountains, but the cloud detail has started to disappear. You'll need to fine tune the highlights in the sky to restore the clouds.

15 Create a new corrector node *before* node 02 (but after node 01) and label it **Sky**.

16 Switch the Color Wheels palette to Log, and decrease the Highlight master wheel (0.25). Drag the HR value (0.85) in the adjustment controls to limit the tonal correction to the brightest clouds.

Before

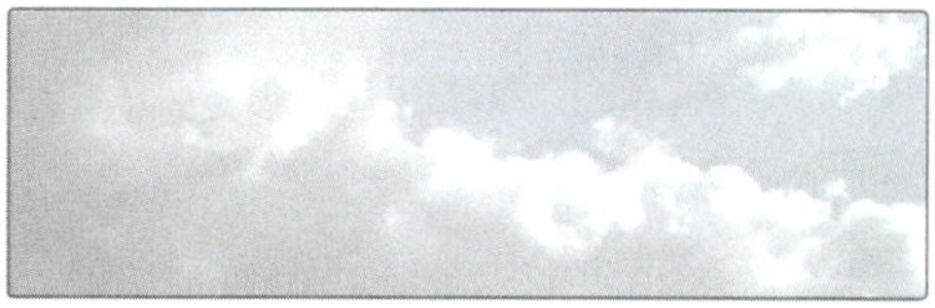

After

With the tonal range creatively optimized, you can add a colorful look to the scene.

17 Add a final node (04) at the end of the pipeline called **Look**.

18 In the curves palette, isolate the red channel and draw a subtle s-curve.

19 Isolate the blue channel, and draw a reverse s-curve that mirrors the red curve.

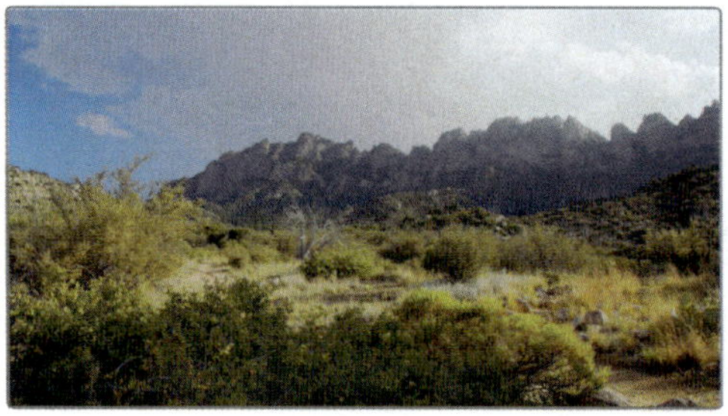

Bypassed

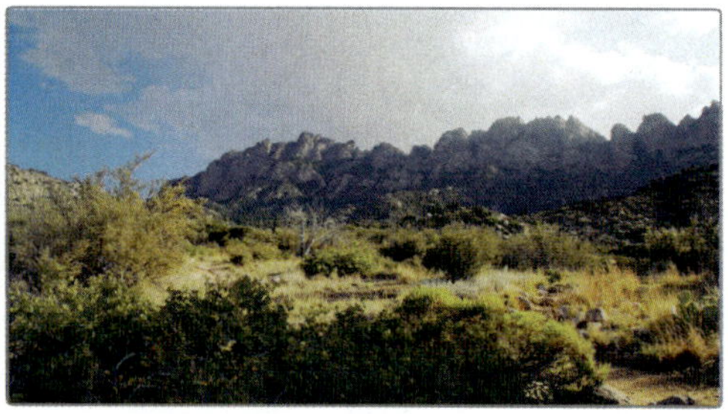

Graded

The result is a dynamic shot with natural-looking but enhanced colors.

20 Press Shift-D to bypass the pipline and compare to the original RAW clip.

The Camera RAW palette is best used for establishing the color gamut and ISO of RAW media prior to grading, rather than for actual grading.

In fact, it is highly advisable to avoid balancing or creating looks in the Camera RAW palette. The standard grading tools in the Color page have the same level of impact on the raw image and are far easier to keep track of in the context of the node tree, which will reduce instances of destructive grading.

TIP When saving stills from clips with manually adjusted Camera RAW settings, you can specify that you do not want their camera RAW settings included in the still grade data. Right-click in the Gallery, and choose Copy Grade: Preserve Camera Raw Settings to enforce this.

Updating Sidecar Data

Blackmagic RAW media carries descriptive metadata for look management in-camera and during post-production. You can generate a sidecar file to back up or share debayer settings and for previewing rushes in the Blackmagic RAW player. As a rule, sidecar metadata files always take precedence over the embedded metadata in a .braw file. However, if the sidecar is deleted or moved, the decoding of the .braw file will fall back on the embedded metadata.

1 Click clip 03 (C001).

2 In the Camera RAW palette, change Decode Using to Clip.

3. Set the Color Space to Rec.709.
4. Change the Gamma to Blackmagic Design Video.
5. To bring out the detail in the midtones, reduce the Exposure by three and a half f-stops (-3.5).
6. Increase the ISO Sensitivity to 400 to brighten the image.
7. Select Highlight Recovery under the ISO pop-up menu to restore the clipped highlights in the clouds.

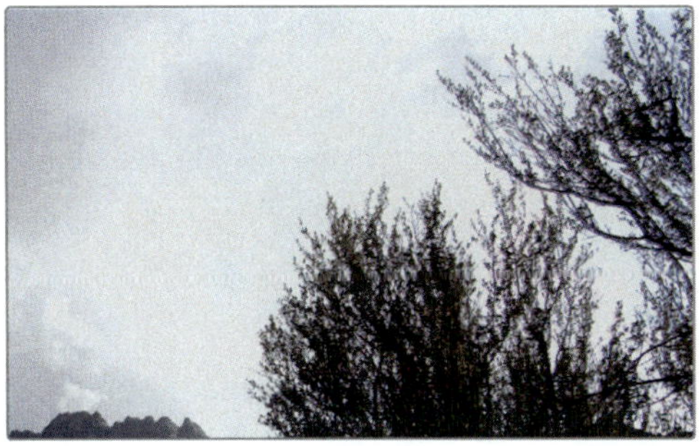

Without Highlight Recovery

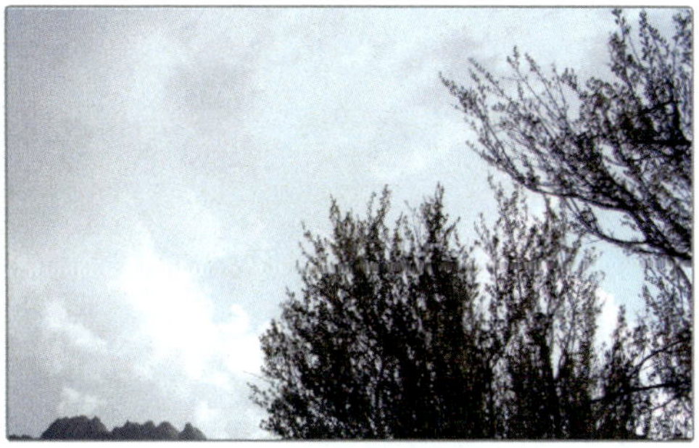

With Highlight Recovery

Highlight Recovery is another feature unique to RAW video formats. It performs a dramatic highlight rolloff to reveal additional data in the brightest parts of the footage.

You will save these RAW settings in a sidecar file and use them to review the clip in the Blackmagic RAW player.

8. At the bottom of the palette, click Update Sidecar.
9. Open your file browser, and locate the Media folder with the three .braw clips.

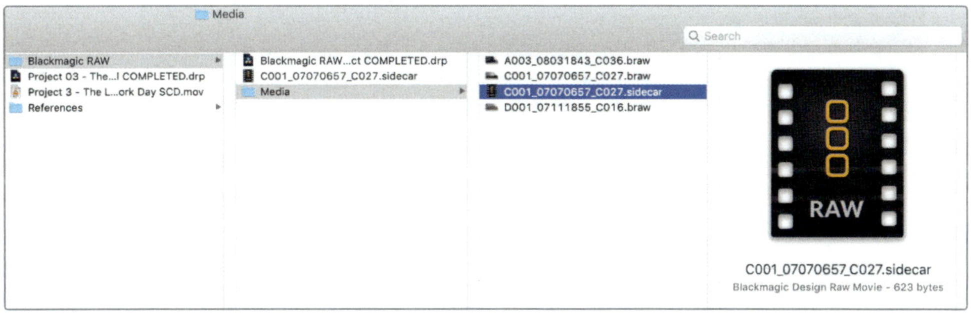

The sidecar you created is located next to the original clip (C001).

Viewing Sidecar Metadata in the Blackmagic RAW Player

When viewing .braw clips in the Blackmagic RAW player, the appearance of the video is determined by the debayer settings saved in the sidecar.

> **NOTE** To complete this exercise, you will need to install the Blackmagic RAW player on your computer. The Blackmagic RAW player is currently available only for MacOS and is available for free download at BlackmagicDesign.com

1 In Finder, open the Media folder, and double-click the clip you previously worked on (C001).

Doing so opens the clip in the Blackmagic RAW player.

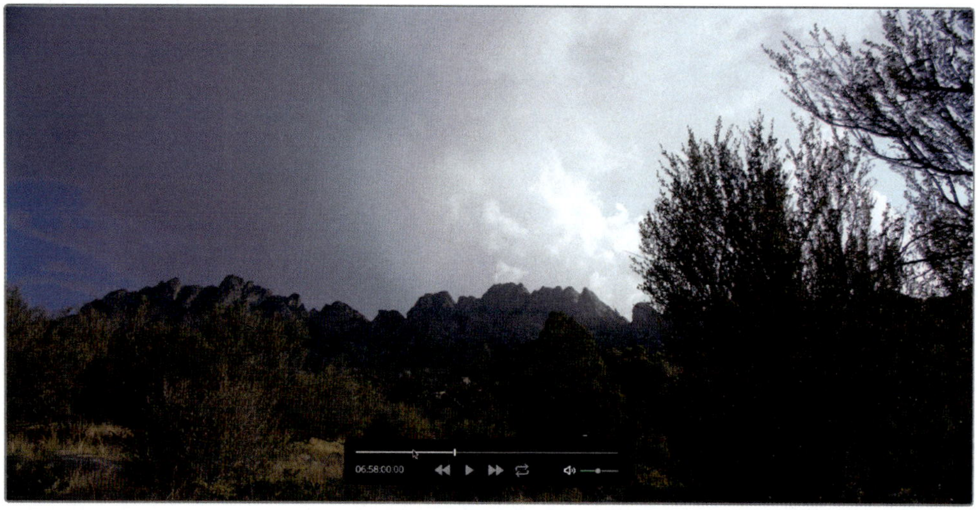

The video in the player features all the changes you made in the Camera RAW palette—exposure, ISO, highlight recovery, and so on.

2 Stop the video, and return to the Media folder.

3 Delete the .sidecar file.

4 Double-click clip C001 to reopen it in the Blackmagic RAW player.

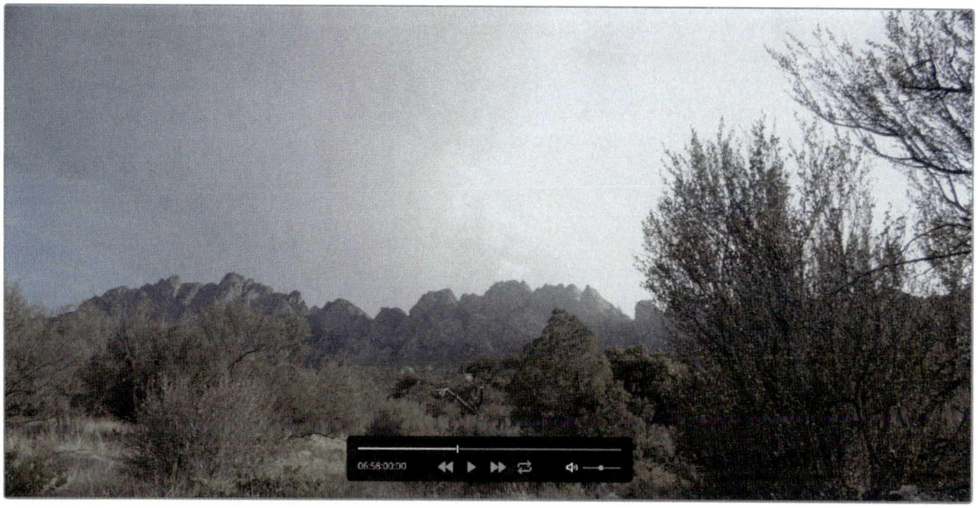

This time, the clip appears flat. This was the original metadata setup (log gamma) that you encountered when you began working on the RAW video.

5 Browse up one folder until you are in the Blackmagic RAW folder. There you will see a .sidecar file that was previously generated for this lesson.

Clip 001 will not adopt its metadata until both files in the same folder.

6 Drag the .sidecar file into the Media folder.

7 Open clip C001 in the Blackmagic RAW player one more time.

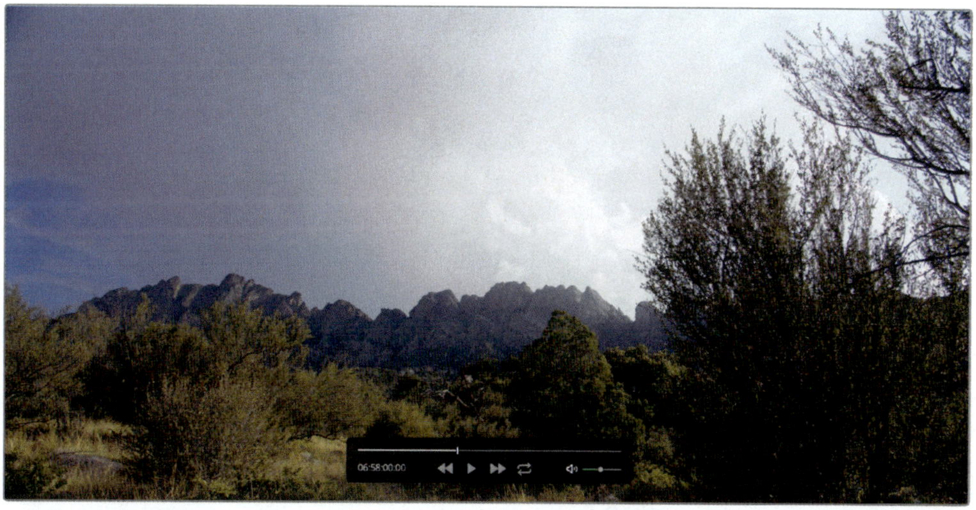

Once again, the video's appearance changed to reflect the dominant metadata source (the sidecar). This look is similar to the one you created but with higher exposure and more saturation.

Viewing Sidecar Metadata in a Text Editor

Sidecar metadata is written in a deceptively simple-looking code that is human-readable and easily modifiable. So, you can manually adjust the sidecar metadata outside of the DaVinci Resolve Color page.

1 Right-click the .sidecar file currently associated with clip C001.

2 Open it in a simple text editor app such as TextEdit (macOS) or Notepad (Windows).

C001_07070657_C027.sidecar

```
{
        "tone_curve_contrast": 1.350000,
        "tone_curve_saturation": 1.300000,
        "tone_curve_midpoint": 0.600000,
        "tone_curve_highlights": 0.999000,
        "tone_curve_shadows": 1.001000,
        "tone_curve_black_level": 0.000000,
        "tone_curve_white_level": 1.000000,
        "tone_curve_video_black_level": 1,
        "highlight_recovery": 1,
        "post_3dlut_mode": "Disabled",
        "viewing_gamma": "Blackmagic Design Custom",
        "viewing_gamut": "Rec.709",
        "viewing_bmdgen": 4,
        "exposure": {
                "06:57:58:23": -2.900000
        },
        "white_balance_kelvin": {
                "06:57:58:23": 5200
        },
        "white_balance_tint": {
                "06:57:58:23": 15
        },
        "iso": {
                "06:57:58:23": 200
        }
}
```

As you can see, the metadata fields and their values are easy to identify in the code.

3 Change the contrast field to 1.55 to increase the contrast.

```
"tone_curve_contrast": 1.550000,
"tone_curve_saturation": 1.300000,
"tone_curve_midpoint": 0.600000,
```

4 Change the white balance field to 6000 to make the image warmer.

```
},
"white_balance_kelvin": {
        "06:57:58:23": 6000
},
```

5 Save the document and close it.

6 If you have Blackmagic RAW player, open the clip to see the changes.

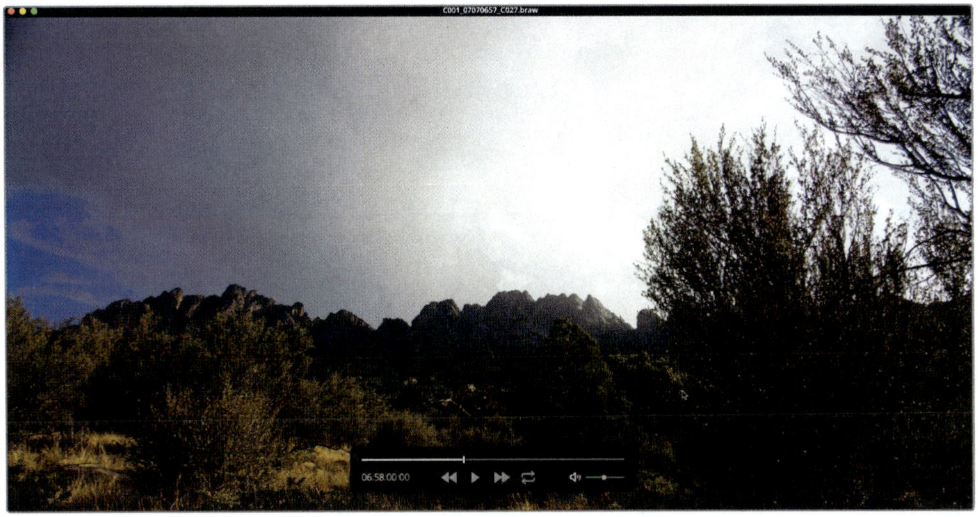

The ability to make these manual adjustments can come in handy when working in the field and needing to quickly adjust ISO/temp data without opening DaVinci Resolve. Also, note that some of the parameters are accompanied by a timecode. Blackmagic RAW supports frame-based metadata which allows for frame-by-frame value adjustments in clips with temporal changes such as camera movement or focal shift.

Using Resolve Color Management with RAW Media

You can easily incorporate RAW media into a color-managed workflow. As with non-RAW media, color management offers the benefit of quick color space and gamma remapping while still giving you access to the full dynamic range of the source image. It also allows for easy switching between different deliverable color standards and the ability to work with multiple video formats in one Timeline.

To ensure a clean workflow, set up color management prior to doing any grading or RAW camera set up—note that the color space and gamma fields will no longer be available in the Camera RAW palette though you will retain control over ISO, temp, tint, exposure, and so on.

In the Project Settings, it is highly advisable to set the Input Color Space of RAW media to Bypass to ensure the full range of the RAW signal is debayered to the Node editor. The preset color gamuts and camera makes/models listed in the Input Color Space pop-up menu are intended for transcoded/compressed media, not RAW video signals, and clipping may occur.

Using Color Space Transform FX with RAW Media

Another method for managing and switching your deliverable color standards is to use the Color Space Transform FX in the Node editor in place of, or in collaboration with, color management.

For best practice, place the Color Space Transform FX at the end of the pipeline in the Timeline Node editor. Leave the Input fields set to Timeline, and adjust the Output Color Space and Gamma per your requirements, which are usually the standard of your grading monitor or final video deliverable.

Setting up a Render Cache for RAW Media Projects

In Lesson 8, you set up your project render cache to a full-quantization (444 or 4444), 12-bit depth codec, but the exercise did not go into detail about the effect this had on the grading process. In this exercise, you will adjust the render cache quality and perform a simple grade test to fully understand why the render cache format matters when working with RAW video.

1. Choose Playback > Render Cache > Smart to ensure that caching is enabled.
2. Click clip 03 (C001), and reset its grades and nodes.
3. Open Project Settings, and click the Master settings tab.
4. Scroll down to the Optimized Media and Render Cache section, and set the Render Cache format to a lower-quality codec such as ProRes 422 (macOS) or DNxHR SQ (Windows).
5. Click Save to close the Project Settings.
6. Open the Camera RAW palette, and change the Gamma to Blackmagic Design Custom to gain access to the Gamma controls in the palette.
7. Reduce the Black Level to -1.00.

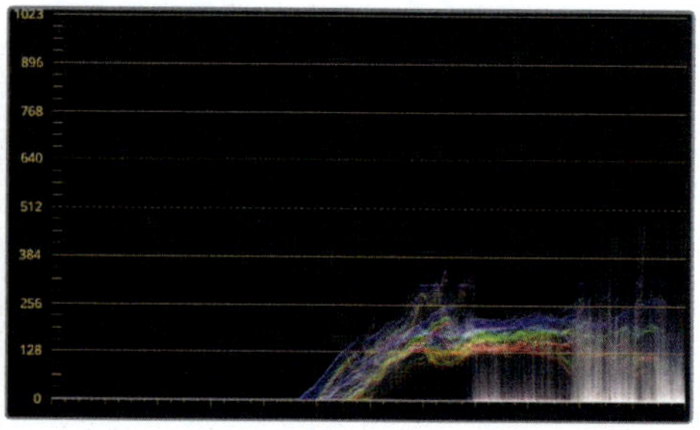

This change significantly darkens the image, leaving only the clouds and sky behind the trees visible.

In Lesson 5, you learned that, when used correctly, the node pipeline is non-destructive. So, raising the Lift master wheel or the black point of the custom curve should completely restore the crushed data in this image.

8 In the Custom Curves palette, drag the YRGB black point halfway up the graph.

The result is an image with severely clipped shadows. In the waveform scope, you can see that the bottom of the trace appears flat where the Camera RAW palette crushed it during the debayering stage.

At first, it might appear that grading RAW media (or using the Camera RAW palette) results in image degradation. But what is actually happening is that the rendered cache is generated at a bit depth that is too shallow to represent the full gamut of the debayered raw image in the Viewer.

> **NOTE** This behavior is not exclusive to the Camera RAW palette. If you construct two nodes with opposing gamma adjustments, you will see the same clipped result when working with any wide dynamic range footage.

9 Open Project Settings, and click the Master settings tab.

10 Set the Render cache format to one of the full-quantization (444 or 4444) or HDR formats.

11 Click Save to close the Project Settings.

12 Click the Custom curves black point, and adjust it slightly to force the clip to regenerate the cache.

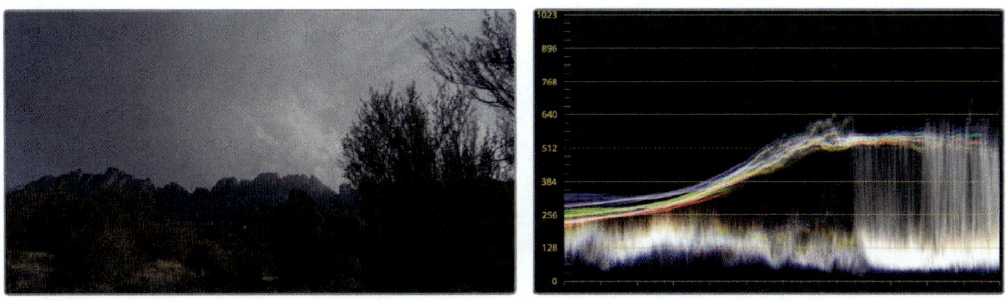

Instantly, the shadows are restored and you can see most of the original image data. (In this case, the restoration cannot be perfect because the Black Level parameter of the Camera RAW palette targets a slightly different tonal range from the curves black point.) The trace in the waveform is also restored and no longer appears flat at the bottom of the graph.

Though you did not change the Camera RAW settings or the Custom curves grade, the render cache is now generated at a greater bit depth and is capable of displaying the full gamut of the restored image.

When setting a Render cache format, always remember that it affects only what you see in the Viewer. If you were to render a clip from the Deliver page while caching in a low-quality codec, the exported image would not have clipped shadows and highlights. This behavior makes it particularly important to set up a high-quality cache when grading HDR and high bit depth footage. If you don't, your final project could end up looking very different from what you are seeing in the Viewer.

TIP 12-bit codecs (such as DNxHR HQX, DNxHR 444, and ProRes 4444) are HDR compliant and can be used for cinema and UHD 4K delivery.

Due to its level of quality, you can use a 12-bit cache in the final export of a project. When adjusting the Render Settings, in the Advanced Settings, select "Use render cached images".

The intermediary codecs available in the Master settings are all relatively high quality for editing and review work; but as you can see from this exercise, not all of them are suitable for grading media with a wide dynamic range. Due to their lower bit depths, most codecs are incapable of displaying the full scope of your grading work and could seriously impede the quality of your qualifier selections and clip details in the highlights and shadows.

Check Your Work

Open and view the Blackmagic RAW Project COMPLETED.drp if you need help understanding the node structure or grading tools used in this lesson.

Lesson Review

1 Which decode method in the Project Settings will utilize a clip's sidecar?

2 True or False? You can change ISO and white balance of RAW media at any time.

3 True or False? The Camera RAW palette gives you much finer control over RAW media than the standard grading tools in the Color page.

4 True or False? Enabling Resolve Color Management will not affect RAW media.

5 True or False? Changes in the Camera RAW palette could permanently clip the gamma range of the image before it enters the node pipeline.

Answers

1. Blackmagic RAW Default
2. True. Due to the wide dynamic range of RAW media, it is possible to adjust the ISO and white balance in the Camera RAW settings of any clip and at any stage of the grading process.
3. False. The standard grading tools in the Color page give you the same level of access to the visual properties of the image.
4. False. Resolve Color Management is one of the methods used to set up RAW projects.
5. False. The Camera RAW palette is no more destructive than any of the other grading tools in the Color page. Clipping is a possibility if you alter a range of the image and fail to retrieve it correctly at a later stage.

Lesson 10

Delivering Projects

When you're ready to export a project—whether at the end of a workflow, at an intermediate point, or when generating dailies—the render settings are configured in the Deliver page of DaVinci Resolve.

In this lesson, you will look over existing presets, prepare a project for delivery, output for digital cinema, and set up your own renders.

Time

This lesson takes approximately 40 minutes to complete.

Goals

Using Lightbox to Check Timeline Prior to Delivery

The Lightbox is a feature in the Color page that gives you an alternative, expanded representation of the Timeline. It provides a general overview of clips in the edit rather than over the Viewer-focused layout of the standard Color page. It is particularly powerful when combined with filters, and and you can use it to quickly assess the grade status of Timeline clips.

1. Open DaVinci Resolve 16.
2. Import and open Project 03 - The Long Work Day Commercial COMPLETED.drp. Relink the media, if necessary.
3. Open the Lesson 10 Timeline.
4. Enter the Color page.
5. In the upper-right of the Color page, click the Lightbox button.

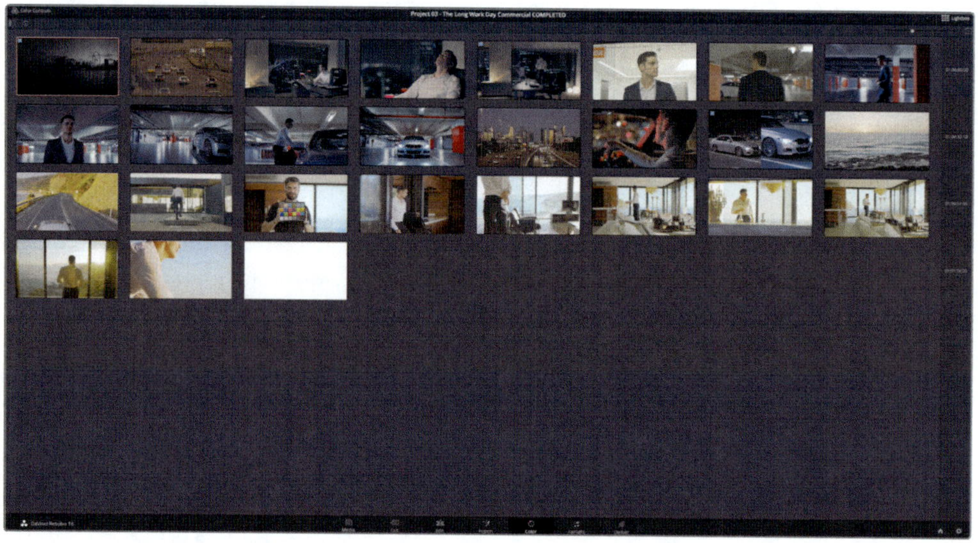

The Lightbox displays a full-screen representation of your project Timeline from left to right, top to bottom. A ruler to the right of the window indicates the timecode of the clips and turns into a scrollbar when the Timeline includes more clips than can be displayed in a single page.

The Lightbox provides a more expanded overview of the Thumbnail Timeline and can be helpful for colorists who find the Clip Timeline in the regular Color page too restrictive. With a single glance at the Lightbox, you can determine which clips are graded and which aren't.

6 Click the Clip Info button in the upper-left corner of the Lightbox panel to display clip numbers, timecodes, codecs, source names, and version information.

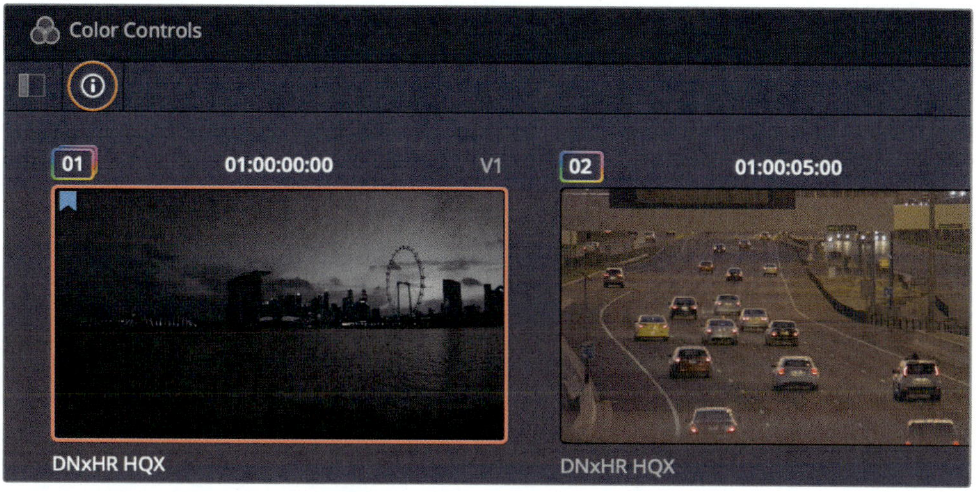

7 Next to the Clip Info button, click the Sidebar button to expand the filtering options.

8 In the filter options, click Ungraded clips.

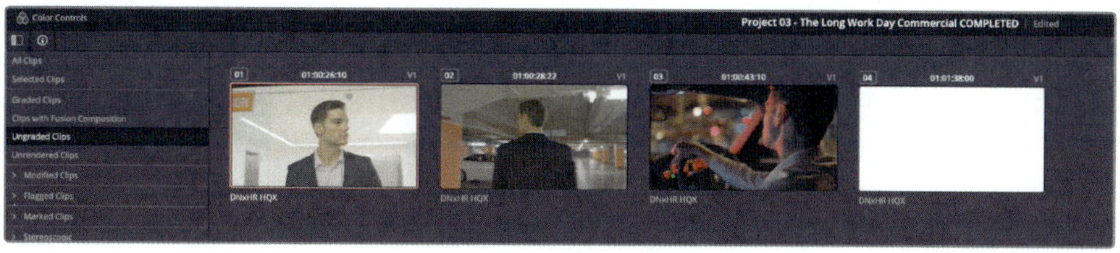

The Timeline is reduced to just four clips. The first two clips clearly belong in the Garage group, but must have been overlooked during grading.

9 Select both clips, and choose Groups > Garage > Assign to Group.

The majority of the grading in the Garage group was carried out in the pre-clip and post-clip stages, so the two clips will immediately adopt the look of the rest of the group. They will remain in the Lightbox results until the next time you change the filter, after which their new status as graded clips will be acknowledged.

The third clip in the ungraded filter results has not been touched at all.

10 In the upper-left of the page, click the Color Controls button to open the grading palettes in the lower half of the screen.

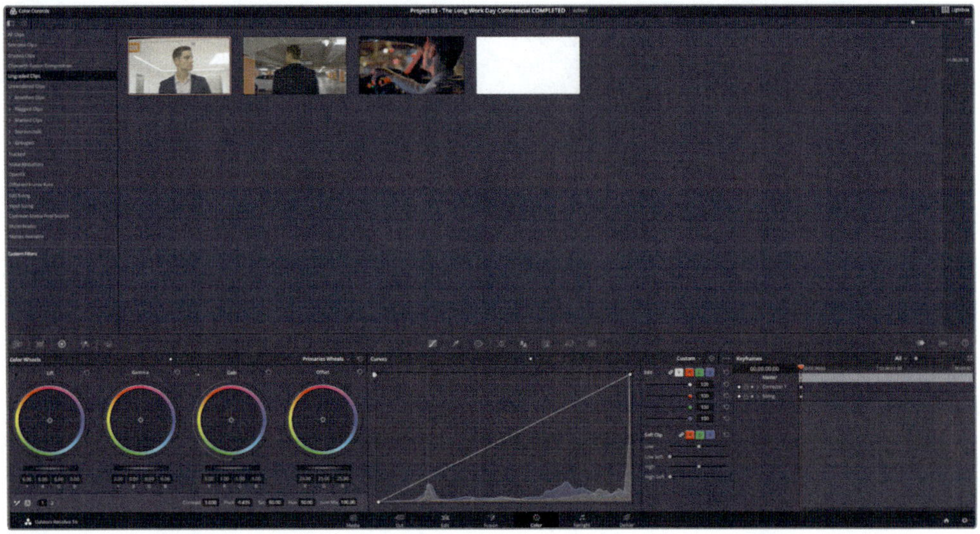

If you are working with an external monitor, you will see a full-screen output of the selected clip in the Lightbox. You can continue to grade and tweak your media in Lightbox mode.

11 Set the Contrast of the interior car shot to 1.1.

The final result in the filter is the solid white matte at the end of the sequence which doesn't require grading.

12 In the sidebar filter, select Noise Reduction.

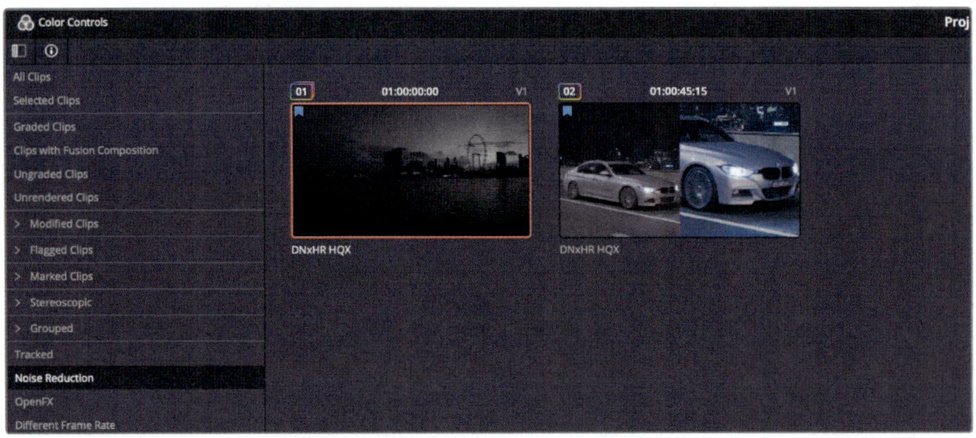

When performing noise reduction in Lesson 8, you learned that bypassing the Denoise node would facilitate faster playback during the remainder of the grade and result in a more efficient workflow.

If you use this method of performance optimization, you must remember to re-enable the Denoise nodes before outputting the project.

Click the Lightbox button in the upper-right corner to close the Lightbox interface.

13 The Noise Reduction filter is still active in the Timeline on the Color page. Click the two clips one-by-one and verify that their Denoise nodes are not bypassed.

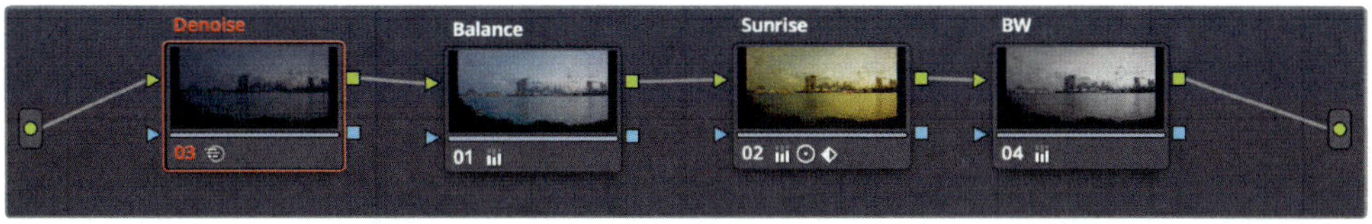

14 Select Clips > All Clips to remove the filter and return to the entire Timeline.

> **TIP** The Timeline Thumbnail mode is another great option for visually assessing the status of clips in the Timeline while in the Lightbox panel. Choose View > Timeline Thumbnail Mode > Source (C Mode) to switch the order of the clips in the Timeline from their edit order to the order in which the media was created. When working with original camera footage, this will display the order in which the footage was recorded. C Mode will place clips that were captured on the same day/location next to each other which enables faster copying of grades and visual comparisons. When done, remember to set the Timeline Thumbnail mode back to Record (A Mode).

The media is now checked to ensure that grades were applied to all relevant clips and that all nodes are active. When working on your own projects, think about the types of workflows you use and what is important to verify before delivering a project.

As well as the standard filters already present in the sidebar, you can also use the Smart Filters option at the bottom of the list to design your filters based on the metadata of the clips on the Timeline.

Understanding the Render Workflow and Presets

The Deliver page is optimally designed to help you quickly set up one or more render jobs. Only four steps are needed to export a video from Resolve:

1 In the Render Settings panel, set up the video output format. These settings include the file type, codec, and audio format of the rendered video; its name and location on your workstation; and a variety of advanced controls to optimize the render speed and file size.

II Define the range of the Timeline you want to export. By default, each job is set to render the entire timeline, but you can use In and Out points to define a custom range.

III Click Add to Render Queue to send the job(s) to the Render Queue.

IV Click Start Render to begin the render process.

In the following exercise you will create a render job based on a preset in the Render Settings of the Deliver page.

1 Enter the Deliver page.

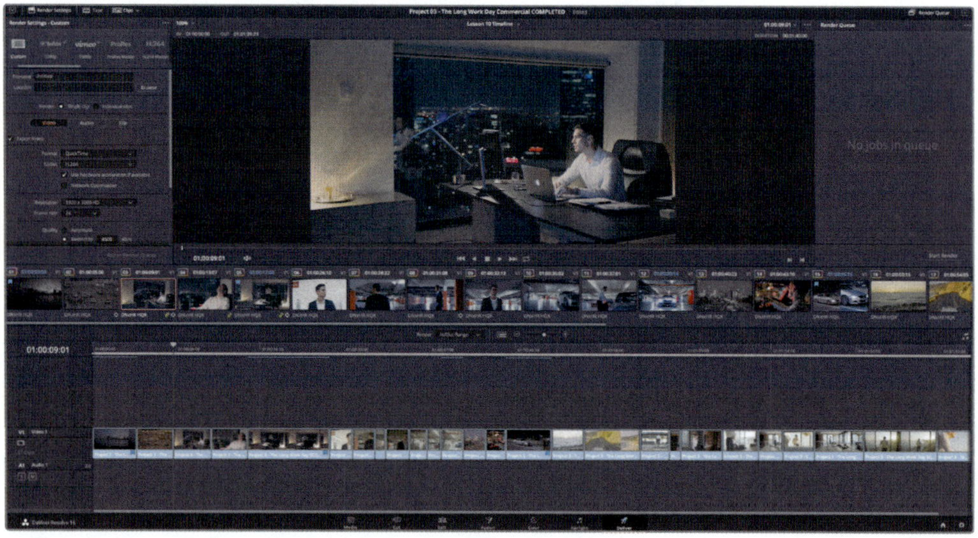

At the top of the Render Settings panel, you will find a horizontal list of render presets.

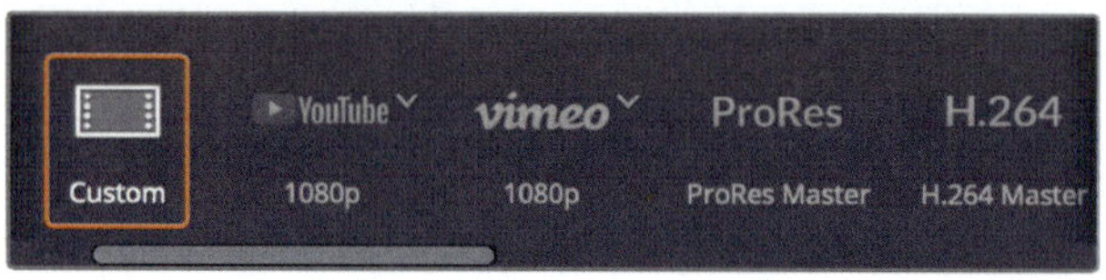

Custom provides access to the full range of render settings in the panel below.

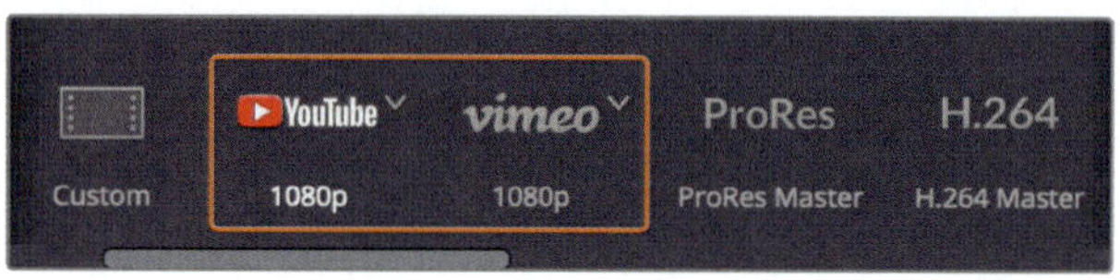

YouTube/Vimeo sets up the render settings based on video configurations recommended by user-generated content websites such as YouTube and Vimeo.

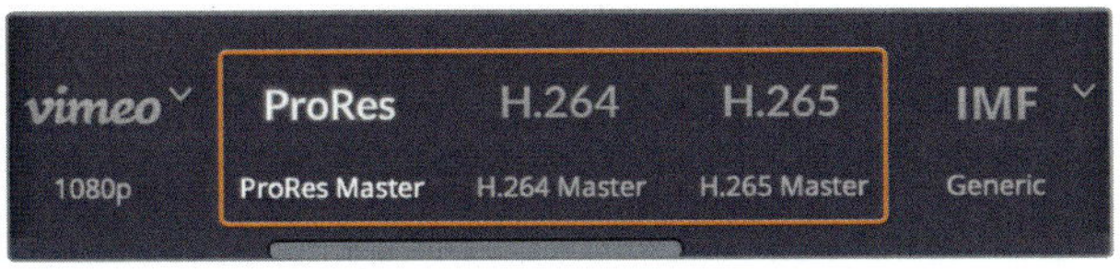

ProRes, **H.264** and **H.265 Masters** deliver several versions of a video file for a client: from high-end exports appropriate for broadcast (ProRes) to compressed HD/UHD files for review or online playback (H.264 and H.265). Note that the ProRes Master preset is available only on macOS systems.

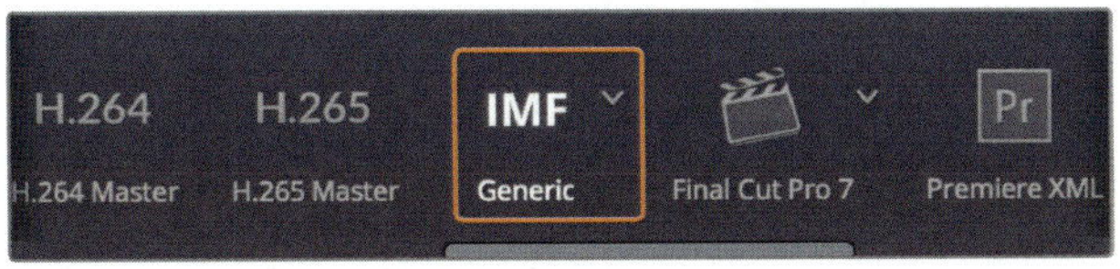

IMF features a set of SMPTE ST.2067-compliant resolutions and codecs for tapeless deliverables to networks. In DaVinci Resolve Studio, this option does not require a license and supports multiple media streams for video, audio, and subtitle tracks.

NOTE The Interoperable Mastering Format (IMF) is used for broadcast distribution and submitting content to Netflix.

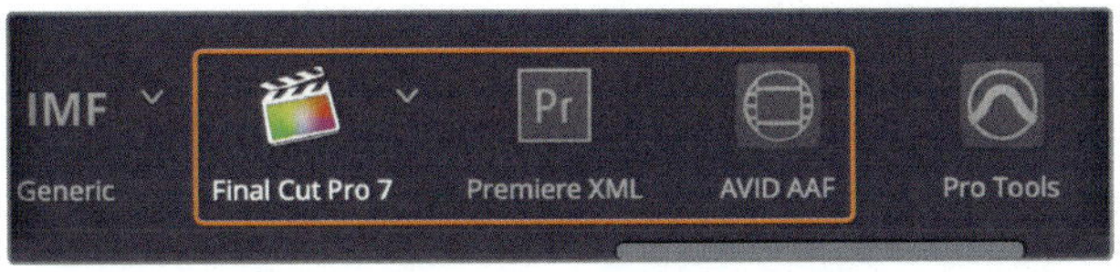

Final Cut Pro 7/X, **Premiere XML**, and **AVID AAF** accommodate a return trip to the respective NLE software. This assumes a workflow in which media was originally edited in an NLE, migrated to Resolve for grading/VFX, and is returned to the same NLE for final delivery.

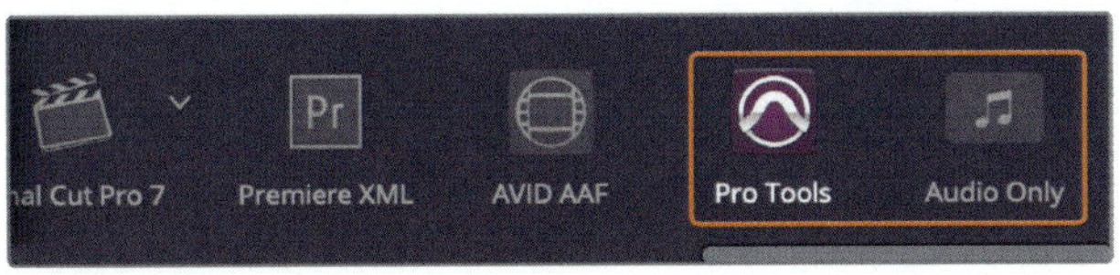

Pro Tools renders out three files: a self-contained video for reference, individual exports of all audio clips and their channels, and an AAF file for Avid Pro Tools migration. This preset accommodates workflows in which the final audio mix is mastered by an external audio engineer in Pro Tools.

Audio Only disables video output and delivers a single audio-only file. You can specify the audio file format in the Audio tab of the Render Settings.

Clicking the icon of a preset will load its settings into the Render Settings panel.

2 Click the disclosure arrow next to the YouTube preset, and choose 2160p to load the 4K UHD version of the preset.

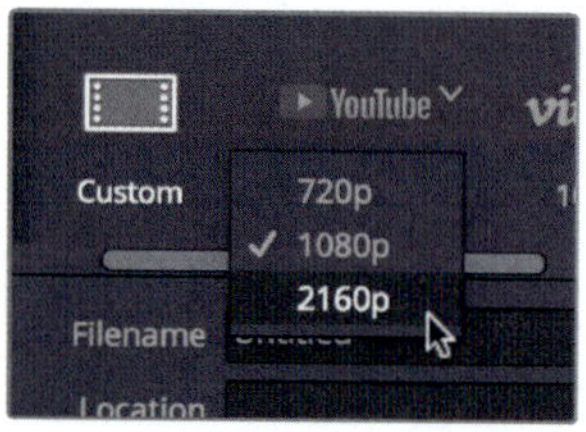

The Render Settings panel changes to display the most relevant values for the YouTube preset.

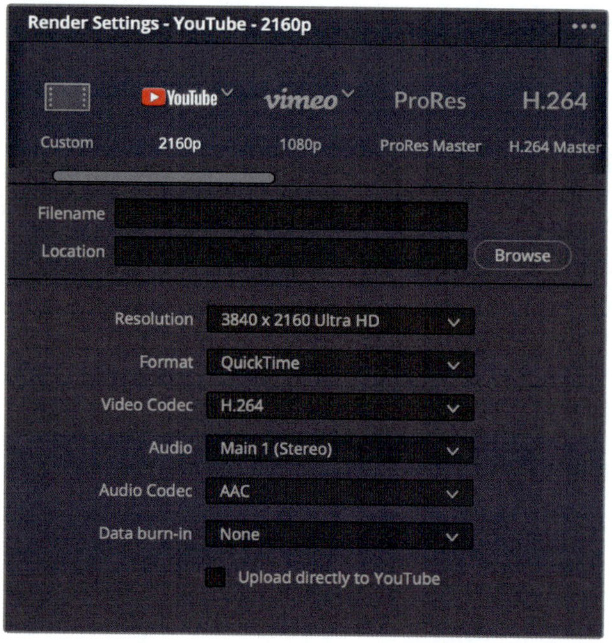

Presets are convenient for quickly setting up project renders but remain fully customizable for further refinement. In this case, you'd like to produce a video with a lower data rate than the default.

3 At the top of the panel, click the Custom button next to the YouTube preset.

4 The panel reverts to its custom layout, but has adopted all the YouTube settings: the file format and codec, and the 4K resolution.

5 Scroll down the settings panel, and change the Quality to Restrict to 7500 Kb/s. Doing so will reduce the data rate of the file, significantly lowering the file size while still maintaining a good level of visual quality.

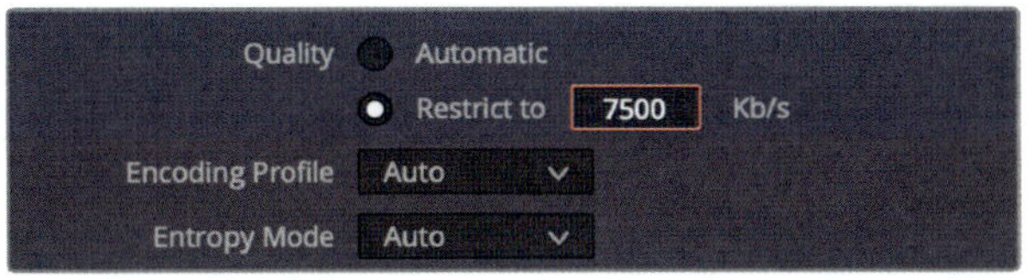

6 To name the video file, scroll up to the Filename and Location fields.

7 Click the empty field next to Filename, and enter **WorkDay_YouTube_1.1**.

The Location field identifies where the rendered file will appear after rendering. A job cannot be sent to the Render Queue without an assigned location.

8 Click the Browse button next to the Location text field.

9 In the File Destination window, navigate to your Desktop, and click Add New folder.

10 Name it **Exports**, and click OK.

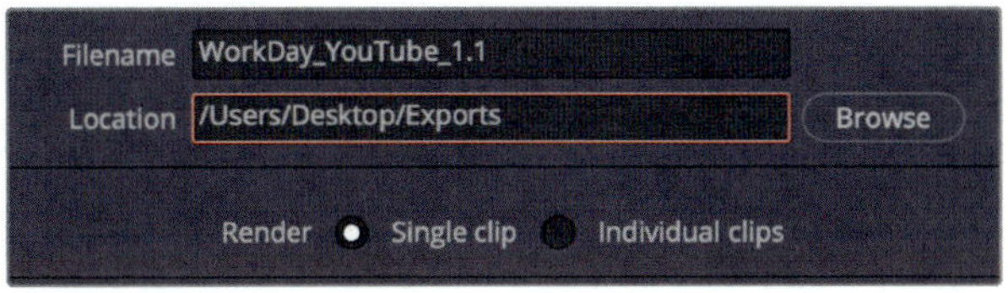

11 With the render settings completed, click Add to Render Queue at the bottom of the panel.

A pop-up dialog asks if you want to export the project at a higher resolution than your Timeline. It also informs you that this type of resizing is best performed in the Project Settings under Timeline Format. For the purpose of this exercise, you will accept the job as it is.

12 Click Add.

13 In the Render Queue panel, click the Job 1 title and rename it to **YouTube**.

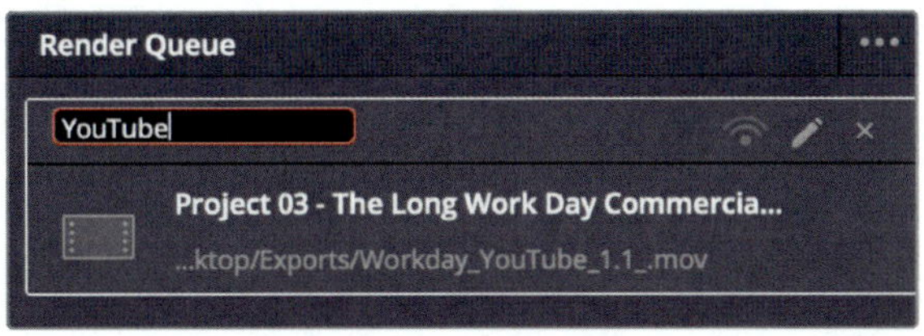

Supporting Multiple Resolution Options for User-generated Content Websites

Video players on user-generated content (UGC) websites such as YouTube or Vimeo often offer the option to choose a playback video resolution. A lower-resolution video will enable smoother playback on a low-bandwidth Internet connection, whereas a higher resolution will produce a more detailed image.

This change in resolution does not occur in real time within the UGC player. Instead, every resolution of every video is generated at the time of the video's upload, which is why a wait period usually occurs before an uploaded video goes live. When switching between resolution options, the user is actually switching between separate renders of the video as generated by the host website.

For this reason, it is advisable to render and upload your video in the highest quality possible and leave it up to the UGC website and the end user to determine which resolution is best suited for playback.

Presets offer an efficient way to export projects quickly and have confidence that the settings are appropriate for the intended destination. However, it is valuable to understand how and why certain settings are used and to be able to configure them more specific needs, especially when your project deliverable extends beyond the destinations targeted in the presets list.

Creating Custom Renders and Saving Presets

You create custom renders as soon as you make changes to the fields in the Render Settings panel. Editors and colorists adjust render settings based on a wide range of factors including the requirements of the receiving software and hardware, and the collaborative workflows they are engaged in.

In this exercise, you will set up a render job to deliver dailies to an editor who is working on a PC.

1. At the top of the Render Settings, click the Custom button.
2. Under the Filename and Location fields, choose Individual Clips. Doing so will export every clip in the Timeline as its own video file. In the case of dailies, you will want to place untrimmed clips on the Timeline to ensure that the editor receives the full media for every take.
3. Set the Video format to MXF OP-Atom.

4 Set the Codec to DNxHD 1080p 145/120/115 8-bit.

TIP Click the Expand button in the interface toolbar at the top of the page to expand the Render Settings panel to the height of the Deliver page.

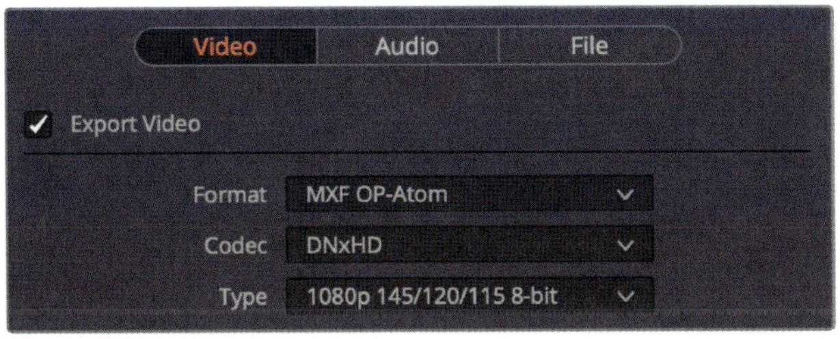

The exercises in this lesson did not focus on audio syncing or editing; however, in a dailies workflow, it is assumed that the audio from an external recorder would have been synced to the video files. The option to export audio can remain selected under the audio tab, using the high quality Linear PCM codec.

5 Click the File tab to configure the naming convention of the dailies.

By default, Filename Uses is set to Custom name. When working with dailies, it is highly advisable that you preserve the original filenames (Source Name in the Render Settings). Doing so will enable you to quickly switch between offline and online media, as well as maintain consistency between post-production departments.

In this case, you do not want to use the source name because all the clips have come from the same video file and will overwrite one another.

6 Enter the Custom name as **WorkDay_Dailies**.

7 Select "Use unique filenames".

8 Choose Suffix as the method by which the files will be distinguished from one another.

9 At the top of the panel, click Browse to change the Location.

10 In the Exports folder on the Desktop, create a subfolder called **Dailies** and select it as the location. Click OK to confirm.

11 In the option menu of the Render Settings panel, choose Save as New Preset.

12 Name the preset **Dailies for PC**.

The custom preset appears in the horizontal menu at the top of the Render Settings panel.

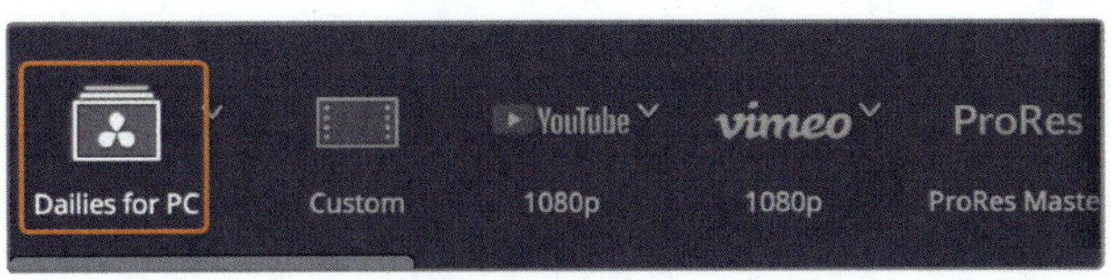

13 Click Add to Render Queue.

Configuring a Timeline for Digital Cinema

A digital cinema package, or DCP, is a collection of media and metadata files used to project digital movie files in a theatrical venue. Resolve makes it convenient to create a digital cinema package with its integration of the DCP plug-in. Still, just because the process is simplified doesn't mean you needn't know what the plug-in is doing. This exercise will combine some practical information about the DCP with the few configuration steps required in the Deliver page.

When creating a DCP, the Timeline in Resolve must be set to one of three 2K resolutions:

- 2K Native (1.90:1) 2048 ×1080 @ 24, 25, 30, 48, 50, or 60 fps
- 2K Flat (1.85:1) 1998 ×1080 @ 24, 25, 30, 48, 50, or 60fps
- 2K CinemaScope (2.39:1) 2048 × 858 @ 24, 25, 30, 48, 50, or 60 fps

Or one of three 4K resolutions:

- 4K Native (1.90:1) 4096 × 2160 @ 24, 25, 30, 48, 50, or 60 fps
- 4K Flat (1.85:1) 3996 × 2160 @ 24, 25, 30, 48, 50, or 60 fps
- 4K CinemaScope (2.39:1) 4096 ×1716 @ 24, 25, 30, 48, 50, or 60 fps

1 In the Edit page, ensure that the Lesson 10 Timeline is open.

  This is a Rec.709, full HD resolution project. But, as is often the case, you may have to output deliverables in multiple formats. In this exercise, you will output a DCP format file.

  The resolution for your DCP will be 2K flat because it is the closest resolution option when starting from full HD. You will need to scale up the project and crop the top and bottom of the frame.

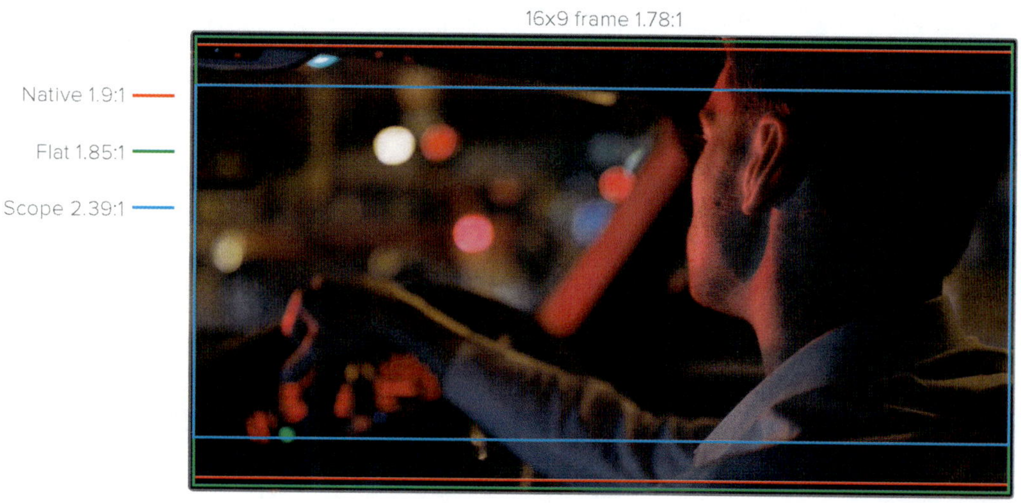

TIP 4K DCPs use a lower bit rate when played on 2K projectors than do 2K DCP's. For that reason, when your target projector is 2K, always make a 2K DCP, even if your content supports higher resolutions.

2 Choose File > Project Settings.

3 In the Master settings, set the "Timeline resolution" to 1998 x 1080 DCI Flat 1.85.

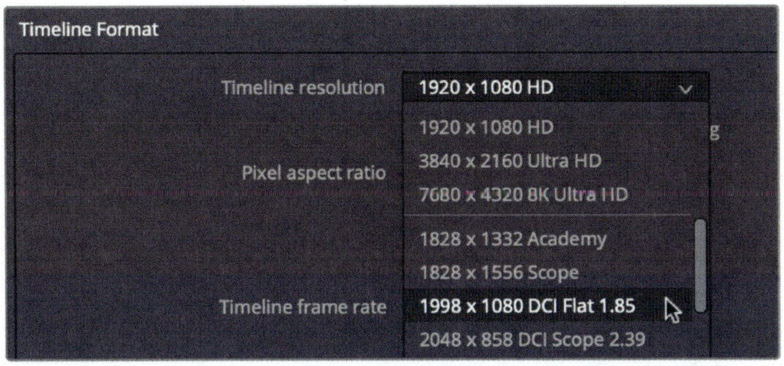

4 In the Image Scaling settings, set the Input Scaling to "Scale full frame with crop".

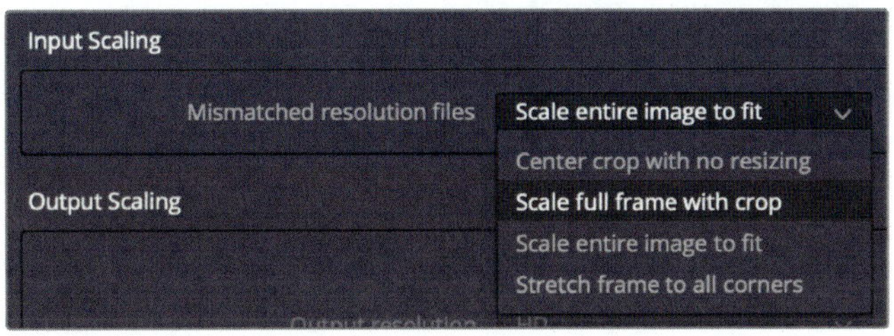

Scaling full frame with crop ensures that the longest dimension of the Timeline Viewer is filled with the source media, omitting letterboxing or pillars. However, it does crop a small portion off the top and bottom of the image.

5 Click Save to close the window.

Your frame size is now DCP compliant. The project Timeline is 24 fps, which is also appropriate for DCP delivery. However, if you were working on a project at 23.976 fps, DCP would still interpret it as 24 fps, and audio playback would be pulled up to match.

Now you can move onto the Deliver page to set up some DCP-specific parameters.

Rendering a DCP

When the resolution and frame rate are appropriately set up, all further output parameters are configured in the Deliver page.

The DCP plug-in in DaVinci Resolve 16 Studio features two sets of codecs. The Kakadu-based JPEG 2000 standard requires no license and delivers unencrypted digital cinema packages. The easyDCP format allows for the encryption of digital media but requires that you purchase a licensing package.

1. Enter the Deliver page.
2. In the Render Settings, click Custom.
3. Near the top of the panel, select Single Clip. Unlike the dailies, you want this Timeline to be rendered as a single, self-contained video file.
4. In the Video tab, set the Format to DCP.
5. Set the Codec to Kakadu JPEG 2000.
6. Set the Type to 2K DCI Flat.

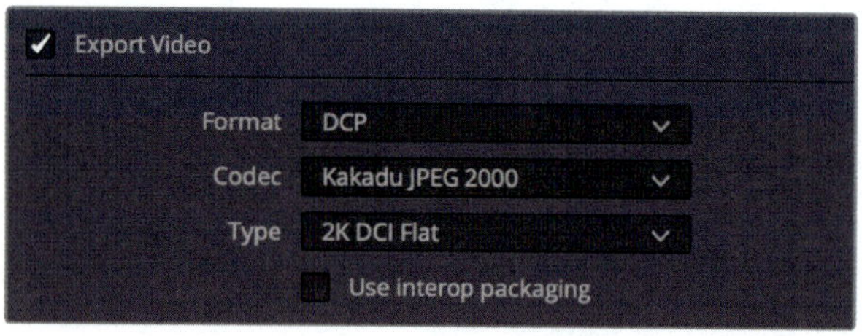

> **TIP** DCP uses the XYZ color space. The conversion of your project color space to XYZ is done during the creation of the DCP file. The project color space is determined by the Timeline color space setting in the Color management settings, even when DaVinci YRGB color management is not in use.

The next checkbox determines whether you are generating the DCP based on the older but more widely supported Interop standard, or the more current and feature-rich SMPTE standard. One of the benefits of using the SMPTE standard is that it supports a wider range of framerates. The major benefit of using the Interop standard is that it will work on more theatre projectors, even though it is limited to 24 or 48 fps.

7. Select "Use interop packaging."
8. Leave the Maximum Bitrate at 250 Mb/sec.

TIP The alternative available codec to DCP is easyDCP, which can be activated with a license. This codec displays an additional "Encrypt package" checkbox. When delivering a DCP file to a film festival, you might want to consider bypassing encryption. Encryption keys are linked to a specific theater and projector, so if a screening room or location is changed at the last minute, as is often the case in festivals, the encryption would prevent your film from being screened.

Naming and Outputting a DCP

DCPs follow a somewhat specific, yet voluntary, Digital Cinema Naming Convention for the content title. For each version of a movie you create (such as the English 5.1 version, the Spanish 5.1 version, the stereo version, the in-flight version, and so on), a composition playlist (CPL) is created that contains the appropriate content name. The DCP preset create this CPL for you and includes a straightforward way to generate a name that follows the appropriate naming convention.

1. Ensure that you are still in the Video tab of the Render Settings.
2. Scroll down to find and expand the Composition Settings.
3. To ensure that the project has a DCP appropriate name, click the Edit button next to the "Composition name" field.

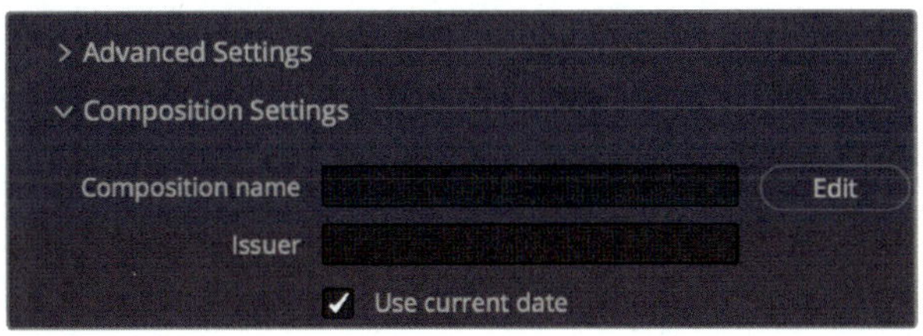

The Composition Name Generator window opens. Here you can enter the metadata that you will use to create a content title compatible with DCP servers and theater management systems.

TIP Separate the words in your movie's title using initial caps—not spaces, hyphens, or underscores.

4 Enter the Film Title as **TheLongWorkDay**, leave the Content Type as ADV (Advertisement), and set the Audio Language to EN (English).

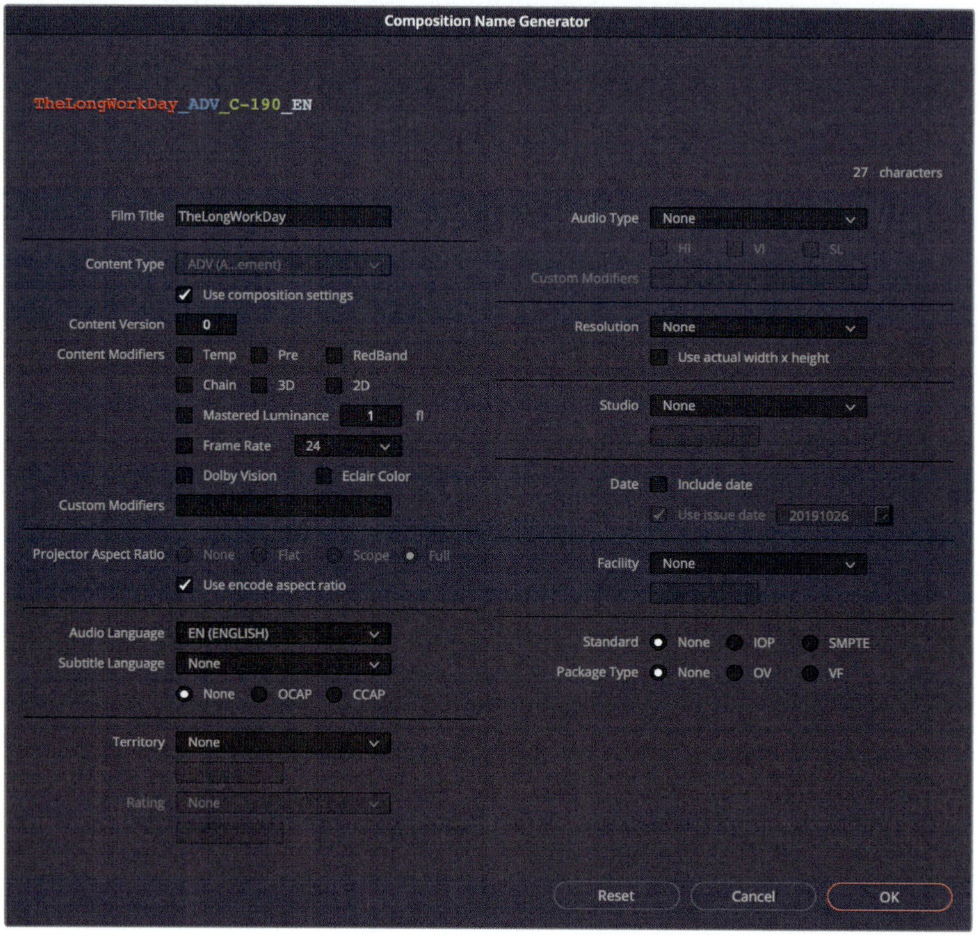

The selected metadata is added to the composition name.

5 Click OK to close the window.

The composition name is not to be confused with the package name that contains the DCP. That custom name is managed in the File tab of the Render Settings panel.

6 Click the File tab, and enter the Custom name as **Long Work Day DCP test**.

Lastly, you need to select a destination for this DCP.

7 Click the Browse button, and select a location.

You can output the DCP to a hard drive in a Cru Dataport DX-115 enclosure that will load directly onto many digital cinema servers and is often required by some film festivals. More conveniently, you can output to a USB 2 or 3 hard drive, or even a USB stick if it accommodates the film's file size. No matter which storage device you choose, the device must be formatted as a Linux ext2 or ext3 drive. There are various ways do so on macOS and Windows workstations.

TIP Some projection servers do not have enough power for certain USB-powered drives to mount. In those scenarios, be sure to use a USB drive that uses an external power source.

8 When you are done selecting your drive destination, click "Add to Render Queue".

After your DCP is rendered, you'll want to test it. The only definite way to test your DCP is to rent a theater and run it just as it would be projected for an audience. That is the only way you can absolutely verify that the color conversion (from your Timeline color space to XYZ) worked correctly.

Using the Commercial Workflow to Export Versions

In Lesson 6, one of the uses listed for versions was color experimentation. When working with clients or directors, the colorist might spend time at the beginning of the post-production workflow establishing the look of key shots and submitting them for review and approval.

Another, practical application of sharing multiple versions of a grade involves VFX migration workflows that require reference grades be used for reconstruction or matching. You can export these different looks or versions using a single job in the Render Queue.

1. Ensure that you are in the Lesson 10 Timeline.
2. Open the Color page.
3. Right-click clip 01, and check its list of local versions.

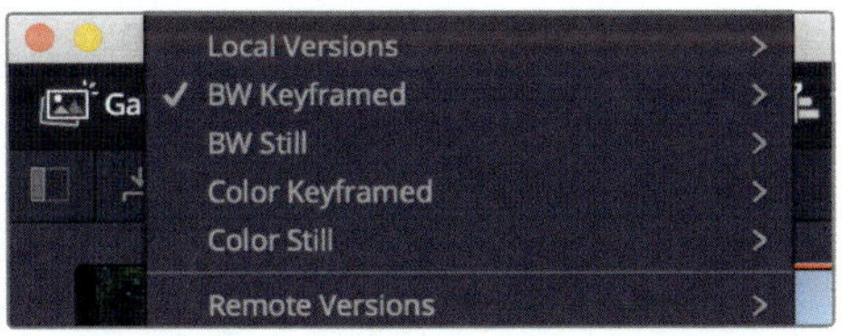

Note that it has four versions, all featuring variants of the grade with and without color, and with and without keyframed sizing. You will export all four versions for review and approval.

4. Open the Deliver page.

5 Right-click clip 01, and choose Render This Clip to place In and Out markers around the clip in the Deliver page Timeline.

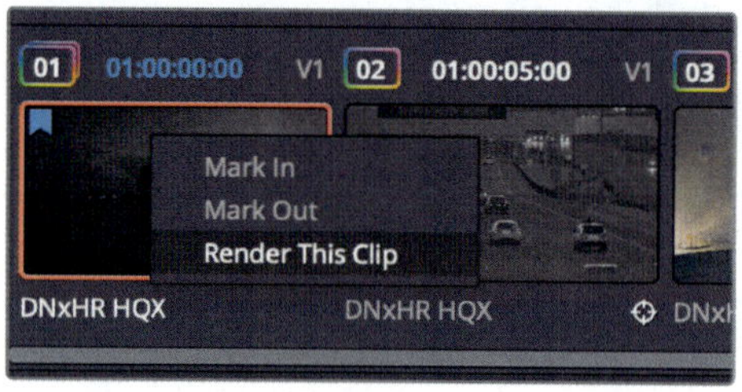

TIP One of the options in the Versions contextual menu is Render Disabled. Choosing it will prevent a version from being rendered out during a Commercial Workflow export.

6 In the Render Settings panel, change the Render Focus to Individual clips.

NOTE You will not see the option to select "Use commercial workflow" when exporting media as a single clip.

7 In the Location field, find the Exports folder on the Desktop, and create a new subfolder called **Sunrise Versions**.

8 In the Video section of the Render Settings, specify the Format as QuickTime and the Codec as H.264 to output a compressed video with a small file size.

9 Set the Resolution to Full HD (1920x1080).

10 In the Audio section, deselect Export Audio.

11 In the File section, ensure that "Filename uses" is set to Source Name.

12 Select "Use unique filenames" to ensure that the rendered media does not overwrite earlier versions of itself.

13 Select Suffix to place a unique identifier after the name of the clip.

14 Scroll down the panel and select "Use commercial workflow". This option exports all available versions of your selected clips.

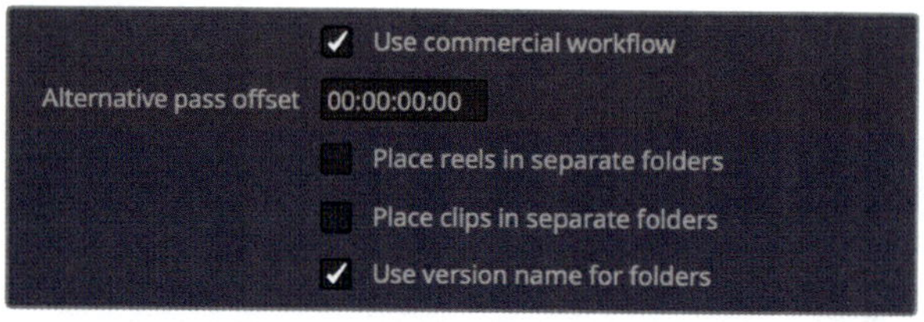

15 Select "Use Version name for folders" to quickly differentiate between the version types.

16 Click Add to Render Queue.

17 In the Render Queue palette, click to select the newly created job, and click the Start Render button.

Note that the other, unselected jobs will not be rendered.

18 Open your computer's file manager, and locate the Sunrise Versions folder.

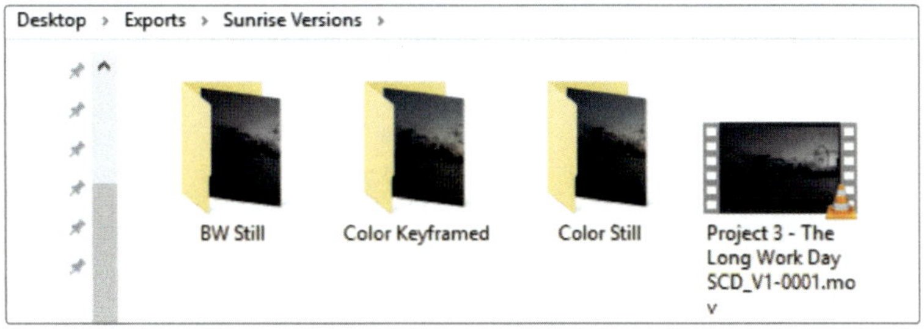

Version 1 is at the root of the folder, while all additional versions are contained in their own subfolders. You can use this structure to great effect in a workflow in which version 1 is the designated ungraded version of every clip on the Timeline, and the graded versions are output into their own subfolders through the commercial workflow.

Also, the subfolders themselves are vital when working with DPX file formats that can produce hundreds, or even thousands, of still images during render.

TIP Versions also have an Enable Flat Pass option in the contextual menu. When this option is chosen, the grade on the version is disabled if Enable Flat Pass > "With clip settings" is selected in the Render Settings panel.

Exploring Advanced Render Settings

In addition to choosing how your footage is compressed, you have additional control over more nuanced aspects of the rendering process. This exercise is designed to familiarize you with these settings, and enable you to set up your custom renders with more purpose.

1 In the Render Settings, change the render focus to Single clip.

2 In the Timeline panel, set the render range to Entire Timeline.

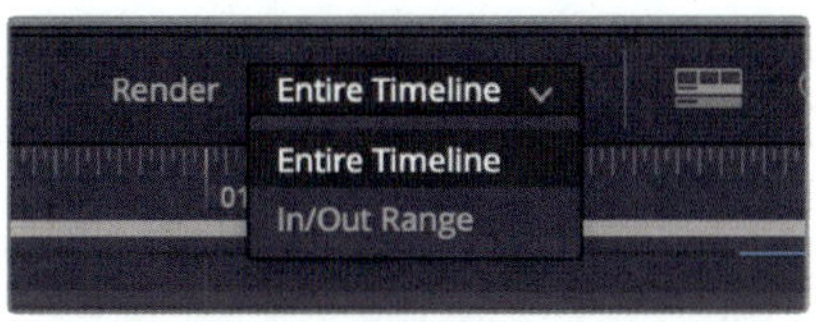

3 In the Render Settings panel, select the Vimeo preset at 720p resolution. Leave the Video format as QuickTime and the codec as H.264.

The Quality value in the Render Settings panel specifically refers to the data rate of the digital data—that is, the data-per-second required to transmit the audiovisual stream. A higher data rate contains more visual information which results in better motion representation and detail quality, whereas a lower data rate selectively discards some data in the interest of generating a smaller file size.

4 Restrict the Quality setting to 4500 Kb/s. Doing so will substantially reduce the file size of the final render, albeit at the expense of its visual quality.

Key frames are full-data, intra-coded frames, or ***i-frames***, inserted into a lossy video stream at regular intervals, such as every 12 frames. These i-frames are reference points for recreating the temporally compressed p- (predicted) and b- (bi-directionally predicted) frames that make up the majority of the moving image in a distribution codec (sch as H.264).

5 Restrict the Key Frames to be grabbed every 12 frames to ensure less distortion during the temporal compression and playback of the video.

6 Click the disclosure triangle to see the Advanced Settings options.

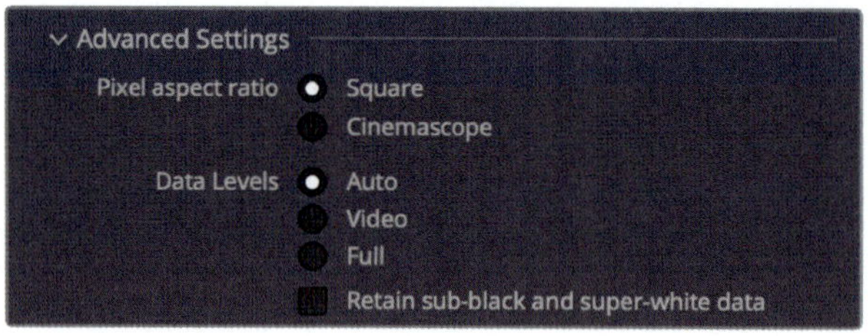

The “Pixel aspect ratio” allows you to indicate whether the video pixels are Square or Cinemascope (rectangular). This option pertains to older workflows in which digital footage recorded for analogue television (at a rectangular 1.33:1 aspect ratio) was converted for computer displays (which have a square 1:1 aspect ratio). If your video looks horizontally distorted (too squashed or stretched out), change the pixel aspect ratio.

7 Since you are working on digitally recorded and encoded media, you can leave the “Pixel aspect ratio” as Square.

Data Levels specify the data range of an image based on its source. The default Auto setting renders the media at the data level that is appropriate for the selected codec. Video refers to YCbCr formats that constrain to pixel data values between 64-940 on a 10-bit system in formats using a Rec.709 video standard. Full expands the range to the film standard of 4-1023 values utilized in high-end digital film formats. If you find that your final video looks substantially darker or lighter than it appears in the Viewer of the Color page, it is likely that the data levels are incorrectly assigned.

8 Leave the Data Levels on Auto.

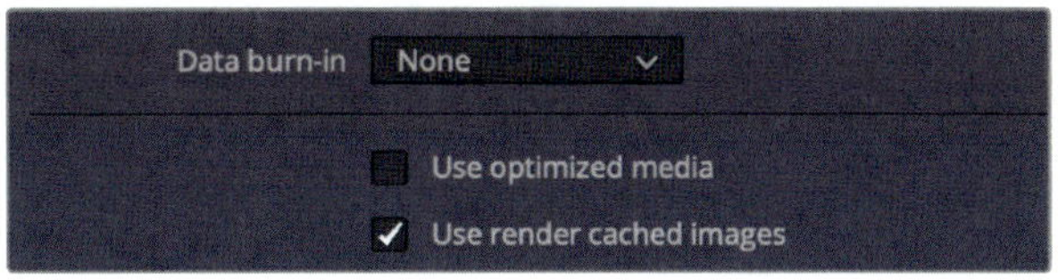

9 Set the "Data burn-in" to None to ensure that the Viewer's data burn-in information will not appear in the rendered video.

The following options, "Use optimized media" and "Use render cached images," allow you to employ previously-generated renders of the footage in the export process. It makes sense to select these options when your optimized media and render cache are set to a high or lossless quality such as 444 or HDR.

The project is currently using a lossless render cache code, so it makes sense to use it in the final render for faster output.

10 Select "Use render cached images".

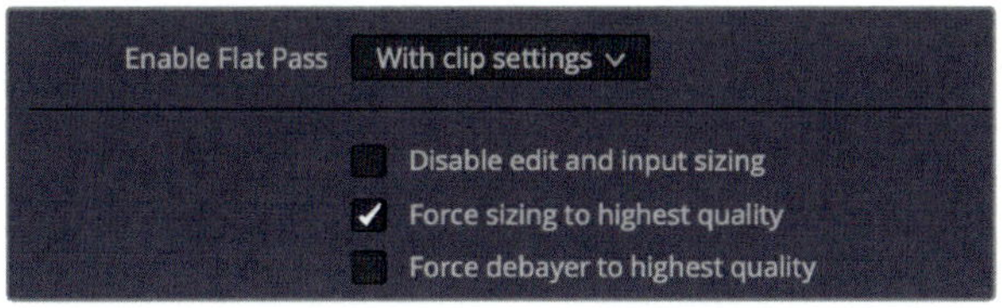

"Enable Flat Pass" allows you to bypass grades applied to versions of clips in the Timeline. The default choice is Off, which ensures that all grades remain intact. Choosing "With clip settings"' ensures that the render will take into account the bypass status of each clip's version. Choosing Always On will disable all the grades in the Timeline, thereby providing a quick way to export an edited Timeline or a set of dailies without a grade.

11 Set Enable Flat Pass to "With clip settings".

12 Selecting "Disable edit and input sizing" removes any transform changes that were applied to the clips in the Edit or Color pages. Leave it deselected.

The "Force sizing to highest quality" and "Force debayer to highest quality" settings bypass the quality settings for resizing and debayering in the Project settings. Selecting one of these is convenient when working on a processor-intensive Timeline that uses high-quality images or RAW footage. You can adjust the Project settings to ensure a lower-quality visual output during editing, but bypass such settings to ensure the highest possible quality output upon final render.

13 The Resize filter in the Project Settings hadn't been reduced to the lower bilinear format in this project, but you can still keep "Force sizing to highest quality" selected for safety.

14 You also don't need to change the debayer for this exercise because the Timeline does not contain any RAW media.

15 Click Add to Render Queue.

16 In the Render Queue, in the options menu, choose Show All Projects.

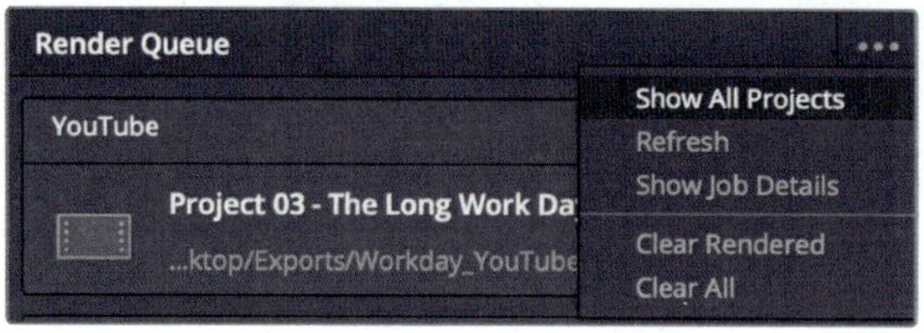

You should now see all the jobs that were added to the Render Queue in any project currently associated with the database you are using. If you split longer projects into reels, or you are working on Timelines with different frames rates, you might want to access all of the jobs in the queue to render them from a single project, instead of waiting for a batch to render before launching other projects.

17 In the options menu, deselect Show All Projects to return to the current project's Render Queue.

Editing Render Jobs

Even after you add jobs to the Render Queue, you can still update their settings or remove them from the queue entirely.

1 Your Render Queue still displays the Versions job, which was already rendered. Click the X in the upper-right corner of the job to delete it from the queue.

2 In the Render Queue, click the pencil icon on the YouTube job you created in the first exercise.

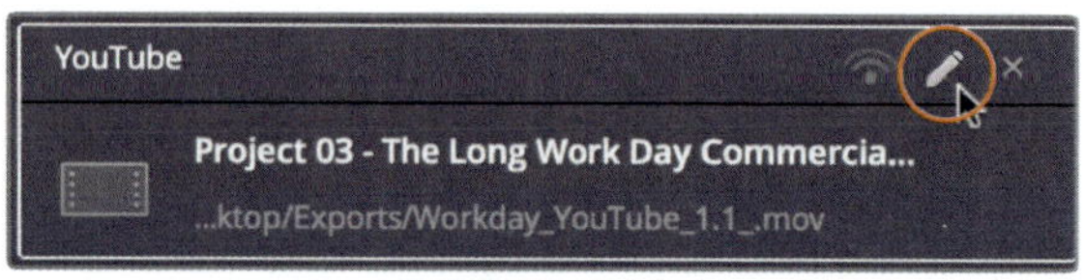

The Render Settings change to reflect the settings of the custom YouTube job. The presence of additional Cancel, Update Job, and Add New Job buttons at the bottom of the panel indicates that a job is currently being edited.

3 Change the Resolution to 1920x1080 for Full HD.

4 Under that, change the Quality to Restrict to 8500 Kb/s.

5 Click Update Job at the bottom of the Render Settings panel to exit the Edit mode.

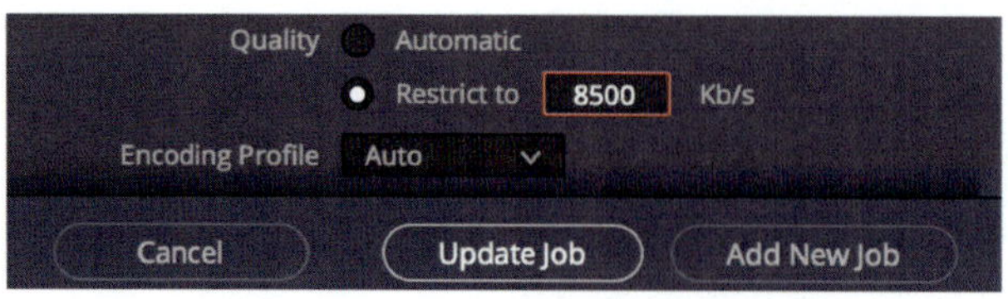

The change overrides the original YouTube job with the new settings.

Remote Rendering

DaVinci Resolve Studio allows you to offload rendering to another Resolve workstation. Remote rendering requires that all workstations have a copy of DaVinci Resolve 16 Studio installed, a shared Postgres database, and access to all necessary media files using the same filename paths. With one computer acting as a render station, all other Resolve stations can continue to be used for further editing and grading.

Utilizing the correct render settings is vital to delivering an aesthetically correct and technically functional video project. Understanding these settings has even greater benefits. It elevates your skillset as a colorist and imbues confidence that your projects are delivered at their optimal quality and adhere to industry standards.

Lesson Review

1. Yes or no? You can continue to view and grade media in the Lightbox.
2. True or False? The Deliver page supports roundtrip workflows with other NLE programs.
3. What does the commercial workflow in the Deliver page do?
4. How do you save a custom render preset?
5. True or False? It is possible to continue editing a render job after it has been added to the Render Queue.

Answers

1. Yes, if you enable color controls and have an external monitor
2. True. The presets at the top of the Render Settings panel allow you to select an NLE program for a roundtrip delivery of individual video clips and an XML Timeline.
3. Renders all versions of individual clip grades
4. Render Settings options menu > Save as New Preset
5. True. Clicking the pencil icon in the upper-right corner of a render job allows you to continue modifying its settings.

Congratulations!

You have completed **Color Correction with DaVinci Resolve 16** and are ready to explore more editing, visual effects, color grading, and audio mixing functionality using the additional certified books in this series. Completing all the lessons in this book has prepared you to become a certified DaVinci Resolve user. You can take the online exam by following the link below to earn your certificate.

We also invite you to become part of the DaVinci Resolve community by joining the web forum on the Blackmagic Design web site. There, you can ask further questions about the creative aspects of editing, color correction, visual effects, and audio mixing.

We hope that you have you have found DaVinci Resolve 16's professional non-linear editing and world-class color correction tools to be intuitive to learn and a perfect fit for your creative workflow.

Test your skills by taking the online assessment: **http://bit.ly/2zehjWk**

Appendix

Setting Up and using the Blackmagic Design Mini Panel

Using DaVinci Resolve Panels

The DaVinci Resolve Panels allow you to make incredibly detailed, subtle, and nuanced changes to the color of your images. Instead of being limited to color grading one click or drag at a time, the panels let you effect multiple controls in different direction at the same time. It could be the difference between taking one minute and five minutes to complete a shot before moving on to the next.

The role of the colorist isn't only about creativity, it's about efficiency. To meet the time requirements of your budget as well as the expectations of your client, you'll have to find ways to quickly save, copy, apply, and tweak numerous looks throughout your projects. Having a set of panels will help you meet those time-sensitive demands.

DaVinci Resolve Mini Panel

The DaVinci Resolve Mini Panel is a compact panel that's packed with a massive combination of features and controls. As with the Micro Panel, you get three professional trackballs along with a variety of buttons for switching tools, adding color correctors, and navigating your node tree. In addition to every tool and feature available on the Micro Panel, the Mini Panel features two 5" color LCD screens that display menus, controls, and parameter settings for the selected tool, along with 8 soft buttons and 8 soft knobs that give you direct access to the menus for specific features. The Mini Panel is ideal for users who regularly switch between editing and color grading, users who wish to access both primary and secondary color correction tools from their panel, or for freelance colorists who need to carry a panel with them when moving between facilities. It's also great for colorists working on location shoots, for corporate and event videographers, for houses of worship, and more.

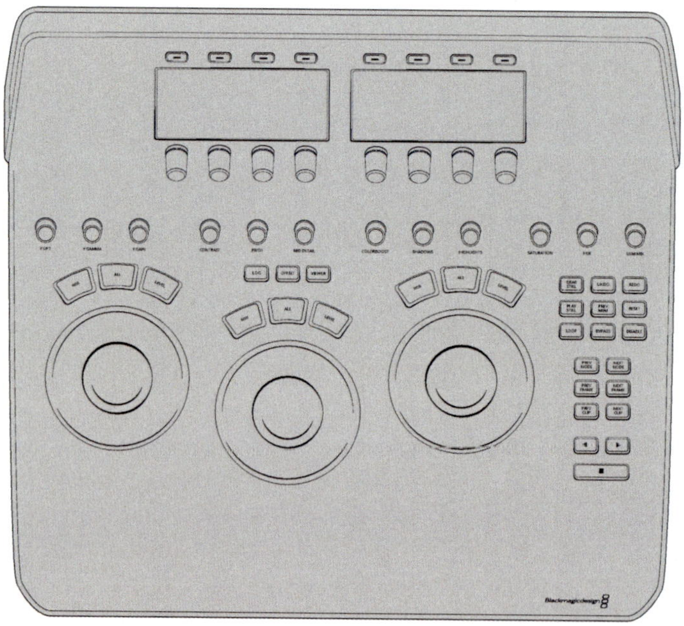

DaVinci Resolve Micro Panel

The DaVinci Resolve Micro Panel is a high-quality, portable, low-profile panel that features three high-resolution trackballs and 12 precision-machined control knobs for accessing essential primary correction tools. If you're using a Micro Panel, it's important to know that all of the instructions regarding the primary color tools and setup are identical to the Mini Panel. Above the center trackball are keys for switching between Log and offset color correction, as well as a key to display DaVinci Resolve's full-screen viewer, which is great for use with laptops. Eighteen dedicated keys on the right side of the panel also give you access to many commonly used grading features and playback controls. The Davinci Resolve Micro Panel is perfect for anyone that needs a truly portable solution. It's great for use on set to quickly create looks and evaluate color, it's ideal for grading in broadcast trucks, excellent for education, and ideal for anyone who's work relies mostly on the primary color correction tools.

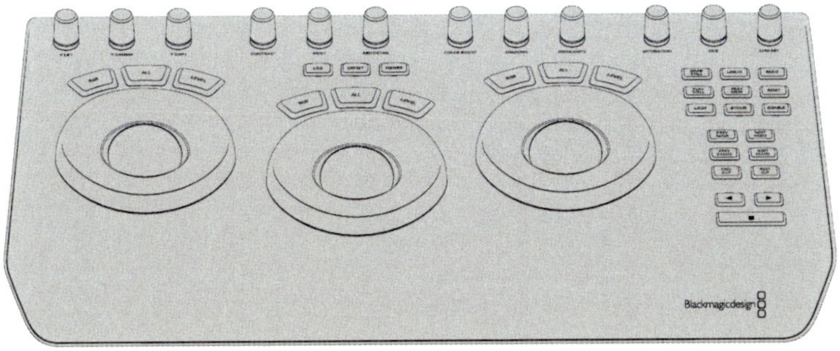

DaVinci Resolve Advanced Panel

For the ultimate in speed, power and control, there is the DaVinci Resolve Advanced Panel. The Advanced Panel has been designed in collaboration with professional colorists to work together in total harmony with the software. This large panel consists of left, center, and right consoles that give you quick, one touch access to virtually every parameter and control in the software. The DaVinci Resolve Advanced Panel lets colorists instinctively reach out and touch every part of the image, adjusting multiple parameters simultaneously with complete responsiveness for a smooth grading experience. While the Mini Panel gives you access to nearly all of the color correction tools in Davinci Resolve, the Advanced Panel gives you even more flexibility with physical buttons and knobs to control Memories, OpenFX tools, Dolby Vision HDR, and many other speed and workflow based tools that will increase your efficiency even more. The Advanced Panel also features a unique T-Bar used for playing back gallery stills, shuttle controls for cycling through frames and speeding through your timeline, as well as a slide out keyboard. Used in many of the top color grading facilities across the world, the Davinci Resolve Advanced Panel is the ultimate control surface for Davinci Resolve.

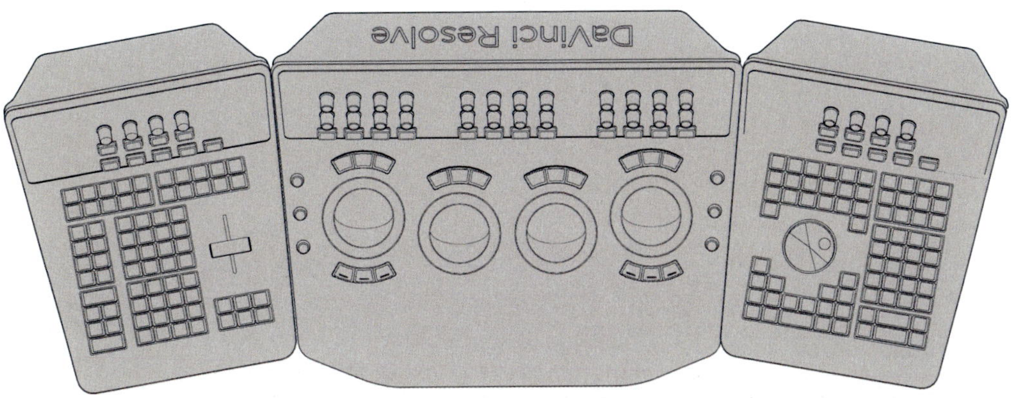

DaVinci Resolve Mini Panel Overview

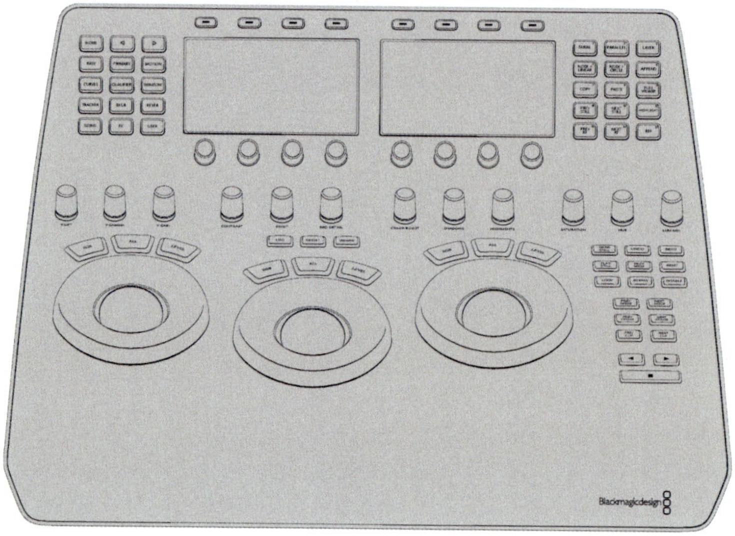

The lower-half of your Mini Panel contains the primary control tools. These tools are identical to the Micro Panel. The largest controls on the Mini Panel are the three wheels and three trackballs that control (from left to right) Lift, Gamma, and Gain. Whereas the wheel controls brightness, the trackball controls color. Look at the Color wheel on your user interface as you move the trackballs and wheels. When you move the Lift wheel to the left, the darker areas of your image grow darker. When you move the Gain trackball to the upper-left, you'll notice that the brighter areas of your image become warmer.

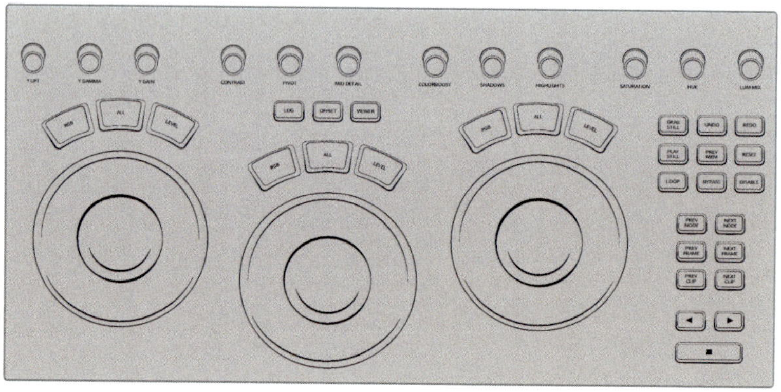

Above the Lift, Gamma, and Gain controls are your Primary knobs, which control the Primary sliders below your Color wheel in the user interface. They control frequently used Resolve tools such as Contrast, Pivot, Saturation, Color Boost, and Hue. These knobs (as well as all knobs on the panel) have 4,098 points per turn, and you can push them in to reset the tool they control.

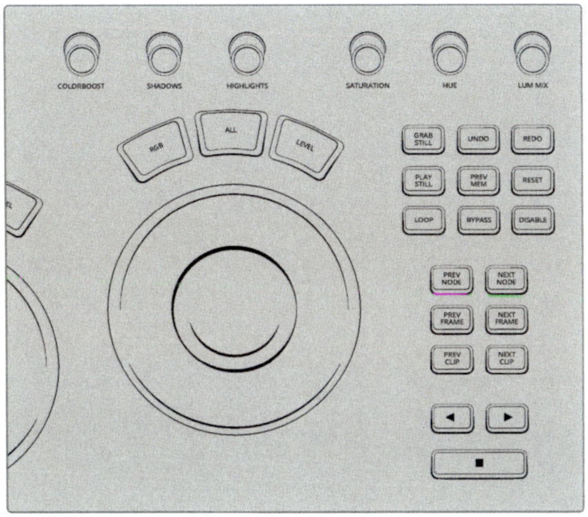

To the right of your Gain trackball and wheel, you'll find useful playback and shuttle controls to help you navigate quickly between clips, nodes, frames, and playback options. Some important controls to remember are Loop, which will loop the currently selected clip; Bypass, which will temporarily bypass all of the nodes/color corrections applied to a shot; and Disable which will temporarily disable the current node selected on a clip.

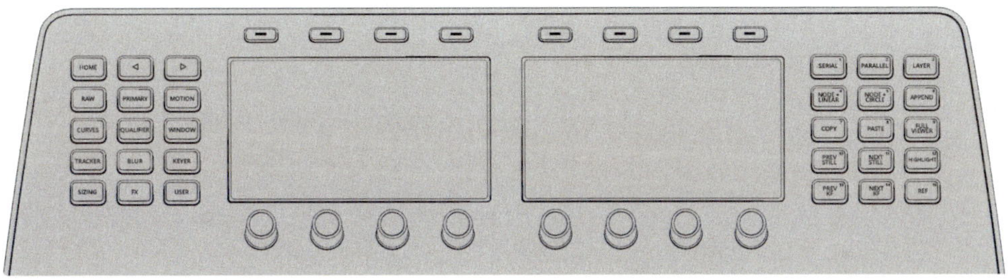

The lip of the Mini Panel consists of your tool palettes; two five-inch high-resolution displays; and even more node, keyframing and selection controls. The color tools in Davinci Resolve are accessed in the user interface through a series of icons between the timeline and color tools. All of these tool palettes are mirrored into their own buttons on the Mini Panel. If you need to access curves, just press Curves. The two displays—as well as the eight soft buttons and eight soft knobs above and below the displays—will control and manipulate whatever palette button you have selected to the left of them.

Index

D

E

F

G

H

I

J

K

T

U

V

W

X

Y

Z

About the Author

Daria Fissoun is a colorist and compositor in east London. She specialises in commercial video projects (past clients include Microsoft, Nike, and Konami) and has worked on a number of short and feature films through UK-based production companies.

Alongside industry work, Daria is also involved in the educational sector. She currently instructs on a variety of post production topics, including compositing, motion graphic animation, and color grading. She has been a staff member or guest lecturer at film and media schools throughout London: SAE Institute London, MET Film School, Central Film School and London South Bank University. In her spare time, she records and uploads video tutorials on post production techniques in Davinci Resolve under her channel name *Goat's Eye View.*

Made in the USA
Columbia, SC
13 October 2020

22743416R00188